Mission from Cape Coast Castle to Ashantee, with a statistical account of that kingdom, and geographical notices of other parts of the interior of Africa

T Edward 1791-1824 Bowdich

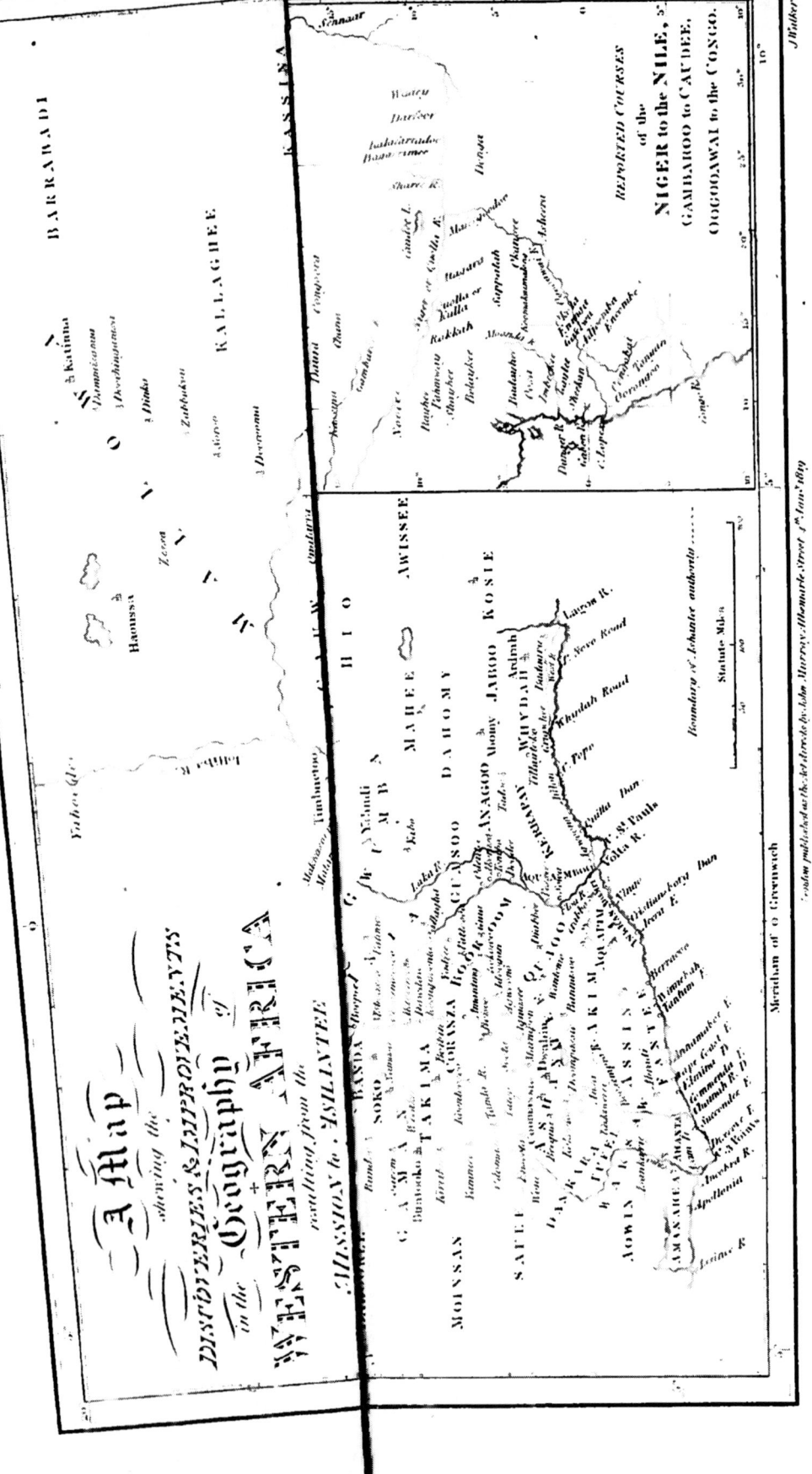

A Map

shewing the

DISCOVERIES & IMPROVEMENTS
in the
Geography
of
WESTERN AFRICA

resulting from the

MISSION to ASHANTEE.

REPORTED COURSES
of the
NIGER to the NILE, &c.
GAMBAROO to CAT-DEE,
OOGOOLAWAI to the CONGO.

ASBEN

BARRABADI

KALLAGHEE

HAOUSSA

KASSINA

Fishes Gle.

Zirra

Skatinna
Yammicama
Drohingoama
Drinka
Zabbokeen
Advona
Drocoama

Timbuctoo
Matuksoo
Maliya

GW IMBA
Mandi
Kebo

SOKO

BANDA

G A L M A N
Bantoko
Yanaba

YAMB

TAKIMA

AWISSEE

MAHEE

DAHOMY

GUNSOO

ANAGOO

JABOO

KOSIE

Lagon R.

WHYDAH

AKIM

Accra

Volta R.

St. Pauls

C. Pope

Christianborg Dan

MOINSAR

SAFEE

FANTE

ASSINE

AMOKAOE

Apollonia

Statue R.

Boundary of Ashantee authority

Statute Miles

Meridian of O Greenwich

MISSION

FROM CAPE COAST CASTLE

TO

ASHANTEE,

WITH A

STATISTICAL ACCOUNT OF THAT KINGDOM,

AND

GEOGRAPHICAL NOTICES OF OTHER PARTS

OF THE

INTERIOR OF AFRICA.

=====

BY T. EDWARD BOWDICH, ESQ.

CONDUCTOR.

=====

" Quod si præ metu et formidine pedem referemus, ista omnia nobis adversa
futura sunt."

LONDON:

JOHN MURRAY, ALBEMARLE-STREET.
1819.

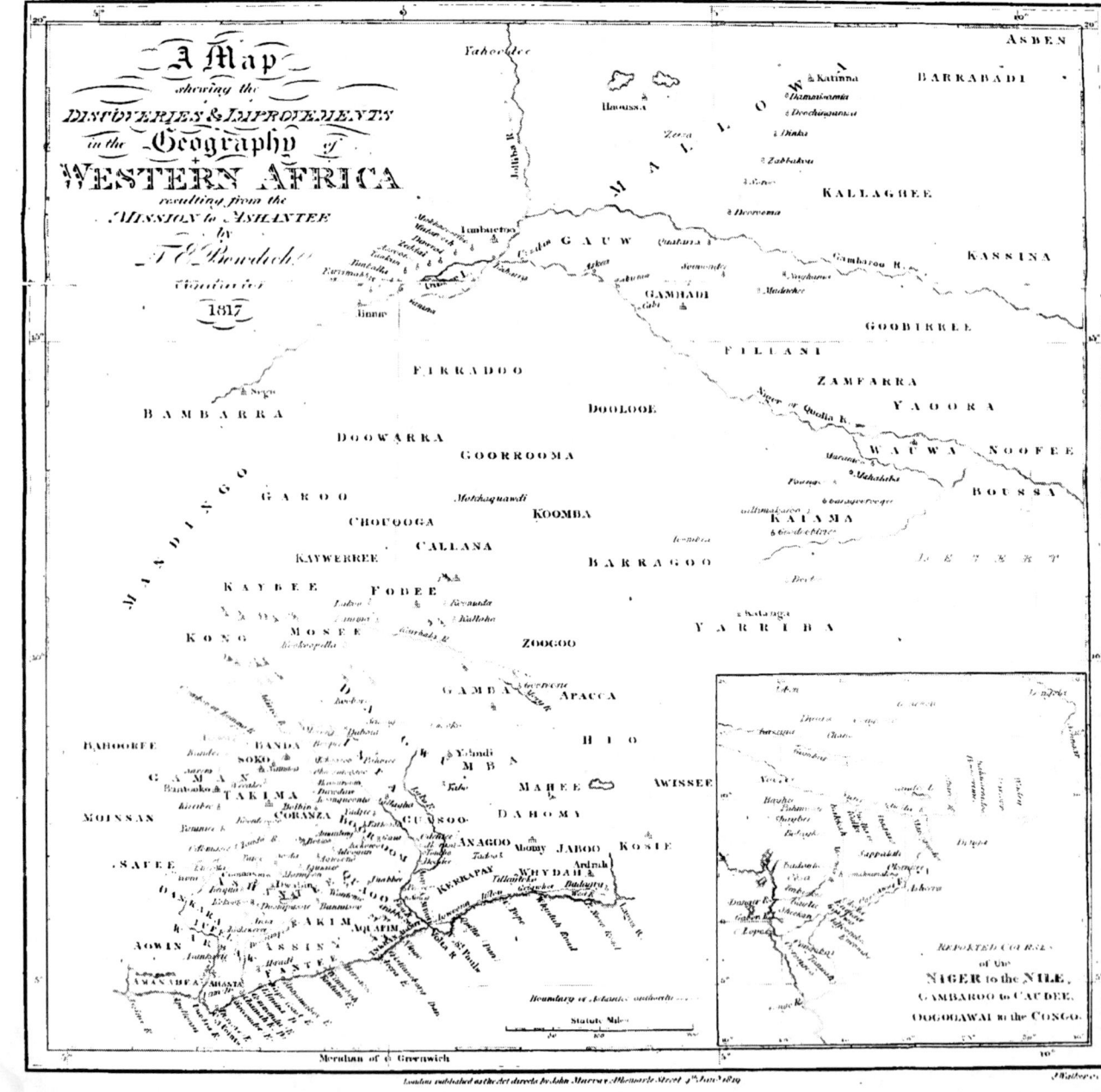

A Map shewing the DISCOVERIES & IMPROVEMENTS in the Geography of WESTERN AFRICA resulting from the MISSION to ASHANTEE by T E Bowdich Commissioner 1817

REPORTED COURSE of the NIGER to the NILE, GAMBAROO to CACDEE, OOGOOAWAI to the CONGO.

Boundary of Ashantee authority

Statute Miles

Meridian of Greenwich

London published as the Act directs by John Murray Albemarle Street 4th Jan 1819

MISSION

FROM CAPE COAST CASTLE

TO

ASHANTEE,

WITH A

STATISTICAL ACCOUNT OF THAT KINGDOM,

AND

GEOGRAPHICAL NOTICES OF OTHER PARTS

OF THE

INTERIOR OF AFRICA.

BY T. EDWARD BOWDICH, ESQ.

CONDUCTOR.

" Quod si præ metu et formidine pedem referemus, ista omnia nobis adversa futura sunt."

LONDON:

JOHN MURRAY, ALBEMARLE-STREET.
1819.

London: printed by W. Bulmer and Co.
Cleveland-Row, St. James's.

INTRODUCTION.

A CURIOSITY throughout Europe, proportionate to the ignorance of the Interior of Africa, exacts the publication of the proceedings and researches of every Exploratory Mission, from its Conductor, as a duty to the Public : " mandat fieri sibi talia."

The Public, in acknowledgment of the performance of the duty, reflecting that it constrains literary efforts which the Author otherwise might never have presumed to expose, should sympathise in his diffidence and anxiety, and receive and review them as a task imposed, and not as a spontaneous essay.

If this indulgence is due even to gentlemen who have had the most enviable opportunities of qualifying themselves at the expense of a liberal Government, it is surely secure to one who never enjoyed those advantages ; but, being suddenly called to the immediate conduct of a Mission, originated by a public Board of very contracted means, when estranged from all facilities, had no resource to aid his realization of the scientific desiderata, beyond the acquirements common to most private gentlemen.

The vessel in which I am making my passage to England having been chartered to trade in the River Gaboon, which is immediately on the Line, I diverted a tedious delay of seven weeks in so unhealthy a situation, by visiting Naängo, a town about fifty miles from the mouth of the River, where I collected Geographical Accounts of the Interior, from several intelligent traders, and numerous slaves from different countries. I have added this compilation, (as it may borrow some interest from the adjacency of the Congo,) with a few notices of the customs and productions of this ruder part of Africa.

CONTENTS.

PART I.

PART II.

APPENDIX.

DIRECTIONS FOR PLACING THE PLATES.

ERRATA.

Map.—Affix the name Leeasa to the river flowing from the Niger by Boussa.

Page 9.—After Frederick James, Esq. add, Member of Council, and Governor of Accra.

Page 72.—For dated, read *dictated.*

GLOSSARY.

Croom. A town or village.

Caboceer. A chief or magistrate.

Pynin. An elder or counsellor.

Palaver. A dispute, debate, argument, or suit.

Book or Note. A certificate of a monthly pension of the African Committee, paid in trade to the Fantee Kings and Chiefs in the neighbourhood of the British settlements, in consideration of their attachment, influence, and services; which Books or Notes were claimed by the King of Ashantee, as his by right of conquest.

Stool. Throne, seat in council, inheritance.

Custom. A festival, carnival, public ceremony, funeral rite.

Panyar. To seize or kidnap.

A Benda. Two ounces four ackies, or £9. currency.

A Periguin. Two ounces eight ackies, or £10. currency.

An Ackie. Five shillings currency.

A Tokoo. Ten pence.

A Dash. A present.

Fetish. A charm, amulet, deity. Any supernatural power or influence. Any thing sacred.

MISSION TO ASHANTEE.

PART I.

MISSION TO ASHANTEE.

CHAPTER. I.

The Objects, and Departure of the Mission.

BOSMAN and Barbot mention the Ashantees as first heard of by Europeans about the year 1700; the latter calls it Assiantee or Inta, and writes, that it is west of Mandingo, and joins Akim on the east; he asserts its pre-eminence in wealth and power. Issert, a physician in the Danish service, who meditated a visit to Ashantee, writes, " this mighty king has a piece of gold, as a charm, more than four men can carry ; and innumerable slaves are constantly at work for him in the mountains, each of whom must collect or produce two ounces of gold per diem. The Akims formerly dug much gold, but they are now forbidden by the King of Ashantee, to whom they are tributary, as well as the Aquamboos, previously a very formidable nation." Mr. Dalzel heard of the Ashantees at Dahomey, as very powerful, but imagined them, the Intas, and the Tapahs, to be one and the same nation. Mr. Lucas, when in Mesurata, was informed that Assentai was the capital of the powerful kingdom of Tonouwah. In Mr. Murray's enlarged edition of Dr. Leyden's discoveries in Africa, we find, " the northern border of Akim extends to Tonouwah, denominated also Inta, Assientè, or Assentai, from its capital city of that name, which stands about eighteen days journey from the Gold Coast."

In 1807 an Ashantee army reached the Coast for the first time. I would refer the reader to the extract in the Appendix, from Mr. Meredith's account of the Gold Coast, as the particulars are introductory as well as interesting; and also serve to correct the misstatement in the work last quoted, that in 1808 the King of Ashantee destroyed the English fort of Annamaboe; originating, probably, from the storm of the Dutch fort at Cormantine, at that time.

The Ashantees invaded Fantee again in 1811, and the third time in 1816. These invasions inflicted the greatest miseries on the Fantees. Few were slain in battle, for they rarely dared to encounter the invaders; but the butcheries in cold blood wer incredible, and thousands were dragged into the interior to be sacrificed to the superstitions of the conquerors. Famines, unmitigated by labour, succeeded the wide waste of the Fantee territory, the wretched remnant of the population abandoning itself to despair; and the prolonged blockade of Cape Coast Castle in the last invasion, engendered so much distress and hazard, that the Government having averted imminent danger by advancing a large sum of gold on account of the Fantees, earnestly desired the Committee to authorise and enable them to venture an Embassy, to deprecate these repeated calamities, to conciliate so powerful a monarch, and to propitiate an extension of commerce. By the store ship which arrived in 1817, the African Committee forwarded liberal and suitable presents, and associated scientific with the political objects of the Mission, in their instructions, which I submit in explanation.

" In order to enable you to redeem the promise to the King of Ashantee (and as we are sanguine in our hopes of the good that may result from it), we send you sundry articles as presents for him, to which you may add such others from the public stores as you may deem desirable, provided they will not materially increase the expense. The Committee are extremely anxious (and in this respect the wishes of all classes of people in this country go with them) that no exertions should be spared to become better acquainted with the Interior of Africa; and we consider the existing state of things to be most favourable for undertaking an exploratory Mission into the dominions of the King of Ashantee. If, therefore, nothing shall have transpired in the interim of this dispatch being received by you, to make the measure objectionable, we wish you to obtain permission from the King to send an Embassy to his capital : if granted, you will select three Gentlemen (one of them from the medical department*) for that service ; and let them be accompanied by a respectable escort, you giving them the fullest instructions for their government. In particular, it will be necessary for them to observe, and report upon, the nature of the country ; its soil and products ; the names, and distances, and the latitude and longitude of the principal places ; and its most remarkable natural objects : the appearance, distinguishing characters, and manners of the natives ; their religion, laws, customs, and forms of government, as far as they can be ascertained ; and by whom each place is governed. When at Ashantee, they should

* We recommend his being well supplied with dressings, &c. for wounds, and bruises, so that he may be able to assist any natives whom he may meet with requiring his aid: services of this sort give Negroes an exalted idea of white men, and are always gratefully remembered.

endeavour to obtain the fullest information of the countries beyond, in each direction; particularly whether any high mountains, lakes, or large rivers are known; and the width, depth, course, and direction of the latter; and whether the water, as well of the lakes as the rivers, is salt or fresh : and how far, and under what circumstances, white men may travel with safety, especially in a northerly direction. They should collect the most accurate information possible of the extent, population, and resources of the Ashantee dominions, and should report fully their opinion of the inhabitants, and of the progress they may have made in the arts of civilized life. They should be directed also, to procure and bring away (with the consent of the chiefs) any specimens of vegetable and mineral productions they may be able: and to ascertain where and how the natives collect the gold, and the extent to which the trade in that article, and in ivory, might be carried on. It would, we conceive, be a most important advantage, if the King of Ashantee, and some of his chiefs, could be prevailed upon to send one or more of their children to the Cape, to be educated at the expense of the Committee (to be attended by their own servants, if required), under the guarantee of the Governor and Council for their personal safety, and that they should be sent back when required.

" Another great object would be, to prevail upon the King to form, and keep open, a path not less than six feet wide, from his capital, as far as his territories extend towards Cape Coast, you engaging on the part of the Committee, to continue it from that point to Cape Coast, which we presume may be done at a very small expense, by means of monthly allowances to the chiefs of such villages as be in that line; upon condition that they shall not allow the path to be overgrown with underwood, or otherwise obstructed.

" It may perhaps be found, that high mountains, or a large river, may be not many days journey beyond Ashantee ; in which case, if the Gentlemen composing the Embassy feel themselves secure in the attempt, they may probably be disposed to proceed so far. In such event, we authorize you to pay their drafts for any moderate sums which they may find it necessary to expend, as well as for the general objects of the Mission.

" Besides the escort of which we have spoken, we think it necessary, or at least extremely important, that the Embassy should be accompanied by natives of character and consequence, conversant with the Ashantee language, in whom you have perfect confidence, selected, one from each of the towns of Cape Coast, Accra, and Apollonia, to whom you may make reasonable allowances for their time and trouble.

" We have said that you should obtain the permission of the King of Ashantee to send the Embassy: we have doubts of the expediency of requiring hostages ; but, we presume you will concur with us in thinking, it will be necessary, before it leaves Cape Coast, that a man of consequence should be specially sent down by the King, to serve as a guide and protector ; and who, on his journey to Cape Coast, may arrange with the messenger whom you may send to the King, respecting the places at which the Embassy may stop to refresh, and give directions to open the paths that may be overgrown.

" The Gentlemen whom you may select, will of course be well advised by you not to interfere with any customs of the natives, however absurd ; or in any way to give them offence. And they cannot too strongly impress upon the minds of the King and people of Ashantee, that the only objects his Britannic Majesty has in view, are, to extend the trade with that country ; to prevent all interruption to their free communication with the waterside ;

and to instruct their children in reading, writing, &c. from which, as may be easily pointed out, the greatest advantages must arise to the Ashantees.

" From what has been said, you, Gentlemen, will perceive, that in selecting the Embassy, it is important that one of the persons composing it should be able to determine the latitude and longitude of places, and that both shall be seasoned to the climate; of ability, physical and mental; of cool tempers, and moderate habits; and possessed of fortitude and perseverance; and that in the selection of their escort also, regard be had to the qualifications of the parties in those respects. Among them there should be a bricklayer, carpenter, blacksmith, gunsmith, and cooper, with proper tools; if these persons can be spared for the purpose. We wish also they should take with them a number of *certificates regarding Major Peddie*, and his companions, to be circulated as distinctly as possible in the Interior; for though the period may be past when they might have been useful to those travellers, it is yet possible that they may be of use in making generally known the object of Government in sending white men to explore that country."

The suggestion of hostages was wholly impracticable, for there was not even time for a communication with the King. A variety of circumstances conspired to urge the immediate dispatch of the Mission; our interests, to say the least, imperiously demanded its early interference; and had we waited for a formal permission from the King to relieve the difficulties of the enterprise, the rainy season would have been too far advanced, and the critical moment have escaped us. The Governor thought it more advisable to dispatch the Mission without an escort, and two native soldiers only were added to the bearers of the baggage. The perusal of the Governor's instructions will be satisfactory to the reader:

Cape Coast Castle, April 19th, 1817

FREDERICK JAMES, Esq.

SIR,

IN accepting your voluntary offer of conducting the Embassy to the King of Ashantee, I have every reason to believe, that from your long experience in this country, and your knowledge of the manners and habits of the natives, it will terminate in a manner highly creditable to yourself, and eventually prove of the greatest importance to the commercial interest of Great Britain, which is the more immediate object of the Mission; however, as many subjects of scientific research may be associated with it, they are particularly recommended to your attention. For this purpose Mr. Bowdich will accompany you; and I have no doubt he will be found perfectly qualified to make the necessary observations, in which you will afford him every facility and assistance. He is provided with instruments for determining the latitude and longitude of places. Mr. Hutchison, writer, and Mr. Tedlie, assistant surgeon, will also be attached to the expedition.

The Ashantees, who are appointed your guides, have been selected by the Ashantee Captain who is now here. They will, I hope, aid and assist you in every thing that lays in their power.

In addition to the Committee's instructions, a copy of which you have herewith, you will attend to the following:

On the subject of your journey, I have nothing to observe further, than, that I hope you will take every opportunity of travelling when there will be the least exposure to the sun, as the officers who accompany you have been but a short time in the country, and every precaution will be necessary for the preservation of their health.

As soon as may be convenient after your arrival at the Ashantee

c

capital, you will of course see the King, and deliver him the various presents in the name of the African Company, to be received by him as pledges of the harmony and friendship which is ever to subsist between them; and also of his good will towards the natives residing under the protection of their different forts. You will not fail to impress upon his mind, the great power, wealth, and consequence of the British nation, and how much it is the interest of himself and his subjects, to promote and perpetuate their present free intercourse with the water side. In the course of your interview many circumstances will doubtless occur, which will suggest various other matters proper to be mentioned to the King, all which I shall leave entirely to your own discretion.

You will acquaint the King, that in order to secure a correct communication between him and myself, I request his permission to allow an officer to reside constantly at Commassey, who will defray all his own expenses, and for whom you will build a house without loss of time. A carpenter, bricklayer, and cooper are sent with you, and you will leave them with Mr. Hutchison, who will remain as Resident. On your departure you will give him full instructions in writing for his future government, a copy of which you will deliver me upon your return.

You will keep an exact diary of every circumstance possessing the least interest, a copy of which you will transmit me by every opportunity.

In the course of your stay in the Ashantee country, you will embrace every occasion of becoming acquainted with the politics of that nation, of ascertaining its extent and boundaries, the power of the King over the lives and property of his subjects, the probable force he could bring into the field, the number of his allies, the sources and amount of his revenues. Whether he is tributary to any other power, and what nations in his neighbourhood are tributary to him? The amount of tribute, and in what articles paid? The rule of succession to the throne? What are the punishments for crimes of all descriptions? Who are the persons of most consequence next to the King? The names of their offices, and the extent of their power: by whom, or how paid? What are the most prominent features in the character, manners, and habits of the people, &c. &c. &c.?

Are any human sacrifices made? Upon what occasions, and to what extent? How are prisoners of war now disposed of?

Of what nation are the Moors that frequent the Ashantee country, and for what purpose do they go there?

Ascertain the current medium of exchange, whether gold, or cowries; also the usual prices at which the Ashantees sell the goods they purchase from the Europeans on the sea coast; and the extent of their commercial relations with the Interior.

You will enquire whether any European travellers have ever been seen or heard of in any of the countries to the northward; and what became of them? Whether any thing be known of the river Niger, or Joliba, as it is called by the natives? This information you will probably obtain from the Moors.

Ascertain the position of the Doncoe country, and the city of Kong; also the mountains of that name. Refer to Park's Travels, and acquire as much information as possible of the regions lying between Ashantee and the last places he visited. In short, leave nothing undone that may add to our present imperfect geographical knowledge of the Interior.

You will receive herewith copies of certificates relative to Major Pedde's expedition, which you will distribute amongst any persons you find travelling into the Interior from Ashantee.

It would be of the first importance to have a road cut directly down to Cape Coast; and this you will urge to the King in the strongest manner. Your observations will, of course, enable you to point out the proper directions.

I inclose a sketch of a treaty, and it would be highly desirable if you could procure its ratification by the King. He might perhaps make some objection at first, but may be persuaded at length, by your address, and reasoning. If he wished any trifling alteration made, you might use your discretion in this respect.

You will acquaint the King, it is my wish that in future he receive his company's pay at this Castle, and not at Accra, as formerly. Should he say any thing of an increase to his present allowance, you may give him hopes that it will be granted to a reasonable extent, provided the objects of this Mission be fulfilled, and after twelve months experience shall have proved the sincerity of his friendship to the British Government, and to the natives resident under its protection at the various forts on the Coast.

From the jealous disposition of the natives of Africa, it is highly probable, that in the prosecution of your enquiries, you will be subject to many unfavourable suspicions. These you will take all possible care to remove, by the most candid explanations on every point that may be required.

You will particularly explain to the King, the ill treatment the people of Cape Coast have experienced from those of Elmina, which has added very much to the distresses they have for some time suffered from the extreme scarcity of provisions; and there is reason to believe, that this unjust persecution has been induced, from their presuming on their connection with the Ashantees. Being perfectly aware that it has been done without the concurrence of the King; I have no doubt but he will, by a proper representation of the affair from you, exert his influence, and prevent what is at present to be apprehended, and what the

Elminas are endeavouring to provoke — a war between the two people.

In all cases not provided for in these Instructions, you have of course a discretionary power, which I am convinced you will make use of with deliberation and prudence, and with becoming zeal for the service upon which you are employed.

Wishing you a prosperous journey and a safe return,

I am, Sir, your most obedient Servant,

JOHN HOPE SMITH.

CHAPTER II.

The Route, and Reception of the Mission.

Tʜᴇ Mission left Cape Coast Castle on the morning of the 22d of April, with the intention of quitting the water side at Moree, three miles and a half to the eastward ; but on reaching it, we were told that the path thence to Payntree's croom, always bad, was then impassable from the rains; and that we must proceed to Annamaboe before we struck into the bush for the Interior.

The reluctance of the carriers, who had been pressed into the service by the authorities of the town, became thus early almost insuperable; the consideration of pay and subsistence, and the reflection, that the dearth inflicted by the invasions the Mission was to deprecate, allowed them but a bare existence at home, were entirely lost in their aversion to the undertaking, which was equally influenced by jealousy and indolence: eleven deserted the first day; and the slender authority of the King and caboceers of Annamaboe, delayed the procuring of others to replace them until the next evening. One party was then started, attended by a soldier and a messenger, as they persisted in laying down their loads, even in the town; and many of the Annamaboes who had been procured, after lifting their packages, which were of moderate weight, walked off again, with the most insolent indifference. The devices by which these people displayed their ill will were peculiarly their own, and none could be more ingeniously tormenting. At four o'clock on Thursday morning we started the remainder of the packages, and followed them at half past six. Proceeding about two miles in a N. N.W. direction, we descended a steep hill, a quarter of a mile in length, and entered a beautiful valley, profusely covered with pines, aloes, and lilies ; and richly varied with palm, banana, plantain, and guava trees : the view was refreshed by gentle risings crowned with cotton trees of a stupendous size. I never saw soil so rich, or vegetation so luxuriant.

The first croom we reached was Quama's, about three miles and a half from Annamaboe ; it presented but a few hovels ; and we passed through three others, Simquoi, Taphoo, and Nasmam, just as wretched and insignificant, before we reached Booka, romantically situated amidst the luxuriant foliage of a high hill, terminating the valley. Abra is about three miles eastward of this croom : it has been entirely deserted since the last invasion, the Ashantee army under Appia Nanu having made it their head quarters. It formerly exceeded Annamaboe, but the little that now remains is in ruin, the inhabitants having retired to the small crooms of their caboceer, or Captain Quaggherce.

Passing through Tachradi, which scarcely existed but in name, we ascended a gentle rising, with a small croom, called Acroofroom, on the left hand. The astonishment of its miserable inhabitants engaging our attention, the extensive area of the summit burst upon us with the more effect. It was environed by small groves ; and clumps of cotton trees rose so happily in frequent spots, as to afford all the scenery of a romantic little park ; the broken rays of the sun stealing through the small trees in the distance, to make the deep shade of the foreground more imposing. The path then became more hilly, and the landscape fuller of wood : our descents and risings frequently through long vistas, so

richly gilded with the sun on the summits, that, impressed with
the description of Issert, we naturally yielded to the expectation,
in ascending each eminence, that it would afford us the delightful
prospect of an open country; but we were disappointed, and
passing through Dunnasee and Assoquah, both small crooms, the
latter situated on a long level, about three miles and a half from
Acroofroom, we shortly after arrived at Payntree's.

On the higher hills the soil was generally gravel, with large
stones; on the lesser, white flint and whinstone abounded: the
levels presented few stones, and the earth was black, strong, and
rich, producing grass from four to ten feet high. The country was
very thinly inhabited, and more sparingly cultivated, the cassada
frequent, but producing little from the want of cultivation.

I made Payntree's croom barely fifteen miles from Annamaboe;
judging from time, it was guessed to be eighteen or twenty; but
the impediments which the path almost incessantly presented to a
hammock, the inequalities of the ground, and many delays which
insensibly consumed the time, conspired to make such a calculation of distance very fallacious. The plan I adopted throughout,
though laborious, entitled me to more confidence; and the observations confirmed the pretension. Mr. Tedlie, who was always
just ahead of myself, took the angles of the path by his compass,
which I pencilled as he uttered them, with their several lengths,
allowing four yards and a half for every six paces. It is allowed
too by the natives to be an easy four hours walk. Several hours
elapsed before all the carriers came up; most of those who had
been started by us the preceding day, slept in the bush, and one
more had deserted.

The prevailing courses and their proportions were N.$\frac{1}{4}$; N.bW.$\frac{1}{8}$;
N.N.W.$\frac{1}{8}$; N.N.E.$\frac{1}{8}$; the rest of the distance being made up of
small lengths, in every point of the compass, from S.W. to S.E.;

the variation $17\frac{3}{4}°$ W. The latitude of Payntree, by two altitudes of the sun, was 5° 20' 30" N.; the longitude, by the course and distance, as afterwards corrected, 1° 47' W.

We received the compliments of Payntree and several caboceers, under a large tree, and were then conducted to a neat and comfortable dwelling, which had been prepared for us : a small square area afforded a shed for cooking in on one side, and a sleeping room in each of the others, open in front, but well thatched, and very clean : from this we passed to our sitting room, the floor of which was elevated about two feet from the ground.

The croom was prettily situated on a level, encircled by very fine trees, and consisted of a very broad and well cleaned street of small huts, framed of bamboo, and neatly thatched. Just beyond the north end of the croom, there was a stream running to the N. N. E. and more than a mile of marshy ground was distinguished by the deeper shade and luxuriance of the foliage. We observed a great number of small birds, which were even more beautiful from their delicate symmetry, than their brilliant plumage ; they were generally green, with black wings, and their nests hanging from the trees.

The Ashantee captain, who expected to continue there some months, on the king's business, sent us a sheep, pleading the scarcity, and his being a stranger, as apologies for so small a present. Old Payntree was attentive and obliging ; he dashed us some fowls, yams, and palm wine. We remained there the next day, to allow our people to procure four days subsistence, as they would not be able to meet with provision on the path during that period.

I walked with Mr. Tedlie along a very neat path well fenced, and divided by *stiles*, to a corn plantation of at least twenty acres, and well cultivated. Payntree's farm house was situated here, and afforded superior conveniences ; a fowl house, a pigeon house, and a large granary raised on a strong stage. As we returned we paid him a visit, and were refreshed with some excellent palm wine: his dwelling was a square of four apartments, which were entered from an outer one, where a number of drums were kept; the angles were occupied by the slaves, and his own room, which had a small inner chamber, was decked with muskets, blunderbusses, cartouch belts fantastically ornamented, and various. insignia. The order, cleanliness, and comfort, surprised us; the sun had just set, and a cheerful fire on a clean hearth supported the evening meal. The old man was seated in his state chair, diverting himself with his children and younger wives, the elder one was looking on from the opposite apartment with happy indifference; it was the first scene of domestic comfort I had witnessed among the natives. There was a small plantation or garden neatly fenced in, near the house, for the supply of the family.

On Saturday the 26th we left Payntree's croom, and proceeded through two romantic little valleys, with a few huts in each: the variety of trees increased with the number, and ornamented the hills with almost every tint and character of foliage: the path was frequently covered with water. Just before we reached Cotta-coomacasa, a most beautiful landscape opened, the fore-ground darkly shaded with large cotton trees, and the distance composed of several picturesque little hills; their fanciful outlines, and the beautiful variety of fresh and sombre tint of the small groves which encircled them, forcibly reminded me of the celebrated ride by Grongar hill, from Carmarthen to Llandilo.

Cottacoomacasa is about six miles and a quarter from Payntree's croom, and consisted but of a few miserable huts and sheds, which scarcely afforded shelter, and were close and filthy. I took the angles of a cotton tree near us, and the height proved to be 139 feet; generally speaking, those we had passed were, to appearance, much higher. The bearers had all settled themselves here, and not contented with a long rest, refused for some time to proceed until the next day; several were intoxicated with the rum from some ankers they had designedly broken. We started again however about half past three, and almost immediately entered a large forest impervious to the sun; the risings were frequent but gentle; the path, crooked and overgrown, presented such constant obstacles to a hammock, that Mr. Hutchison, Mr. Tedlie, and myself, were glad to dismount, and found it was much more comfortable as well as more expeditious to walk; the only inconvenience was the troops of large black ants, which were too thick to be avoided, and stung us sadly. We passed two little streams running E. N. E. About six miles from Cottacoomacasa we found all the baggage, the people making their fires, and settling themselves for the night; it was almost dark; Quamina, our Ashantee guide, had gone on without us, and Mr. James we knew must be far behind; we therefore determined to halt for the night, and our hammocks were slung to the trees. The distance marched this day was twelve miles. The longitude of Cottacoomacasa was one mile E. of that of Payntree by account, that of our resting place 1° 46′ 30′ W. and the lat. 5° 28′ N.

The next morning we continued our march through the same dark solitude, and passing three small streams running E. we reached Mansue soon after ten o'clock. We had scarcely seated ourselves under a tattered shed, which could not defend us from the burning sun, when we were encircled by the cooking fires of the party, and nothing but violence could remove them to a proper distance.

Mansue had been the great Fantee market for slaves from the Interior, and its former consequence was evident from the extent of its site, over which a few sheds only were now scattered.

We proceeded again at one o'clock, and passing through a small river, Assooneara, running eastward, we came to a second, called Okee, running in the same direction to the Amissa, which falls into the sea between Annamaboe and Tantum. We passed five or six swamps, one nearly half a mile long; in these the soil was a dark clay, but otherwise gravelly. We halted in the woods at a spot where our guide Quamina was busied in cutting down the underwood to accommodate himself and his women; the bearers, resolute in their perverseness, had gone on with our provisions and clothes. The ground of our resting place was very damp, and swarmed with reptiles and insects; we had great difficulty in keeping up our fires, which we were the more anxious to do after a visit from a panther: an animal which, the natives say, resembles a small pig, and inhabits the trees, continued a shrill screeching through the night; and occasionally a wild hog bounced by, snorting through the forest, as if closely pursued. This day's distance was eight miles, and the course N. ¼ N. b. E. ⅙. Lat. and long. by account 5° 34′ N. and 1° 48′ W. Thermometer in shade 6 A. M. 74.

We started the next morning at seven o'clock, and after three miles and a half crossed a small river called Gaia, and sometimes Aniabirrim, from a croom of that name being formerly in its neighbourhood; it was ten yards wide and two feet deep, and ran to the E. just across the path, but afterwards N. N. E. to the Amissa. Here Mr. Hutchison waited for Mr. James to come up, whilst Mr. Tedlie and myself walked on to overtake the people. The doom and iron-wood trees were frequent; the path was a labyrinth of the most capricious windings, the roots of the cotton trees obstructing it continually, and our progress was generally by stepping and jumping up and down, rather than walking; the stems or caudices of these trees projected from the trunks like flying buttresses, their height frequently 20 feet. Immense trunks of fallen trees presented constant barriers to our progress, and increased our fatigues from the labour of scaling them : we were also frequently obliged to wait the cutting away of the underwood before we could proceed, even on foot. The large trees were covered with parasites and convolvuli, and the climbing plants, like small cables, ascending the trunks to some height, abruptly shot downwards, crossed to the opposite trees, and threaded each other in such a perplexity of twists and turnings, that it soon became impossible to trace them in the general entanglement. We passed through two small streams running S. and several swamps, richly covered with palm trees. Parrots and crown birds were numerous. At the end of ten miles we came to a small river called Quatoa, four yards wide, also running eastward to the Amissa ; and immediately after to a few sheds bearing the same name, where we found the last party of the bearers all lying down, and a soldier ineffectually endeavouring to rouse them : we started them with difficulty. A mile and a half thence we met with the Okee again, running over its rocky bed in a transparent stream, which reflected the richest foliage ; its course S.W. $\frac{1}{2}$ W., the breadth nine yards, and we stepped across it from rock to rock. We soon afterwards walked through the Antoonso, a smaller river running W. S.W., which probably crossed the path to the eastward in one of the small streams near Cottacoomacasa, as every report confirmed its also running to the Amissa ; it was very near Fousou, where we had scarcely arrived, before the Fantees, such was their perverseness, insisted upon going on, the Cape Coast messengers either had no influence or would not exert it ; we soon stopped them with the assistance of Quamina, our Ashantee guide, Mr. James not coming up until late in the evening. Fousou was formerly a large town, but had been destroyed by the Ashantee invasion of 1807 ; it presented but a few sheds, in one of which we observed the Ashantee traders to deposit yams and plantains to subsist them on their return ; so severe was the scarcity in the Fantee country : we could purchase nothing, and were admitted to the best hovel with reluctance. This day's distance was 14 miles. The courses N. ½ N. N.W. ¼ N. b W. ⅛. The latitude of Fousou by observation, was 5° 43′ 20″ N. and the longitude by account 1° 52′ W.

The next morning, the 29th of April, we marched seven miles to Ancomassa, a name given to half a dozen sheds ; the path was still of the same rugged nature, and the gloom unvaried. A strong fragrance was emitted from the decaying plants and trees of the mimosa kind, whilst others in the same incipient state of putrefaction were very offensive. We passed through two small rivers, Bettensin and Soubin, six yards wide, and shallow ; they both ran eastward to the Owa, of which I could not learn more than that it emptied itself into the Boosempra.

We proceeded at four o'clock, and had not gone two miles on our gloomy route before it became dark. The path was level, but very swampy, and generally covered with water. The fire-flies spangled the herbage in every direction, and from the strength of their light, alternately excited the apprehension of wild beasts, and the hope that we approached the resting place our guide, whom we never saw after starting, had told us of in the morning. The greatest fear of the people was of the spirits of the woods, (whom Mr. Park's interpreter, Johnson, propitiated by a sacrifice between Jing and Gangaddi) and the discordant yells in which they rivalled each other to keep up their courage, mingled with the howls and screeches from the forest, imposed a degree of horror on this dismal scene, which associated it with the imaginations of Dante. Three or four times we suddenly emerged from the most awful gloom into extensive areas, on which the stars shed a brilliancy of light gradually softened into the deep shade which encompassed them; they were the sites of large and populous crooms destroyed in the Ashantee invasions. About nine o'clock we discovered a few miserable sheds, which the noise of the bearers, who had long arrived, convinced us to be Accomfodey. We had passed two small rivers, the Aprinisee and Annuia, both running to the Boosempra. This day's distance was 11 miles, and the courses N. $\frac{1}{3}$ N. b W. $\frac{1}{5}$. The lat. and long. by account 5° 49′ N. and 1° 55′ W. Thermometer 11 a. m. 80.

We marched early the next morning. The scenery of the forest, excepting on the banks of the small rivers, was very naked of foliage, and only presented a harsh and ragged confusion of stems and branches intricately blended. We passed a small river soon after leaving Accomfodey, bearing the same name and running eastward; and shortly after another, six yards wide and two feet deep (the Berrakoo), running N. E. to the Boosempra. The path was sometimes trackless, and appeared to have been little used since the invasion of 1807; several human skulls were scattered through this dark solitude, the relics of the butchery. We halted about two o'clock by Mr. James's direction, and passed the night in the forest. This day's distance was eight miles, the prevailing courses N. $\frac{1}{4}$, N. b W. $\frac{1}{8}$, N. N. W. $\frac{1}{8}$, N. b E. $\frac{1}{8}$. The latitude and longitude by account 5° 58′ N. 1° 55′ W. Thermometer 2 p. m. 88$\frac{1}{2}$, 7 p. m. 82$\frac{1}{2}$.

The next morning we passed some sheds, on the sites of the crooms Dansamsou and Meakirring. At the end of five miles and a quarter, the herbage to the right disclosed the cheerful reflections of the sun from the water; and we descended through a small vista of the forest, to the banks of the Boosempra or Chamah river. Nothing could be more beautiful than its scenery: the bank on the south side was steep, and admitted but a narrow path; that on the north sloping; on which a small Fetish house, under the shade of a cachou tree, fixed the eye; whence it wandered over a rich variety of tint and foliage, in which light and shade were most happily blended: the small rocks stole through the herbage of the banks, and now and then ruffled the water: the doom trees towering in the shrubbery, waved to the most gentle air a rich foliage of dark green, mocking the finest touch of the pencil; the tamarind and smaller mimosas heightening its effect by their livelier tint, and the more piquant delicacy of their leaf: the cotton trees overtopped the whole, enwreathed in convolvuli, and several elegant little trees, unknown to me, rose in the background, intermixed with palms, and made the coup d'oeil enchanting. The bright rays of the sun were sobered by the rich reflections of the water; and there was a mild beauty in the landscape, uncongenial to barbarism, which imposed the expectation of elegance and refinement. I attempted a sketch, but it was far beyond my rude pencil; the expression of the scene could only have been traced in the profile of every tree; and it seemed to defy any touches, but those of a Claude or a Wilson, to depict the life of its beauty. I took two angles from a base on the south side, which gave the width of the river, forty three yards; the depth was 7 feet, and the course N.W.$\frac{1}{2}$W. with a very strong current. A small river called Nimeä, ran into it, close to our right as we landed: we crossed in the hollow trunk of a tree, thirty feet long, the ends plastered up with sticks and swish.

Mansue was said to have been the last town of the Fantee territory; but we had no opportunity for comparison until we passed the river, the country thitherto presenting all the gloom of depopulation, and the forest fast recovering the sites of the large towns destroyed in the Ashantee invasions. The inhabitants of the few wretched hovels, remotely scattered, seemed as if they had fled to them as outcasts from society; they were lost even to curiosity, and manners were brutal and sullen.* We could purchase nothing for our subsistence.

The scene brightened from our crossing the Boosempra; the path improved, and Prasoo, the first town, only three quarters of a mile from the river, presented a wide and clean street of tolerably regular houses; the inhabitants clean and cheerful, left their various occupations to gratify their curiosity, and saluted us in a friendly and respectful manner: indeed the Assins may be considered, collectively, a more mannerly and orderly people than the Ashantees. Kickiwherree, one mile and a half distant, was a larger town, not so regular, but presenting the same neat appearance, improved by the white-washing of many of the houses. We halted here under the ganian† tree, used, generally speaking, for recreation only, palavers being talked in the open fronts of the houses. We were conducted to a comfortable dwelling, affording us four very clean rooms, about 12 feet by 7, in which there were shelves containing many articles of superior domestic comfort; a curtain or skreen of bamboo let down in the open front, and the floors raised about a foot and half from the ground, were washed daily with an earth of the neighbourhood, which coloured them Etruscan red. The iron stone abounded. Kickiwherree was 7 miles from the previous resting place, and the prevailing courses N.¼ N.b.W.⅐. The latitude by observation was 5° 56′ 40″ N; the longitude by account 1° 57′ W. Thermometer 8 a. m. 77; 1 p.m. 91.

My observations had not been so frequent as I wished; the nature of the country, and the season of the year were both very

* Every account I received afterwards, confirmed the boundary of the Fantee and Assin territories to be between Mansue and Fousou; also that Ancomassa, Accomfodey, Dansamsou, Meakirring, &c. &c. had all been large Assin crooms, destroyed with many others in their neighbourhood, in the Ashantee invasion of 1807.

† This is the same tree as the banian or India fig.

unfavourable to them.   I worked the double altitudes, invariably by Dr. Pemberton's rule in Keith's trigonometry, which requires no assumed latitude, and is in all cases accurate.

Mr. James having determined to rest the next day at Kicki-wherree, we did not proceed until Saturday the 3rd of May.   We passed through a small river close to the town, called the Ading, six yards wide and two feet deep; and soon after a second, the Animiasoo, nine yards wide, and three feet deep, both running to the Boosempra; close to the latter was a large croom of the same name, the seat of Cheboo's government.   Pagga and Atobiasee were also large crooms near each other, and within four miles of Kickiwherree.   At Atobiasee was a small river called Prensa, five yards wide, and two feet deep, which ran E.S.E. to the Boosempra: two miles thence we came to Becquama, a very old croom, with a river nine yards wide, called Prapong, running E. by S. to the Boosempra; and at the end of nine miles we halted at Asharaman, a small croom on an eminence, where the Assins under Apootey and Cheboo, first engaged the Ashantees in 1807.   There was a small plot of corn near this croom, the first we had seen since we left Payntree, though every croom was surrounded by a tract of cultivated land, or plantation of plantains.   The path continued through forest.   Distance 8 miles.   Courses N. $\frac{1}{4}$.   Latitude by observation, 5° 59′ 20″.   Longitude by course and distance 1° 57′ 40″ W.   Thermometer 6 a. m. 76, p. m. 89.

The next day we passed through Ansa, a large croom, where Amoo had governed; north-west of which, at a little distance, was Aboiboo, the residence of his enemy Apootey.   A small river near Ansa, called Parakoomee, eleven yards wide, and three feet deep, ran south to a larger, called Ofim or Foom, which rises six days northward of Coomassie, and falls into the Boosempra some miles westward of our crossing.   The path was very swampy, and we did not reach Akrofroom until three o'clock : this was by far the largest croom we had seen. The heavy rains during the night floated us in our lodgings, and, as Quamina reported, rendered the path to Moisee impassable for the next day; consequently we did not proceed until Tuesday the 6th. Distance 12 miles. Courses N.⅕, N. N.W.¼. Latitude by observation, 6° 5′ 40″. Long: C and D 2° 2′. W. The path still through forest, presented frequent acclivities, and the iron stone, and a soft grey rock abounded; the soil was sometimes gravelly, but generally of a red coloured clay used in the native pottery. We passed the Parakoomee again twice, and at the end of 11 miles halted at Moisee,

" Cingebant silvæ ; quem collibus undique curvis,"

the last Assin town, at the foot of three high hills covered with wood, bearing W. N. W., N., and N. N. E.; the barriers of the Ashantee kingdom. Course N.⅕, N. W.b. N.⅐. N.b. E.⅛. Latitude by observation 6° 8′ 50″ N. Longitude C and D 2° 4′ 20″ W. The thermometer was broken on the 4th.

We passed the northern boundary the next morning; the ascent was a mile and a half in length, and very rocky; a small river called the Bohmen ran S.W. to the Jim, which falls into the Ofim : the water of the Bohmen is said to instil eloquence, and numerous Ashantees repair annually to drink of it: it flowed in a very clear stream, over a bed of gravel, and was three feet deep, and eight yards broad. The expectation of an open country was again disappointed ; I bore several eminent points, in the hope of being able to do so again at some distance, and of thus, with the intermediate course, checking the distance computed by paces ; but the forest soon shut them out entirely. The first Ashantee croom was Quesha; and we soon after passed through Fohmannee, which had been a very considerable town. We stopped there awhile at the request of a venerable old man, who regaled us with some palm wine and fruit: his manners were very pleasing, and made it more painful to us to hear that his life was forfeited to some superstitious observances, and that he only waited the result of a petition to the king to commiserate his infirmities so far as to allow him to be executed at his own croom, and to be spared the fatigue of a journey to the capital: he conversed cheerfully with us, congratulated himself on seeing white men before he died, and spread his cloth over the log with an emotion of dignity rather than shame: his head arrived at Coomassie the day after we had. On ascending the hill, the soil became a dark brown clay, and very productive.   We passed the first large plantation of corn we had seen since we left Payntree, and halted at Doompassee. Distance 6 miles.   Courses N. $\frac{1}{3}$. N. N.W. $\frac{1}{5}$. N. W. $\frac{1}{6}$:   Latitude by observation, 6° 11′ 30″.

Doompassee had been a very large croom, but the caboceer having intrigued with one of Sai Cudjoe's wives, who had permission to visit her family in this place, the greater part of it was destroyed in consequence, and the caboceer decapitated: the woman possessing irresistible art in practising upon the numerous admirers of her beauty, the king spared her life, and employed her thenceforth to inveigle those distant caboceers, whose lives or properties were desirable to him.   It was the most industrious town on the path; cloths, beads, and pottery were manufacturing in all directions, and the blacksmiths' forges were always at work. The intelligence of the beginning of the King's fetish week, and Mr. James's attack of fever, delayed us at Doompassee, and a messenger was dispatched in the interim to announce our approach. During our stay, I observed an eclipse of Jupiter's first satellite, which gave the longitude 2° 6′ W.

We did not leave Doompassee until the 14th of May; after two miles, passing a small stream running N.W. we ascended a high hill, on which a large croom, called Tiabosoo, was situated. I looked into a pit here six feet deep; the first stratum was vegetable mould, the second gravel, the third, a kind of potter's clay, and the remaining of brittle stone of a reddish brown, resembling that they call cabouc in the East Indies. The next croom was San-quanta, where the path took an easterly direction, and about seven miles from Doompassee we passed Datiasoo, where large quantities of pottery were manufacturing, exclusively: it was not more than a mile distant from Dadawasee, where we found a messenger from the king, expressing his regret that we had come up in the rainy season, as he had heard it was a very unhealthy one for white men, and appointing us to enter the capital on the Monday following; he sent us a present of a sheep, forty yams, and two ounces of gold for our table; he had also given six ackies to our messenger, who returned at the same time. The path had been cleared by the king's order, the plantations became more frequent and exten-sive, and numerous paths branching off from that we travelled, shewed that the country was thickly inhabited, and the intercourse of the various parts direct and necessary for an interchange of manufacture and produce: the crooms hitherto had appeared insulated. The Acassey or blue dye plant grew profusely. Distance seven miles. Courses N. $\frac{1}{4}$, N. b W. $\frac{1}{7}$, N. N. W. $\frac{1}{7}$, N. N. E. $\frac{1}{6}$. Latitude by observation 6° 16′ 20″ N. long: C and D 2° 7′ 30″ W.

The next day, leaving Dadawasee, close to which was another large croom called Modjawee, we descended a very steep hill, and passed the Dankaran or Mankaran, a small river, in the rainy season eleven yards wide and four feet deep, running to the Birrim: not far from this river was Sabnfoo, and a short distance from that croom, a smaller river called Yansee, running N. N. W. We then passed through Korraman, near which was the small river Dansabow, running westward, and three other large crooms,

Aquinasee (having a neatly fenced burial ground,) Amafou, and Agabimah; crossing another small river called Soubirree, near the latter, we reached Assiminia, distant eight miles from Dadawasee. The path was frequently eight feet wide, and kept as neatly as that of a garden in the environs of the crooms, which now disclosed themselves very prettily at some distance. Courses N. $\frac{1}{5}$, N.bE. $\frac{1}{6}$, N.N.E. $\frac{1}{6}$. Latitude by observation 6° 22′, longitude C and D 2° 7′ 50″ W.

There was a violent tornado in the night, during almost the whole of which the rain continued in torrents, increasing the small streams near the town from ancle to three feet deep. Almost all the inhabitants were employed in weaving the staple manufacture of Assiminia, which was formerly of much greater extent. Mr. James rested here the whole of the next day, and on Saturday we proceeded through Boposoo (on a very high hill), Agemum, Yoko, and Abountum; near which we crossed the Biaqua, running west to the Jim, and about seven yards wide and two feet deep; between this and Sarrasou, where we halted, were two large crooms, Pootooaga and Fiasou.

The path was continually well cleared: each croom presented one wide central street, with the ganian or cachou trees at the extremities. The soil ceased to be sandy, and became a reddish earth: we observed some quartz, but silex prevailed. Distance 11 miles. Courses N.$\frac{1}{4}$, N. N. E.$\frac{1}{5}$. Lat. by observation, 6° 30′ 20″. Long. C. and D. 2° 6′ 30.″

The river Dah runs close to Sarrasou, rising at Sekooree near Dwabin, and falling into the Ofim at Measee in the Warsaw path; it is generally about sixteen yards wide, and four feet deep. There was an ingenious fishing weir in this river; two rows of very strong wicker work were fixed across it, supported against the rapidity of the stream by large stakes, driven into the ground obliquely on each side of them, and connected above and below by the trunks of two large trees. The funnel-shaped baskets, thickly inserted at the bottom, were of split cane, and about twelve feet long. There are large plantations of corn around Sarrasou, which is a great nursery for pigs. We left it on Monday morning, the 19th, and passing through a small croom, Oyoko, stopped at another, Agogoo, about four miles distant, to dress ourselves in full uniform. The soil from Sarrasou was a rich black mould, and there were continued plantations of corn, yams, ground nuts, terraboys, and encruma: the yams and ground nuts were planted with much regularity in triangular beds, with small drains around each, and carefully cleared from weeds.

Two miles from Agogoo, we crossed the marsh which insulates Coomassie ; the breadth at that part forty yards, and the depth three feet. Being within a mile of the capital, our approach was announced to the king, who desired us by his messengers to rest at a little croom, called Patiasoo, until he had finished washing, when captains would be deputed to conduct us to his presence. Distance 6½ miles. Courses N.⅙, N. N.W.⅙.

We entered Coomassie at two o'clock, passing under a fetish, or sacrifice of a dead sheep, wrapped up in red silk, and suspended between two lofty poles. Upwards of 5000 people, the greater part warriors, met us with awful bursts of martial music, discordant only in its mixture ; for horns, drums, rattles, and gong-gongs were all exerted with a zeal bordering on phrenzy, to subdue us by the first impression. The smoke which encircled us from the incessant discharges of musquetry, confined our glimpses to the foreground ; and we were halted whilst the captains performed their Pyrrhic dance, in the centre of a circle formed by their warriors ; where a confusion of flags, English, Dutch, and Danish, were waved and flourished in all directions ; the bearers plunging and springing from side to side, with a passion of enthusiasm only equalled by the 'captains, who followed them, discharging their shining blunderbusses so close, that the flags now and then were in a blaze; and emerging from the smoke with all the gesture and distortion of maniacs. Their followers kept up the firing around us in the rear. The dress of the captains (see drawing, No. I.) was a war cap, with gilded rams horns projecting in front, the sides extended beyond all proportion by immense plumes of eagles feathers, and fastened under the chin with bands of cowries. Their vest was of red cloth, covered with fetishes and saphies* in gold and silver; and embroidered cases of almost every colour, which flapped against their bodies as they moved, intermixed with small brass bells, the horns and tails of animals, shells, and knives; long leopards tails hung down their backs, over a small bow covered with fetishes. They wore loose cotton trowsers, with immense boots of a dull red leather, coming half way up the thigh, and fastened by small chains to their cartouch or waist belt; these were also ornamented with bells, horses tails, strings of amulets, and innumerable shreds of leather; a small quiver of poisoned arrows hung from their right wrist, and they held a long iron chain between their teeth, with a scrap of Moorish writing affixed to the end of it. A small spear was in their left hands, covered with red cloth and silk tassels; their black countenances heightened the effect of this attire, and completed a figure scarcely human.

This exhibition continued about half an hour, when we were allowed to proceed, encircled by the warriors, whose numbers, with the crowds of people, made our movement as gradual as if it had taken place in Cheapside; the several streets branching off to the right, presented long vistas crammed with people, and those on the left hand being on an acclivity, innumerable rows of heads

* Scraps of Moorish writing, as charms against evil.

Drawn by T.E.Bowdich Esq.

Nº 1.

CAPTAIN in his WAR DRESS.

rose one above another : the large open porches of the houses, like the fronts of stages in small theatres, were filled with the better sort of females and children, all impatient to behold white men for the first time ; their exclamations were drowned in the firing and music, but their gestures were in character with the scene. When we reached the palace, about half a mile from the place where we entered, we were again halted, and an open file was made, through which the bearers were passed, to deposit the presents and baggage in the house assigned to us. Here we were gratified by observing several of the caboceers pass by with their trains, the novel splendour of which astonished us. The bands, principally composed of horns and flutes, trained to play in concert, seemed to soothe our hearing into its natural tone again by their wild melodies ; whilst the immense umbrellas, made to sink and rise from the jerkings of the bearers, and the large fans waving around, refreshed us with small currents of air, under a burning sun, clouds of dust, and a density of atmosphere almost suffocating. We were then squeezed, at the same funeral pace, up a long street, to an open-fronted house, where we were desired by a royal messenger to wait a further invitation from the king. Here our attention was forced from the astonishment of the crowd to a most inhuman spectacle, which was paraded before us for some minutes ; it was a man whom they were tormenting previous to sacrifice ; his hands were pinioned behind him, a knife was passed through his cheeks, to which his lips were noosed like the figure of 8 ; one ear was cut off and carried before him, the other hung to his head by a small bit of skin ; there were several gashes in his back, and a knife was thrust under each shoulder blade ; he was led with a cord passed through his nose, by men disfigured with immense caps of shaggy black skins, and drums beat before him ; the feeling this horrid barbarity excited must be imagined. We were soon released by

F

permission to proceed to the king, and passed through a very broad street, about a quarter of a mile long, to the market place.

Our observations en passant had taught us to conceive a spectacle far exceeding our original expectations ; but they had not prepared us for the extent and display of the scene which here burst upon us : an area of nearly a mile in circumference was crowded with magnificence and novelty. The king, his tributaries, and captains, were resplendent in the distance, surrounded by attendants of every description, fronted by a mass of warriors which seemed to make our approach impervious. The sun was reflected, with a glare scarcely more supportable than the heat, from the massy gold ornaments, which glistened in every direction. More than a hundred bands burst at once on our arrival, with the peculiar airs of their several chiefs ; the horns flourished their defiances, with the beating of innumerable drums and metal instruments, and then yielded for a while to the soft breathings of their long flutes, which were truly harmonious ; and a pleasing instrument, like a bagpipe without the drone, was happily blended. At least a hundred large umbrellas, or canopies, which could shelter thirty persons, were sprung up and down by the bearers with brilliant effect, being made of scarlet, yellow, and the most shewy cloths and silks, and crowned on the top with crescents, pelicans, elephants, barrels, and arms and swords of gold ; they were of various shapes, but mostly dome ; and the valances (in some of which small looking glasses were inserted) fantastically scalloped and fringed ; from the fronts of some, the proboscis and small teeth of elephants projected, and a few were roofed with leopard skins, and crowned with various animals naturally stuffed. The state hammocks, like long cradles, were raised in the rear, the poles on the heads of the bearers ; the cushions and pillows were covered with crimson taffeta, and the richest cloths hung over the sides.

Innumerable small umbrellas, of various coloured stripes, were crowded in the intervals, whilst several large trees heightened the glare, by contrasting the sober colouring of nature.

"   Discolor unde auri per ramos aura refulsit."

The king's messengers, with gold breast plates, made way for us, and we commenced our round, preceded by the canes and the English flag. We stopped to take the hand of every caboceer, which, as their houshold suites occupied several spaces in advance, delayed us long enough to distinguish some of the ornaments in the general blaze of splendour and ostentation.

The caboceers, as did their superior captains and attendants, wore Ashantee cloths, of extravagant price from the costly foreign silks which had been unravelled to weave them in all the varieties of colour, as well as pattern; they were of an incredible size and weight, and thrown over the shoulder exactly like the Roman toga; a small silk fillet generally encircled their temples, and massy gold necklaces, intricately wrought; suspended Moorish charms, dearly purchased, and enclosed in small square cases of gold, silver, and curious embroidery. Some wore necklaces reaching to the navel entirely of aggry beads; a band of gold and beads encircled the knee, from which several strings of the same depended; small circles of gold like guineas, rings, and casts of animals, were strung round their ancles; their sandals were of green, red, and delicate white leather; manillas, and rude lumps of rock gold, hung from their left wrists, which were so heavily laden as to be supported on the head of one of their handsomest boys. Gold and silver pipes, and canes dazzled the eye in every direction. Wolves and rams heads as large as life, cast in gold, were suspended from their gold handled swords, which were held around them in great numbers; the blades were shaped like round bills, and rusted in blood; the sheaths were of leopard skin, or the shell of a fish like shagreen.

The large drums supported on the head of one man, and beaten by two others, were braced around with the thigh bones of their enemies, and ornamented with their skulls. The kettle drums resting on the ground, were scraped with wet fingers, and covered with leopard skin. The wrists of the drummers were hung with bells and curiously shaped pieces of iron, which gingled loudly as they were beating. The smaller drums were suspended from the neck by scarves of red cloth; the horns (the teeth of young elephants) were ornamented at the mouth-piece with gold, and the jaw bones of human victims. The war caps of eagles feathers nodded in the rear, and large fans, of the wing feathers of the ostrich, played around the dignitaries; immediately behind their chairs (which were of a black wood, almost covered by inlays of ivory and gold embossment) stood their handsomest youths, with corslets of leopard's skin covered with gold cockle shells, and stuck full of small knives, sheathed in gold and silver, and the handles of blue agate; cartouch boxes of elephant's hide hung below, ornamented in the same manner; a large gold handled sword was fixed behind the left shoulder, and silk scarves and horses tails (generally white) streamed from the arms and waist cloth : their long Danish mukets had broad rims of gold at small distances, and the stocks were ornamented with shells. Finely grown girls stood behind the chairs of some, with silver basins. Their stools (of the most laborious carved work, and generally with two large bells attached to them) were conspicuously placed on the heads of favourites; and crowds of small boys were seated around, flourishing elephants tails curiously mounted. The warriors sat on the ground close to these, and so thickly as not to admit of our passing without treading on their feet, to which they were perfectly indifferent; their caps were of the skin of the pangolin and leopard, the tails hanging down behind; their cartouch belts (composed of small gourds which hold the charges, and covered with leopard or pig's skin) were embossed with red shells, and small brass bells thickly hung to them; on their hips and shoulders was a cluster of knives; iron chains and collars dignified the most daring, who were prouder of them than of gold; their muskets had rests affixed of leopard's skin, and the locks a covering of the same; the sides of their faces were curiously painted in long white streaks, and their arms also striped, having the appearance of armour.

We were suddenly surprised by the sight of Moors, who afforded the first general diversity of dress; there were seventeen superiors, arrayed in large cloaks of white satin, richly trimmed with spangled embroidery, their shirts and trowsers were of silk, and a very large turban of white muslin was studded with a border of different coloured stones: their attendants wore red caps and turbans, and long white shirts, which hung over their trowsers; those of the inferiors were of dark blue cloth: they slowly raised their eyes from the ground as we passed, and with a most malignant scowl.

The prolonged flourishes of the horns, a deafening tumult of drums, and the fuller concert of the intervals, announced that we were approaching the king: we were already passing the principal officers of his houshold; the chamberlain, the gold horn blower, the captain of the messengers, the captain for royal executions, the captain of the market, the keeper of the royal burial ground, and the master of the bands, sat surrounded by a retinue and splendor which bespoke the dignity and importance of their offices. The cook had a number of small services covered with leopard's skin held behind him, and a large quantity of massy silver plate was displayed before him, punch bowls, waiters, coffee pots, tankards, and a very large vessel with heavy handles and clawed feet, which seemed to have been made to hold incense; I observed a Portuguese inscription on one piece, and they seemed generally of that manufacture. The executioner, a man of an immense size, wore a massy gold hatchet on his breast; and the execution stool was held before him, clotted in blood, and partly covered with a cawl of fat. The king's four linguists were encircled by a splendor inferior to none, and their peculiar insignia, gold canes, were elevated in all directions, tied in bundles like fasces. The keeper of the treasury, added to his own magnificence by the ostentatious display of his service; the blow pan, boxes, scales and weights, were of solid gold.

A delay of some minutes whilst we severally approached to receive the king's hand, afforded us a thorough view of him; his deportment first excited my attention; native dignity in princes we are pleased to call barbarous was a curious spectacle: his manners were majestic, yet courteous; and he did not allow his surprise to beguile him for a moment of the composure of the monarch; he appeared to be about thirty-eight years of age, inclined to corpulence, and of a benevolent countenance; he wore a fillet of aggry beads round his temples, a necklace of gold cockspur shells strung by their largest ends, and over his right shoulder a red silk cord, suspending three saphies cased in gold; his bracelets were the richest mixtures of beads and gold, and his fingers covered with rings; his cloth was of a dark green silk; a pointed diadem was elegantly painted in white on his forehead; also a pattern resembling an epaulette on each shoulder, and an ornament like a full blown rose, one leaf rising above another until it covered his whole breast; his knee-bands were of aggry beads, and his ancle strings of gold ornaments of the most delicate workmanship, small drums, sankos, stools, swords, guns, and birds, clustered together; his sandals, of a soft white leather, were embossed across the instep band with small gold and silver cases of saphies; he was seated in a low chair, richly ornamented with gold; he wore a pair of gold castanets on his finger and thumb, which he clapped to enforce silence. The belts of the guards behind his chair, were cased in gold, and covered with small jaw bones of the same metal; the elephants tails, waving like a small cloud before him, were spangled with gold, and large plumes of feathers were flourished amid them. His eunuch presided over these attendants, wearing only one massy piece of gold about his neck: the royal stool, entirely cased in gold, was displayed under a splendid umbrella, with drums, sankos, horns, and various musical instruments, cased in gold, about the thickness of cartridge paper: large circles of gold hung by scarlet cloth from the swords of state, the sheaths as well as the handles of which were also cased; hatchets of the same were intermixed with them: the breasts of the Ocrahs, and various attendants, were adorned with large stars, stools, crescents, and gossamer wings of solid gold.

We pursued our course through this blazing circle, which afforded to the last a variety exceeding description and memory; so many splendid novelties diverting the fatigue, heat, and pressure we were labouring under; we were almost exhausted, however, by the time we reached the end; when, instead of being conducted to our residence, we were desired to seat ourselves under a tree at some distance, to receive the compliments of the whole in our turn.

The swell of their bands gradually strengthened on our ears, the peals of the warlike instruments bursting upon the short, but sweet responses of the flutes; the gaudy canopies seemed to dance in the distant view, and floated broadly as they were springing up and down in the foreground; flags and banners waved in the interval, and the chiefs were eminent in their crimson hammocks, amidst crowds of musquetry. They dismounted as they arrived within thirty yards of us; their principal captains preceded them with the gold handled swords, a body of soldiers followed with their arms reversed, then their bands and gold canes, pipes, and elephants tails. The chief, with a small body guard under his umbrella, was generally supported around the waist by the hands of his favourite slave, whilst captains holla'd, close in his ear, his warlike deeds and (strong) names, which were reiterated with the voices of Stentors by those before and behind; the larger party of warriors brought up the rear. Old captains of secondary rank were carried on the shoulders of a strong slave; but a more interesting sight was presented in the minors, or young caboceeers, many not more than five or six years of age, who overweighed by ornaments, were carried in the same manner, (under their canopies), encircled by all the pomp and parade of their predecessors. Amongst others, the grandson of Cheboo was pointed out, whom the king had generously placed on the stool of his perfidious enemy. A band of Fetish men, or priests, wheeled round and round as they passed with surprising velocity. Manner was as various as ornament; some danced by with irresistible buffoonery, some with a gesture and carriage of defiance; one distinguished caboceer performed the war dance before us for some minutes, with a large spear, which grazed us at every bound he made; but the greater number passed us with order and dignity, some slipping one sandal, some both, some turning round after having taken each of us by the hand; the attendants of others knelt before them, throwing dust upon their heads; and the Moors, apparently, vouchsafed us a blessing. The king's messengers who were posted near us, with their long hair hanging in twists like a thrum mop, used little ceremony in hurrying by this transient procession; yet it was nearly 8 o'clock before the king approached.

It was a beautiful star light night, and the torches which preceded him displayed the splendor of his regalia with a chastened lustre, and made the human trophies of the soldiers more awfully imposing. The skulls of three Banda caboceers, who had been his most obstinate enemies, adorned the largest drum: the vessels in which the boys dipped their torches were of gold. He stopped to enquire our names a second time, and to wish us good night; his address was mild and deliberate: he was followed by his aunts, sisters, and others of his family, with rows of fine gold chains around their necks. Numerous chiefs succeeded; and it was long before we were at liberty to retire. We agreed in estimating the number of warriors at 30,000.

We were conducted to a range of spacious, but ruinous buildings, which had belonged to the son of one of the former kings, and who had recently destroyed himself at a very advanced age, unable to endure the severity of disgrace: their forlorn and dreary aspect bespoke the fortune of their master, and they required much repair to defend us from the wind and rain, which frequently ushered in the nights.

CHAPTER III.

*Proceedings and Incidents until the Third Dispatch to Cape Coast
Castle.*

Coomassie, May 22nd, 1817.

To the Governor and Council, Cape Coast Castle.

Gentlemen,

THE important objects of the Mission, and the safety and prosperity of the Settlements, have this day demanded our public
dissent from our superior officer, Mr. James; to prove the act
tutelary to these objects, can be our only justification.

The Mission has engrossed our thoughts and exertions from the
moment we were honoured by the appointments; we have felt that
the credit of the Committee, the character of the service, and the
good of our country were associated in the enterprise; and that
we were personally responsible for these important objects, to the
extent of our industry, fortitude, and ability. Our reflections
naturally associated obstacles commensurate with the importance
of the objects affected; and to overcome the former in a manner
auspicious to the latter, we conceived to be the duty expected
from us, as composing a Mission originated to remove a portion of
the formidable barriers to the interior of Africa. We anticipated
prejudice, intrigue, and difficulty, as inevitable; as obstacles to
invigorate and not to sicken our exertions.

At Dadasey, on Wednesday the 14th instant, we received a present from the King, of two ounces of gold, a sheep, and thirty yams, with a second appointment to enter his capital the succeeding Monday. When within a short distance, the messenger who announced us, returned, to desire us to wait at a croom until the King had washed. We were permitted to enter soon after two o'clock, and the King received us with the most encouraging courtesy, and the most flattering distinction. We paid our respects in turn, (passing along a surprising extent of line) to the principal caboceers, many of remote, and several of Moorish territories; and all of these encircled by retinues astonishing to us from their numbers, order, and decorations. We were then requested to remove to a distant tree to receive their salutes; which procession, though simply transient, continued until past eight o'clock. It was indescribably imposing from the variety, magnificence, and etiquette: its faint outline in Mr. Bowdich's report, will impart our impression of the power and influence of the monarch we are sent to conciliate. The King as he passed, repeated his former condescensions.

The next morning (Tuesday) the King sent to us to come and speak our palaver in the market place, that all the people might hear it: we found him encircled by the most splendid insignia, and surrounded by his caboceers: we were received graciously. Mr. James, through his linguist, declared to the King's, (who are alone allowed to speak to him in public) that the objects of the Mission were friendship and commerce; impressed the consequence of our nation, and the good feelings of the Committee and Governor towards the King, as would be testified by our presents; he submitted the wish of a Residency, and of a direct path. The King enquired if we were to settle the Commenda palaver; the reply was, no! He rejoined, " that he wished the Governor of Cape Coast to settle all palavers for him with the people of the forts, and that he had thought we came to make all things right, and so to make friends with the Ashantees." The King had previously observed, as literally rendered, that " the forts belonged to him," meaning (as the context, and the whole of his sentiments and conduct have confirmed) nothing humiliating to our dignity and independence; but simply, that the advantages derived by the Fantee nations from the forts, should now be his. He desired the officer to be pointed out to him who was to be the Resident; and then enquired if that was all our palaver, he was told yes: he said he would give us his answer the next day.

Soon after we returned to our house, the King's linguist delivered this message. " The King knows very well the King of England has sent him presents; if you wish to be friends with him you must bring these presents to his own house, and shew them to him and his friends, and not give them before all the people." This, in our judgment was a policy, to prevent any favourable bias of the body of caboceers and people anticipating the King's and his councils satisfaction of our motives and professions.

We attended: all the curiosity the packages excited could not incline the King to regard them, until he had desired distinctly to understand who had sent them, the King of England, or the Governor. He was told, the Company to whom the forts belonged under the King; the interpreter seemed to render it the King individually; it was more intelligible, and the agreeable impression it made was striking. The presents were displayed. Nothing could surpass the King's surprise and pleasure, but his warm yet dignified avowal of his obligations. " Englishmen," said he, admiring the workmanship of the different articles, " know how to do every thing proper," turning to his favourites with a smile as auspicious to our interests, as mortal to the intrigues of our rival. Much of the glass was broken ; Mr. James expressed his regret, and offered to procure more ; the King replied, " the path we had come was bad and overgrown, that we had many people to look after;" and waved our excuses with superior courtesy. He desired the linguists to say, " this shewed him that the English were a great people, that they wished to be friends with him, to be as one with the Ashantees; that this made him much pleasure to see, (and to repeat again and again,) " that he thanked the King of England, the Governor at Cape Coast, and the officers who brought the presents much, very much." He made very liberal presents of liquor to our people, and delivered the distinct presents to his four principal caboceers in our sight.

We learned from Quashie, the Accra linguist, the favourable reports he had collected through his intimacy with some of the principal men. All the caboceers, he said, had thought we had come for bad, to spy the country ; the King thought so too a little, but much fetish was made, and all shewed that we meant well, and now the King thought so ; the mulatto sent by General Daendels, directly after Mr. Hydecoper, and who arrived just before us, had sent to the King for a pass to go back, and the King told him, that he would give him this message, " that the King had thought to do good to the Dutch, but now he sees their white mens faces, he should do good to the English." This mulatto man (who is not in the service, but a free man of Elmina town) visited us afterwards, and his complaints and sentiments confirmed these reports in our favour.

On Wednesday morning the King's sisters (one the caboceer of the largest Ashantee town near the frontier) paid us a visit of ceremony, and retired to receive our's in return ; their manners, were courteous and dignified, and they were handed with a surprising politeness by the captains in attendance.

Mr. James being indisposed, we went by invitation to see the chief captain's horse, when the King sent to us to say, he was walking that way, and requested us to get our chairs and wait, that he might bid us good morning. Directly he saw us he ordered the procession to alter its course, and stopped to take us by the hand. The procession consisted of about 2000 men, and was marked by all the suit and parade of royalty. The caboceers that day in attendance appeared as warriors, being divested of the rich silks of the preceding day; the executioner, the master of the bands, and the cook, were in the train, with suits which shewed the importance of their offices; the latter was preceded by a massy service of plate. Mr. Bowdich's report will be more particular.

The king sent his messenger this morning to repeat, that he thanked the King of England and the Governor very much for yesterday.

The King was much pleased when Quashie, the Accra linguist (who is our only intelligible medium,) attempted to describe the use of the sextant; consequently, when Mr. Bowdich saw the King's chief captain this morning, he offered to shew it to the King, with the camera obscura and telescope; the captain said it would please the King, and reported, that the King was much pleased with us, that he liked to be friends with the English, that he wished to make pleasure with us, and would send for us by and by to do so. We have been particular in these lesser circumstances, as they are the evidence of the King's good feelings, and of the fair prospect of the consummation of the Mission, superior to all the prejudice and intrigue opposed to it.

We were sent for to the King's house; he was only attended by his privy counsellors; he expressed much delight at the camera obscura and instruments. He said, " the Englishmen knew more than Dutchmen or Danes—that black men knew nothing." He then ordered our people to be dismissed, said he would look at the telescope in a larger place, that now he wished to talk with us. He again acknowledged the gratification of Tuesday, and desired Mr. James to explain to him two notes which he produced, written by the Governor in Chief at the request of Amooney, King of Annamaboe, and Adokoo, Chief of the Braffoes, making over to Saï, King of Ashantee, four ackies per month of their company's pay, as a pledge of their allegiance and the termination of hostilities. The impression seemed instantly to have rooted itself in the King's mind, that this was the Governor's individual act, or that he had instanced it; his countenance changed, his counsellors became enraged, they were all impatience, we all anxiety. "Tell the white men," said the King, "what they did yesterday made me much pleasure; I was glad we were to be friends; but to day I see they come to put shame upon my face; this breaks my heart too much. The English know, with my own powder, with my own shot, I drove the Fantees under their forts, I spread my sword over them, they were all killed, and their books from the fort are mine. I can do as much for the English as the Fantees, they know this well, they know I have only to send a captain to get all the heads of the Fantees. These white men cheat me, they think to make 'Shantee fool; they pretend to make friends with me, and they join with the Fantees to cheat me, to put shame upon my face; this makes the blood come from my heart." This was reported by his linguist with a passion of gesture and utterance scarcely inferior to the King's; the irritation spread throughout the circle, and swelled even to uproar.

Thus much was inevitable; it was one of our anticipated difficulties; it was not a defeat, but a check; and here originates our charge against Mr. James, whom we declare to have been deficient in presence of mind, and not to have exerted those assurances and arguments which, with a considerate zeal, might at least have tended to ameliorate the unjust impression of the King, if not to have eradicated it. Mr. James said, " the Governor of Cape Coast had done it, that he knew nothing about it, that he was sent only to make the compliments to the King, that if the King liked to send a messenger with him, *he was going back and would tell the Governor all that the King said.*" This was all that was advanced. Was this enough for such a Mission to effect? the King repeated, " that he had expected we had *come* to settle all palavers, and to *stay* and make friends with him; but we came to make a fool of him." The King asked him to tell him how much had been paid on these notes since his demand—that he knew white men had large books which told this. Mr. James said he had seen, but he could not recollect. Nothing could exceed the King's indignation. " White men," he exclaimed, " know how many months pass, how many years they live, and they know this, but they wont tell me; could not the other white men tell me." Mr. James said, " we never looked in the books."

We were not so indiscreet as to expect or wish Mr. James to commit himself by *promising the satisfaction* of the King's wishes; but dwelling on the expense and importance of the Mission, on the expectations it had excited, and feeling the reason of the King's argument, that its object should be to settle all palavers if we wished to be good friends, we conceived we but anticipated the feeling of the Council and of the Committee, in our anxiety for Mr. James to offer to communicate with the Governor by letter, and to wait his reply, with a confidence that his good feeling towards the King, his instructions from England, and his own disposition, would lead him to do every thing that was right to please him.

Mr. James's embarrassment had not only hurried him to extricate himself as an individual at the expense of his own dignity and intellect, but, which was worse, he had thrown the whole onus of this invidious transaction on the shoulders of the Governor in chief, against whom the King's prejudice would be fatal to all, and whose interest in his honour was most flattering to the King, most auspicious to us, and the hopes of the Mission ; not only the future prosperity, but the present security of the Settlements hung upon this, and the dagger was at this moment suspended from a cobweb. Mr. Bowdich urged this in the ear of Mr. James, urged the danger of leaving the King thus provoked, the fatal sacrifice of every object of the Mission, the discredit of the service, the disgrace of ourselves ; Mr. James replied, " he knew the Governor's private sentiments best." The Moors of authority seized the moment, and zealously fanned the flame which encircled us ; for the King looking in vain for those testimonies of British feeling which presence of mind would have imposed, exclaimed, as he turned his ear from the Moors, " I know the English come to spy the country ; they come to cheat me ; they want war, they want war." Mr. James said " No! we want trade." The King impatiently continued, " They join the Fantees to put shame upon my face ; I will send a captain to-morrow to take these books, and bring me the heads of all the Fantees under the forts ; the white men know I can do this, I have only to speak to my captains. " The Dutch Governor does not cheat me ; he does not shame me before the Fantees ; he sends me the whole 4 oz. a month. The Danes do not shame me, and the English 4 ackies a month is nothing to me ; I can send a captain for all ; they wish war." He drew his beard into his mouth, bit it, and rushing abruptly from his seat exclaimed, " Shantee foo! Shantee foo! ah! ah!" then shaking his finger at us with the most angry aspect, would have burst from us with the exclamation," If a black man had brought me this message, I would have had his head cut off before me." Mr. James was silent.

H

Gentlemen! imagine this awful moment, think what a fatal wound menaced the British interests; the most memorable exertion of the Committee, the pledge to the Government of their energies, of the zeal and capabilities of their officers, this important and expensive Mission falling to the ground, the sacrifice to supineness; the Settlements endangered instead of benefited, ourselves disgraced as officers and men, our key to the Interior shivered in the lock, and the territories of a great and comparatively tractable prince shut against us for ever. Could we be expected to look with indifference on these sacrifices, to risk nothing to avert them; to be auxiliary to the triumph of the intrigues and duplicity of our rival, which you know to have been exerted even to our destruction? Not a moment was to be lost; Mr. Bowdich stood before the King, and begged to be heard; his attention was arrested, the clamours of the council gradually abated: there was no interpreter but the one Mr. James brought from his own fort, and no alternative but to charge him promptly in the Governor's name, before reflection could associate the wishes of his master, to speak truly. Mr. Bowdich continued standing before the King, and declared, " that the Governor wished to gain his friendship more than he could think;" that we were sent, not only to compliment him, but to write what he had to say to the Governor, and to wait to tell his answer to the King, and to do all he ordered; to settle all palavers, and to make Ashantees and English as one before we went back. That the Governor of Accra was sick, and in pain, and naturally wished to go back soon, but that himself, and the other two officers would stay with the King, until they made him sure that the Governor was a good friend to him. That we would rather get anger, and lose every thing ourselves, than let the King think the Governor sent us to put shame on him; that we would trust our lives to the King, until we had received the Governor's letter, to make him think so ; and to tell us to do all that was right, to make the Ashantees and English as one ; and this would shew the King we did not come to spy the country, but to do good." Mr. Bowdich then assured Mr. James that no outrage on his dignity was meditated ; that we should continue to treat him as our superior officer, but that we felt the present act imperative, as our duty to the Service and our Country.

Conviction flashed across the countenance of the interpreter, and he must have done Mr. Bowdich's speech justice, for the cheerful aspect of the morning was resumed in every countenance. The applause was general ; the King (who had again seated himself) held out his hand to Mr. Bowdich, and said, " he spoke well; what he spoke was good ; he liked his palaver much." The King's chief linguist came forward and repeated his commendations with the most profound bows ; every look was favourable ; every where there was a hand extended. The King then instructed his linguist to report to Mr. Bowdich, personally, his arguments respecting the books. " That he had subdued the Fantees at the expense of much powder and shot ; and that, in consequence, all their notes were his : that he had only to send a Captain to bring all their heads, that he did not want to do no good, and keep the books ; he would do more for the forts than the Fantees could ; that the Dutch Governor did not cheat him, but gave the four oz. a month. That he wished to be friends with the English ; but that the 4 ackies a month put shame upon his face." To this Mr. Bowdich replied, that he could only say he knew the Governor would do what was right ; that he could not say more until he heard from him ; but that he would write every word the King said ; and he was sure the King would see that the Governor would do what was right. We shook hands and retired.

All the Fantees being detained by the King, Mr. Bowdich and

Mr. Hutchison went in the evening to the chief captain to request a messenger from the King to Cape Coast; about two hours afterwards he reported the King's reply almost literally as follows: " The King wishes you good night; this is his palaver and yours, you must not speak it to any one else, the white men come to cheat him. The King recollects the face of the white man who spoke to him to day, he likes him much, he wishes he would talk the palaver; the King likes the other white men who stood up with him very much; he thinks the Governor of Accra wishes to put all the wrong on the Governor at Cape Coast, and not to tell any thing. The King thinks that not right, and he sees you do not like that. You must not speak this palaver again; 'tis the King's palaver, and yours; the King's captain will speak right to the King what you say, and you shall have a messenger."

We again affirm positively, that Mr. James made no offer to communicate with the Governor, but spoke only of his return, which we know he was meditating at the expense of the treaty, and every object of the Mission.

Referring to our detail previous to the serious business of to day, you will find every circumstance to have been encouraging, and in our opinion, auspicious to the consummation of the Mission. Yet at that moment, unclouded as it was, we know Mr. James, by his own confession, to have written to head quarters with a gloom which existed only in his own imagination; this letter did not go from the detention of the Fantee bearers. We believe firmly, that had there been no interference on our part at the critical moment, Mr. James would have returned forthwith to Cape Coast, without effecting one object of the Mission, and that the future good of the Settlements would not only have been sacrificed, but their present security endangered.*

* " The government of the country is a military despotism, and I have this day re-

Mr. James may write that Mr. Bowdich rose with great warmth: this we deny, and affirm that he displayed no more than a temperate zeal, considerate in its declarations, and respectful even in its dissent from Mr. James. The attention of the King was arrested by the novelty of a white man addressing him in the oratorical manner of his own country, but it was not until the linguist had conveyed the arguments, that the King held out his hand and the applause was general. Mere observations whispered in the ear of the linguists had lost all effect, and would not have answered the crisis.

Mr. James has talked, and perhaps written much of the King's suspicion, but we must contend that much of this is misnamed, and is no more than that deliberate policy which is a pledge of the durability of the confidence it precedes. Certainly there has been suspicion, but not more than must have been expected, not more than was commensurate with the important novelty which challenged it. It has been confessed here, that our political rival has exerted all his address to vitiate our objects in the eyes of the King, to convince him our ostensible views were pretences; our real ones dangerous and unjust; that we sought sovereignty, not commerce. The Moorish chiefs and dignitaries by whom the King is surrounded, whose influence is powerful, not only from their rank but their repute, naturally urged these arguments against unbelievers and competitors in trade, and their extensive intercourse has unfortunately possessed them of facts to the point of our ambition. Let these considerations be weighed, let our account of the King's general deportment be again referred to; let us impress, that he has never once adverted to our destruction of his

ceived private information, that it is already settled, that if the refusal of the notes occasions a war, and any one is hurt or killed by the forts, our lives will be the forfeit." Mr. James's Dispatch.

troops before Annamaboe, or of the critical situation of the fort; that he has evinced a disposition to a sound understanding, by veiling every irritating retrospect, by acknowledging ... conciliatory circumstance.

We do not presume to enter our opinions into the important question of the King's demand of the whole of these two notes; we have advanced nothing but our assurance that the Governor will do what is right, and we have pledged our lives to convince the King of this; the importance of the Mission would have claimed a more valuable pledge.

Whilst we impress the surprising power and influence of the King, we must do him the justice to acknowledge the convincing manner in which he urged the injuries and forbearance which preceded the Fantee war; his willingness to do every thing for the forts, and the conduct of the Dutch Governor in giving him the whole of the four ounces, were impressively and ingeniously associated.

To wear away suspicion, Mr. Bowdich has ceased his enquiries and observations for a time. The resources for intelligence of the Interior are infinite. Timbuctoo has been visited by most of the sojourners, and a mass of valuable information may be gathered with caution.* The eclipses of Jupiter's satellites will be regularly observed by Mr. Bowdich, and the mean longitude reported; the want of a good watch imposes considerable trouble.

We have reflected on what we have done, and if we are so unfortunate as to be visited by your and the Committee's displea-

* " In the present suspicious state of the King's mind respecting us, I fear it would be impolitic to make the enquiries you ordered in your instructions. I think it will be more prudent to leave them to time. Mr. H. if he remains, will be able, from time to time, to obtain such information as they can give, without creating that suspicion which would certainly arise from any questions put at the present moment. I have kept Mr. H's hammock men, as it is yet uncertain whether he will remain." Mr. James's Dispatch.

sure, we shall console ourselves in our reluctant change of pursuit, by the satisfaction of our own minds of the honourable zeal of our motives.

We most respectfully solicit our recall, as we cannot implicate our character and our responsibility with Mr. James's judgment and perseverance in prosecuting the Mission, of the consummation of which we cannot agree to despond. We could not reconcile ourselves to the sacrifice of one of its important objects to our personal apprehensions (supported as we are by authority and circumstances) whilst the recollection of the illustrious energies of an enterprising traveller, forlorn and destitute, appeals to our spirit, and impresses the expectations of our country. We are, &c.

(Signed)
T. EDWARD BOWDICH.
W. HUTCHISON.
HENRY TEDLIE.

Coomassie, May 24, 1817.

To THE GOVERNOR AND COUNCIL, CAPE COAST CASTLE.

GENTLEMEN,

THE act our former letter has avowed, and we would presume (after the most deliberate reflection) to add justified, has made it our duty to communicate (independently of Mr. James) the circumstances of the interval we may await your pleasure.

If this duty had not been imposed on us by the act in question, the imminent fatality engendered in the debate of to day, and quickened by the ardor of the captains, would have demanded from our private as well as our public feelings, the most energetic representations (as auxiliary to those of Mr. James,) in impressing the calamities and the sacrifices which menace the Settlements and the Mission, to secure your serious deliberation, as the only preventive we can look to with confidence.

Yesterday we were conducted some way without the town to an assembly of the Moorish caboceers and dignitaries, who exert every device against us. A chapter was read from the Koran, and we were ordered to swear by that book that we had no rogues palaver, and that we had put no poison in the King's liquor. We severally refused to swear on the Koran, but offered to do so on our own prayer books. The King's linguist mediated, and asked us if we would only strike that book three times, and then declare as much, because the Moors said, that book would kill us if we lied. We did this, and were about two hours afterwards ordered to sit without our house and receive the following present from the King:

One bullock, 2 pigs, 8 oz. of gold, for Mr. James.

One sheep, 2 oz. 4 ackies of gold, for each of us.

To each of the numerous Fantee messengers, 10 ackies of gold.

To our cooks, a large assortment of pots and country vessels, 100 large billets of wood, 100 yams, 100 bunches of plantains, four of sugar cane, four (24 gallon) pots of palm oil, three jars of palm wine.

To the soldiers, 10 ackies of gold.

To the Accra linguist, 10 ackies of gold.

On Saturday we were summoned to the King, and waited as usual a considerable time in one of the outer courts of the palace, which is an immense building of a variety of oblong courts and regular squares, the former with arcades along the one side, some of round arches symmetrically turned, having a skeleton of bamboo; the entablatures exuberantly adorned with bold fan and trellis work of Egyptian character. They have a suit of rooms over them, with small windows of wooden lattice, of intricate but regular carved work, and some have frames cased with thin gold. The squares have a large apartment on each side, open in front, with two supporting pillars, which break the view and give it all the appearance of the proscenium or front of the stage of the older Italian theatres. They are lofty and regular, and the cornices of a very bold cane work in alto relievo. A drop curtain of curiously plaited cane is suspended in front, and in each we observed chairs and stools embossed with gold, and beds of silk, with scattered regalia. The most ornamented part of the palace is the residence of the women. We have passed through it once; the fronts of the apartments were closed (except two open door ways) by pannels of curious open carving, conveying a striking resemblance at first sight to an early Gothic screen; one was entirely closed and had two curious doors of a low arch, and strengthened or battened with wood-work, carved in high relief and painted red. Doors chancing to open as we passed, surprised us with a glimpse of large apartments in corners we could not have thought of, the most secret appeared the most adorned. In our daily course through the palace there is always a delay of some minutes, before the door of each of the several distinct squares is unlocked; within the inmost square is the council chamber.

. To day, after the delay of nearly an hour (which seems an indispensible ceremony) in the outer court, (where different dignitaries were passing to and fro with their insignia and retinues,) we were conducted to a large yard, where the King, encircled by a varied profusion of insignia, even more sumptuous than that we had seen before, sat at the end of two long files of counsellors, caboceers, and captains; they were seated under their umbrellas, composed of scarlet and yellow cloth, silks, shawls, cottons, and every glaring variety, with carved and golden pelicans, panthers, baboons, barrels, crescents, &c. on the top; the shape generally a dome. Distinct and pompous retinues were placed around, with gold canes, spangled elephants tails to brush off the flies, gold headed swords, and embossed muskets, and many splendid novelties too numerous but for a particular report, which will not be neglected Each had the dignitaries of his own province or establishment to his right and left; and it was truly " Concilium in Concilio." When we recollected the insignificant, though neat appearance of the few Ashantee towns we had passed through on the southern frontier, and even the extent and superior character of the capital, this magnificence seemed the effect of enchantment.

We have intruded this sketch to impress the power and resources of the monarch we are to conciliate, and to anticipate in some degree the delay of Mr. Bowdich's report, the transcription of which must yield to the present momentous communication.

The King having decided a cause then in course, by which one of his captains was condemned to death for cowardice, ordered the question of the Annamaboe and Braffoe notes to be resumed. The several Fantee messengers were heard, the King of Annamaboe's, Amooney's, and Payntree's (the interior caboceer) having joined us in the path. They appeared all equivocation and embarrassment, as Quashie's interpretations confirmed; they were incompetent to answer the King's linguists, and unable to use the few uninterrupted intervals which were allowed them to any purpose : it seems they would not acknowledge what the full amount of these notes was. Mr. James was asked, he said " white men's heads were not like black men's, and he could not recollect; but he thought 4 oz. and 2 oz." He did not offer to learn from the Governor. Several impassioned harangues were made by the King's linguists and counsellors : the King said, " he had 4 oz. from Elmina, and 2 oz. from English Accra; was it not putting shame upon him to send him 4 ackies from Cape Coast?" The Cape Coast messenger (Quashie Tom had absented himself) spoke again with great trepidation; the King could not conceal his emotions; his counsellors became clamorous; in an instant there was a flourish of all the horns; all the captains rose and seized their gold headed swords from their attendants; the head general snatched Mr. Tedlie's from his scabbard; numerous canopies crowded one upon the other in the background, as if some considerable personages had arrived; there was nothing but commotion, wrath, and impatience. The captains, old and young, rushed before the King, and exclaimed, as Quashie reported, (who seems to have been afraid to tell us all, and was restrained by Quamina) " King, this shames you too much; you must let us go to night and kill all the Fantees, and burn all the towns under the forts." They then presented themselves successively with their bands of music and retinues, and bowing before the King, received his foot upon their heads; each then directed his sword to the King (who held up the two first fingers of his right hand) and swore by the King's head, that they would go with the army that night, and bring him the books, and the heads of all the Fantees. Each captain made the oath impressive in his own peculiar manner; some seriously, some by ridicule, at our expense, and that of the Fantees, pointing at our heads and ears, and endeavouring to intimidate us by the most insolent action and gesture as they held out their swords. The old general (Apokoo) who swore the last, after he had done so in the most expressive manner, threw Mr. Tedlie's sword to him, over the heads of the people with contemptuous defiance. The number was so great, that we thought this awful ceremony would never finish.

The King left the council a short time. In the interval, Quamina Bwa (our guide) told Accra Quashie to beg Mr. James to speak to the King when he came back, and try and appease him. Mr. James did so, but without the zeal, presence of mind, or argument the crisis demanded; it was not adequate even to ameliorate the King's impression of the Governor and the English; it was no more than he said at first. The King took not the least notice of it, but declared angrily, that " if he did not see white men's faces he would cut off the heads of every Fantee messenger on the spot." Some sheep and gold were then brought forward and presented to the Captains, and the King rose abruptly from his chair. In this anxious moment we reflected that the mulatto of General Daendels had a long audience of the King just before we were received ; no resource was to be left untried, that was manly and appropriate. Mr. Bowdich stepped before the King, and declared through the linguist, " that he wished to speak what he knew would make the King think that the Governor would do him right, and was his good friend." The King said he would hear him speak in the house ; we retired amidst the insults and menaces of the assembly.

About two hours after, we were summoned, and, as is the etiquette, kept some time in waiting; in this interval, Mr. James said that our situation being very critical, it was a pity any difference should be observed, and that he thought it much better to be reconciled. Mr. Bowdich replied, that he could not think it possible our sentiments to be delivered to the King could differ at such a moment; that if they did we should assimilate ours to his as much as possible ; but feeling the necessity for the greatest energy, for every address and argument for the conviction of the King, we must, for the public good, continue our assumption of the privilege of strengthening his declarations by our own until our recall, that we should be tender of his dignity, but that it being a difference on a point of public duty, we could not compound it, but would take the consequences. We were received ; the King's aspect was stern; he prefaced that " he did not wish to make war with the English; but that the 4 ackies a month shamed him too much; that the captains said to him, King! they cheat you, they put shame on you; we will go to night and bring you the heads of all the Fantees; that he was forced to say to them, I beg your pardon, but as I see the white men's faces, I beg you to stay till to-morrow, when they can write to the Governor, and they will tell me themselves what he says; then if he does not send me Amooncy's and the Braffoes books, you shall go and kill all; that he had been obliged afterwards to dash them sheep and gold to make them stay until the white men got the Governor's letter." Mr. James assured the King " that the King of England and the Governor wished to be friends with him, to do all that was right; and he thought in his own mind that the Governor would give up the books." The King took no notice, and continued serious: the moment called for the most energetic appeal to his reason, for every imposing argument and circumstance. There was a long pause; Mr. Bowdich rose, and charged Mr. James's linguist to interpret truly. We took the precaution of making notes of this speech, feeling we should be particular where we pledge our honour, and volunteer our affidavit; it was as follows.

" We swore yesterday as the King wished, to day we wish to swear as we should before our own King." The King held up the two first fingers of his right hand as he did to the captains. " We swear" (presenting our swords and kissing the hilt, as the most imposing form that occurred to us) " by our God, and by our King, and we know the Governor of Accra will do the same, that we mean no bad to the King, that the King of England and the Company ordered the Governor to send us to make the Ashantees and English as one, that we are sure the Governor will do the King right, and that when we write him all the King says, we will write also that we think the King's palaver good. We were sent to make the English and Ashantees as one, because our's is the greatest white, your's the greatest black nation, and when two great nations are friends, it makes good. I came out in the ship that was sent to tell the Governor this, and when he heard it, he said it gave him very much pleasure. The King of England and the Company thought the Governor should send to the King, to send some of his great men to Cape Coast, that we might be safe; but the Governor said, no! there was no occasion, and wrote to the King and the Company that he could trust all his officers in Ashantee, because the King's honour made them safe, so we came without sending, because we knew the King was our true friend.

" The Governor, wished always to do the King right, but the Fantees never would tell him what was right, so he wrote to the King of England to send him some presents, that he might send his own officers to the King, and hear properly from the King's own mouth what was right, because the Fantees never would tell him what was true, or what the King said. When the Governor reads what we shall write him, then he will know the truth for the first time. We shall stay to make the Ashantees and English one, and we pledge our lives to the King, that we speak a proper palaver, and when we speak true before God and the King we cannot fear."

There were repeated and general applauses as each sentence was interpreted; the King. smiled, and desired his linguist to say to Mr. Bowdich as Quashie interpreted, " The King likes you, you speak a proper good palaver, you speak like a man, the King wishes to be a friend to white men; he thinks white men next to God." Here the King raised his hands to heaven, and then covering his face, Quashie continued to interpret. " The King thanks God and his own fetish, that they have sent him white men to talk proper like this to him, and when you three white men go back to Cape Coast, and the Governor has bad put into his head, and think you did wrong, then if you want any thing to eat, send a messenger to him and he will send you plenty, for the King thinks you do right to God and him, and to your King, and to the Governor, and that you will get much honour when you go back; so the King thanks you, and says you speak well." The King then asked Mr. James if he would swear on his sword like us, as we said; Mr. James did so. The King made an observation which it seems we cannot convey to you in its full force, or nearer than, that he liked the three white men because they always stood up to speak, and pushed forward to get what they wanted. Many auxiliary observations were afterwards offered casually by each of us, to confirm his change of sentiment. The Fantee linguists attempted to intimidate the linguist Quashie of Accra, but ineffectually; this man is invaluable from his influence and intelligence, he is our only safe medium, and interprets to the King anxiously and impressively.

The King appeared much pleased, and made us a long speech. "The King says the Fantees are all rogues, the Governor knows that very well; the King thinks they always put bad palaver in the Governor's head, he always tells his captains so; he is sure you come to do him right. The King wishes all good for the English; he swears by God and by the fetish, that if the English could know how the Fantees serve him, and all the bad they do, they would say his palaver was good. The King speaks true." He then gave us an ouline of the Fantee war, which must have convinced even the most prejudiced, of his injuries and forbearance, and their injustice and cruelty.

The King says, " if the English trust to him, he will take more care of the forts than the Fantees can, he will do them great good, he does not want to do nothing. He will send the English his trade; he will send them good gold like what he wears himself, (shewing his armlets,) not bad gold like he knows the Fantees make, his people don't know how to do that, the Fantees do it in their own houses before they give it to white men. If at any time the English in the forts are in want of any thing to eat, and send to him, he will send them every thing. To morrow is Sunday, but the next day is Monday, then he will give you a proper messenger."

We cannot do justice to the King's sentiments either in detail or in expression; they were incredibly liberal, and would have ennobled the most civilized monarch; they seemed to break the spell which has shut the Interior. He begged us to drink with him, and Mr. James agreed in the toast of " May the Ashantees and English always be one ;" it pleased him, and he begged us to touch his glass with ours. He then turned suddenly to the Fantee messengers (who were trembling in the rear) and said, " you made me very angry with you, and I am very angry with you, but never mind, come and drink some of my liquor."

Our critical situation demands the delivery of our sentiments on the subject of these notes; we do so with diffidence and respect. The services of the Braffoes, who hold the one, are merely nominal, their enmity nugatory from their political situation; the issuing of a fresh note to Amooney will be but a small addition to the expenditure, and even the expense of renewing them both cannot be weighed with the prevention of another Fantee war, of the destruction of a whole people, and the ruin of our Settlements in their defence, with the defeat of the intrigue and devices of our rival, and the acquisition of the confidence of a powerful and liberal monarch, whose influence may perfect the views of the British Government on the Interior. We hail the circumstances as auspicious, even in the present serious moment.

Mr. James confesses that he desponds of consummating the objects of the Mission; we do not; we would be responsible for all of them, but we diffidently await your decision. We must claim this momentary calm of the King to ourselves, because it only affords us the credit, or rather the justification of having done our duty, which we are resolute in repeating Mr. James has not. What has been said through Mr. Bowdich is here reported faithfully; we have not committed the Governor or ourselves.

Gentlemen, our situation is critical; if your answer determines the King on war, we are his prisoners; if, as we cannot doubt, the valour of our countrymen again retards his progress by defences as memorable as that of Annamaboe, we may be the victims of an irritated soldiery, though we feel it would be with the reluctance of a generous prince, who is not independent, but, unfortunately, controlled by a military despotism, which deposed his brother and invested him.

But, Gentlemen, if in your better knowledge and reflection, you cannot consistently with your honour and your trust, meet the King's demand, the history of our country has fortified our minds with the illustrious example of a Vansittart, and his colleagues, who were situated as we are, when the dawn of British intercourse in India was scarcely more advanced than its dawn in Africa now; and their last request to their Council is our present conclusion to you —" Do not put our lives in competition with the honour and interests of our country."

We are, &c. &c.

(Signed)   T. EDWARD BOWDICH.

W. HUTCHISON.

HENRY TEDLIE.

K

Coomassie, May 28th, 1817.

To the Governor and Council.

Gentlemen,

On Sunday the King visited us at our quarters, and expressed much gratification with the trifles we presented him individually, and our solicitude in explaining some plates of botanical and natural history, which he sends for frequently.

On Monday we had a public audience before the Captains, (whose ill-will has been acknowledged,) when two messengers were ordered to accompany one of ours to Cape Coast, with the letters to the Governor, and were impressively sworn; they received their instructions in a speech from the linguist of nearly two hours; it seemed to be intended to conciliate the Captains at the same time.

In the afternoon the King sent for us again, and said he wished to dictate a letter to the Governor. Mr. James wrote the sense of the King's expressions, but was obliged to leave off from indisposition. The King would not trust it out of his hands. Yesterday evening it was concluded, when the King proposed to make his mark, and insisted on repeating it in the direction. We have taken the pains to preserve this curious letter verbatim, which from its length, and our constant interruption, we are compelled to reserve with many curious particulars for the General Report.

We are anxiously waiting a summons to hand our dispatches to the messenger. Nine days are allowed for the journey to Cape Coast, and nine for the return. The whole time has been gradually extended, by intreaty of the Fantee messengers, from eighteen to thirty days.

Mr. Hutchison is ill with a bilious attack, and several of the people with a fever and dysentery. The heat is very powerful here, but Mr. Bowdich and Mr. Tedlie continue in excellent health.

We would recommend the sending up a common green silk umbrella, and a Company's dirk, as presents to the King's favourite nephew.

Our confinement to the house is rather irksome; we are not allowed to walk in the town without Captains accompanying us.

12 o'clock. The King sent to say Mr. Bowdich must come to the palace, and mount the chief captain's horse, and shew him how Englishmen ride. Mr. Bowdich went, and by the King's desire gallopped up and down the opposite hill. The King expressed great anxiety when the horse was made to play his tricks; and when Mr. Bowdich persevered, and made him gallop back and alighted, the King sent him word that " he rode like a proper man, that he stayed on the horse well, and made him do proper."

4 o'clock. The King sent for us at two, to make some additions to the letter, and to seal it in his presence. A long prayer was uttered by a Moor after the sealing of the letter, and we were called back to be again impressed with the example and justice of the Dutch as regards the books. Mr. Hutchison's illness prevented his attendance to day. The messengers are to go to night.

May 29th, 3 p. m. The messengers and the Fantee bearers, have been delayed in consequence of the death of a person of rank, and their assistance in the custom. I am now assured that they will leave Coomassie at 4 o'clock.

In reply to the request we urged to Mr. James, that he would dismiss our hammock men, as they had been of so little service to us in coming up, and were a considerable expense; he impressed that it would be contrary to your instructions.

Only one message from the King to day, and that a private one to Mr. Bowdich, with permission for him to ride: he went all round the town, which he considers to be about three miles in circumference: the King afterwards sent him word, that to-morrow he must ride on a cloth only, as he had heard the English did.

We are, &c. &c.

(Signed)　　　　　　T. E. BOWDICH.

H. TEDLIE.

P. S. Mr. James had a severe relapse of fever last night, and was very ill this morning; at 10 o'clock a. m. he had the cold bath, and some febrifuge medicine. Mr. Hutchison is rather better, the soldiers also, but the hammock men continue much the same.

SAï TOOTOO QUAMINA, *King of Ashantee and its Dependencies, to* JOHN HOPE SMITH, *Esquire, Governor in Chief of the British Settlements on the Gold Coast of Africa.*

THE King sends his compliments to the Governor, he thanks the King of England and him very much for the presents sent to him, he thinks them very handsome. The King's sisters and all his friends have seen them, and think them very handsome, and thank him. The King thanks his God and his fetish that he made the Governor send the white men's faces for him to see, like he does now; he likes the English very much, and the Governor all the same as his brother

The King of England has made war against all the other white people a long time, and killed all the people all about, and taken all the towns, French, Dutch, and Danish, all the towns, all about. The King of Ashantee has made war against all the people of the water side, and all the black men all about, and taken all their towns.

When the King of England takes a French town, he says,

" come, all this is mine, bring all your books, and give me all your pay," and if they don't do it, does the Governor think the King of England likes it?* So the King has beat the Fantees now two times, and taken all their towns, and they send and say to him, you are a great King, we want to serve you; but he says, Hah! you want to serve me, then bring all your books, what you get from the forts, and then they send him four ackies, this vexes him too much.

The first time he made war against the Fantees, two great men in Assin quarrelled, so half the people came to Ashantee, half went to Fantee. The King said, what is the reason of this, so he sent his gold swords and canes to know why they did so, and the Fantees killed his messengers and took all their gold.† After they fought with the Elminas and Accras, the Fantees sent word to the King they would serve him; the King sent word to the Assins, if it is true that the Fantees want to serve me, let me hear; after that they sent to say yes! they tired of fighting, and wanted to serve him, he said, well, give me some gold, what you get from the books, and then you shall hear what palaver I have got in my head, and we can be friends; then he sent some messengers, and after they waited more than two years, the Fantees sent word back, no! we don't want to serve the King, but only to make the path open and get good trade: this vexed the King too much.

Then the Fantees sent to a strong man, Cudjoe Coomah, and

---

* This is an extraordinary impression, that all the towns in Europe are supported like those under the forts, holding notes from their governments for annual stipends.

† Here the King's linguist ceased, and by his desire requested us to repeat all the King had said, he was much pleased with our accuracy, and begged us to take some refreshment, (spirits and palm wine were introduced in silver bowls) fearing he had kept us too long without eating, and would continue the letter to-morrow. He locked up what had been written, and heard it read again the next day, before his linguists continued.

said, " come, let us put our heads together against the King ;" after that, when the King heard this, he sent one, not a great man, but his own slave, and said, well you will do, go kill all the people, all the Aquapims, and Akims, and all ; and so he killed all, and after he killed all he came and told him.

When he sent against Akim, the people in Akim sent word, that they told their head men not to vex the King, but they would not mind them, so he killed the head people, and the others begged his pardon.

When the King went to fight with the Fantees they sent this saucy word—we will kill you and your people, and stand on you; then they did not kill one Ashantee captain, but the King killed all the Fantee captains and people. They do not stand on him.

· That time, after the King fought, all the Fantees sent word, well we will serve you, but you must not send more harm to hurt us, we don't want to fight more, but to make good friends with you. Then the King said, what caboceer lives at Cape Coast and Annamaboe, what books they get from the forts, let them send all, and then we can be friends. And the King sent word too, if my messengers go to Cape Coast fort, and if they bring pots of gold, and casks of goods, then I can't take that, *but I must have the books.*

After that the King sent word to the Governor of Cape Coast and the Governor of Annamaboe, well! you know I have killed all the Fantees, and I must have Adocoo's and Amooney's books, and I can make friends with you, good brother and good heart ; but now they send four ackies, that is what makes the King's heart break out when he looks on the book and thinks of four ackies, and his captains swear that the Fantees are rogues and want to cheat him. When the white men see the Fantees do this, and the

English officers bring him this four ackies, it makes him get up very angry, but he has no palaver with white men.

All Fantee is his, all the black mans country is his; he hears that white men bring all the things that come here; he wonders they do not fight with the Fantees, for he knows they cheat them. Now he sees white men, and he thanks God and his fetish for it.

When the English made Apollonia fort he fought with the Aowins, the masters of that country, and killed them; then he said to the caboceer, I have killed all your people, your book is mine; the caboceer said, true! so long as you take my town, the book belongs to you.

.He went to Dankara and fought, and killed the people, then he said; give me the book you get from Elmina, so they did, and now Elmina belongs to him.*

The English fort at Accra gave a book to an Akim caboceer, called Aboigin Adjumawcon. The King killed him and took the book. The Dutch fort gave a book to another Akim caboceer, Curry Curry Apam. The Danish fort gave a book to another Akim caboceer, Arrawa Akim; the King killed all and took their books.

This King, Saï, is young on the stool, but he keeps always in his head what old men say, for it is good, and his great men and linguists tell it him every morning. The King of England makes three great men, and sends one to Cape Coast, one to Annamaboe, and one to Accra; Cape Coast is the same as England. The King gets two ounces from Accra every moon, and the English wish to give him only four ackies for the big fort at Cape Coast, and the same for Annamboe; do white men think this proper?

When the King killed the Dankara caboceer and got two ounces from Elmina, the Dutch Governor said, this is a proper King, we

* The King always spoke of the acts of all his ancestors as his own.

shall not play with him, and made the book four ounces. The King has killed all the people, and all the forts are his; he sent his captains to see white men, now *he* sees them, and thanks God and his fetish. If the path was good when the captains went, the King would have gone under the forts and seen all the white men. The Ashantees take good gold to Cape Coast, but the Fantees mix it; he sent some of his captains like slaves to see, and they saw it; ten handkerchiefs are cut to eight, water is put to rum, and charcoal to powder, even for the King; they cheat him, but he thinks the white men give all those things proper to the Fantees.

The King knows the King of England is his good friend, for he has sent him handsome dashes; he knows his officers are his good friends, for they come to see him. The King wishes the Governor to send to Elmina to see what is paid him there, and to write the King of England how much, as the English say their nation passes the Dutch; he will see by the books given him by both forts. If the King of England does not like that, he may send him himself what he pleases, and then Saï can take it.

He thanks the King and Governor for sending four white men to see him. The old King wished to see some of them, but the Fantees stop it. He is but a young man and sees them, and so again he thanks God and his fetish.

Dated in the presence of,

   T. Edward Bowdich,

   William Hutchison,

   Henry Tedlie.

May 30. Apokoo sent us a present of 30 ackies of gold and some fruits.

June 1. The King sent to desire Mr. Tedlie to bring his instruments and medicines, and explain their uses to him; he was shrewdly inquisitive, and presented Mr. Tedlie with 6 ackies of gold in approbation of his intelligence

June 4. The King paid us a visit at our quarters, and expressed himself highly gratified with some botanical engravings: he said white men tried to know so much they would spoil their heads by and by. We were allowed to take a walk in the town to day, in charge of two captains. We had scarcely passed the palace when two men were decapitated for cowardice: three others had been executed during the night.

June 5. Bakkee, to whom our house formerly belonged, had been sent the second in command of the army with which Appia Danqua invaded Fantee the second time, in pursuit of the Akim and Aquapim revolters. Wearied of the procrastination and labours of the campaign, he inconsiderately observed to a public messenger, that, as the King had declared when he invaded Fantee in person, that he would have the head of every Fantee caboceer, and yet returned with a part only; so he could not be expected to forego the enjoyment of the riches and luxuries of his home, until every revolter was killed. On his return to the capital without leave, he was charged with this, and not denying it, was stripped of all his property, and hung himself. Aboidwee our present house master was raised to Bakkee's stool, or seat in council, to which 1700 retainers are attached.

June 9. The King sent us two sheep and a large quantity of fruit; his nephew also sent us a sheep.

June 11. We were invited to attend the King's levee, on the Adai custom, and were presented with a flask of rum and a fat sheep. This walk was a great relief, for the longest court in our quarters was not more than 14 feet.

June 12. The King sent us a large Hio sheep to look at; it measured 4½ feet from the head to the insertion of the tail, which was two feet long, its height was three feet, and it was covered with coarse shaggy hair.

June 13. The King sent for us late at night; he assured us he wished to think well of the English; and that if Cape Coast was not so far off, he should send messengers daily to wish the Governor good morning, but the Crambos (Moors) and his great men thought we came to do bad, and spy the country; so he sent for us when it was dark, that they might not know it. He had only two persons with him. Mr. James was too ill to attend.

17. The King sent a present to our quarters of

   2 ounces of gold to the officers.
   20 ackies to our people.
   10 ackies to our linguists.

   1 hog, 1 sheep, and a profusion of plantains and oranges. This was his reproof of a disgraceful attempt to borrow money of him for our subsistence; of which Mr. Hutchison, Mr. Tedlie, and myself, had publicly disclaimed our knowledge and sanction. Nothing could be more injurious to our dignity.

18th. Mr. Tedlie having ventured to walk a few yards without the town, was arrested by a captain, with about 100 followers, who detained him in his house whilst a message was sent to the King, who desiring Mr. Tedlie to be brought before him, enquired if he had his small box (compass) in his pocket, and finding he had not, affected to reprove the captain severely, for supposing either of us could wish to run away, whilst the King was our friend. After this we seldom went out.

21st. Bundahenna, one of the King's uncles, begged him for

permission to go and make custom for some relatives whom he had lost in the last Fantee war, as he feared their spirits were beginning to trouble him. The King subscribed four ounces of gold, two ankers of rum, one barrel of powder, and four human victims for sacrifice, towards this custom. We received a present of 11 ackies of gold from Quatchie Quofies household.

26th. We received a present from a captain called Oöossa Cudjo, of 10 ackies of gold, and another from Jessinting, of the same quantity, a sheep and some plantains.

28th. The King sent us a large quantity of plantains and oranges. Apokoo, one of the four greatest men in the kingdom, hearing his mother's sister was dead, killed a slave before his house, and proceeded to her croom to sacrifice many more, and celebrate her funeral custom; but, when he found, on opening her boxes, that the old woman from her dislike of him, had thrown almost all her rock gold into the river, and that he should only inherit a number of hungry slaves, he sacrificed but one more victim, and made but a very mean custom.

29th. Attended the King's levee, and were presented with a flask of rum, and a fat sheep. The King sent us word that he would be glad to let us walk out, but there were many bad people who would kill us if they could. We were gratified by an invitation to visit Odumata, one of the four aristocrats; he begged us to drink palm wine with him, and ordered a large jar of it to be sent to our servants. He told us he was the first captain who fought with the English at Annamaboe; and that if the books were not sent, he would be the first to do so again; he asked us if we would take him to England to see our King, and engage to bring him back again; for, having sold an immense number of captives as slaves, he expected some of them might recognise him, and call out to the King of England to stop him, because he had sent them out of their own country.

July 2. A girl was beheaded for insolence to one of the King's sons, and a man for transgressing the law by picking up gold which he had dropped in the public market place, where all that falls is allowed to accumulate until the soil is washed on state emergencies.

3rd. This morning one of the King's sons (about 10 years of age) shot himself: his funeral custom was celebrated in the afternoon, and a smart fire of musquetry was kept up until sun-set, amidst dancing, singing, and revelry; two men and one girl were sacrificed, and their trunks and heads were left in the market place till dark. The mother of this child, a favourite wife of the King's, having added crime to a continued perversity of conduct, had been put to death; the boy was banished the King's presence from that time. This morning he had stolen into the palace for the first time, and the King desiring him to be removed, observing that he had, doubtless, as bad a head towards him as his mother had shewn; he replied, that if he could not be allowed to come and look at his father, he had better die; half an hour afterwards he destroyed himself privately, by directing a blunderbuss into his mouth, and discharging it with his foot. The keeper of the royal cemetry was this day imprisoned. His wife was soon after charged by the council with making fetish to turn the King's head; she replied that it meant no more than to make the King think better of her husband; but they insisted that she invoked the Fetish to make the King mad, and she was executed.

5th. A loud shout from our people announced the return of the messengers from Cape Coast Castle, after an absence of thirty-eight days.

CHAPTER III.

Proceedings and Incidents until the Third Dispatch to Cape Coast Castle.

Cape Coast Castle, June 21, 1817.

Sir,

M R. J AMES being ordered to return here as soon as possible, will deliver you his instructions, and you will immediately on receipt of this letter, take upon yourself the management of the Mission. I have every reliance on your prudence and discretion, and still firmly hope that the termination of the Embassy will be attended with success, and that the sanguine expectations which we have entertained as to the result of it, will not be disappointed.

The King has received a very erroneous impression of the affair of the Fantee notes, which I regret to hear was the cause of a serious disturbance: I am glad however to find that by your prompt mode of conduct, you were in some measure able to repress the unfavourable bias it seems to have occasioned, and I have no doubt that an explanation of the circumstance will effectually remove any remaining prejudice. This transaction was entirely between the Ashantee messengers and Fantees, negociated, and determined on by them at Abrah, and afterwards ratified here by their mutual consent. Hearing that messengers from the King were at Abrah, I invited them down, wishing through their medium to communicate with him concerning the conveyance of the presents I had received from the Committee.   After some delay they arrived, and on their first interview made known their errand to the Fantees, and the manner it had been arranged, applying at the same time for two notes to be made out in favour of Zey, at four ackies each, which were to be deducted from the notes of Amooney and Aduecoe; not being perfectly satisfied from the representation of these people as to the justness of the claim, I delayed complying until it was stated to be a pledge of good faith and allegiance on the part of the Fantees, and a confirmation of the final adjustment of all differences between the two parties, and as such they were given them.   The nature of the claim having been fully and satisfactorily explained, I have no hesitation in complying with the wishes of the King; and this I do the more readily, knowing that by the extension of his authority, good order and subjection will be better preserved.

This will, I hope, evince to the King my friendly intention towards him; and you will impress upon his mind, that it is my earnest desire to cultivate his friendship, the establishment of which will be mutually beneficial; and in order that the union between us may be more closely cemented, I am particularly desirous that Mr. Hutchison be permitted to reside at Ashantee, which will be the means of preventing any interruption to the good understanding which, before you leave, will, I hope, be firmly settled.

I have no objection to you returning by way of Warsaw, but your undertaking the journey on foot, I am apprehensive, you will find too fatiguing. The hammock-men are engaged for the trip, therefore the only additional expense will be their subsistence; I however leave it to you to dismiss them or not.

The Accra linguist being so very useful, and the only man who will interpret faithfully, you will retain him until you return.

I have sent you, by the King's messenger, 40 oz. of gold to defray your expenses; should any loan have been granted by the King, you will of course repay him.

I send you a piece of muslin and 10 danes for presents to the Moors, whose friendship it will be highly necessary to conciliate. I have also at your request, sent a dirk and umbrella, intended for the King's chief captain and his favourite nephew.

Quamina, the Ashantee captain at Abrah, has refused to allow any letters to pass that place which may be given in charge to Ashantee traders, on the plea that by so doing he would incur the displeasure of the King; who, he says, expects that especial messengers will be engaged here to proceed with all letters to the capital. Not long ago a trader who had received a letter, was detained by him at Abrah, and the letter returned. The expense of employing messengers here on every occasion would be material, which is quite unnecessary, as opportunities almost daily occur for forwarding letters by the different traders going from hence. I therefore hope your representation of this affair to the King, will induce him to countermand his orders to Quamina, if any such have been given him.

I am, Sir,

your most obedient Servant,

JOHN HOPE SMITH.

To *Thomas Edward Bowdich, Esq.*

JOHN HOPE SMITH, *Esquire, Governor in Chief of the British Forts and Settlements on the Gold Coast of Africa,* to SAÏ TOOTOO QUAMINA, *King of Ashantee.*

SIR,

I HAVE received your letter of the 26th ult. and am happy to find that you are sincerely desirous of cultivating the friendship of the British nation. Both inclination and duty urge me to reciprocate the sentiments expressed by you, and I shall be anxious at all times to promote the harmony and good understanding which, I hope, will now be established between us respectively, and which cannot fail to be mutually advantageous.

I regret to find there has been so much trouble about the Fantee notes, and I am sorry you did not apply to me in the first instance, as the affair should have been settled immediately to your satisfaction; but I knew not of it, except from the Fantees having begged me to take four ackies per month from each note, which they said they had agreed for with your messengers at Abrah.

I observe by the many instances quoted in your letter, that the notes of conquered countries have been transferred to your ancestors, therefore it shall be the same on the present occasion. Herewith I send you two notes, one for two oz. per month, formerly held by Amooney, also one from the caboceer at Abrah for two oz. the latter was only 12 ackies per month, and I have added 1 oz. 4 to it. These, and the notes you hold from Accra, will make your Company's pay six oz. per month, which shall be regularly paid at the Castle.

I hope my ready compliance with your wishes will convince you of the good will of the British nation, but I have every reason to believe that attempts have been made to prejudice you against it, however your own good understanding will readily suggest to you that the only motive is jealousy in trade.

The conduct of the English you will always find very different; they enter into fair competition with the other European residents here, but they never, by clandestine means or false assertions, endeavour to injure their character with the natives of this country.

I have learned with regret that the people of Elmina are using their influence to induce you to make a palaver with the Commendas. They are a mere handful of people, extremely poor and not worth your notice; besides they are under my protection, therefore I hope you will not think further of the affair, and I shall consider your compliance in this instance, as the greatest possible proof of the sincerity of your intentions towards the English.

I wish you health and happiness, and I hope you will reign many years, enjoying the love of your subjects, and the respect of all the Europeans resident in this country.

I am, Sir,

your faithful friend,

(Signed)   J. H. SMITH.

Cape Coast Castle, 20th June, 1817.

P. S. The abolition of the slave trade was an act of the King and the Parliament in England, in which the government in this country had no concern.

Coomassie, July 9, 1817.

To John Hope Smith, Esq. Governor in Chief, &c. &c. &c.

Sir,

The messengers returned on Saturday the 5th instant.

To be confirmed by your approbation, in the opinion that my zeal for the public good had not exceeded my duty, is a most flattering satisfaction. The appointment you have conferred on me, is an acknowledgment so far transcending my conduct, that it must stimulate every ability to exert itself for the success of the Mission, to justify such an honourable distinction.

The box containing the letters was opened in the King's presence, but being engaged in a custom on the death of a son, he deferred the reading of your letter, retaining it with the notes. His acknowledgments of your justice were associated with the declaration, that, although you had sent him the notes, still, if I could not fortify him with the prices of the various articles to be received in payment, you would have it in your power (though he did not suspect you) to reduce the intrinsic of the whole, to that of the moiety rejected. The proposition of the same prices as those attached to the Accra note, was annihilated by the argument, that Accra was a small fort, and not like Cape Coast or *Elmina*. So much stress was laid on the instance of the latter, that I felt called upon to declare, as the only striking conviction, that you did not wish, in the payment of these notes, to treat the King like a trader, and therefore would not allow the Elmina Governor to act more liberally in prices than yourself: the conviction was entire and instantaneous.

The next audience did not take place until Monday, Mr. James being present. I did justice to the utmost of my ability to your impressive letter; the effect was honourable to you, and encouraging to myself; the King ordered me to take his hand, in his sensibility to the strong appeal of the several paragraphs, and again at the conclusion, as a pledge of his cordial satisfaction of the whole ; his linguist followed his example, (as did the whole council) when he laid his fore-finger on his head and breast, as the invocation to Heaven for the vouchsafement of your several good wishes, as I concluded with them. I was reluctantly compelled to yield a minor object to a custom consecrated by their constitution. The laws of the three first Kings (who were brothers, and cotemporary leaders of the colony, whose conquests established the Empire) are sacred ; and it was a law of Saï Cudjo, the younger brother, and the grandfather of the present King, which granted to particular captains the honourable patent of receiving the pay of small forts, distinctly, each being responsible for his. separate duties to his settlement. If this law were not inviolable, the King pleads, that it would be an invidious act, and unjust to the merits of the Captain of English Accra, (Asquah Amanquah) to remove the payment of the Accra note to Cape Coast; but as the other appointments originate in him, he will respect your wish, by constituting one captain to receive both the Abra and Annamaboe notes at Cape Coast. He enquired if it was your wish that no Ashantee trader should go to Accra? I replied no! you were only desirous to induce as many as possible to come to Cape Coast.

The Cape Coast linguists, and our guide, Quamina Bwa, confirmed your report of the conduct of Quamina Bootaqua, the captain now at Payntree, in the negociation of the notes; it excited the greatest surprise and indignation ; his interception of letters was disclaimed, and will be done away with. I submitted to the King, on retiring, that in my next audience, I should be desirous of declaring the purport of the official instructions transferred to me (which had not been yet avowed) with other credentials, explanatory and impressive of the good wishes and intentions of the Government, the Committee, and yourself. I was favoured with my first separate audience at 8 o'clock this morning. I first impressed from the dispatches of the Committee, every motive and sentiment that was convicting or imposing; urging your waving the hostages and escort; as the demonstration of your confidence in the King's honour and friendship; and insinuating that the establishment of a school at Cape Coast, was solely in anticipation of the King's committing some of his children to your care for education, as the foundation of the pre-eminence of Europeans. I then passed to your instructions, rendering them in a manner as persuasive and auspicious as possible; associating in favour of the Residency, the commanding motive of facilitating political interests, with the imposing one of securing justice to the Ashantee traders. Lastly, I introduced the Treaty, as a pledge from the King to give force to your application to the Government at home, for the increase of his pay; for, as he continued to dwell on the grant of 4 ounces from Elmina, I availed myself of this liberty of my instructions, to divert the impression, and to propitiate his ratification of the Treaty. I considered the pretence of your being obliged to address the British Government on the subject, as preservative of the opportunity of judging of the sincerity of his professions, and of the duration of the union.

I think I may pledge myself for three great pillars of our commercial intercourse, by the accomplishment of the Residency, the Education, and the Treaty.

I reconcile myself to fresh difficulties by the reflection that they are inseparable from all great political views; and that without them, I should be deprived of the satisfaction of proving myself, in a small degree, worthy this confidence and distinction, by patience and perseverance. A letter accompanies this, written in the King's presence, on the subject of the Commenda palaver, which wears so decided an aspect, that whilst I pledge all my energy and address, and look with hope to the aid of your suggestions, I must candidly confess, I do not think it can be compounded in any thing like a reasonable way. I appealed to the King's magnanimity, and depicted the poverty of the Commendas, but every appeal and every argument was ineffectual; their aggravated offences admit of no amelioration of the King's feelings. I depreciated the plea of General Daendels' repeated messages, by submitting that they were addressed to the Town, and not to the Fort, and I succeeded in retiring him from the negociation, as an interference inconsistent with your dignity, and the present good understanding.

I did not discourage the King's great anxiety for clothes of the English costume, considering that his example would be more auspicious than any thing else, to the introduction of these manufactures. I have distributed the muslins, &c. as politically as possible, including with the Moors of repute, the aristocracy, or four captains controuling the King, his four linguists, his brother and successor, our housemaster, and some other captains of superior influence. I made a point of conciliating a Moor of influence, about to return through Sallagha or Sarem (the capital of the Inta country, and the grand emporium of the merchandize of the interior) to Houssa, feeling the policy of communicating every favourable impression to the neighbouring kingdoms. In my second interview I obtained permission from the King to dismiss the remaining Fantees. It was one of the first considerations, for the sake of our dignity, to avoid the humiliating circumstances and impressions, which have ensued from the want of foresight, and the consequent inability to meet the demands of our people. Their conduct since has been so mutinous and insulting, with the exception of six, that to preserve the impression of the firmness of an English officer, I secured one who encouraged the others, by persisting in some insulting indecencies, in contempt of my remonstrances, and ordered him to be punished.

The others (with the above exception) having refused in a body, aggravating their disobedience with the grossest insolence, to go with a cane to Payntree, and bring the biscuit which had been deserted there; I have disclaimed them, and left them to act for themselves, only securing them the King's permission to depart.

I shall request the King to furnish me with his own people, on the conclusion of the business of the Embassy. Such an arrangement favours œconomy, and impresses the confidence I affect.

The frequent presents had enabled me to present the Fantees with large supplies of plantains and hogs; and on paying them their arrears, which I did the same evening I received your gold, I gave them a bullock which fell to my share in a division with Mr. James.

You will see by the balance of the annexed account, that (preserving our dignity) every expense should be avoided that can be; and I assure you, that in making the present arrangement for bearers for our baggage only, I do not disregard your solicitude for our health. I shall order one Cape Coast messenger to attend Mr. James, and also the bearers left behind, being sufficiently recovered.

The statistical and scientific desiderata so impressively recommended to my attention, are daily realising beyond my expectations. Mr. Tedlie has had a severe attack of fever and dysentery, but is convalescent: Mr. Hutchison and myself are in perfect health.

I am, with respect, Sir,

Your most obedient Servant,

T. E. BOWDICH.

Saï Tootoo Quamina, *King of Ashantee and its Dependencies, to* John Hope Smith, *Esquire, Governor in Chief of the British Settlements on the Gold Coast of Africa.*

The Commenda palaver now rests with you and the King of Ashantee only, the Dutch Governor has no more to do with it, so the King recals the captain sent to him, and sends a proper messenger to treat with you individually.

The conduct and messages of the Commendas have been so irritating and insolent to the King, that nothing but believing you to be his good friend, could induce him to treat at all with them, or do any thing but kill them ; but for your sake, he will settle the palaver, and you must help him properly.

The King wants to begin the union without any palaver remaining, and as this Commenda palaver is the only one, it must be settled, and if you do this, he will take care the Elminas shall not do wrong to the Fantees, but he will help you in all your palavers.

The Elminas are always sending him messages about the insulting conduct and expressions of the Commendas towards him, and this is very vexatious to him, so he wishes to put an end to it with your help.

Adoo Bradie, his favorite nephew, the son of the former King Saï Quamina, is sent with a proper captain; Quantree, to help you settle the palaver.

Two thousand ounces is the demand.

The origin of the palaver is, that after the King returned from his own campaign against the Fantees, the Commendas went to the Elminas and said, " well, you help'd the King, and now he is gone back we will fight for it."

Again, when a war was about to take place between the Cape Coast people and the Elminas, the Commendas went to the latter and said, well, we will help you if you will give us plenty of powder to fight for you: they did so, and immediately the Commendas used it to seize 98 Elminas, and sold them as slaves—this the King thinks you will say is very bad.

The Cape Coast people and the Fantees having joined against the Elminas, they sent to tell the King, stating, when he demanded the reason, that it was because they had not resisted him when he came down against the Fantees; adding, that the Commendas, who were their natural allies before, had now joined their enemies, and begging the King to revenge this act of perfidy. The King much angered, immediately sent a captain for the purpose of their destruction (Yaquokroko,) but the Dutch governor sent to him, and then sent to the King to beg him to stop, because the English and Dutch being one, it would put shame on his face.

Col. Torrane by giving up Cheeboo, induced the King to consider the Cape Coast people as his friends, and they took fetish accordingly, but their joining the Fantees afterwards to fight against Elmina for assisting the King, has made him distrust them always since.

He considers his favourite nephew as the adopted son of Col. Torrane, to whom he gave him, and the Colonel gave him English clothes, so he is all the same as a Cape Coast Boy.

Col. Torrane being dead, he considers his nephew to stand in the same relation to you, and that he is therefore the proper messenger to send to you about this palaver.

You must write in your great book, that the King is your good friend, that he likes you too much, that he thanks God very much, so that every future Governor may read that in the Cape Coast Books.

The mark ✕ of Saï Tootoo, King of Ashantee,

Present.   Per T. E. Bowdich.

WM. HUTCHISON.
HENRY TEDLIE.

Coomassie, July 9th, 1817.

Coomassie, July 12th, 1817.

John Hope Smith, Esquire, Governor in Chief, &c. &c.

Sir,

I am just returned from reading your letter to the King, and extracts from that to myself, before the assembly of the captains: the effect was satisfactory; and Quamina Bootaqua is ordered up to answer for his conduct. The King enquired if the pay now due on the two notes would be liquidated on application; I replied, immediately; he is anxious for it, on account of the approaching yam custom.

I am, &c.

(Signed)   T. EDWARD BOWDICH.

I will not continue to copy the rude diary before submitted, it is only a register of dull or disgusting circumstances, illnesses, human sacrifices, and ceremonious visits. I would not anticipate the better arrangement of my reports, or break the thread of the correspondence on the political difficulties opposed to the Mission. I will abridge some passages of my diary, merely to give an idea of the nature of our conversations, and the biography of the leading men. Mr. Hutchison has sent me copious extracts from his diary, as Resident, his leisure and tranquillity having afforded him better opportunities of social intercourse and domestic observation, than I had, or could afford time to cultivate, without neglecting my reports. I shall adjoin these extracts, expecting they will contribute to the rational entertainment of the public, and to the credit of an active and intelligent officer.

A captain called Asofoo, sent us a present of seven ackies of gold, and we also received twelve from Amanquateä, and three from our house master. On the 9th of July the King sent us ten ackies of gold, and repeated his satisfaction of the result of the late correspondence, and daily presents of meat and fruits from various quarters, evinced the better opinion of his chiefs.

I paid my first private visit to Baba the chief Moor, and took some pens, paper, ink, and pencils with me as a present; the paper and pencils were much esteemed, but he preferred his reed and vegetable ink. He received me courteously, and was contemplating a curiously intricate figure like a horoscope; the ms. was filled with them; he laid his finger on it, and said, if you have any hard palaver, this can make me settle it for you when no other person can; or if you have any dear friend in England you wish to see, tell me the name, and this shall bring him to you. I thanked him, observing, that when Englishmen knew their palaver was right, they always left it to God, and that England was too good a place for me to wish any one I regarded to leave it. His disciples and pupils were writing on wooden boards, like those Mr. Park describes. When a charm was applied for, one of the oldest wrote the body of it, and gave it to Baba, who added a sort of cabalistical mark, and gave it a mysterious fold; the credulous native snatched it eagerly as it was held out to him, paid the gold, and hurried away to enclose it in the richest case he could afford. I had a long conversation with Baba, and he begged me to visit him frequently; he was much gratified with the specimens of African Arabic at the end of Mr. Jackson's work, and read them fluently. I visited him the next day, when he sent hastily for a Moor, who he told me was very learned, and just come from Timbuctoo. This man expressing no surprise when he first saw me, · Baba explained it, by telling me, spontaneously, that this Moor had seen three white men before, at Boussa. I eagerly enquired the particulars of the novelty, and they were again repeated to Baba, and were thus interpreted : " that some years ago, a vessel with masts, suddenly appeared on the Quolla or Niger near Boussa, with three white men, and some black. The natives encouraged by these strange men, took off provisions for sale, were well paid and received presents besides : it seems the vessel had anchored. The next day, perceiving the vessel going on, the natives hurried after her, (the Moor protested from their anxiety to save her from some sunken rocks, with which the Quolla abounds) but the white men mistaking, and thinking they pursued for a bad purpose, deterred them. The vessel soon after struck, the men jumped into the water and tried to swim, but could not, for the current, and were drowned. He thought some of their clothes were now at Wauwaw, but he did not believe there were any books or papers." This spontaneous narrative, so artlessly told, made a powerful impression on my mind. I saw the man frequently afterwards, his manners were very mild, and he never asked me for the most trifling present. He drew me a chart before he went away, and I dispatched some certificates for Major Peddie by him, endorsed with Baba's recommendations. I heard exactly the same thing afterwards from another Moor, but he had not been an eye witness. I begged Mr. Hutchison, when I left Coomassie, to note any other report on the subject of Mr. Park's death, and he afterwards sent me the ms. a translation of which is in the appendix. I continued to call on Baba three or four times a week; these visits afforded much information, for at each I found strange Moors just arrived from different parts of the interior, sojourning with him. They always affected to deplore the ignorance of the Ashantees, and presumed it must be as irksome to me as to them. Baba telling one that I could speak different languages, he said that he would try me, and addressed me in several, all very uncouth to my ear, and their names even unintelligible, except one, which he called Hindee or Hindoo; neither had I heard of any of the great cities he enumerated, until at last he pronounced Room (Rome) and said, if I did not know that I was not a Christian. I never saw the Shereef Brahima (to whom I was introduced about this time by a Jenné Moor) at Baba's, they did not appear to be on terms; I think the latter was envious of the greater learning and intelligence of the former, who had been to Mecca and Medina. One day I requested Baba to draw me a map of the world, he did so, encircling one large continent with a sea, bounded by a girdle of rocks. Old Odumata's notion of geography was as strange; for he mentioned one day, that when on the coast above Apollonia, he had an idea of walking to England, for he was told he should reach Santonec (Portugal) in 30 days, and that after that, the path was very good. He greatly enjoyed our singeing the hair of a foppish attendant of his, with a burning glass; the man's amazement was inconceivable, Mr. Hutchison was at some distance, and not suspected.

We were now permitted to walk four or five miles beyond the city, and felt quite at home. We seldom went out in the morning, lest an occasion for an audience should occur. Apokoo and several other daily visitors diverted us with their anecdotes, and in the afternoon we made our round of calls. Apokoo was always facetious, and looked with much anxiety for our entry, as his greatest recreation; he was very desirous of learning tennis and sparring, and daily made some essays, so comical, that neither we nor his attendants could contain ourselves. Apokoo became very communicative of Ashantee politics, and asked innumerable questions about England; particularly, why the King of England did not send one of his own sons to the King of Ashantee, with the presents, and why so great a King sent such a small force to Africa.

The Spanish campaign was gone through, again and again, and never tired him. He gave us an excellent dinner, as did Odumata repeatedly. Both were extravagantly enraptured with the miniature of an English female, and called all their wives to look at it.

Having been advised by a note from the Governor, of the arrival of an Ashantee boy and girl at Cape Coast Castle, sent by the King without any explanation, I desired an audience on the subject, and forwarded the following letter, which also communicates the baseness of one of the King's messengers, just returned from the Coast, and other inauspicious circumstances.

Coomassie, 10th Aug. 1817.

JOHN HOPE SMITH, ESQ. GOVERNOR IN CHIEF, &c. &c. &c.

SIR,

THE King has explained to me that he sent the boy and girl you mention to have arrived at Cape Coast, to become the property of the Committee or Government, conceiving it to be obligatory on him, in justification of his possession of the notes, to allow an Ashantee family to rear itself under the Governor's protection, for the service of the Settlement, and as an acknowledgment of the duties he owes it. He begs me to observe that he put the same plates of gold around their necks which distinguish the royal attendants.

I had reason to believe, from a coolness and some invidious comparisons on the part of the King, that the messenger lately arrived, Ocranameah, who was so particularly recommended to your favour, had been unjust in his report of the treatment he had experienced. I did not hesitate to avow my impression to the King, having solicited an audience for the purpose. The King confessed he had felt his private feelings hurt ever since the return of that messenger, having received his assurance, that you would scarcely admit him to your presence; that he received no present or compliment from you, and was wholly neglected during his stay at head quarters. I instantly pledged my honour to the King that Ocranameah (who was present) was guilty of falsehood and ingratitude, adding, that I was not prepared to confront him with the particulars of the presents he received from you and the officers; though I was positive, from private letters, as well as my own conviction, that you had not slighted the opportunity of evincing your private friendship for the King; and as I might possibly identify some trifle, I wished the King to allow a search to be made. On the messenger's box being sent for and opened, two engravings appeared, to the surprise of the King, and which I recognised; but as the messenger still persists in *your* entire neglect of him, and of his not having received any present or compliment worth mentioning, I must trouble you for the particulars of his treatment at Cape Coast Castle, for the entire conviction of the King. The King expressed his suspicion (founded on reports) that many Ashantees imposed on your generosity, by introducing themselves as attached to him in various capacities; and hoped that you would only listen in future to such as he recommended to your notice by letter, which his three messengers above had been; the second (Ocranameah) the more particularly, and that recollection had made him so sensible of the neglect. You will regret, with myself, that this inauspicious circumstance has been unvoidable.

The recent intelligence respecting the Buntooko war, has imposed serious anxiety, in the place of the King's former confidence. The revolt of that people, as may be expected in all revolts from arbitrary controul, has gradually induced the secessions of some other tributaries; and the King feels called upon by these unexpected difficulties, to conduct the war in person; not with his former expectation of witnessing their rapid subjugation, but from his present conviction of the necessity for every stimulus and energy. His precaution has dictated some popular acts, ameliorating the condition of the lower order of his subjects. The confidential ministers have been instructed to hint to me, that it would be indiscreet in the King to expose even his temporary reverses in an arduous war, by the residence of a British officer; and that he would most probably defer that part of the mutual wish, until the contest was terminated. I used the same medium to impress upon the King, that such a feeling towards the delegate of a friendly power was misplaced; that you had expedited his ex-parte views in the confidence of his consummation of the reciprocal objects of the Mission, without which (as they had been instituted for his benefit and aggrandisement) I could not think of returning; since a protraction would be construed into a slight of the friendly overtures of the British Government, which (from its dignity and pre-eminence in Europe) could not be vouchsafed whenever they might be solicited.

I anxiously await your communications on the Commenda palaver, to further my exertions for the full accomplishment of the Mission. The King and his Council labour under so much anxiety and[i] business at the present moment, that though we pay and receive visits of ceremony, it is almost impossible to effect an audience, but on the receipt of dispatches.

I am, &c. &c.

T. EDWARD BOWDICH.

The most entertaining *delassement* of our conversations with the chiefs, was, to introduce the liberty of English females ; whom we represented, not only to possess the advantage of enjoying the sole affection of a husband, but the more enviable privilege of choosing that husband for herself. The effect was truly comic, the women sidled up to wipe the dust from our shoes with their cloths, and at the end of every sentence brushed off an insect, or picked a burr from our trowsers ; the husbands suppressing their dislike in a laugh, would put their hands before our mouths, declaring they did not want to hear that palaver any more, abruptly change the subject to war, and order the women to the harem.

One of the King's linguists was a very old man, called Quancum; he spoke but seldom, yet the greatest deference was paid to his opinion; the King appeared to consult him more than any other. I was so much interested by this man's deportment, that I enquired his history. He had been the linguist of two former Kings, who paid frequent, and large sums of gold, as damages for his intrigues; neither had age corrected his fault, until very lately, though the present King used the most friendly remonstrances ; and urged, that from his paying large sums so frequently for him on this account, his subjects thought, that he countenanced the depravity. Quancum confessed to the King, that his ardour for women was perpetuated by the sensual devices of one of his wives. Soon afterwards, he was detected in an intrigue with the wife of, a captain of great consequence, and the King refused to interfere. The captain declaring that the punishment of Quancum, and not gold, was his object, the King permitted him to be despoiled of all his property, even to his bed. The favourite wife was amongst the spoil, and the injured captain being much smitten with her, assured her of an indulgence and preference, even greater than that she had enjoyed with Quancum ; she replied, she must always hate him, and intreated to be sold. After much importunity the captain agreed to do so, provided she would put him in possession of all the presents Quancum had lavished on her; she produced them, stipulating, that her son might retain a small sum of gold, which Quancum had lately presented to him; this was agreed to, and she was immediately sold to a distant caboceer; but her son followed her, and buying her with his little property, presented her again to his father. On this, the King gave Quancum a house, and some furniture, and takes care to continue small supplies of gold daily, adequate to his and this woman's comfort; having exacted a solemn oath from him, that he would devote himself to this one wife, and never try to recover any of the others.

Mr. Tedlie's interesting interview with the King, when he desired his attendance to exhibit and explain his surgical instruments, and medicines, is best described in his own words.

" The King sent for me this morning, saying he wished to see the medicines, books, and instruments. I went immediately, and explained through Quashie, the Accra linguist, the proper use and advantage of each instrument: he was very particular in his enquiries, and asked if I had performed the operations I described : I assured him that I had, and as a proof, exhibited a piece of bone that I had taken out of an Indian black man's head in Ceylon, who had been wounded, and who lived. The King held up his hand as a mark of approbation, and all his attendants were astonished. I applied the instruments first on myself, then on the linguists, afterwards on the King's two captains, and lastly on the King : nothing could exceed the King's approbation. He then desired me to shew him the medicines; he enquired the virtues and doses of each, what time in the day they should be taken, and whether it was proper to eat or drink after taking them? I told him: he asked if I would sell them? I said no. I brought these medicines for the officers; I could not sell them, but I would give him as much as I could, keeping in view that some of the four officers might be sick; he said that I was right, but he could not help coveting the greater part of the medicines; he viewed them all over five or six times, and asked me to give him some of them. I did give him as much innocent medicine as I could with propriety afford; he thanked me " very much." I then shewed him the botanical books; he was astonished, held up his hand and exclaimed hah! at every brilliant or high coloured plant which he saw. All his attendants were closely arranged around: the two captains laid hold of a volume each, and were admiring the flowers; when either of them ejaculated an admiration, the King would seize it, and ask me what that tree was? After I had told him the use of them, I said all these trees grow in England; and the reason the English write all these in a book is, that they may know which is a good tree, and which is bad. He expressed the greatest astonishment at the flax (linum), oak " that we build our ships with," poppy " that makes a man sleep," and the sensitive plant (mimosa), which he pointed out and described himself. During this time he whispered to one of his attendants, who went out, and returned in a short time with a bit of cloth containing 9 ackies of gold; the King presented it to me; I accepted it, and returned thanks. He then asked me if I would come and see him at any time he sent for me; I assured him I would do every thing to please him, consistent with my duty. He shook hands with me and went into his house. He returned in a short time, leading his sister by the hand, in a manner that would shame many beaux in Europe, saying, " this is the white doctor I told you of; go, and take his hand; you are sick, tell him your complaint, and he will do you good: the lady complied with his request. He then said " give me that gold I gave you, the cloth is not clean; I want to put it in a clean cloth for you." He then put it in a piece of rich silk, and after he returned the gold he said " I like you; I like all the English very much; they are a proper people, and I wish to drink health with you." He retired to his own apartment, and returned with a flask of gin, and two servants with a silver vase and water and glasses; he helped himself and me, made a bow and said " Saï wishes you good health." I returned the bow, saying, I wish good health to the King, and hope he never will require any of my medicine: when this was explained to him he held out his glass to me, we touched and drank. He then took my hand, saying, " If I send my sister to you will you talk with her?" I assured him I would talk with and advise all the King's friends whenever he wished. After I gave all the medicine I could conveniently part with, he sent for a small Dutch liqueur case; he desired 10 or 12 of his attendants, and his eunuch, to keep in their heads what I said; and requested me to repeat again the use and dose of each medicine I gave him, with the proper time and method of using it. I did so. He placed his hand on his head saying " Saï recollects what the white doctor says;" then placing the medicines in the case himself said " that good for my head, that good for my belly, that good for my stomach," &c. One of the King's sisters sent a message that she wanted to come and see the white gentlemen; and shortly afterwards arrived with her stool and retinue, being head caboceer of a large town. After exchanging compliments, she complained that her left hand pained her very much. I examined it, but must confess I could not see any thing the matter with it; however I rubbed a little liniment on her hand, which seemed to gratify her; she asked if I would come and see her in the evening? I answered yes. Quamina, our Ashantee guide, came to conduct me: he said I must dress, put on my sword and hat, as this woman was a caboceer, and the King's sister ; he would carry my umbrella. When I arrived I found the princess lying on a mat in one of the inner apartments of the house she occupied ; she ordered a stool for me ; I rubbed some more liniment on her hand ; she wished me to stop and drink palm wine ; this I declined, alledging the English did not like palm wine in the evening, because it is sour."

CHAPTER V.

Proceedings and Incidents until the Signing of the Preliminaries to a
General Treaty.

[The Governor's reply to my communication on the subject of the Commenda
palaver, reached me on the 27th of August.]

Cape Coast Castle, August 11, 1817.

T. E. BOWDICH, Esq.

SIR,

I ENTERTAINED a confident hope that no further mention would
have been made by the King concerning the Commendas, after the
receipt of my letter, and I am sorry that he should allow so insignificant a set of people to protract in the least the settlement of our
union. As it is my particular wish to remove this impediment, I
have used every endeavour to bring the affair to a conclusion, and
trust the King will not suffer it to be invincible. The Commendas
are also naturally anxious for its termination, but their poverty is
so great, that they have it not in their power to comply with his
demand. They have acknowledged their fealty to the King, and
have agreed to pay the sum of 120 oz. of gold, of which, messengers are sent by his nephew to enquire whether he will accept. This,
with the sum they have been unavoidably obliged to promise the
principal persons deputed to negociate this business, will increase
the sum to at least 150 oz. The many proofs the King has had of

my friendly intentions towards him, and the consideration of the benefits that will accrue to him from his alliance with the English, will, I hope, induce him to concede to the terms offered by the Commendas. A refusal must be considered as an avowal of his determined resolution not to conciliate the affair, and as the indigent circumstances of these people, make it utterly impossible for them to pay a larger sum, you will, should he persist in exacting more, procure his permission to leave the country, and return with the other officers as soon as you can. To sacrifice the Mission, after the heavy expences which have been incurred, and when we are induced to believe that every other object is propitiated to our utmost expectations, should be avoided if possible; but if he insists on a larger sum being levied from the Commendas than has been offered, there remains no other alternative. The dignity of the flag must be the superior consideration to all others.

The King has no need to doubt in the least the sincerity of the Cape Coast people, they are his friends, and have every inclination to continue so; and I am convinced his nephew will, on his return, confirm this report to him.

I will make known to the Committee his request for a crown and clothes, and I have no doubt but it will be complied with.

I am, Sir,

your most obedient Servant,

JOHN HOPE SMITH.

Coomassie, Aug. 29, 1817.

JOHN HOPE SMITH, ESQ. GOVERNOR IN CHIEF, &c. &c. &c.

SIR,

I HAVE the satisfaction to enclose a copy of the Preliminaries to the general Treaty, as signed this day by the King in Council, adjusting the Commenda palaver, agreeably to your letter of the 11th, which did not reach me till the 27th instant.

I proceed to acquaint you with the transactions of the interval.

The charge of a political Embassy, in a part of the world where respect and security are founded upon the opinion imposed by our conduct, exacted a spirit and dignity, which might have been abated in insinuating a Mission through the country for scientific purposes, but the inviolability of which was inseparable from the improvement and safety of neighbouring settlements. Since my last dispatch, I have been obligated to resist various encroachments, of which I shall mention two or three to justify my treatment of them.

The death of Quamina Bwa, our Ashantee guide, in the early part of the last week, creating an idle, but popular superstition that he had been killed by the fetish for bringing white men to take the country; I was applied to in the King's name, to ameliorate this impression, by contributing an ounce of gold towards the custom to be made by the King for his repose. I refused on two grounds; first, that Quamina Bwa had himself unjustly incensed the people against us, by panyaring* their provisions in the King's name, for our subsistence, and defrauding them of the gold we gave him for the payment: secondly, that the rites of customs were unnatural to our religion, which bound us, at least, not to encourage them. Fifteen persons had been sacrificed the

* Seizing.

week before (in a custom for the mother of a captain) with aggravated barbarity.

Several of the principal men having applied to me to send to Cape Coast for silks, to be paid for on receipt at Coomassie (a very dangerous and impolitic indulgence), I impressed, indignantly, that I was not sent as a trader to make bargains with them, but as an officer to talk the palavers with the King.

These circumstances, and a personal chastisement of some insults from inferior captains, which was provoked after much patience, influenced ex parte representations, which, though they may not have sickened the King's regard, induced hauteur and neglect. In proceeding to the King's house on public occasions, which I never did without the flag, canes, and soldiers, we had been expected to make way for the greater retinues of superior captains, who would rudely have enforced it; and after soliciting audiences for two days, I was kept in waiting above an hour in the outer courts of the palace. On the last occasion of the latter treatment, knowing that it was affected, I returned to our quarters until I received the King's invitation; representing to him, that as an officer dignified by an authority to make a treaty with him in the name of the British Government, I could not submit to disrespectful treatment at the Palace, nor allow the English flag to give place to any but himself; that, if it merely affected myself as an individual, my esteem for the King would induce me to compromise these points of etiquette with his captains; but, according to the custom of England, I dared not; for if I did, my sword would be taken from me on my return to Cape Coast Castle. It produced the desired effect; the gong gong proclaimed in every street that all captains must make way for the flag; and at the monthly levee of the captains (the Adaï custom) the King's linguists were deputed to us first, with the customary present of a sheep and rum ; and presented us the first to pay our compliments to the King, being followed by Amanquatcä, Quatchie Quophi, Apokoo, and Odumata ; the four captains composing the Privy Council, or Aristocracy, which checks the King. The first (whose power approximates to that of the Mayor of the Palace under the early French dynasty) sent his linguist and gold swords to compliment us on the ground. I determined to take advantage of this impression, and of the comparative facility of intercourse, and demanded an audience to discuss the treaty, a copy of which I enclose, and hope my additions will be satisfactory. I have the King's assurance that it shall be formally executed in eight days ; when all his tributaries will be present for the yam custom, and when I hope to make the King of Dwabin and its dependencies a party, whose power is equal to the King of Ashantee's.

To resume—the audience was granted ; and I read the treaty before the King and his Council, submitting it article by article, to their consideration. It was debated the whole of that and the succeeding day. I considered that if I could get the treaty discussed and executed in this favourable interval, removing the Commenda palaver from the situation of an obstacle, and reserving it as the first proof of the King's disposition to coincide with you in what was reasonable and just, I might, on the receipt of dispatches, gain the better terms for that people.

On Saturday the 22d instant, I was summoned to declare the articles of the treaty before the assembly of captains, who were seated with their attendants and warriors in the large yard of the palace, with all the imposing pomp and military parade, which had before been collected to subdue us, in the scene of the declaration of war. The King's sisters, with the females of his family, were seated, with their numerous attendants, on an elevated floor behind. The deputies from the Fantee towns in the interior, were

P

placed within hearing, and the crowd was almost impervious: the most ghastly trophies were mixed with this blaze of ostentation. We were seated near the King immediately opposite to his linguists.

In reading the treaty, I paused after every article, leaving it to be formally repeated to the King through his linguists, and then sat down whilst it was discussed by the assembly. It is not necessary to repeat the various debates; and I will only notice that Amanquateä, through his linguist, proposed the renewal of the Slave Trade as a sine qua non;* this, however, as I had all along declared it to be impossible, was at length over-ruled, but with considerable difficulty. It was also proposed to attach a fine to the infraction of the treaty; but this I resisted as derogatory to the dignity of the contracting parties; and urged, that as the King and his dignitaries would consider his oath as sacred, as you and the Government would mine, I considered no *infraction* of the treaty could take place; though it might possibly be *offended* by the conduct of his subjects, or of individuals under British protection, which was provided for, and must be visited accordingly by the authorities pledged to the treaty.

I had declared from the first, that it would be expected that the King should swear in the form of his country to the fulfilment and preservation of the treaty, and that his oath should be attested by his principal captains, from my anxiety to fortify to the utmost, a

---

* Presents from two Spanish slave ships were received through the Mulatto Brue on the 16th instant; they were general, but I can only particularise the following:

To the King, 3 pieces of cloth, 1 umbrella, and a hat.

To the chief linguist, 1 piece, do. 2 flashes liquor.

To the 4th do. (Otee) 1 do.　　2 ditto, do.

To Odumata, 2 do.　　　　　　2 ditto, do.

To Quamina Bwa, agent for the purchase of the slaves, 2 pieces of cloth, 1 umbrella, and 1 Dane gun.

measure not only valuable to commerce but to humanity, in averting the renewal of a war, recorded by indelible marks of carnage and devastation.

At the moment I expected the King to execute the treaty, a fresh design was disclosed, in a long speech from the chief linguist, setting-forth the wrongs the King had just received from the people of Amissa, who had scourged his messengers, and couched their insulting defiance in the foulest language; yet, he said, the King did not want to invade the Fantee country for the sake of one town, and therefore I must stay and assist him to settle that palaver; he would then readily swear to the treaty. I replied at length, declaring particularly that I could not, and would not recognize the Amissa palaver; that the King vitiated the compliments he had been pleased to pay me, in expecting me to be such a fool as to involve you in the palaver of a people, over whom you neither possessed nor desired authority; and that if I had not a right to think better of the King, I should view such a proposal as evasive of the treaty, and final to the hope of a thorough understanding.

The chief linguist rejoined, that I had declared in announcing the treaty, that it was the wish of the British Government to put an end to war, and for the King to have no occasion to trouble the Fantees; whereas, if the people of Amissa were not persuaded to retract, the King must send a captain to destroy them, which could be done at a word, and this perhaps would make another war. I urged that the Fantee towns under the British forts must be considered distinctly, and that those, and those only, were viewed by the Government and the treaty; yet, for the cause of humanity, I would request you, for the King, to advise the people of Amissa better, through some medium, which I hoped might do good, but if disregarded, you could not even repeat it: that was all I could promise, and if that was not enough, our negociations were at an end. No! that was not enough, I must stay and see the palaver settled.

We immediately rose, and I declared as impressively as I could, that as the officer of the King of England, your orders only could be obeyed by me, that I dared not remain or allow myself to be stopped, even if I should be killed on the path, for my life was not my palaver, but the King of England's. As I bowed to retire, the linguist exclaimed, that the King promised to see me again in an hour.

I used the interval for reflection, and resolved to act upon the conclusion, that nothing but an undaunted resolution could check these encroachments, which were to be attributed to the Government rather than to the King.

The hour having fully expired, I sent a cane to Adooçee, the chief linguist, to desire the audience; he sent me word that the King was asleep, and no one dared to awake him. I then went to Odumata (who resides within the palace) and repeated to him, that I was determined to go, if the King did not keep his word and see me; he said I could not; I rejoined, I would, and left him. I then went to Adoocee's house, declared the same, and received the same reply. I left a cane in waiting at the palace, with orders to quit and return to me at 4 o'clock, (which allowed altogether four hours instead of one) if he was not dispatched with a message in the interval. No notice was taken; there was no alternative to my making good what I had said. The views of the Mission were at risk, but they would have been too dearly purchased by such concessions, and I was sanguine, rather than apprehensive of the success of the measure I adopted; without spirit and fortitude nothing was to be done.

I ordered all the baggage out, planted the flag, and giving the soldiers' muskets to the officers, converted them and the artificers into bearers, as well as our own servants, for I saw the previous dismissal of my own people was considered a hold on me. I ordered the linguists to declare to the party publickly, that I would flog any man who attempted to leave the town in debt; I paid all they confessed, by advances on their pay to the amount of 10 ackies: this gave the greatest publicity to our movements.

The King's uncle, Bundaenha, and another superior captain came in form to entreat me to stay, whilst they affected to address the King. I saw through this, and that I might presume on it; holding the watch in my hand, I promised to wait half an hour, and no longer. They returned within the time to conduct me to the King, but after being kept unusually long in waiting, the answer to my remonstrance through the linguists, was, that the King was very busy hearing a great palaver; I saw they lingered still in their hope of my submission. I sent the two canes to tell the King that mine was a great palaver, and ought to be heard, not only from its importance, but because he had passed his word that it should; that after a King disregarded his promise, it was useless to wait any longer. Returning to our quarters, I ordered the people to load the baggage.

At the moment of starting, a royal messenger ran up, to say the King was waiting to see me. I dismissed him with the message, that I could not stop, unless a person of consequence was sent to *promise* for the King. The King's uncle came, and assured me the King would receive me himself at the entrance of the palace. We went, and were instantly ushered into the presence of the King and his captains, who were debating by torch light: the clamour and deportment of this assembly might have been subduing, had it been novel. -The uproar having abated, the King demanded, through his linguist, why I had determined to leave so suddenly, and whether he had not behaved well to me, adding to much declamation, that he knew the King of England and the Governor wished to please him, and would not countenance the act. I replied, that " I had not only gone the full length of my instructions to please the King, but exceeded them; and all that I had to fear was, that you would not approve my remaining a moment after he had trifled with me. The King's behaviour to me, as an individual, I should always be proud to speak of, but his respect of the Embassy was a very superior consideration. Every thing he wished had been done, and now he tried to impose a palaver on me, with which you had no more to do than with the Buntooko war. The King had promised me to settle the point of the treaty, I waited the discussion patiently, he pledged his word to see me that evening, he had avoided it; I had said I would wait no longer if he did not keep his word; no English officer dared to break his word, if he did, he lost his sword." Much declamation ensued, but the King's conviction silenced the assembly, and realized the triumph I expected. He said, what I told him was true, that he was very sorry, but he had too much to think about; he liked the Law (the Treaty) very well, but begged me to wait a little longer till all his captains came. I received his promise to see me the following day. The next morning the head linguist came in form to acquaint me that some palavers had arrived in the night, which had made it necessary for the King to go to Berramang (a croom about five miles to the N. E. on the road to Sallagha, the capital of the Inta country) but he had orders to furnish us with the King's hammock-men, if we were inclined to follow him the next day. We did so, and I enclose an extract from my diary, with the circumstances of the day, as they do not affect the point in question: on taking leave in the evening, the King promised that I shoul hear from him the next day.

Apokoo, who had been left in charge of the town, visited me in form by the King's orders, with the criers and insignia, to assure me there should be no more impediments to the treaty, and that the King would return the next day. The evening was productive of another disturbance, from my resistance of an indignity. The Cape Coast messenger arriving, informed me that the dispatches and letters were retained by Adoo Bradie's messenger, who accompanied him. I sent the canes to Apokoo's to demand them, but ineffectually; I then went myself, and insisted on the delivery; he said it could not be allowed until the King returned to the capital. I protested so strongly against the act, that he sent for the chief linguist (Adoocee) and after a palaver, they promised to send me the letters on my return to the house: I left the canes in waiting. The time allowed having expired without the receipt, I went again to Apokoo's, who referred me to Adoocee. I went to him, and he said he dared not interfere in the business. The Cape Coast messengers refusing to do so, we proceeded instantly to Adoo Bradie's house, and finding the messenger, demanded the letters, and obtained them. I had scarcely read them, before Adoocee came with some captains, and about 100 persons, (being then 9 o'clock) to demand my delivery of your letter to his charge, until the King's return. I indignantly refused, asserting my authority, and criminating such a request as injurious to the rights of the meanest subject of the King of England, and an insuperable affront to you. He tried threats and entreaties alternately; the former I treated with contempt, the latter I regretted I dared not yield to. The palaver was prolonged till 10 o'clock at night. I determined not to lose ground. The King did not arrive until the evening of the next day, I sent three canes with my compliments on his return, and received his with an appointment of an audience the next (this) morning.

We were sent for early, the affair of the letters was opposed to me. I repeated my declarations to Adoocee, and added, that I should not think of leaving a Resident, if such were the forms of the Ashantee Court. The Ashantee messengers declared that you had ordered your letters to be delivered to the King. I said that was impossible. The King was very gentle, but such was the sus‑picion of the assembly, that they requested me to swear on my sword, that I had not altered any part of your letter; I did so, prefacing the act as such a suspicion merited. I then read your letter, abating nothing of its spirit and firmness, and laying stress upon your disposition to benefit the King, and the proofs you had given. I concluded my illustrations with the declaration, that you did not settle the King's palaver from fear, but from friendship, as it remained with him to prove. I submitted the preliminaries in form, for rejection or acceptance. After an ardent debate among the captains, they were executed and attested, and I lose no time in forwarding the copy. I left a duplicate with the King, as I shall of the treaty.

The King intends to dispatch a messenger directly to empower Adoo Bradie to receive the gold, and hopes you will recommend the people of Commenda to restore any of the slaves in their pos‑session belonging to Elmina, although that is not his palaver.

The King desired me to communicate his best thanks for your handsome treatment of his nephew, whose reports have been very flattering.

I urged my intercessions for Quamina Bootaqua, until the King vouchsafed me his assurance that he would pardon him.

I have the satisfaction to inform you, that I have been able, privately, so far to conciliate the Moors, as to have witnessed their forwardance of the certificates* to the Interior, with their own letters of recommendation indorsed.

* For a copy of these certificates vide the opposite engraving.

I advocated the merits of the Castle linguist, De Graff, as you desired, and successfully. I flatter myself this will anticipate the arrival of the King's, and the Cape Coast messengers.

I am, &c. &c.

T. E. BOWDICH.

Preliminaries of a General Treaty, to be made and entered into by Thomas Edward Bowdich, *Esquire, for the Governor and Council of Cape Coast Castle, and on the part of the British Government, with* Saï Tootoo Quamina, *King of Ashantee and its Dependencies.*

1st. The King accepts the offer of the people of Commenda, through the Governor in Chief; namely, one hundred and twenty ounces of gold for himself, and the customary fees to his embassadors, as a settlement in full of all demands.

2nd. The people of Commenda shall acknowledge their fealty to the King, and be entitled to all the benefits of his protection.

3d. The King shall authorize · some responsible captain to receive the gold, from the hands of the deputies of the people of Commenda, at Cape Coast Castle.

4th. It is hereby agreed, that every palaver is now settled preparatory to the General Treaty, which shall be executed forthwith.

Signed and sealed this twenty-ninth day of August, in the year of our Lord one thousand eight hundred and seventeen.

The mark of SAÏ TOOTOO QUAMINA. ⋈ (L. S.)

T. E. BOWDICH. (L. S.)

In the presence of

William Hutchison.
Henry Tedlie.
Adoocee, Chief Linguist.
Apokoo, Keeper of the Treasury.
Quamina Quatchie, } Linguists to the Mission.
Quashee Apaintree, }

Q

Extract from Diary.—Monday, 25th August, we started soon after seven o'clock, and proceeding in a N. E. direction, crossed the marsh close to the town, where it was about two feet deep and one hundred and fifty yards broad. We travelled the path to Sallagha, through a beautiful country, abounding in neat crooms (of which we passed through seven), the sites spacious, and environed by extensive plantations. The path was wide and so nearly direct, that the eye was always in advance through beautiful vistas varied by gentle risings. The iron stone still prevailed.

The King received us in the market place, and enquiring anxiously if we had breakfasted, ordered refreshment. After some conversation we were conducted to a house prepared for our reception, where a relish was served (sufficient for an army) of soups, stews, plantains, yams, rice, &c. (all excellently cooked) wine, spirits, oranges, and every fruit. The messengers, soldiers, and servants were distinctly provided for. Declining the offer of beds, we walked out in the town, and conversed and played drafts with the Moors, who were reclining under trees ; the King joined us with cheerful affability, and seemed to have forgotten his cares. About two o'clock dinner was announced. We had been taught to prepare for a surprise, but it was exceeded. We were conducted to the eastern side of the croom, to a door of green reeds, which excluded the crowd, and admitted us through a short avenue to the King's garden, an area equal to one of the large squares in London. The breezes were strong and constant. In the centre, four large umbrellas of new scarlet cloth were fixed, under which was the King's dining table (heigthened for the occasion) and covered in the most imposing manner ; his massy plate was well disposed, and silver forks, knives, and spoons (Colonel Torrane's) were plentifully laid. The large silver waiter supported a roasting pig in the centre; the other dishes on the table were roasted ducks, fowls, stews, pease pudding, &c. &c. On the ground on one side of the table were various soups, and every sort of vegetable; and elevated parallel with the other side, were oranges, pines, and other fruits; sugar-candy, Port and Madeira wine, spirits and Dutch cordials, with glasses. Before we sat down the King met us, and said, that as we had come out to see him, we must receive the following present from his hands, 2 oz. 4 ackies of gold, one sheep and one large hog to the officers, 10 ackies to the linguists, and 5 ackies to our servants.

We never saw a dinner more handsomely served, and never ate a better. On our expressing our relish, the King sent for his cooks, and gave them ten ackies. The King and a few of his captains sat at a distance, but he visited us constantly, and seemed quite proud of the scene; he conversed freely, and expressed much satisfaction at our toasts, " The King of Ashantee, the King of England, the Governor, the King's Captains, a perpetual union (with a speech, which is the sine qua non) and the handsome women of England and Ashantee." After dinner the King made many enquiries about England, and retired, as we did, that our servants might clear the table, which he insisted on. When he returned, some of the wine and Dutch cordials remaining, he gave them to our servants to take with them, and ordered the table cloth to be thrown to them and all the napkins. A cold pig, cold fowls (with six that had not been dressed) were dispatched to Coomassie for our supper. We took leave about five o'clock, the King accompanying us to the end of the croom, where he took our hands, and wished us good night. We reached the capital again at six, much gratified by our excursion and treatment.

Mr. Tedlie had brought Quamina Bwa (our guide) into a very advanced state of convalescence; but he so eagerly betook himself from low diet to palm oil soups, and stews of blood, that he soon relapsed, and a gathering formed on his liver, aggravated not a little by the various fetish draughts he swallowed. Seeing there was no other chance, Mr. Tedlie, who is a very skilful operator, would have scarified the liver; but although I had great reason to rely confidently on his judgment and ability, I thought our situation too critical to run such a risk. A Fantee boy having fractured his leg, and his dissolution appearing inevitable, the parents, in great distress, applied to the surgeon of an English outfort, who amputated the limb, and after much wearying attendance, to the surprise of every one, restored the boy to health. The family then brought him into the fort, and laying him down in the hall, addressed the surgeon (who was in charge of the fort) thus; " As Master cut off poor boy's leg, and so spoil poor boy for work, we come to ask Master how much he think to give poor boy to keep him."

Quamina Bwa was fetished until the last moment, and died amidst the howls of a legion of old hags, plastering the walls, door posts, and every thing about him, with chopped egg and different messes. I forget how many sheep he had sacrificed to the fetish by the advice of these harpies. The King sent him a sheep and a periguin of gold, when he heard he was ill. This man had settled the palaver with Mr. White, after the blockade of Cape Coast, in 1815, the third invasion of the Ashantees, and was universally odious, for his cruel extortions; these being reported to the King, he was disgraced; and being very extravagant, became much involved. Being at Payntree, he prevailed on Quamina Bushmaquaw to allow him to conduct us, to retrieve his finances a little. Excepting Adoocee, the King's chief linguist, he was the most plausible villain I ever met with.

The head of an Akim caboceer arrived in Coomassie about this time. The King and the Ashantee government had proposed that every croom of Akim should pay 20 periguins of gold as an atonement for their late revolt. Ten periguins were advanced immediately by each, and the other moiety was excused until after the harvest; but Aboidedroo caboceer of Manasoo resolutely refused to pay a tokoo. The King's messengers, however, appealed to his people with so much address, that they rose upon their caboceer, killed him, and sent his head to the King, with the 20 periguins required.

CHAPTER VI.

Proceedings and Incidents until the Ratification of a General Treaty.

T H E report of an Ashantee having been flogged to death in Cape Coast Castle, which was aggravated every hour to our prejudice, was explained by the following letter:

Cape Coast Castle, August 17, 1817.

T. E. Bowdich, Esq.

Sir,

The day before yesterday an Ashantee man was guilty of a most daring insult to the fort. On passing the gate, he was desired by the sentinel to take his cloth off his shoulders, but instead of complying, he turned round and struck him. The offender was instantly secured, and I ordered him to be put in irons. Last night about nine o'clock, the captain of the guard came to me to say, that the sentry on duty had reported the Ashantee to have hung himself. The place in which he was with others confined, was immediately opened, and he was found in a room adjoining to that in which the prisoners sleep, with his under cloth attached to a beam not more than three feet high, and very tightly drawn round his throat, part of his body was lying on the ground, and it must have been by the most determined resolution that he succeeded in strangling himself. The surgeon was present, but his efforts to recover him were ineffectual. This is the second offence of a similar nature that has occurred; the first person, I most assuredly should have punished, had he not ran past the sentry and made his escape.

The King's displeasure will no doubt be excited when he hears of such acts of insolence, and I hope he will issue such orders to his people, as will make them more circumspect in future.

I am, Sir,

your most obedient Servant,

J. H. SMITH.

Coomassie, 31*st August*, 1817.

JOHN HOPE SMITH, ESQ. GOVERNOR IN CHIEF, &c. &c. &c.

SIR,

I RECEIVED your letter last evening respecting the suicide of the Ashantee. I procured an audience this morning, and have just returned from the palace, where I had the honour to address you a letter, in the name of the King, on this, and other subjects.

The messenger sent up by Adoo Bradie, was the brother of the deceased, and declared before the King upon oath, that he had been killed by the officers. The master (our landlord) proposed a fine to the captains assembled, but after the audience was gone through, the King retired to council, which is the form, and returning, dictated the sentiments I had the honour to communicate to you, and rebuked our house-master severely for his proposition. Of course I impressed the insult to the fort, as the superior consideration of your letter.

The insolence of the lower orders here became insufferable, they proceeded even to pelting us with stones; after every effort on our part to conciliate them by the exhibition of the telescope and other novelties. As may be expected in a military government, they are beyond the King's control, out of the field. He declared however, that he would behead any man I would point out to him, and begged me to punish them as I thought proper: a summary chastisement of two inferior captains repressed this spirit.

All the captains of consequence have become friendly and respectful; Apokoo was deputed in form yesterday, in the name of the whole, to thank me for my conduct in negociating with the King.

The Treaty will be brought forward to be executed in six days, before the annual assembly of Kings, caboceers, and captains. All the Kings tributaries and allies being compelled to attend him at the yam custom.

The King intends your linguist De Graff, to take fetish with his five linguists, to be just to both the powers to be pledged to the treaty, and is convinced of his probity.

> I am, with respect, Sir,
> your most obedient Servant,
> T. EDWARD BOWDICH.

Coomassie, 31st Aug. 1817.

Saï Tootoo Quamina, *King of Ashantee, &c. to* John Hope Smith, *Esquire, Governor in Chief, &c. &c. &c.*

Sir,

The King assures you, that, anticipating the permanent union of the English and Ashantees, so far from allowing the death of one man to retard it, he should take no notice if a thousand were flogged to death by you, as reported here, well knowing the insolent disposition of the lower order of Ashantees, which is as vexatious to him as to you. He is satisfied however, that this man came to his death by his own hands.

The King wishes you to adjust the palaver between the Commendas and Elminas, as soon as convenient to you; that all the people who serve him may be united, relying entirely on your justice.

The King will thank you very much if you will make the people of Cape Coast, Elmina, and Commenda " *all one together.*"

The little palaver between these people, is the only one remaining; and therefore, though it is not his, he wishes you to settle it.

The King hereby, and by his messenger, empowers his nephew Adoo Bradie, and the Captain Quantree, to receive the gold from the deputies of Commenda in your presence.

You must settle the compliments and fees, which the Commendas send to the King's linguists and captains.

The King hopes you will advise the people of Amissa, through some medium, to retract their insolent message to the King, that the whole of the Fantee territory may be quiet.

The King has condescended personally to solicit Mr. Bowdich to protract his stay fifteen days, and obliged all his captains to the same condescension, so that you will consider it the King's act from the wish to send him down with an honourable escort, and other marks of his favour.

The King wishes you health and happiness.

The mark ⋈ of Saï Tootoo Quamina, &c.

In the presence of
    WM. HUTCHISON.
    HENRY TEDLIE.

A few only of the many curious observations of our Ashantee friends recur to me. One captain told us he had heard that the English were so constantly in palavers, one with another, that their houses, which he understood to be made of wood, the same as their ships, were always fixed on wheels; so that when a man had quarrelled with his neighbour, he moved to another part of the bush. Another insisted that monkies (whom the Moors said sprung from the Israelites, who disobeyed Moses) could talk as well as men; but they were not such fools; for if they did, they knew men would make them work.—This is better than Pliny's account of monkies playing chess.

The King walked abroad in great state one day, an irresistible caricature; he had on an old fashioned court suit of General Daendels' of brown velveteen, richly embroidered with silver thistles, with an English epaulette sewn on each shoulder, the coat coming close round the knees, from which the flaps of the waistcoat were not very distant, a cocked hat bound with gold lace, in shape just like that of a coachman's, white shoes, the long silver headed cane we presented to him, mounted with a crown, as a walking staff, and a small dirk round his waist.

The King presented one of our servants with six ackies of gold, for making trowsers for his child, and mending him a pair of drawers, which he thought it extravagant to put on under trowsers or small clothes, and therefore wore them alone.

I fixed a rude leaping bar in the outer yard of our house, and trained the horse to it, preparatory to getting him over the trunks of trees on the path: this brought even greater levees than the camera obscura, or the telescope. Sometimes a gazer would start from the eye piece of the latter, to lay hold of the figure at the end, as he expected; and they all insisted on both being taken to pieces in their presence, that they might see what was inside   At length, being inexplicable, it was pronounced fetish. A captain had told the King, that with the telescope we saw, when at Doompassie, all that he was doing at Coomassie : and happening, in a sudden and heavy rain, to gallop from Asafoo to our house, with Mr. Tedlie on the horse behind me, holding the umbrella, it was immediately reported to the King as our plan of travelling to Cape Coast.

Our Accra linguist pointed out a man to me named Tando, whom he recollected to have visited the Coast some years, in great pomp, never going the shortest distance, but in his taffeta hammock, covered with a gorgeous umbrella, and surrounded by flatterers, who even wiped the ground before he trod on it. This man had now scarcely a cloth to cover him. He had been retired from his embassy to Akim, in consequence of a dispute with Attah, then the king of that country ; for though Attah was adjudged to be in fault, after the palaver was talked at Coomassie, the Ashantee government thought it politic to displace Tando, though he had become disagreeable to the other, only for his vigilance and fidelity. After a long interval of the most luxurious life the capital could afford, he was instructed to proceed to Elmina, to talk a palaver for the King ; but thinking it would be a coup d'éclat much more important and agreeable, if he could settle the Warsaw palaver as well, he visited the country on his return, and persuaded them to conciliate the King, and avert their ruin, by carrying a considerable sum of gold to Coomassie, and agreeing to pay twenty-four slaves for every Ashantee subject killed or injured by one of Warsaw. Deputies returned with this man for this purpose ; but the King dismissed them contemptuously ; and to the disappointment and surprise of Tando, declared that no man must dare to do good out of his own head, or perhaps he would find he did bad, as Tando had done, in spoiling a palaver which he and his great men meant to sleep a long time. Tando was immediately stripped of all his property for his presumption, and from a noble became a beggar.

The Moors now became friendly, and sent us some very good coffee, and choice pieces of meat.

Coomassie, Sept. 8th, 1817.

JOHN HOPE SMITH, ESQUIRE, GOVERNOR IN CHIEF, &c. &c.

SIR,

I HAVE the satisfaction to inform you, that the treaty was signed and sworn to yesterday, by the King of Ashantee, and this day, by the King of Dwabin. The whole of the caboceers, captains, and tributaries having arrived, the treaty was finally discussed on Saturday, and two of the four members of the Aristocracy, with the two oldest captains (Ashantee and Nabbra) were deputed to swear for that assembly, with the King, whose oaths (being very rare) are solemnized by the presence of his wives.

The King sent a handsome procession of flags, guns, and music, to conduct us to the palace on the occasion ; and meeting us in the outer square, preceded us to the inmost, where about 300 females were seated, in all the magnificence which a profusion of gold and silk could furnish. The splendour of this coup d'oeil made our surprise almost equal to theirs. We were seated with the King and the deputies, under the large umbrellas in the centre, and I was desired to declare the objects of the Embassy and the Treaty, to an old linguist, peculiar to the women. The King displayed the presents to them ; the flags were all sewn together, and wrapped around him as a cloth.

I was afterwards desired to stand before the King, and swear on my sword that I had declared the truth : I did so, with the other officers. The next form dictated was, that I should seat myself, and receive the oaths of the deputies, and lastly, of the King himself, for his brother the King of England. They advanced in turn, extending their gold swords close to my face, as they declared their oaths. I rose to receive the King's, all the women holding up two fingers, as their mark of approbation when he received the sword, and one of his counsellors kneeling beside him with a large stone on his head. The King swore very deliberately, that his words might be fully impressed on me, invoking God and the fetish to kill him ; first, if he did not keep the law, if we had sworn true ; and secondly, if he did not revenge the Ashantees to the full, if we had bad in our heads, and did not come for the purpose I avowed. The assurances, and the menaces of the oaths of the captains were equally forcible. The King sent an anker of rum to our people to drink on the occasion, and paid each captain the customary fee, of a periguin of gold on his oath.

The King having communicated my wish, by a formal message, to Boïtinnee Quama, the King of Dwabin, who holds his temporary court on the north side of the town, I seconded it, by sending the canes to request an audience; at which I had again formally to declare the objects of the Embassy and the Treaty, which, after a great deal of form and enquiry, received his signature, with the attestations of his chief linguists, Quama Saphoo, and Kobara Saphoo, who are his principal counsellors. His court was equally crowded with the King of Ashantees, who sits on his right hand when he visits Dwabin ; a reciprocal etiquette.

By an addition to the 4th article of the treaty, I reconciled the point of the Amissa palaver; and the securing you the opportunity of mediation, (without attaching any thing like responsibility) I considered to be not only a precaution due to humanity, but a prudent and legitimate measure for the extension of our influence.

The value of this treaty is enhanced by the reflection, that the justice, dignity, and spirit, of the British Government have been preserved inviolate; and that it has been the result of the impression, and not of the abatement of these characteristics.

We are flattered by your acknowledgment of our offer to accompany the King to the Buntooko war, and feel the force of your reason in the present view of the invasion of that country. The lake proving to be southward instead of northward, and close to the Accra path, I did not think it prudent to aggravate suspicion, for so secondary and well defined an object, whilst every day exacted some exertion (beyond vigilance) to wear away the difficulties opposed to the more important views of the Mission.

I expect the King will permit me to take leave on Saturday next. To-morrow Apokoo gives us a dinner in public.

I am, with respect, Sir,
your most obedient Servant,
T. E. BOWDICH.

Treaty made and entered into by Thomas Edward Bowdich, *Esquire, in the name of the Governor and Council at Cape Coast Castle on the Gold Coast of Africa, and on behalf of the British Government, with* Saï Tootoo Quamina, *King of Ashantee and its Dependencies, and* Boïtinnee Quama, *King of Dwabin and its Dependencies.*

1st. There shall be perpetual peace and harmony between the British subjects in this country, and the subjects of the Kings of Ashantee and Dwabin.

2nd. The same shall exist between the subjects of the Kings of Ashantee and Dwabin, and all nations of Africa residing under the protection of the Company's Forts and Settlements on the Gold Coast, and, it is hereby agreed, that there are no palavers now existing, and that neither party has any claim upon the other.

3rd. The King of Ashantee guarantees the security of the people of Cape Coast, from the hostilities threatened by the people of Elmina.

4th. In order to avert the horrors of war, it is agreed, that in any case of aggression on the part of the natives under British protection, the Kings shall complain thereof to the Governor in Chief to obtain redress, and that they will in no instance resort to hostilities, even against the other towns of the Fantee territory, without endeavouring as much as possible to effect an amicable arrangement, affording the Governor the opportunity of propitiating it, as far as he may with discretion.

5th. The King of Ashantee agrees to permit a British officer to reside constantly at his capital, for the purpose of instituting and preserving a regular communication with the Governor in Chief at Cape Coast Castle.

6th. The Kings of Ashantee and Dwabin pledge themselves to countenance, promote, and encourage the trade of their subjects with Cape Coast Castle and its dependencies to the extent of their power.

7th. The Governors of the respective Forts shall at all times afford every protection in their power to the persons and property of the people of Ashantee and Dwabin, who may resort to the water side.

8th. The Governor in Chief reserves to himself the right of punishing any subject of Ashantee or Dwabin guilty of secondary offences, but in case of any crime of magnitude, he will send the offender to the Kings, to be dealt with according to the laws of his country.

9th. The Kings agree to commit their children to the care of the Governor in Chief, for education, at Cape Coast Castle, in the full confidence of the good intentions of the British government, and of the benefits to be derived therefrom.

10th. The Kings promise to direct diligent inquiries to be made respecting the officers attached to the Mission of Major John Peddie, and Captain Thomas Campbell; and to influence and oblige the neighbouring kingdoms and their tributaries, to befriend them as the subjects of the British government.

Signed and sealed at Coomassie, this seventh day of September, in the year of our Lord one thousand eight hundred and seventeen.

The mark of SAÏ TOOTOO QUAMINA ⋈   (L. S.)

The mark of BOÏTINNEE QUAMA ⋈   (L. S.)

THOMAS EDWARD BOWDICH.   (L. S.)

In the presence of

WILLIAM HUTCHISON, Resident.

HENRY TEDLIE, Assistant Surgeon.

The mark of APOKOO   ⋈   ⎫
        ODUMATA ⋈   ⎪ Deputed from the General Assem-
        NABBRA   ⋈   ⎬ bly of caboceers and captains to
        ASHANTEE ⋈   ⎭ swear with the King.

        KABRA SAPHOO   ⋈ ⎱ Linguists to the King of
        QUAMINA SAPHOO ⋈ ⎰   Dwabin.

        QUASHEE APAINTREE ⋈ Accra Linguist.

        QUASHEE TOM ⋈   ⎱
        QUAMINA QUATCHEE ⋈ ⎰ Cape Coast Linguists.

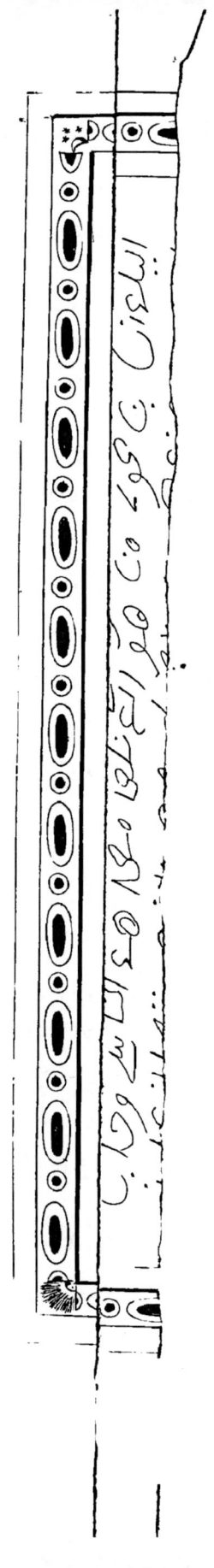

as the object of the British Government in sending these persons to Africa, and that any Person who may happen to meet with these Gentlemen, and shall to the Bearer of a Letter to the Governor of CAPE COAST CASTLE on the Gold Coast from either of them, shall receive five Ounces of Gold, and to literally rewarded for any service or kindness which it may appear by such Letter may have been rendered to either of them.

Witness my hand at .... the Capital of the Kingdom of Ashantee the 2d day of July 1817
Wm Hutchison Resident

T. E. Bowdich Conductor of the Mission from Cape Coast Castle

بسم الله الرحمن الرحيم ...

T. E. Bowdich

We were present at the trial of Appia Nanu, who had accompanied his brother Appia Danqua in the last invasion of Fantee, and was ordered by the King, on his death, to take the command of the army, and prosecute the campaign. In the irritation of the moment, he exclaimed, before the royal messengers, that though the King did not prevent him from succeeding to the stool, and the honours of his brother, he kept back all the rock gold which belonged to the inheritance, and desired to wear him out in the pursuit of the revolters, to prevent his claim and enjoyment of the property of his family. From this time he was very inactive, and became suspected of cowardice; however, having succeeded in getting the head of one of the revolters, he returned to Coomassie; where he was coolly received, but not accused until the 8th of July. The witnesses were the messengers the King had sent to him, who had been concealed in a distant part of the frontier ever since, that Appia Nanu, believing the general report of their death, might be the more confounded when they burst upon him at the moment of his denial of the charge. He was deprived of his stool and the whole of his property, but permitted to retire with three wives and ten slaves; the King hearing the next day that he still loitered in the capital, exclaimed, that no proper man would bear so much shame before all the people, rather than leave his home, and ordered only one wife to be left to him, whereupon Appia Nanu hung himself. The King considers, that none but the basest spirits can endure life after severe disgrace.

The Moors celebrated the feast of Ramadan in this month: there was nothing curious in this ceremony. Men and women were dressed in their richest suits, and seated on large skins before their houses, for they occupy one street exclusively. They rose occasionally in small troops, made short circuits in different directions, saluted each other, and then sat down again. In the evening, the superiors exchanged visits at their houses; the one visited always accompanied the other some distance along the street on his way, where they exchanged blessings, and parted. The slaves who carried their small umbrella's over their heads, seemed thoroughly jaded by this incessant parading.

The King regretted in one of his visits about this time, that they were not more frequent; he said, our conversation entertained him more than any thing else, because it told him of so many things black men never heard of, but when he wished to see us on that account, his great men checked him, and said, it did not become him as a great King to want us, but that he should only send his compliments, see us, and make us wait a long time when he sent for us to the palace.

CHAPTER VII.

Proceedings and Incidents until the completion of the Mission and its return to Cape Coast Castle.

On the 11th of September I received the Governor's reply to my letter of the 10th of August.

Cape Coast Castle, August 25, 1817.

T. E. Bowdich, Esq.

Sir,

I have received your letter of the 10th instant. The boy and girl shall be disposed of under the protection of the Government here, agreeable to the King's wishes.

The messenger (Ocranameah) has grossly misrepresented to the King, the reception he met with at Cape Coast; he was treated with the greatest civility during his stay, and on leaving, expressed himself gratified by the attention which had been shewn him.

For the King's satisfaction, I have subjoined a list of the articles I made him a present of;* the three first which I gave him, on taking leave, will, when produced, convince him how much he has been deceived, and prove to him, that his recommendation of the messenger was not unattended to.

The Buntooko war, I consider a mere pretext for getting rid of

---

* One piece of silk. 10 handkerchiefs of Dane. 1 umbrella. 4 gallons of rum. 20lbs. of pork. 1 basket of rice. Biscuit. 1 sheep.

the Resident; it cannot be the true motive: to oppose however, any disinclination to the measure, either on the part of the King or his principal men, would be entirely useless; the aversion to it has no doubt originated in the latter, with whom, under the present order of things, the Resident would be very unpopular; consequently unsafe. The eager desire which the King has manifested for enquiring into every trivial occurrence, is another cause of its being objectionable. The residence of a British officer would afford him the opportunity, not only of doing this, but of making demands which he might otherwise not have thought of. These and other circumstances, which were entirely unforeseen, have materially altered my opinion in regard to the Residency, which is certainly not so desirable as I before considered it. You will therefore, on your return, bring Mr. Hutchison with you.

I am not aware of any Ashantees having introduced themselves here, but such as were duly authorised by the King; you will however inform him, that none will be attended to unless they bear his cane.

As Mr. Hutchison is to return, it will be a most important point that you bring down two of the King's sons for education, and I am very solicitous that you should accomplish this object if possible.

The Commenda palaver being terminated, there will be nothing to detain you longer at Ashantee. Your returning by way of Warsaw will be desirable, and I hope the King will not object to your so doing.

I am, Sir,

your most obedient Servant,

JOHN HOPE SMITH.

Coomassie, Sept. 16, 1817.

John Hope Smith, Esq. Governor in Chief, &c. &c. &c.

Sir,

I did not receive your letter of the 25th of August, until the 11th instant, four days after I had advised you of the execution of the treaty. I considered it my duty to acquaint you of every variation in the prospects of the Embassy, although, even when communicating the discouraging circumstances of my letter of the 10th ult. I could not abate my hopes, or allow doubt to sicken my exertions. I valued on the reflection, that I had not been heard before the King in vindication of the Residency ; the motives of which I knew to have been grossly misrepresented by our natural enemies the Moors, to whose arts the suspicion of the natives have been suitably auxiliary. My confidence was justified by the favourable impression the King and the Government manifested, when the subject was publicly advocated ; since which I have never heard of an objection to it : it has indeed, become a favourite measure with the superior captains, who, as far as may be judged from the respect and deference with which they have treated us from that time, seem not only to have been conciliated, but won by the recent circumstances of the negotiation. The terms of the treaty, by exceeding your expectations, will compensate for the accumulation of difficulties which have been opposed to us. We are taught to believe that no law has ever been enacted in this kingdom with equal solemnity, or an oath, so serious, been before submitted to by the King, or imposed on the captains. Had the treaty disappointed, instead of exceeded our expectations, I must have viewed it as inviolable, and submitted myself to your candour ; which I would now, and justify myself by answering the reasonable apprehensions which have recently affected your opinion of the Residency, rather than by the plea that the treaty was executed before I received them.

If I had been convinced that it was dislike, and not suspicion, which actuated the opposition to the Residency, I should not only have considered it imprudent, but derogatory, to have persevered in the view; but, sensible that it was the latter, (from the evidence of the King's deportment, and the knowledge of the intrigue and calumny excited against us,) I felt the greater anxiety for its accomplishment; since, to have yielded to suspicion, without every labour to eradicate it, would have been to have excluded ourselves from the kingdom hereafter.

If the King had been actuated, individually, by the desire of detecting the frauds of his messengers, I should have viewed the measure as pernicious; but the Government itself having anxiously recommended it, for the sake of their own interest, (Fort pay, and purchases from the treasury being always divided amongst the superior captains) I considered it harmless; and not solely from the power of its advocates, but also from the impotence of the royal messengers in state affairs, being generally attendants on the King, and therefore jealously watched by the other parts of the Government. This desire has only been addressed to me in two instances, both of which I think justified it: first, respecting the fort pay; it having been since proved, and confessed, that, out of 62 oz. paid at Christiansburg Castle in 1816 and 17, the Ashantee Government has been defrauded of 23 oz. by the messenger: and secondly, respecting the goods purchased by Ocranameah, where the fraud could not escape notice. Such peculations have probably, in the first case, given rise to doubts of our honour; and in the latter, have certainly proved a prejudice to the trade. On the occasion of Ocranameah's baseness, I myself requested the King to allow me to address you for the particulars of his treatment; and if you consider the mischievous influence of the report, the fatality of the impression that the King's Embassy had been subjected to contempt, whilst we had been treated with generosity and respect, you will admit that the disproof was imperious on me: he has been disgraced, and owes his safety to my intercession. Nothing but the most decisive conduct can arrest villainy here. The reports of Adoo Bradie have been highly flattering. The King will certainly have a better opportunity of making demands from the residence of a British officer; neither can I lessen the probability further than by my opinion, which though only indulgent of the people in general, is certainly favourable of the honour of the King, and the superior captains. The advantages and prospects of our preserving our footing by a Residency, have been too fully suggested by your experience, to require my dwelling on them.

I will proceed to acquaint you of the circumstances subsequent to my receipt of your letter, one of which had nearly been serious. After the settlement of the Commenda palaver, the King requested me to wait 10 days, which were afterwards extended to 15, as you were advised in his letter of the 31st ult. This time expired on Saturday last, but the King said then that we must not go until Monday. Accordingly, on that day, I delivered Mr. Hutchison written instructions (a copy of which I enclose) and sent several messages to the King to remind him of his promise. We were not sent for until six o'clock in the evening, when the King said he could not let me go then, nor before he had time to send me away properly. This I considered to be the mere affectation of state; I pleaded that your orders were binding, and that it was insulting to you, as well as dangerous to me, to prevent my respect of them, now every thing like business was settled. The King said he would only ask me to stop until Wednesday. I replied, that if he would give me his hand, and promise that I should go then, I would wait. No! he could not, but he would promise me for the Monday following. I saw that yielding to this would subject me to an indefinite delay. I told the King that I should be obliged to go, though unwillingly, without his approbation, and that not only my duty but his promise justified me. I had only to ask him if he still wished me to leave Mr. Hutchison? All the reply I could get was, that I might break the Law if I thought proper. I told them the Law would never be broken by an English officer, but still, if they were sorry that they had sworn to the Law, I would send for it and tear it in pieces before them; we did not make laws from fear. No! they liked the Law, and could not break it, but I might if I chose. I repeated my willingness to stay till Wednesday; the promise could only be given for the Monday: the King and the council retired abruptly. I followed them, told them I was obliged to be determined, and begged the King to shew his respect for you, and the friendship he had condescended to profess for myself, by considering your orders: this was construed as indecision; and Monday, or when the King has time, was the reply. I thanked him formally for all his kindnesses, told him I must go, and retired. It was necessary, at least, to make the attempt, although it was then eight o'clock. I left all the luggage in the charge of Mr. Hutchison, except two portmanteaus, the sextant, and the box containing my papers. We had scarcely proceeded fifty yards before the gong-gongs and drums were beat all around us, and we were attacked by a crowd of swords and muskets, headed by our house master Aboïdwee, who in the first rush seized the luggage and the flag. I felt myself compelled to attempt to regain the flag; and the value of my papers, and the impolicy of being intimidated by the outrage, were also considerations. I begged the officers not to draw their swords till the last moment, and taking the muskets, the butt ends of which cleared our way to the luggage, we fastened on it, with the soldiers, artisans, and our servants, who supported us vigorously. The Ashantees did not attempt to fire, but attacked us only with their heavy swords and large stones. We kept our ground nearly a quarter of an hour, though our belts and caps were torn away, and we frequently fell. At this time, Mr. Tedlie (who had regained his sword, which had been torn from his side) was stunned by a blow on the head, and as all were much bruised, and some of the people cut, I contented myself with the recovery of the flag, the sextant, and the papers, and we retired slowly to the house, not expecting they would follow us; but they did so, with a fury which led me to believe they intended our destruction. We posted ourselves in the door-way, and I immediately dispatched the canes by a back way to the King, to tell him we had not yet drawn our swords, but we must do so unless he rescued us immediately. The tumult did not allow expostulation, we had no alternative but to defend ourselves, which the narrow passage favoured. The captain, Aboïdwee, who was quite mad with fury and liquor, made a cut at me as I held him from me, which would have been fatal but for the presence of mind of one of the soldiers, through which it only grazed my face. We were soon rescued by the presence of Adoocee, the chief linguist, and Yokokroko, the King's chamberlain, with their retinues. Nothing could exceed their servility, they offered to swear the King was not privy to the outrage, ordered Aboïdwee before them, and threatened him with the loss of his head. I told them I knew the King's controul, and was not to be treated as a fool; he had forcibly detained us as prisoners, and must take the consequences; I should say no more. They continued their professions and entreaties upwards of an hour, and did all they could by their menaces to Aboïdwee, and their deference to the evidence of our

T

people, to convince me of their discountenance of the outrage.   I divided the people into watches for the night.

By day light the next morning all our luggage was returned, I refused to receive it. Yokokroko and Adoo Quamina then sent to say they waited below until we had done breakfast; a long palaver succeeded, of the same tenour as that of the preceding night. About 11 o'clock, the linguists, Adoocee, Otee, and Quancum; Yokokroko, and a crowd of captains came from the King with a present of 20 ackies, two flasks of liquor, and a large hog. I asked them if they came to put more shame on my face, by bribing me to settle the great palaver they had made the night before with the King of England. They flattered and menaced by turns to make me take it, and urged, that to refuse the King's present was to declare war. I persisted in refusing every thing short of an interview with the King. The Cape Coast messengers, impelled by their apprehensions and their avarice, had the temerity to declare at this moment, that you had sent them as a check upon me, and that they knew I was not doing as you wished in talking so to the King, and that you would make a palaver with me for not waiting the King's pleasure. It was necessary to annihilate the impression of such language immediately. I deprived them of their canes, and threatened to put them in irons. The King not long after sent his eunuch and followers to conduct us to the palace, where he had assembled the superior captains. We went in plain clothes, alleging that we dared not wear our uniforms as prisoners. The King said, I must not say that; he was my good friend, and would do me right; he did not think I would have tried to go without his leave, and never meant his people to fight with us, he would give me the heads of all those who led them on, and beg me himself for the rest, as I begged him for Quamina Bootaqua; he never begged any body before; he did not send the gold, as I thought, he sent it to pay for any thing the people had spoiled, and meant to do us right all the same; it would break his heart if the King of England heard he had used his officers ill, and if I liked him, I must settle the palaver easy.

Of course I would not hear of any heads being cut off, though they all pressed it repeatedly, and doubtless would not have regarded sacrificing a few inferior captains to varnish their allegation; yet, I must declare, it is my firm opinion, and it is supported by the evidence of our private friends, that the King and his principal men merely intended Aboïdwee to stop us, by placing his numbers before us and pleading the King's orders, not dreaming of any outrage, or that the impetuosity of this man, irritated by the loss of his retainer at Cape Coast,* would hurry him to order his soldiers to assault us: he has not an atom of influence; but the King selected him as a near relative of his own, to succeed to Bakkee's stool, to which 1700 men are attached: the King repeatedly offered me his head. To resume, the King requested us to drink with him, and then to shake hands, begged us to resume our uniforms, and ordered his own people to attend us at our house. I renewed the subject of our departure. The King said this was a bad week, and he did not like us to go in it, he would thank me very much to stay till Monday, and then he could get a proper present ready. Sunday too was the Adaï custom, and then I must put Mr. Hutchison's hand in Adoocee's, and Adoocee place it in his, and he would promise to take proper care of him before all the captains. Odumata and Adoocee came forward to give me their hands, as a pledge of their responsibility. I said I could receive no one's hand but the King's on such an occasion, but I ordered Quashie Apaintree to do so, and it was sworn to. The King then said Adoocee had told him the Cape Coast messengers

* The man who hung himself.

had tried to put shame on my face—he was very angry with them—they ought to know God made white man's head better than black man's, and they must come before him, and put my foot on their heads. I told him, I could not let any one do so, but I sent for their canes, and entrusted them to them again, with a suitable reprimand. The King then begged me to receive his present, which I did, giving the people the hog and liquor, they had received another on the Friday before, which the King sent me, with 39 yams.

I have observed that the Government's anxiety for the force of the Treaty, and for the Residency, has heightened in proportion to the indifference I have affected. I consider the affair of yesterday to have perfected the impression of our spirit. I certainly would not think of leaving any but an officer of the most considerate conduct as a Resident, and, I believe, Mr. Hutchison, by tempering his spirit with judgment, may safely realize the objects of the situation; if, however, on my return, you consider I have left him in a precarious situation, I volunteer my services to replace him, and deliberately to retire the Residency.

It occurs to me, the Amissa palaver may possibly be the design of this interval, if it should, you may rely on my remaining resolute on the subject.

I am, &c.

(Signed)   T. EDWARD BOWDICH.

Coomassie, Sept. 1817.

To WILLIAM HUTCHISON, *Esquire, British Resident.*

SIR,

I AM directed by the Governor in Chief to leave you written instructions for your future government.

The conviction of the honour and justice of our public negotiations, having procured us a footing in opposition to the arts which have been practised upon the suspicion of the natives, your conduct is looked to, with confidence, to support it, by originating an opinion of our moral character, equally auspicious to the benevolent views of the British Government. The simplicity of our religion, tolerating the calumny of the Moors, that we are destitute of any, you will have the satisfaction of perfecting the confutation, by a regular retirement to its duties, and by the practice of that benevolence and forbearance, equally congenial to the policy prescribed to us.

It would be premature, as well as dangerous, to direct any other than the tacit reproof of your own conduct and sentiments, to the cruelties consecrated by the superstitions of the Ashantees; you must be content to avoid the countenance of them by your presence, by adhering to the plea of the repugnance of your religion. This conduct, associated with a humanity always inclining you to induce mercy, whenever the offence, or prudence, may admit of an interference, will propitiate your own wishes, and the expectations of the Government.

The friendship and respect which the King, and the superior captains have manifested, will not only be preserved, but strengthened, by a dignified deportment, and a considerate use of the private intercourse these feelings have established; and you will cultivate the frequent opportunities of instilling into their minds, that education originated the pre-eminence of Europeans; and that peace is most auspicious to the greatness of a Nation, directing all its powers to commerce and the arts, and thereby founding its superior comfort, prosperity, and embellishment. The power and resources of your own country should be quoted to illustrate this truth; and you will impress that it is the experience of it, which has imposed the benevolent anxiety of the British Government, to improve the condition of the people of Africa, through the legitimate medium of commerce. This impression you will extend, deliberately, to the visitors from other kingdoms, particularly to those from the Sarem and Mallowa countries.

In encouraging the trade with the Coast, your measures must disprove any view but that of a fair competition; and your vigilance of the British interests must be distinct from any thing like jealousy, suspicion, or intermeddling: you will act as the advocate of the views of Europe, but not allow any interference to be imposed on you, without the sanction of the Governor in Chief, whose letters will be, exclusively, attended to, and to whom you will candidly communicate any circumstance or reflection, affecting our new connection.

You will repress, rather than encourage the disposition of the King and the Council, to detect imposition through your assistance, by confining your justifications, as much as possible, to public transactions; for although the Government is gratified by it, it may tend to make the Residency unpopular.

I enclose you a copy of the Treaty, and particularly direct your attention to the 4th article, which authorizes you to submit to every thing like a mediation, separable from responsibility, to the discussion of the Governor in Chief, for the sake of peace and humanity; but you will do this, invariably, with diffidence; without betraying any sanguine expectations.

You will be more sensible to insult than injury; and the most politic conduct will be, to declare that the British Government exacts from all its officers, on pain of disgrace, a firm repulse of the former; and that they dare not admit the influence of their private feelings, as in the latter case.

I leave you in possession of the esteem of the King, and the friendship of the superior Captains, and with every thing favourable to the objects of the Residency; but, should any caprice in the Government make you invidious to any thing like a party, or diminish their respect, you will immediately address the Governor in Chief, who will order your presence at Head Quarters. Another important consideration will be your health; also the character of the captain who may be left in charge of the capital, should the King go himself to the Buntooko war. Your personal safety is out of the question at present, but should the least doubt arise in your own mind hereafter, you must consult the Governor's solicitude, rather than your own spirit.

You see the necessity of keeping in with the Moors; the flattering their intelligence is most conducive to this, and also elicits valuable information.

I shall afford you a perusal of the dispatch of the Committee, and the instructions of the Governor in Chief, to perfect the present.

I have directed Mr. Tedlie to leave you a supply of medicines, and you will take charge of the Resident's flag.

I am, Sir,

your most obedient Servant,

(Signed)   T. EDWARD BOWDICH.

Baba had a great number of Arabic manuscripts; I have preserved a leaf finely illuminated. Apokoo astonished us by offering
to lend us some books to read; he shewed us two French volumes
on geography, a Dutch bible, a volume of the Spectator, and a
Dissuasion from Popery, 1620. It was gratifying to recollect that
this chief, now become so much attached to us, was the man
mentioned in our early dispatches as snatching Mr. Tedlie's sword
from him, on the declaration of war, to make his oath against us
the more inveterate. Telling the King one day that Mr. Hutchison's and Mr. Tedlie's countries, Scotland and Ireland, were
formerly distinct from mine, he begged directly to hear specimens
of the different languages, and was reluctantly persuaded that it
was the policy of England to get rid of all national distinctions
between her subjects. Apokoo was very fond of scribbling, and
with a smile frequently begged to know what he had written.
They could not comprehend how any hieroglyphic that was not a
picture, could express an object. My name, said the King, is not
like me. He was rather uneasy at my sketching; the Moors, he
hinted, had insinuated that I could place a spell on the buildings
I drew. I told him, without drawings, the people in England
could not be convinced that I had visited him; he appeared
satisfied, and begged to be drawn handsome.

There are only four direct descendants now living of the noble
families which accompanied the emigration of Saï Tootoo, the
founder of the Ashantee monarchy; none of them are wealthy,
and Assaphi, who is one, is a beggar, wandering in the bush,
having been disgraced from the highest favour, for the following
fraud. An old linguist of the former King's (Saï Quamina) having
died at a distant croom, the King, according to custom, sent
Assaphi with four periguins of gold, and a quantity of expensive
cloths and mats to bury him; Assaphi kept the gold, and substi-

tuted inferior cloths of his own. The wife urged the great and zealous services of her husband to Saï Quamina, and her indignation at such a mean acknowledgment as the King had sent. Assaphi returned, reported her gratitude, and that every thing had been handsomely done, to the credit of the King. The wife privately dug up the cloths buried with the corpse, and suspecting the fraud, secretly conveyed them to the King, with a full account. The King sent for Assaphi and again enquiring the particulars, with seeming indifference, suddenly required him to swear to the truth, which he advanced to do, when the King said no! you must not swear, and the woman was immediately discovered to him with all the cloths. He then confessed the particulars, was stripped of every thing, and is now the more despised for not killing himself; and the King could not put him to death, as the direct descendant of one of Saï Tootoo's peers. Part of the King's reproach to him was curious: " my brother's linguist did him great good, so when he and my brother, who now live with God, make God recollect all, and tell him the shame you put on him for me, in so burying him, God will kill me."

A man and a woman were beheaded on the 17th of this month, for an intrigue: the woman was very handsome, and the wife of a captain: on their being suspected, both were ordered to drink doom, which choking them, they were immediately executed. The King's sister sent for Mr. Tedlie to go and see her, he enquired into her complaint and recommended some medicine, which she very thankfully agreed to take; he prepared some for her, and went to give her the proper directions; upon which, she handed the cup to her husband, who beginning to swallow it very fast, Mr. Tedlie stopped him, and said he had only prepared sufficient for one person; the lady replied, " let him drink this to day, and I can have more to-morrow " he told her that he had very little medicine, and could not afford to give it to people that were in good health: she did not appear pleased with this reasoning. A man of Assiminia, who had received medicine and advice from Mr. Tedlie on our march up, sent him a third present about this time, of fruit, vegetables, and wild deer, with the account that he was quite well.

Apokoo enquired very anxiously, why the King of England had not sent one of his sons with the presents to the King of Ashantee. He said he had himself conquered five nations, during the present and the preceding reign, and he named twenty one nations which now paid tribute to Ashantee; but he added, there were three countries which would not; two eastward, and one to the north-west; each of those eastward had defeated the Ashantees; the one north-westward, on the King sending for tribute, desired that he would come and take it, and afterwards entirely destroyed an Ashantee army.

Akrofroom, Sept. 26, 1817.

JOHN HOPE SMITH, ESQ. GOVERNOR IN CHIEF, &c. &c. &c.

SIR,

THE King only availed himself of our detention to introduce us to fresh ceremonies, and to augment the testimonies of his friendship. The Amissa palaver was not attempted, and nothing like design has disclosed itself.

On the Monday there was a general assembly of the caboceers and captains, the King of Dwabin being present, with his linguists, also several Dagwumba caboceers, and the Moorish dignitaries. The King announced the execution of the Treaty by himself and the deputies, and impressed, in a long speech through his linguists, that he would visit the least offence against it with the greatest severity. I was then requested to read it for the last time, and the King's duplicate was executed in a similar manner.

In the evening, the King gave us our last audience before all his superior captains: a letter was dictated, which I shall present to you on my arrival; and Adoocee, the chief linguist, was formally deputed to receive Mr. Hutchison's hand from me, and to place it in the King's, who received it with a solemn avowal of his responsibility for the charge. The linguist then presented from the King,

To the Government, four boys for education.

To the British Museum, six specimens of the goldsmith's work. (I had interested the King, by my account of this national repository.)

To the Governor in Chief, one boy, one girl, to be brought up in his service.

To Mr. Bowdich, one boy, one girl, and 2 oz. 6 ac. of gold.

Mr. Tedlie, one boy, and 1 oz. 4 ac. of gold.

Accra linguist, one cloth,	-	10 ditto.

Cape Coast linguists, two cloths, 10 ditto.

De Graaff's messenger,	-	10 ditto.

The officers servants,	-	-	10 ditto.

The soldiers,	-	-	10 ditto.

I afterwards received a Sarem cloth and some trifles as a further dash from Apokoo; one sheep, &c. &c. from Baba the chief of the Moors; and 15 ackies of gold from the King's linguists, with their acknowledgments of my firmness during the negotiation.

The King having a palaver at present with the Warsaws, objected so strongly to our returning through their territory, that after one or two attempts to over-rule his apprehensions, I found it would be imprudent to persevere in the wish, although the disappointment was great; the King assured me the Warsaw path was two days longer, and that he will not spare any labour on that of

Assin directly after the war. I had permission to go some miles on the Warsaw path, to convince myself of its neglected condition.

The King's favorite son (a child about five years old) whom he had dressed in our uniform for the occasion, was so alarmed at the idea of being given over to us, that the King's feelings obliged him to promise me that he would send the children after me ; he is too jealous of the advantages to allow those of his great men to participate, until his own family are first distinguished by them.

The King supplied me with bearers, and pressed me to take six hammock men in case of sickness ; he would not hear of pay for any, and persisted in appointing one of his captains to take care of us. He yielded the point of an escort reluctantly, which I had combated from the consideration of the expense of a present to such a number. The King requested me on taking leave, to wait a short time until his captains had distributed the powder to salute as on our departure, and it being then dark, to proceed no further than a small croom just beyond the marsh, where the people should join us in the morning. The King and his captains were seated by torch light with all their insignia, without the palace, and we quitted the capital, preceded by the King's banners, discharges of musketry, and every flattering distinction that could be thought of.

The King has provided one of the best houses for Mr. Hutchison, very superior to any we could have raised at so short a notice, and has anticipated every thing to make him comfortable, and respected ; nothing could be more considerate or kind, than his speech to him on my taking leave.

A messenger of the King of Dwabin's accompanies me for a suit of our uniform for the King's wear, which I could not refuse.

I am, &c. &c.

(Signed)   T. EDWARD BOWDICH.

Coomassie, September 22, 1817.

SAÏ TOOTOO QUAMINA, *King of Ashantee, &c. to* JOHN HOPE
SMITH, *Esquire, Governor in Chief, &c. &c. &c.*

SIR,

WE are from this time forth good friends, and I shall send all the
trade I can to Cape Coast Castle, and I hope that you will by and
by have confidence in my word.

I beg you will send my best compliments to the King of England, and accept them yourself, in proof of my satisfaction of the
purposes of the Embassy, and its happy termination.

You will call all the Fantee caboceers before you, and impress
the importance of the Treaty, and exact their respect of it, as I
have from all my great men and caboceers.

I hope you will always act towards me as a friend, and I shall
always be ready to protect and support the British interests.

I wish you health and happiness, and all my captains send their
best compliments to you.

    I am, Sir,

      your sincere friend,

    The mark ✄ of Saï Tootoo Quamina.

Present,

W. HUTCHISON.

HENRY TEDLIE.

I will thank you to impress on the King of England that I have
sworn not to renew the war with the Fantees, out of respect to
him, and I shall consider them as his people. I hope therefore he
will, in turn, consider if he cannot renew the Slave Trade, which
will be good for me.

I hope the King of England will now let all foreign vessels come to the coast to trade, and you must say that the path is now clear to do as much English trade as your supplies will allow.

The following letter was sent after me, to Doompassie.

Coomassie, 23d September, 1817.

JOHN HOPE SMITH, ESQ. GOVERNOR IN CHIEF, &c. &c. &c.

SIR,

THE King of Ashantee desires me to request you will write to all the Governors of English forts, on the African coast, to order the caboceers of each town, to send a proper person to Cape Coast, and that you will add one messenger yourself; that they may all proceed to Coomassie to take the King's fetish in his presence, that none may plead ignorance of the Treaty concluded between his Majesty and the British nation.

The King wishes me to express, that he is fully satisfied with the objects of the Mission, and that the Treaty may be read by me to all the Fantee deputies you may send for that purpose.

I am, &c. &c.

(Signed)　　　　　W. HUTCHISON.

My last private letters from Cape Coast Castle had imposed the most painful anxiety; the two lives naturally beyond all others the dearest to me, were imminently endangered by the seasoning illness of the country; one yielded to it before I could arrive, yet, under all the impatience of my affliction, I must confess, when I took

the King's hand for the last time, when I reflected on the benevolence, the solicitude, and the generosity I had exeprienced whilst
my life was in his hands, affected by the most untoward and
irritating political circumstances, by the aggravated suspicions of
his chiefs, and by the poisonous jealousy of the Moors, there was
a painful gratification in the retrospect, which blended the wish to
linger another hour in listening to acknowledgments of esteem and
obligation, more affecting than flattering, and enhanced by the
consoling reflection, that they were the natural emotions of one of
those monarchs we are pleased to call barbarians. Night was
coming on, but as I had so positively declared before the King
and his council, on the former occasion, that nothing should deter
me from keeping my word in quitting Coomassie on this day, it
would not do to delay even until the morning. A strict observance
of your word, is every thing in the eye of a Negro. The King
said, he would not beg me to stay, as I had declared I dared not;
he would only ask me to go no further than Ogogoo, that night,
and his people should join me early in the morning. Our exit was
a brilliant scene, from the reflection of the glittering ornaments of
the King and his captains by the torches; they were seated in a
deep and long line, without the palace, accompanied by their
retinues; all their bands burst forth together, as we saluted the
King in passing, and we were enveloped in the smoke of the
musketry. The darkness of the forest was an instantaneous and
awful contrast, and the howlings and screeches of the wild beasts,
startled us as we groped our way, as if we had never heard them
before. The torches provided for our protection against them
were extinguished in crossing the marsh, which had swollen to
between four and five feet deep, and the descent to it from Coomassie was rocky and abrupt. The linguists and soldiers lost
themselves in the forest, and did not arrive at Ogogoo until long

after Mr. Tedlie and myself. The inhabitants were asleep, but they rose cheerfully, cleared the best house for us, and made fires. The next morning I received the dash of gold from the King's linguists, in a Mallowa bag, with a long compliment; the conclusion of which was, that I must always be ready to use the same spirit and address, in talking a palaver for the King of Ashantee, as I had shewn in talking that of my own King. This testimony of their good feeling and esteem, which they could not avow whilst we were political antagonists, was grateful.

Marching through Sarrasoo, where we were liberally refreshed with palm wine, we halted in the evening at Assiminia. We were received with great hospitality by the principal man, who provided us with excellent lodging, to his own inconvenience, and presented us with some fowls. The path was almost a continued bog, for the rainy season had set in violently. The next day we marched through Dadasey to Doompassie, and occupied our former comfortable dwelling. One party spent the night in the woods. Thursday morning, the 6th, we had a short but most fatiguing march over the mountains dividing the frontiers, to Moisee, the first Assin town. The difficulty of procuring provisions until the people returned from the plantations, detained us in Moisee until four o'clock in the evening. As the stage from Doompassie had been short, (although fatiguing) I determined to proceed to Akrofroom, as we should gain a day by it. The Ashantees remonstrated, knowing the swollen state of the several small rivers, and the aggravated difficulties of the path from the heavy rain; but I was so apprehensive of being detained, by their pleading their superstitious observance of good and bad days for travelling, that I was afraid of seeming to yield to them, lest it might encourage the disposition. I recommended them to go back, and started without them, but they were soon at my heels, declaring, they should lose their heads if they quitted us. Mr. Tedlie, myself, a soldier, and the Ashantee next in authority under the captain, outwalked the rest of the party, and found ourselves out of their hearing when it grew dark. We lost some time in trying to make torches to keep off the beasts, and to direct us in the right track, for we were walking through a continued bog, and had long before lost our shoes. A violent tornado ushered in the night, we could not hear each other holla, and were soon separated; luckily I found I had one person left with me (the Ashantee) who, after I had groped him out, tying his cloth tight round his middle, gave me the other end, and thus plunged along, pulling me after him, through bogs and rivers, exactly like an owl tied to a duck in a pond. The thunder, the darkness, and the howlings of the wild beasts were awful, but the loud and continuing crash of a large tree, which fell very near us during the storm, was even more so to my ear. The Ashantee had dragged me along, or rather through, in this manner until I judged it to be midnight, when, quite exhausted, with the remnants of my clothes scarcely hanging together, I let go his cloth, and falling on the ground, was asleep before I could call out to him. I was awoke by this faithful guide, who had felt me out, and seated me on the trunk of a tree, with my head resting on his shoulder; he gave me to understand I must die if I sat there, and we pursued the duck and owl method once more. In an hour we forded the last river, which had swollen considerably above my chin, and spread to a great width. This last labour I considered final, and my drowsiness became so fascinating, that it seemed to beguile me of every painful thought and apprehension, and the yielding to it was an exquisite, though momentary pleasure. I presume I must have slept above an hour, lifted by this humane man from the bank of the river to a drier corner of the forest, more impervious to the torrents of rain; when, being awoke, I was surprised to see him with a companion and a torch; he took me on his back, and in about three quarters of an hour we reached Akrofroom. This man knew I carried about me several ounces of gold, for the subsistence of the people, not trusting to our luggage, which we could not reckon on in such a season and journey. Exhausted and insensible, my life was in his hands, and infested as the forest was with wild beasts, he might after such a night, without suspicion, have reported me as destroyed by them; this had occurred to me, and was an uneasy feeling as long as my torpor left me any. It was about two o'clock in the morning, and the inhabitants of Akrofroom were almost all asleep, for it was too rude a night for Negro revelry; however, I was directly carried to a dry and clean apartment, furnished with a brass pan full of water to wash in, some fruits and palm wine, an excellent bed of mats and cushions, and an abundance of country cloths to wrap around me, for I was all but naked. After I had washed, I rolled myself up in the cloths, one after the other, until I became a gigantic size, and by a profuse perspiration escaped any other ill than a slight fever. A soldier came up about mid-day, and gave me some hopes of seeing Mr. Tedlie again, who arrived soon afterwards, having left his companions in a bog, waiting until he sent them assistance from the town. Our gratification was mutual, for the only trace he had had of me was by no means an encouraging one; my servant meeting an Ashantee in the forest with fragments of my clothes, which he persisted he had not taken from any person, but picked up on his way. Mr. Tedlie (whose feet were cut and bruised much more than mine, and whose wretched plight made him envy the African toga I had assumed) after we had separated, and the storm had drowned our mutual hollaings, the howlings of the wild beasts meeting his ears on all sides, had just determined to roost in a tree for the night, when an Ashantee appeared with a torch, and conducted him out of the track to the remains of a shed, where four or five of the people had before strayed and settled themselves. Another party arrived at Akrofroom about four o'clock, and the last, with the Cape Coast linguist and the corporal, not until sun set; they had lost the track altogether, and spent the whole day, as well as the previous night, in the woods. We made an excellent duck soup, our grace to which was, " what a luxury to poor Mungo Park;" the name recalled sufferings which made us laugh at our own as mere adventures.

On Saturday the 8th we marched to Asharamang. Here we found great difficulties in getting provisions until the Ashantees came up, for Quamina Bwa's knavery had been ascribed to us; and here, panyaring all we required, he had not given the inhabitants a tokoo of the gold. At length we were well supplied and comfortably lodged. The next day we marched through Kickiwherree to Prasoo, where we occupied a good house, and an Ashantee captain proceeding on an embassy, dashed us a supply of fowls and yams. We crossed the Boosempra early the next morning, and thence began to leave the rains behind us. Persevering in making but one journey of the distances which occupied us two and three days going up, we pressed forward, passing by our former bivouacs in the woods, scarcely distinguishable, until we reached the site of Accomfodey, for only one hut now remained; the wretched inhabitants having deserted it in terror of the Ashantees. The solitary Fantee who occupied it, had the address to assure me, that I should find much better lodging at Ancomassa, where we recollected to have left some comfortable huts going up, and we resolved to try another stage, and were recompensed by finding scarcely a wreck of the place, and some tattered sheds only instead of the sound roof we had quitted. We proceeded early the next morning, passed Foosou, which was entirely deserted, and marched until we found ourselves at sun set on the banks of the Aniabirrim. The people were all behind, and the Ashantees coming up about an hour afterwards, informed us they had settled themselves for the night about two hours walk distant. Unfortunately we had no flint, and after fasting all day, we had the mortification of losing our supper merely for want of a fire; the wood was all so wet that friction had no effect on it, we could find no shelter, and a heavy rain set in as it grew dark; fatigue luckily beguiled us of cold and hunger, and of our apprehensions of a visit from the beasts, who were howling about the banks of their watering place. I wrapped myself up in the Inta cloth Apokoo had given me, and wet as the ground was, I never slept better. Hence the forest visibly declined in height towards the coast. We pressed on by day light, found some excellent guavas to allay our hunger, and reaching Mansue, made a good soup of our fowls, peppers growing luxuriantly all around us. We waited until we heard of the people behind us, and then proceeded; about five in the evening I reached Cottacoomacasa, with the Dwabin messenger only. The place was deserted, and a body of Ashantee traders had occupied the remaining shed. I would not disturb them, but waiting until sun set for Mr. Tedlie, I left him a supply of guavas, and proceeded to Payntree. There was a charm in the name of that place, being but one journey from the sea, superior to the recollection of the former night's adventure. It was a brilliant night, and the dark gloom and hollow echos of the long vistas of the forest, formed a fine contrast to the extensive areas (sites of large Fantee crooms destroyed by the Ashantees) into which we frequently emerged. The wild music and cheerful revelry of the inhabitants of Payntree stole upon my ear, and raised the tone of my spirits in proportion as the sounds strengthened.

A loud and continued shout warned me that I was announced;

torches and music instantly encircled me, and I was conducted to old Payntree's residence, who had built himself a new house somewhat in the Ashantee fashion. An excellent bed was prepared for me of an accumulation of mats and country cloths, and a famous supper of soups, stews, fruit, and palm wine. Quamina Bootaqua paid his respects, and old Payntree, Amooney King of Annamaboe, and two or three other cabocecrs, unknown to me, made a long adulatory speech, complimenting my ability, bewailing my hardships, and magnifying their obligations. I was requested to seat myself on old Payntree's state stool, whilst they stood around me, and he begged me to listen to an air composed by his band on the occasion of the embassy, and its successful termination; " all would now be well, and Fantee revive and flourish." I sat up till midnight, vainly expecting Mr. Tedlie and the soldiers; they awoke me by their arrival before sun rise; they had passed the night in a sound hut, on the path, which from the want of a torch had escaped my notice.

Hearing, as I expected, that there was a path from Payntree to Cape Coast Castle, avoiding Annamaboe (whence the Mission had departed), I determined to explore it, and Payntree furnished me with a guide. The country was beautifully diversified with hill and dale, but the soil was generally lighter and more gravelly than that between Annamaboe and Payntree. We passed through several groves of guava trees, and all the other tropical fruits abounded. Occasionally there were small plantations of Guinea corn, where a few wretched Fantees still lurked in the ruins of the crooms the Ashantees had destroyed. We passed through eleven which had been considerable, and now presented but a few mud houses scattered over extensive sites. Their names were Assequah, Daöoramong, Amparoo, Taächoo, Coorikirraboo, Perridjoo, Abikarrampa, Aquoitee, Miensa, and Amosima. The only water was near

Amparoo; it was a large pond nearly two miles in circumference, and sixty yards broad, impregnated with vegetable matter. After travelling 15 miles, we climbed some very steep and rocky hills, apparently of iron stone, and descended into a flat country, continuing until a small rising about two miles from Cape Coast Castle, (which I judged to be 20 miles from Payntree by this interior path) opened the sea to our view; as delightful to our sight, as land would have been after a prolonged and perilous voyage. The shouts and greetings of the natives were a grateful introduction to the more congenial congratulations of our countrymen.

MISSION TO ASHANTEE.

PART II.

CHAPTER I.

Geography.

THE impression of the Natives that we came " to spy the country" was sedulously strengthened by the Moors, who were actuated
by alarm, jealousy, and a spirit of intolerance unmitigated by a
previous intercourse with Europeans. I felt compelled, therefore,
to suppress all curiosity for a considerable time, lest the anxiety to
detect us in geographical enquiries, to make their calumny more
imposing, might have been gratified. Latterly, when better feelings had been induced through patience and candour, as the
Moorish charts and MSS. evidence, the inaptitude rather than the
reluctance of the natives, made the shortness of our stay unaccom-
modating. I shall pass over a mass of memoranda recorded on
individual report, and only select such, wherein Moors and natives,
unknown to each other, have agreed ; describing their travels in
their own way, without my questions anticipating or directing
them. These routes and observations were further confirmed by
the evidence of children, recently arrived as slaves from the
various countries, whose artless replies decided my credence. It
may be remarked, that the children of the African Negroes, early
accustomed to travel with their parents for their convenience or
their assistance, and unoccupied by the difficulties of incipient
education, observe nature more attentively than European children
of the same age would ; for they have nothing else to think of, or

Y

to divert the fatigue of these reiterated trading journies: their evidence, therefore, was a genuine and acceptable check on the Moorish and Negro adults.

The difficulty of adjusting geography by investigation only, is not diminished by the numerous small states, scarcely less frequent than those of modern Italy, which we find to compose this part of Western Africa.

Any thing like observations of the Sun's place, during a journey, seemed to be so uncommon to the Natives, and so secondary to the Moors, from their confused accounts of the occasional changes, that, after expending much time to no purpose, I was obliged to content myself with placing the different kingdoms in the same direction as their several paths bore from Coomassie, taking every precaution to be convinced that the paths did not cross each other; and afterwards adjusting the positions by the various auxiliary evidence which occurred in the general course of my enquiries. I allow 15 miles for each days journey (which, from observation and report, I have reason to think is the average) and two thirds of the sum to be made good on the horizontal distance, as we found this to be nearly the case in our journey from Annamaboe to Coomassie; the distance travelled being 146 miles, Annamaboe laying in 5° 4' N., and 1° 43' W., and the latitude of Coomassie being 6° 34' 50" N.; and the longitude 2° 11' W. by the mean of the observations of the eclipses of Jupiter's 1st and 2nd satellites.

I procured the numerals of the various countries whenever I could, to assist future enquirers.

There are nine great paths leading from Coomassie, the Dwabin, Akim, Assin, Warsaw, Sauee, Gaman, Soko, Daboia, and Sallagha.

Dwabin is not more than three quarters of a day's journey

eastward, from Coomassie, by the route No. 1.; in which I have retained only the larger towns, omitting the villages; as I shall invariably. The river Dah is crossed close to the westward of Dwabin, and said to be as wide as we found it at Sarrasoo. Two journies beyond Dwabin is a small dependent district called Mohoo. Several names, such as Meäsee, Marmpon, Akrofroom, &c. will be found common to different states, as Larissa, Argos, and Thebes were in antient Greece.

There is an eastern branch of the Akim path, entered immediately on leaving Coomassie, to a country called Quaöo, northward of Akim, (of which it seems formerly to have been a district) and adjoining the Volta. Djabbec is its principal town, and the second Wantomoo, 8 journies from Coomassie by route No. 2. The latter is situated at the foot of a mountain whence the Boosempra issues, with two smaller rivers, the Soobirree and Sesee, running to the Kirradee. This district is entered the 3d day from Coomassie.

There are two routes to Accra through Akim, the capital of which is Bannasoo, 5 journies, and the northern frontier town Feëa, 3 journies from Coomassie. The easternmost route to Accra is 15 journies; the other is made 17 journies to pass near the lake Boosmaquee. This lake, 3 journies from Coomassie, was described as four miles long, and nearly three broad; upwards of thirty small crooms were reckoned situated around it, supported by fishing: the water was said to be unpleasant to drink, and to give a reddish hue to the hair of the people who washed in it. Fish were forwarded thence daily for the King's table, by relays of men. It was called the white mans fetish, there being a popular superstition, nourished by the Moors, that Europeans were to join it with the sea, to introduce vessels for the subjugation of the country. Close to the lake is a mountain called Quashee Boposoo, sometimes seen clearly from Coomassie, abounding in large black stones, described as basaltes. By this route (No. 3.) to Accra, the Akim country is entered the 4th day, the Boosempra is crossed on the 6th, by a tree laid over it, and the Birrim, by a line and raft on the 12th; it is much wider than the Boosempra is where we crossed it, and runs to that river, falling into it just above our crossing. The Aquapim, a clear and mountainous country, is entered on the 16th day. By the eastern route, No. 4, the Akim country is entered the 4th day; a large hill called Abirrawantoo is passed the 9th; thence the Birrim springs, crossing the path twice before it runs to the Boosempra. Three days westward from this mountain, is a second, called Papow, in which the Aïnshue or the Winnebah river rises. A river called Dinshue rises also in this neighbourhood, running to the Saccomo, which falls into the sea 8 miles west of Accra. Isert, who visited Aquapim, called the capital Kommang, but Akropong is so now. The distance from Coomassie to Accra may be estimated at 230 miles, which bears about the same proportion to the horizontal distance, as the path we travelled through Assin from Annamaboe. Dr. Leyden was much imposed on in the extravagant account he has given of the extent, power, and commerce of Akim,* which is placed in the map accompanying his work, eastward of Dahomey, instead of westward of the Volta. Dr. Isert was a Danish gentleman, who had the good fortune to cure the former King of Ashantee's sister of a lingering disorder, after she had exhausted all the skill of the

---

* "On the west of Aquamboe lies the powerful state of Akim, sometimes denominated Akam, Achem, and Accany, which occupies almost all the interior of the Gold Coast, and is supposed by the natives to extend to Barbary. The Accanese are represented as carrying on an extensive commerce with the interior kingdoms of Africa, particularly Tonouwah, Gago, and Meczara, by which Mourzouk the capital of Fezzan seems to be intended."

fetish women, and came to Christiansburg Castle in despair. He afterwards expressed his wish to visit the Ashantee kingdom; and being encouraged, he set out in June 1786, and staying some days in Aquapim, was just about to enter Akim, when he was recalled by the Governor. A dangerous illness, heightened by his disappointment, soon afterwards disgusted him with the country, and he left it for the West Indies. As Dr. Isert's letters are only known in German and Dutch,* and he was an industrious and scientific observer, an extract from his description of the Aquapim country will be acceptable. I am indebted for a Latin translation of this and other passages, adduced on different subjects, to Dr. Reynhaut of Elmina Castle.

" I began my journey early in the morning of the 17th of June, and after walking two hours I arrived at a little village, picturesquely situated, named Aschiama. Two hours behind this lies a chain of mountains, which are composed of granitous stones; flints are but rarely found. The whole prospect shews itself here in a very different manner to that observed in sandy countries; the rocks are covered with lofty trees, which are encompassed with small forests almost impervious. The soil, no longer sandy, becomes argillaceous, and excellent for vegetation. Behind these forests I arrived at a Negro village called Abodee, eight leagues from Christiansburg: the inhabitants of this place are very tenacious of native ceremony and etiquette. Thence I passed by an irregular path through the following villages, Fiasso, Fientema, Futu, Mampon, Odaky, Manno, and Manseng. An hour afterwards I reached a village named Kommong, the residence of H. R. H. the Duke of Aquapim. Here the country is charming, though forests are still to be found. Mountains, rocks, and vallies vary each

* " Reize van Koppenhagen naar Guinea, &c. Door den Heer Isert. Amsteldam, 1797. Naar het Hoog Duitsch."

other in the most striking order; fresh water, so rarely obtained in maritime countries, is found here of an excellent quality. Near this village a stream constantly rushes from the summit of a rock, and affords a fresh and crystalline water. Trees of a very large circumference are also found; I calculated one of the biggest to be 45 feet round and 15 in diameter. These trees are not the same as those of which Adanson speaks in his description of Senegal, (Adansonia digitata) but are of a peculiar species; they much resemble a round tower, as they do not bear either flowers or fruits. Here I found the Ammonium Grana Paradisi, the Ammonium Zerumber, and a new genus in a perpendicular tree ornamented by flowers, which resembled tulips, (Novum Genus Tetandriæ) and of great elegance: also a new species of aloe, of which the inhabitants make thread; a new species of citron with indented leaves, and a multitude of unknown trees and shrubs. In the thickest forests grows a species of Spanish cane, very straight and well proportioned, and often attaining six feet in height; it is to be wished that it could be made use of, treating it as the Chinese do, for if, when dry, an equal degree of tenacity could be induced, it would prove superior in quality. I observed, on the boughs of the trees, the Senna plant (which is parasitic, and consists entirely of a flower), it was almost the shape of a pine when open, and the inside is of a very deep red; the Negroes use it in the syphilitic disorder, when first attacked. I took it for the Aphutcia Hydrora of Thunberg, but on examination it differs much, as it belongs to Icosandria. Palm trees are here very rare, except the oliferous (Elois Guineensis) and the viniferous (an Phœnix) which are cultivated in great numbers; also the true cocoa nut trees (Cocas nucifera) and the false (an Borassus.) In a word, nature entirely changes her form as soon as you reach the summit of the chain of mountains, and I do not believe one twentieth part of the plants found here are the same as those on the Coast. With regard to natural history, I was less happy in making discoveries. The elephant, so abundantly inhabiting the environs of Fidah, (Whydah) and other wild beasts, are here very rare, which may be attributed to the scarcity of grass, the growth of which is prevented by the almost impenetrable forests. Several sorts of birds are here seen, principally paroquets, of which I knew six species, Psittacus, Erythæus and Pullarius (Linn.) the others seem to be new, and I also saw a great number of insects of new species. The mineral kingdom would perhaps be richer if they had mines here. The rocks are solely composed of rough stones like granite and grens, and their species; dry quartz and slate stones are often found; on the other hand I could not discover calcareous earth. The soil is varied, but consists in general of a rich aluminous earth, traced in different colours, and of a rich black earth with which sand is never mixed. The atmosphere seemed more salubrious than on the sea coast, though physicians generally deny this quality to exist near the forests which grow in warm climates. I believe the elevated situation of the country contributes much to it. The Europeans who inhabit the Coast in forts, would do well to establish an hospital and a garden here. The Arum Esculentum, the Banana (Musa sapientum) the Ananas (Bromelia Ananas) the Carica Papaia and Citron all abound here."

The Assin path is that described in the route from Annamaboe to Coomassie, it branches off at Foosoo to Ensabra, two journies from Winnebah, through Anissoo, Asoidroo (the head quarters of the King of Ashantee in the invasion of 1807) and Atoäperrim, which means " to fire a gun." The principal town of Assin is Ansa, through which we passed, Akrofroom, apparently larger, is called the second. A range of stony hills is the boundary of Assin and Akim.

The path to Elmina, through the Warsaw country, makes so considerable an angle to the westward, that the Ashantees invariably declared it occupied more time to travel than the Assin ; it is allowed to be ten journies at Elmina, by route No. 5. The Dah is crossed the first day at its town Adahsoo, and in the evening Becquoi (one of the five large towns built by the Ashantees) is reached. The Dankara country is entered the third day, the Tufel the fourth, the Wársaw the sixth, the Boosempra is crossed the tenth day, the Ofim, which skirts this path to the westward (having received the Dah at Meeäsee) falling into it. The capital of the Dankara country is four journies westward of Coomassie, and the frontier is entered the second by route No. 6 : it is the most productive of gold, but has been extravagantly over-rated in Bosman's report of its population. The river Seënnee, or, as the Portuguese have called it, Ancobra, from its serpentine course, has been thought to rise just beyond the north eastern frontier, but it will presently appear to be a branch of the Tando of the Ashantees. In the Dutch copies of the old Portuguese charts, Dankara is placed eastward of Ashantee. The Warsaw country will be noticed more particularly, in considering the maritime geography from Cape Coast Castle to the river Assinee.

The Warsaw path has two grand branches, one to Apollonia and one to Aöwin, each thirteen journies ; the former is in the small kingdom of Amanähéä. The Aöwin country extends from Apollonia to the river Assinee, five journies in length and three in breadth ; it is governed by seven or eight caboceers, like those of Warsaw, independent of each other : it can furnish about 5000 soldiers. The numerals of Amanähéä and Aöwin will appear in an essay on the Fantee language. Both countries are at the mercy of the Ashantees, who extort gold from them frequently, though they have not yet fixed the tributes.

Sauëe lies eight journies W. N.W. from Coomassie, and Moinsan fifteen. I could not procure the routes, but Wom and Sannasee are two of the largest towns which are passed through.

Buntookoo, the capital of the kingdom of Gaman, is 11 journies N. N.W. of Coomassie by route No. 7. The river Ofim is crossed the second day, the Tando the fifth, thence the country becomes open. Yammee, the frontier town of Gaman, is reached the eighth day. The name of the King of Gaman is Adinkara; the capital, though not so large, is allowed to be better built than Coomassie, and the Moorish influence has been longer established. It is incomparably the richest country in gold, and small pits were described to me, like those Mr. Park saw at Shrondo. The numerals are,

One	Tah.
Two	Noo.
Three	Sah.
Four	Nah.
Five	Taw.
Six	Torata.
Seven	Toorifeenoo.
Eight	Toorifeessa.
Nine	Toorifcena.
Ten	Noonoo.

The four principal Gaman towns, are Sarem, which some call the capital, Bandakeeä, Bundoo, and Nasseä, five journies from Kong, and seven from Buntookoo.

A powerful kingdom called Bahooree, which has hitherto successfully resisted the Ashantees, was described to be westward, and expected to afford refuge to the King of Gaman on the approaching invasion.

I had heard it reported that the Tando formed the Assinee river,

z

about 35 miles westward of Cape Apollonia, but a very intelligent Ashantee satisfied me this was a mistake, arising probably from Seënee being the native name of the Ancobra, which is formed by one branch of the Tando; a second running westward. The Tando is not near so large as the Boosempra, and therefore very unlikely to form so large a river as the Assince; the western branch may possibly run into it. Mr. Meredith, writing from report without sufficiently checking it, has made the Tando and the Chamah or Boosempra the same; yet, p. 225, he adds, " the Volta is more probably a branch of the Tando, a large river reported as running to the eastward, and which the Ashantees are obliged to cross in coming to the Coast:" he did not reflect that he thus laid down a river running out of the sea. The Tando, we have seen, is five days northward of Coomassie, it rises in some rocky hills called Toofeeä, near the large town Aënkroo, between the Banda and Inta paths.

Soko (formerly a province of Gaman) is 11 journies from Coomassie; and Banda, four beyond, and a little to the eastward; see route No. 8. The first day, Tafoo is reached, a large aboriginal Inta town, for, as will be seen in the historical report, the Ashantees emigrated, and subjected several Inta districts now forming the northern part of their dominions, and trenched considerably on that declining kingdom, now entirely at their mercy. If Mr. Dalzel had reflected, it would have occurred to him, that the Taffoe, Tafoe, or Tafu of Snelgrave (placed so absurdly in his map, 60 miles west of the mouth of the Volta) and the In-ta* he heard of at Dahomey, and confounded with Ashantee, were the same: for the In in In-ta is scarcely audible, and only a slight nasal sound barely amounting to n, as N-ta; foo is merely an adjunct equal to people or men in our language, affixed in the present

---

* This induced me to think that In-ta and Ta-pah, as well as Assiantee might mean the same place, as we find of Mahee, Yahon, &c.—Dalzel.

infancy of African language to all names of countries, as if we always said the Scotchmen or Irishmen, instead of the Scotch and Irish. The Ofim is crossed one day beyond Tafoo at its croom Ofeesoo, the Tando four journies beyond at Tandosoo. Takima is reached the eighth day, whence the Fantees are reported, by tradition, to have emigrated, and there is yet but little difference in the languages.

Sixteen journies N. N. E. of Coomassie is Boopee (which I have placed accordingly in 8° 42′ N. and 1° 19′ W.) the frontier town of Inta, hitherto confounded with Ashantee, than which it is more populous and more civilized. The Moorish influence has been long established there, and almost all its caboceers affect to profess that faith. The river Adirri, which we shall presently identify with the Volta, is crossed four hours southward of Boopee, and is described as about 120 yards broad; it rises eight journies N.W. of Boopee, in a large mountain called Kondoongooree, one of the mountains of Kong, which were distinctly and invariably reported not to be a chain, but frequently and individually scattered, from Kong eastward. Seven journies from Coomassie, on the Inta route, is the smaller kingdom Coranza (probably the Corisseno of the old maps) the people of which are of the same origin as the Ashantees by tradition, but, as the King himself assured me, of much more genius and aptitude. Three journies from Boopee is Daboia, the second town of Inta. The first journey is to Minsiroo, where lions are numerous; the second to Moronko, the inhabitants of which are so fearful of being carried off as slaves by the Ashantee traders (who travel in great numbers) that they have no doors to their houses, but ascending by a ladder, which they immediately draw up, they enter through the thatch. Close to Moronko is a river, about as large as the Boosempra, called Adiffofoo. Pahmee, three journies south eastward of Daboia, and Yabo which I cannot place so precisely, are the alternate residences of the King of Inta. There is a constant commercial intercourse between Inta and Dahomey, the frontiers being five journies apart. The numerals of Inta are

One	- -	Koko.
Two	-	Anyoe.
Three	-	Assa.
Four	-	Anna.
Five	- -	Annoo.
Six	- -	Assee.
Seven	-	Assoonno.
Eight	-	Adoobrooa.
Nine	- -	Digrakoono.
Ten	-	Koodoo.

Sallagha, the grand market of the Inta kingdom, is 17 journies north-eastward from Coomassie, by route No. 10. The first is to Marmpon, one of the five large towns built by the Ashantees, and possessing palatine privileges; the second, through five smaller towns to Aphwaguiassie, the largest market in the Ashantee kingdom; the 9th day the rivers Kirradee and Oboosoom are crossed, each about 60 yards wide, and flowing so near together, as to appear one in the rainy season; a high mountain, Aduarreekennee, is just beyond them, the boundary of Ashantee and Booroom. The tenth day the river Sennee is forded, which afterwards enlarges considerably, and runs into the Volta; it rises five journies from Coomassie (by route No. 11) between the Boopee and Sallagha paths. The Booroom country is quite open, and the Ashantees give the river the figurative name of Birrinsoo, which means that its distance is so deceiving, that you will cry before you reach it. The capital of Booroom is Guia, a considerable town, noticed in the route to Odentee, a fetish sanctuary of great repute, and said to be splendidly furnished. The Ashantee language is spoken very commonly in Booroom, but the vernacular numerals are

One	-	-	Ekoo.
Two	-		Enoo.
Three	-		Essa.
Four	-		Enna.
Five	-	-	Annoo.
Six	-	-	Esseä.
Seven	-		Assoono.
Eight	-		Aquiay.
Nine	-	-	Akonno.
Ten	-	-	Edoo.

The tenth day the Adirri or Volta is crossed, more than a mile wide, but much interrupted by rocks, and described to be full of hippopotami (which they call sea elephants,) and alligators. This river divides Booroom from Inta, Sallagha being one day's long march from it. Calculating the 17 journies to Sallagha at 15 miles each, the course as N. E. by E. and supposing two thirds to be made good on the horizontal distance, according to our own experience, which gives 170 B. equal to 147 G. miles, Sallagha will lie in latitude 7° 56' N., and longitude 9" W. As a check upon this position, it will be necessary to follow the Adirri or Volta as far as the natives navigate it from Adda, where it is called the Flou (as the falls of the Senegal.) Isert's report may be interesting as an introduction.

" The people of Adda think it derogatory to cultivate land, and live by fishing, and making salt, which they sell to the people of the Interior. The Volta has no breakers, and therefore may be presumed to be deep." This is an extraordinary mistake; Dalzel says there are high breakers. Colonel Starrenberg (of Engineers) at Elmina Castle, who went about 60 miles up the Volta, accompanied by a Danish officer and flag, and met with no impediment so far, but turned back reluctantly in three or four fathoms of water, observed to me, that he thought the channel between the breakers about a mile wide. Dalzel mentions an American brig making good her passage over the bar, on which there is about two fathoms water; and a Danish schooner has done so since. "An arm goes from the mouth to Quitta." This must be the river running from Lagos into the Volta, near the mouth, as will be shewn in considering the errors in the maritime geography. " Six English miles from the mouth, it forms a lake 60 miles long and 48 broad, whence an arm extends to Pottriba, 3 miles eastward of Quitta : in this lake are more than a hundred islands." Colonel Starrenberg thought the river widened about 9 British miles from the mouth, but the number of small islands prevented even ocular demonstration. So large a lake would certainly have been spoken of by the natives to Europeans ere this; those whom I have questioned, have gone up the river to the extreme navigable point, and crossed it in many parts ; and they all declare that at Ascharee, 2 days from Adda, it is not two miles wide. I never could find either an Ashantee, or a waterside native, who knew of the arm running to Pottriba, a name they had not heard of; neither could Col. Starrenberg learn any thing of it ; no branch appeared as far as he went. Isert probably alluded, from report, to the river Assuafroo, which runs from eastward into the Volta, 7 journies from Adda, as will appear in the natives account. " From May to December the water is good to drink, being then higher than the sea ; in the other months it is not so, but produces more fish. The river overflows in July, and August, and the neighbourhood of its banks is excellent for the cultivation of rice." Rice is abundantly cultivated in the Inta kingdom. " Three miles from the sea is an island, called Bird Island; full of pelicans of peculiar kinds. There is a fish in this river called hardrass, which, when smoked, is exactly like European salmon. There are also hippopotami and crocodiles : quantities of oysters adhere to the mangroves, but when the river is fresh they are good for nothing. There are a great number of singing birds, and a nightingale equal to the Polish, which sings in May and December." Col. Starrenberg heard a nightingale, but saw only one hippopotamus. There is a kind of cedar tree, (Avicenniæ nov. spec.) which shoots up many branches from the ground, about as thick as a pipe, and bare of leaves : this tree is so very salt in its nature, that in the morning a great quantity of liquid salt is found on the leaves, chrystallizing in the course of the day.* Amalfee is on an island, 48 miles from the mouth, the inhabitants of which, and those on the banks of the river, of Agrafee, Wefee, Tophirree, and Bettoo, call themselves river inhabitants. The former are the brokers of slaves for the

---

* " In the province of St. Jago, in Chili, there is a plant of this class and order (Didynamiæ gymnosperma) supposed to be a species of wild basil (Ocimum salinum), resembling the common basil so much as to be hardly distinguished from it, except that the flower stem is round and jointed, and its scent and taste not like the basil, but rather like the sea flag, or some marine plant. It is an annual, shooting forth in the spring, and continuing till the commencement of winter: every morning it is covered with hard and shining saline globules, resembling dew, which the countrymen shake off the leaves to serve them as common salt, and in some respects is thought to be of a superior quality. Every plant produces daily about half an ounce of this salt ; but Molina, a scientific naturalist, to whom we are indebted for this information, says, that it is extremely difficult to account for this phenomenon, as the situation where he found these plants was in the most fertile part of the kingdom, and at a distance from the sea of more than seventy miles. When we see some plants secrete flint, separate and distinct from their fibres, as well as combined with their organic structure; and when we also know that plants secrete alkali, in every situation, I cannot perceive why Molina should consider the contiguity of the sea to be essential to the production of a neutral salt in the Ocimum salinum." Linnæan System, London, 1816, vol. ii. p. 303. .

Riley, whose narrative has recently appeared, saw in the desert, " A dwarf thorn bush from two to five feet high with succulent leaves strongly impregnated with salt."

Creppee country, and receive a vast number from one of its provinces called Acottim, 3 journies eastward."

Mr. Meredith could scarcely have enquired about the Creppee or Aquamboe countries, to have placed them west of the Volta. The natives who carry salt up the Volta, pull the 1st day, by Agrafee, Foomee, and Tefferee to Amanfee, on the banks ; the 2nd to Dofo on an island ; the 3rd, by Ascharee, on the western bank, to Adomë ; the 4th by Assafoo to the Aquamboe country ; the 5th to Sowa ; the 6th to Pessee ; the 7th by Appasoo, to Deyatoompon, where a large river flows into the Volta from the eastward ; to Doodee the 8th; to Tombo the 9th; to Akorosoo the 10th; to Odentee the 11th. Here the river becomes too rocky to proceed conveniently, and hence to Sallagha by land is 4 journies, through the large towns Oboëkee, Akuntong, Enkungquakroo, and Apapassee, famous for making cotton cloth. There is a small state northward, between Aquamboe and Inta, called Anoöchoo, subject to Ashantee, bordering on which is Guasoo, the southern district or province of Inta. The Creppee country borders on Aquamboe eastward, and is independent.

I am not in possession of Colonel Starrenberg's bearings, but the course of the river may be pretty well ascertained from fixing the points of Odentee, Quaöo, and Ascharee. Odentee is 6 journies southward of east (by route No. 12) from Pattooda, in the Booroom country, and mentioned in the route to Sallagha. Quaöo, the country where the Boosempra rises, has already been mentioned as entered 8 journies from Coomassie. Ascharee, 2 days and a half pull up the river, is reached in 1 day's walk from Ningo. The course of the Volta is consequently about W. N. W. to Quaöo, N. E. by N. to Odentee, and N. W. by Sallagha, which course it appears to continue to Boopee, if not to its source in the Kondoongooree mountain. The 10 days pull from Adda to Odentee, and the 4 journies by land thence to Sallagha, agree very well with the distance and position of that place, as before calculated by the 17 days route from Coomassie. The houses of Sallagha and other towns of Inta were mentioned as peculiar from being round. Leo Africanus observed houses built in the form of bells at Timbuctoo.

Seven days from Sallagha, N. E. according to the Moors, through the Inta town of Zongoo, is Yahndi, the capital of Dagwumba, which I have placed, calculating the course at N. E. by E., and allowing 18 miles for each journey, as the country is said to be open, in 55′ E. and 8° 38′ N.: the position is assisted by the common account of its being 8 journies from Daboia, by route No. 13, and that two obscure, but direct paths to Daboia and Yahndi, from Coomassie, occupy the first 19 days, and the latter (described as laying between Daboia and Sallagha) 23 days. Sir William Young, in his Report of the Geography and History of Northern Africa, writes, " the Slatees of Old Calebar are said to carry on their trade to Degombah *northward*," which also supports my placing it more to the eastward than it appears in Major Rennel's map. Yngwa, a district and large town of Dagwumba, is said to lie 8 days northwestward of Yahndi, through Sakoigoo; its distance from Daboia, by report 6 journies, places it about N. N. W. Two journies from Daboia, towards Yngwa, is the river Adiffofoo, about 60 yards wide, running eastward, 2 journies from which is Kooboro, a large Dagwumba town.

North-eastward of Yahndi is Tonomah, of which I do not recollect more than the name, though I think it is a town and district of Dagwumba. The kingdom of Tonowah, of which Assentai has been described as the capital by the Shereef Imhammed,* must

* In the Dutch copies of the old Portuguese charts, Xabunda (perhaps Banda) is

have been derived from this name, being otherwise unknown. Three journies north-eastward of Yahndi is Sokoquo or Ensoko, also a considerable town.

Yahndi is described to be beyond comparison larger than Coomassie, the houses much better built and ornamented. The Ashantees who had visited it, told me, they frequently lost themselves in the streets. The King, Inăna Tanquăree, has been converted by the Moors, who have settled there in great numbers. Mr. Lucas called it the Mahomedan kingdom of Degomba, and it was represented to him as peculiarly wealthy and civilized. The markets of Yahndi are described as animated scenes of commerce, constantly crowded with merchants from almost all the countries of the interior. Horses and cattle abound, and immense flocks are possessed even by the poorer class. The numerals of Dagwumba and Yngwa differing, I submit both.

		Yngwa.		*Dagwumba.*
One	-	Lakoo	-	Yahndo
Two	-	Ayee	-	Ayee
Three	-	Attah	-	Attah
Four	-	Anāhee	-	Nasee
Five	-	Leerennoo	-	Ennoon
Six	-	Ayoboo	-	Yohbee
Seven	-	Ayapaï	-	Poiee
Eight	-	Annee	-	Nehenoo
Nine	-	Awai	-	Whyee
Ten	-	Peä	-	Edoo.

Yahndi is named after the numeral one, from its pre-eminence. Sarem is the name of a region, including Gaman, Inta, and Dagwumba, so called from the open nature of those countries.

placed as the capital of Ashantee, and two or three large Portuguese towns, one St. Lawrence, with several convents and crosses between it and the Coast.

One day from Sallagha, towards Yahndi, and scarcely one journey westward from the latter, is the river Laka, described to be as large and as rapid as the Adirri or Volta, which it joins below Odentee, and may therefore be safely concluded to be the Assua-froo ; for the names of rivers are very mutable in Africa, each country through which they pass naturalising them to its own language, and thus increasing the perplexities of a geography founded on investigation. I could not procure any authorized account of the northward course of this river, the best opportunities had escaped me when I heard of it.

Five journies N. E. from Yahndi is the smaller kingdom of Gamba, the birth place of Baba the chief Moor at Coomassie, and the boundary of the Ashantee authority, though its influence, through the much respected medium of Dagwumba, would extend to the Niger. Seven journies northward of Yngwa is the kingdom of Fobee: the river Koontoorooa is crossed four days from it, being about half a mile broad, it has an eastern and western branch, the former running to the Karhala, one day farther, considerably wider, and the course south-eastward. One journey from the river is a large mountain called Sarraka, the same distance from Fobee, the capital of the kingdom. Lakoo, Lamma, Karhala, and Koomada are the next largest towns. Five journies northward is an independent kingdom called Chouoocha. The position of Fobee is checked by Goorooma, being 15 journies from it, (a kingdom to be noticed presently in the direct northern route from Yahndi to Houssa,) and Kawerree only nine, doubtless Cayree, a kingdom in the route of the Moors from Coomassie to Jinnie. The numerals of Fobee are

One	-	-	Koroom.
Two	-	Nalay.
Three	-	Poompevarra.

Four	-	Leetaynalec.
Five	- -	Kakwassee.
Six	- -	Mannassa.
Seven	-	Noottoosoo.
Eight	-	Borafay.
Nine	-	Pirrifay.
Ten	- -	Nanooa.

Five journies from Yngwa is Mosee, a more warlike but less visited kingdom; it consists of many states, but the superior monarch is named Billa, and the capital Kookoopella. I place this N.W., because, although its traders pass through Yngwa, they do not cross the Karhala, or indeed any river but what they can walk through. The numerals are

One	- -	Yimbo.
Two	-	Ayeeboo.
Three	-	Ataboo.
Four	-	Annasee.
Five	- -	Annoo.
Six	- -	Ayobee.
Seven	-	Owhi.
Eight	-	Ennee.
Nine	- -	Aïhopoi.
Ten	-	Peega.

A few days northward of Fobee, through Chamday and Kobafoo, is Calanna, described as a very large city, rivalling Yahndi as a market, and situated at the foot of a mountain abounding in iron stone, which they manufacture for rude purposes in much the same manner as Mr. Park witnessed at Jeningalla. Calanna is probably the Calanshee of Imhammed, who told Mr. Lucas that it was a dependency of Tounouwah or Assentai, situated mid-way between it and the coast, 18 journies from each. The numerals are

One   -   -   Kodoom.
Two   -   Naboolla
Three   -   Naweedazoo.
Four   -   -   Nabonaza.
Five   -   Nabonoa.
Six   -   -   Lodoo.
Seven   -   Logwa.
Eight   -   Littaïzoo.
Nine   -   -   Nako.
Ten   -   Yewoo.

Kumsallahoo I have not attempted to lay down, having no other guide for placing it than the report that it is one moon's journey from Dagwumba, that its traders pass through Mosee, and cross only one river, the Fachinga, and that not large. The numerals are

One   -   -   Yumbo.
Two   -   Yeeboo.
Three   -   Tabo.
Four   -   -   Nasee.
Five   -   Annoo.
Six   -   -   Yobo.
Seven   -   Poihee.
Eight   -   Nehee.
Nine   -   -   Wahee.
Ten   -   Pega.

We will now return to Coomassie and proceed northwards to Jinnie, or as it was generally pronounced, Jennë. This route to Tombuctoo (or Timbooctoo) is much less frequented by the Moors than that from Dagwumba, through Houssa. They alledge that the people northward, are neither so commercial, so civilized, or so wealthy as those north-eastward. The first 12 journies are to Buntookoo, seven journies whence is a river called by the natives

Coombo, and by the Moors, Zamma; it is described as half a mile broad, and running westward. I could not find any Ashantee who had travelled beyond this river, which is the northern limit of their authority. Five journies eastward of north from the river, is Kong, the King of which is named Asequoo. A large mountain called Toolileseena is near the capital, and a small river, Woora, four journies from it. The kingdom is said to be by no means so wealthy or powerful as that of Ashantee; the market is supplied from Houssa, the country is populous, horses numerous, and elephants killed daily. The people fight with spears, and bows and arrows. Seven journies from Kong several mountains are passed, called Koonkoori. Mr. Park says, that "Kong signifies mountain in the Mandingo language, which language is in use from the frontier of Bambarra to the western sea." The language of Kong seems to be a corruption of the Bambarra or Mandingo: the numerals are

One	-	-	Kiddee.
Two	-	Filla.	
Three	-	Sowa.	
Four	-	Nanoo.	
Five	-	-	Looroa.
Six	-	-	Wora.
Seven	-	Ooranfilla.	
Eight	-	Leeaygee.	
Nine	-	-	Konunto.
Ten	-	-	Tah.

The Ashantees calling all the slaves whom they brought down to the water side Dunkos, it had been, for many years, naturally concluded that there was a large country of that name in their neighbourhood. Isert writes, " the Dunkoers are a people behind Ashantee." On enquiry, however, I found to my surprise, that there is no country of that name, but that it is merely an epithet, synonymous with the barbarian of the Greeks and Romans, which they apply to all the people of the interior but themselves, and implies an ignorant fellow. I first suspected this from observing some Dunkos were cut in the face, and some not, and I presently discovered their vernacular languages were various, and unintelligible to each other. Generally speaking, the bush or country people of Dagwumba have three light cuts on each cheek bone, and three below, with one horizontal under the eye; those of Yahndi, three deep continued cuts; the people of Moscee, three very deep and long, and one under the eye; those of Bornoo are frequently cut in the forehead; of Marrowa all over the body in fine, small, and intricate patterns. In Fobee, Kumsallahoo, and Calanna, the lower orders have a hole bored through the cartilage of the nose. These cuts are made during infancy, to insinuate fetish liquids to invigorate and preserve the child.

Nine journies northward of Kong is Kaybee, the King of which, named Mamooroo, killed the former monarch Dabbira. The country was said to be very populous, the capital behind a mountain called Beseeree, the soil chalky, and asses as numerous as horses. Three journies from the frontier of Kaybee, over a large mountain called Seboopoo, and across a large river, is Kayree, through which country it is very dangerous to pass, the people laying in ambush in small parties to rob or kidnap travellers, and subsisting by rapine. Five journies thence is Garoo (probably Gago*) a very powerful kingdom, the King, Batoomo, lives at Netaquolla. Twenty journies beyond is the kingdom of Doowarra, the people of which are indifferent warriors, but superior agriculturists, and

---

* Gago oppidum amplissimum nullis quoque cingitur muris, distat a Tumbuto meridiem versus quadringentes fere passuum millibus, inclinatusque fere ad Euroaustrum. Leo Af.

plant extensively : the soil is red earth. A smaller kingdom called Filladoo or Firrasoo, is in the neighbourhood. Five journies north of Doowarra is the Niger, and on an island, about a mile from the southern bank, is Jennë. The route from Kong to Jennë is the only one which has not been checked by Negro evidence, but I had reason to think well of the Moor who furnished it, who never contradicted himself, though repeatedly cross questioned during the four months I was at Coomassie. The places reported to Mr. Park on this route, it is true, are none of them mentioned, but, probably, the people who were insuperably adverse to his proceeding, were the least likely to satisfy his curiosity but by imposing on him.* Mr. Park in his route from Sego to Bædoo, has a town called Doowassoo, only four journies from Sego ; but I was assured repeatedly that Doowarra is a powerful kingdom. In the first Mission, Mr. Park reported the kingdom of Gotto to be so close to the Niger, that its chief, Moösee, embarked on it to attack Jinnie, and Major Rennell has placed it accordingly : but, in the second, he writes, " one month's travel south of Bædoo," (which he makes 30 journies southward of Sego) " through the kingdom of Gotto, will bring the traveller to the country of the Christians, who have their houses on the banks of the Ba Sea Feena." He says the Ba Nimma rises in the Kong mountains south of Marraboo, but does not mention the kingdom of Kong in his route, which is about one moon's travel from the sea, as he has described Bædoo to be.

* " To what degree the natives of Silla would have contradicted each other in their accounts of Tombuctoo, Park's short stay there could not have allowed him time to ascertain, even if his knowledge of their language had enabled him to understand their accounts as well as he did those of the slatees on the Gambia.

" Several instances of the contradictory testimony of the Negroes occur in Park's travels, Jennë, for instance, is stated in his first Mission to be situated on the Niger, but on his second journey he renounces that opinion, on the apparently good authority of an old Somonie (canoe man) who had been seven times at Tombuctoo." Adams's Editor.

Now it is very unlikely, if Bædoo had been but 20 journies from Coomassie, that we should not have heard of it; and it is next to impossible, that if any kingdom called Gotto laid still nearer, (which it must have done, to have been passed through from Bædoo to the sea) that it should have been unknown. Indeed, if the kingdom of Bambarra extended 28 days south of Sego, as appears by the route given to Mr. Park, the Ashantees would not have spoken of it from mere report, but would probably have become acquainted with it, either through war, commerce, or negotiation. It is a little extraordinary that the kingdom of Ashantee, reported as eminently powerful to Mr. Lucas even so far distant as Mesurata, and which must be well known in the neighbourhood of Jennë, from the number of Moors who visit it from that city, should not even have been noticed to Mr. Park in this southern route from Silla or Sego to the sea. Mr. Park writes of the Moors not being able to subject Jinbala; I believe they insinuate themselves as residents every where, but I could not hear of their having established themselves by force, or of their composing even the greater part of a population any where.*

* Mr. Hutchison writes, that from Inta to Jennë is said to be 41 journies. This Gentleman, the Resident at Coomassie, merely accompanied the Mission to act in that capacity in case the object could be accomplished, and was not instructed to report: the officer conducting the Mission being responsible to the extent of his industry, and the opportunities, for the various desiderata, excepting the Botanical and Medical, which were expected from the Surgeon, Mr. Tedlie. Mr. Hutchison's time was much employed in making duplicates and copies of the frequent and voluminous dispatches to head quarters. The Moors disliking even a second European to be present at their geographical communications, Mr. Hutchison, through his obliging disposition, which accommodated itself to every thing auxiliary to the pursuits of the Mission, rendered me a great service, and quieted the uneasiness of the Moors by keeping watch, and diverting the various Ashantee visitors who would have intruded, with great patience and address. There was no time even for a communication of the data I had collected before the Mission left Coomassie, for we may be said to have lived in public the latter part of the four months,

Having reached the Niger it is time to observe, that it is only known to the Moors by the name of Quolla, pronounced rather as Quorra by the Negroes, who, from whatever countries they came, all spoke of this as the largest river they knew; and it was the grand feature in all the routes (whether from Houssa, Bornoo, or the intermediate countries) to Ashantee. Mr. Horneman wrote that the Niger, in some parts of Houssa, was called *Gaora*, which must sound very like Quorra. The Niger, after leaving the lake

and Mr. Hutchison's genius inclining more to the cultivation of the Ashantee and Arabic languages, which I had no doubt would yield to his great industry, I did not intrude less congenial pursuits on his attention, (the desiderata having been amply realized,) but merely requested he would let me know what any intelligent Moor, arriving after my departure, might say of the Interior, and, if possible, procure a chart from him, especially if he was not a native of Houssa or Bornoo, which two of the Moors who had drawn for me were. After I had finished my Geographical Report, Mr. Hutchison sent, with some other interesting particulars, added as notes with his initials, a chart drawn by a Jenné Moor just arrived, confirming all I had collected in the most satisfactory manner. The names of the countries from the source of the Niger to Egypt were written in Arabic, with Mr. Hutchison's expression of the pronunciation in English opposite. I particularly recollect that his ear differed somewhat from mine, which accounts for the trifling diffe- rences in our spelling. I shewed Mr. Hutchison my charts as curiosities, but he took no minutes of the names, uninteresting from his never having had an opportunity of reading Major Rennell's Dissertations, which would alone make them so to any one. He gives a better proof of this, than my own impression, by the following extract from his letter to me, accompanying the chart: " The Bornoo you used to talk about, you will find the same as the lake Chaudi, or Al Bahare Noohoo, or else you know a country I I do not recollect hearing of;" but, in the postscript, he writes, " On looking over my memoranda, I find Bornoo is the principal monarchy the Arabs alone stand in awe of, and one of the four kingdoms best known on the Quolla." Mr. Hutchison *unconsciously* confirming what I had learned, is even more satisfactory than if I had left him any basis for his enquiries; indeed, his own object, the acquirement of the language, was too im- portant to be interrupted unnecessarily. Before I attach any quotation from this Gentle- man's letters, I must acknowledge the assistance I had previously derived from his spirited zeal as an officer, as well as that which has since resulted from his interest in intellectual pursuits.

Dibbir, was invariably described as dividing in two large streams; the Quolla, the greater, pursuing its course south-eastward until it joined the Bahr Abiad, and the other branch running northward of east near Timbuctoo, and dividing again soon afterwards; the smaller stream running northwards by Yahoodee, a place of great trade,* and the larger turning directly eastward, and increasing considerably, running to the lake Caudi or Cadi under the name of Gambaroo.† The Moors call the branch running by Timbuctoo the Jolliba, I presume figuratively, as a great water, for I was assured by a native of Jennë, who had frequently visited Timbuctoo, that this branch was called Zah-mer by the Negroes.‡

The variety of the concurrent evidence respecting the Gambaroo, certainly made an impression on my mind almost amounting to conviction. De Lisle, in his map of Africa for the use of Louis XV. (the accuracy of which in one point where our latest charts are in error, the Lagos river, will be shewn towards the close of this Report) makes a branch from the Niger running near Timbuctoo; and what is even more to the point, writes " Gambarou ou Niger." It was not till sometime after my return from Ashantee, that I un-expectedly discovered this solitary European record of such a

---

* The Moors particularly mentioned buying their writing paper there. One told me that the Joliba ran to a river called Hotaiba after it passed Yahoodee, which river ran towards Toonis. Several talked of vessels coming to Yahoodee, navigated by white men, but whence I could not learn, and Brahima had never visited it, though such reports were familiar to him.

† The rivers Arauca and Capanaparo in Cumana form bifurcations similar to those of the Niger. The Arauca divides itself into two rivers, the northern one, the Arauquito, runs through the lake Cabullarito into the Orinoco, and the southern retaining the name of Arauca, also flows to the Orinoco. The Capanaparo falls into the Orinoco in two streams, the northern retaining the original name, and the southern acquiring that of Mina. See Humboldt's map of the eastern part of the province of Verina.

‡ See note, p. 189.

name, and it will at least be allowed that so respectable a character as De Lisle, would neither have laid down the branch from the Niger (for it is as likely to be so in the absence of explanation, as a river running into it) without some authority, nor have invented the name Gambarou: and it will also be allowed, that he must have heard of it as being a very large river, to have confounded it with the Niger. De Lisle has preserved most of the names reported to me, more closely than any other geographer.* In the judicious compendium of Mr. Murray, I observe the following note. " It is but justice to D'Anville to say, that in his map of central Africa, inserted in the 26th volume of the Academie des Inscriptions, he has represented a river passing close to Timbuctoo, running S.W., and falling into the Niger. This delineation has not been copied by others, but it is not the less probable that that excellent geographer may have had positive information on which to found it." Now, I may presume, this is only recorded in delineation, and not noticed by D'Anville in the text, or, his authority would have appeared. I shall be indulged in such a conjecture, when it is

* " No one who compares the maps of De Lisle and D'Anville with the materials then published, can doubt the excellent means of information with which they must have been supplied both by government, and by private individuals." Murray.

We find a remarkable instance of De Lisle's accuracy in Major Rennell's construction of the geography of Mr. Horneman's expedition. " Mr. Horneman was informed that there are 101 inhabited places in Fezzan." It is remarkable that this is precisely the number stated in M. Delisle's map of Africa, drawn in 1707; and, according to Mr. Beaufoy's informant, there are nearly 100.

I have since found an older authority for the name *Gambaroo*, and which also shews that the name *Quolla* and its connection with the Gambaroo, have not been wholly unknown hitherto. It is in the L'Afrique de Marmol, livre viii. chap. 3. " C'est une chose estrange que ce fleuve venant de si loin, car Ptolomée le fait venir du lac *Quélo-nide*, et de celui de Nuba, il n'entraine pas tant d'eaux par ce costé-là, et la marée ne monte pas si avant, *que par l'autre bras que l'on appelle Gamber.*" One may almost fancy Quolla and Quellonide to have been derived from the Chalonides of Ptolemy. .

recollected I am writing where I cannot satisfy myself, in a place destitute of literary facilities. If it is only to be found in the delineation, it is of course, as likely to be a branch running N. E. from the Niger, as a river running S.W. into it. Mr. Park has described the Niger as dividing into two large branches after leaving Dibbie, and their re-union has been admitted by considerate investigators, to be a very improbable addition to that report.* Sidi Hamet assigns no course to the great river which he described as about an hour's ride with a camel south of Timbuctoo, and distinguished from the Niger, or, as he called it, Zolilib, by saying the latter was two hours ride. Adams placed La-mar-Zarah, about three quarters of a mile wide, two miles south of the town, without hesitation, but he only *conceived* that the course was S. W.† Leo, ambiguous as the context may be, certainly writes that there is a *branch* of the Niger passing Timbuctoo, " Vicino a un ramo del Niger." Mr. Beaufoy's Moor says that below Ghinea is the sea into which the river of Tombuctoo disembogues itself; on which Major Rennell observes, " by the word sea, it is well known the Arabs mean to

---

* " The fact of a large lake like the Dibbie, discharging its waters by two streams flowing from distant parts of the lake, and re-uniting after a separate course of a hundred miles in length, has always appeared to us extremely apocryphal, at least we believe that the geography of the world does not afford a parallel case." Adams's Editor.

† " According to these statements of the Moorish traders, Adams would seem to have *mistaken* the course of the stream at Tombuctoo. In fact, I do not recollect that he told me at Mogadore that it flowed in a westerly direction: but, I think, I am correct in saying, that he discovered some uncertainty in speaking upon this subject, (and almost upon this subject alone) observing, in answer to my inquiries, that he had not taken very particular notice, and that the river was steady, without any appearance of a strong current." Dupuis on Adams.

Adams's name, La-mar-Zarah (for of course he did not attach *La* mar to indicate water, but pronounced La-mar-Zarah, as an integral name) seems accounted for by his confounding or connecting the Arabic name of the river, *Lahamar*, with the Negro name *Yça* (for we find these names in Marmol, tom. 3. liv. 8.) making *Lahamar-yça*, La-mar-Zarah.

express a lake also:" this river of Timbuctoo is, doubtless, the branch of the Niger forming the Gambaroo, and the sea below Ghinea, the lake Caude. In the Description de l'Afrique, traduite du Flamand, D'O Dapper, à Amsterdam, 1686, I find " Ce Royaume de Tombut ou Tongbutu environ à quatre lieuës *d'un bras* du Niger." The account, to be submitted presently, that this branch of the Niger passing Timbuctoo is not crossed until the third day going from Timbuctoo to Houssa, is not an argument against its identity with the Zarah of Adams, or the river of Sidi Hamet, only two or three miles from the city ; because, giving a northerly course to the branch, and Houssa laying north eastward 20 journies from Timbuctoo, as will be shewn presently, the direction of the path would not require the river to be crossed immediately, but, evidently, not till the second or third day.

De Barros, who considered the Senegal to be the Niger, wrote, that it received various names,* and was called by the Caragoles (Serawoollies) Collë ; on·which Mr. Murray reasonably observes, " this name seems readily convertible into Joli-ba, the latter syllable being merely an adjunct, meaning a river:" this I was also given to understand.   Now, if the name Joliba had not been reported on the authority of Mr. Park, I might submit that Collë is more readily convertible into Quolla, which approximating even more closely to Kulla, seems to identify the Collë and Kulla under the common name of Quolla.†   Mr. Park in his memoir to Lord

* Les Sénégurs le nomment Sénédec, les Jalofes Dengueh, les Turcorons qui sont plus au-dedans du pays Maye, les Saragoles qui sont plus haut Colle, et en un contrée plus vers l'orient Zimbale : au royaume de Tombut on le nomme Yça. Marmol, tom. 3, livre 8. The name Zimbale must be derived from Jimballa, by which country the river passes ; it occurs in the route from Shégo to Timbuctoo. P. 194.

† Kulla, in the Mallowa, if not in the Kassina language, means *child* ; perhaps, allegory being the character of African language, the southern river may be called Quolla or Kulla, from being a *branch* only of the great river which forms it and the Gambaroo.

Camden, writes, " the river of Dar Kulla, mentioned by Mr. Browne, is generally supposed to be the Niger, or at least to have a communication with that river." The name and course of the Quolla suggested this to me before I observed the above remark, which I did not until my return.* Other arguments will presently appear for the identity of the Kulla and the Niger.†

The Gambaroo seems to me to identify the Gir of Ptolemy,‡ carried by him into the centre of Africa, and which would appear as large as the Niger by the expression, " maximi sunt Gir et Nigir." The river of Bornoo, hitherto assumed, is not adequate to the impression Ptolemy conveys, and the names " Gir et Nigir," seem to indicate a connection. The Niger may be considered to terminate when the smaller stream is lost in the Nile.

Concerning the source of the Niger, there was a difference of opinion amongst the Moors, and not the least notion amongst the Negroes. Some said that it rose in Bambooch, meaning, as I presume, Bambouk, and others in Jabowa, where they described another large river to rise also, running westward. Jabowa was said to be 40 journies from Sego, and Bambooch 43.

From Jabowa the Niger was described to run to Fouta Gollabi, and in six days thence to Fouta Towra; the Moors must certainly have meant Foota Galla, and Footatora, for their pronunciation

* See the account of the large interior river known at Gaboon, under the name of *Wole* or *Wolela.*

† " There is one thing that disagrees with Mr. Park's account, they call the Niger Quolla at Jenné, Sansanding, &c. &c. and describe the Jolliba as falling into the Quolla east of Timbuctoo." W. H.

The Moors invariably reported to me that it ran from it. Mr. H. might perhaps have misunderstood the Jenné Moor, whose single authority cannot be opposed to the concurrence of several.

‡ Illorum verò qui per interiorem Æthiopiam fluant, quique fontes et ostia in continente habent maximi sunt Gir et Nigir. (Lib. 2. E. 1. De maximis *fluminibus.*)

was more imperfect than their knowledge of the native names westward, whither they rarely travelled. I induced a Moor on each side the question, and of different countries, to draw in my quarters, unknown to each other, what they called a chart of the Quolla, for the sake of preserving the several names in their own writing. They were only inferior to one Moor, from whom I never had an opportunity of inducing a chart. Both parties met, apparently, at Hasoo, as will be seen by submitting the names.*

Bambooch.	*Jabowa.*
Journies.	
10 to Gadima, probably Gadoo, little more than 6 journies from the capital of Bambook, according to Major Rennell.	
20 to Hasoo - - - -	Hasoowa.
4 to Jaoora - - - -	Jaoona.
2 to Jamoo - - - - -	Gamsoö.
5 to Mallaïa - - - -	Mallaïu.
2 to Shégo - - - - -	Sego.

Sego was correctly described according to Mr. Park, and the death of the monarch he first knew spontaneously mentioned, with his warlike disposition, and great power. Mr. Park observes that he

---

* The Jenně Moor does not appear to have been so particularly acquainted with the source of the Niger. He has drawn two hills, from one of which springs a large river he could not name, running westward, the other is the source of the Quolla, and Mr. Hutchison has written its name Bieteerilmiloo. Between this source and Mala, the King of which he describes as a great monarch, he mentions no towns or kingdoms. This Mala is the Malay of the Moorish charts I procured, between the source and which five places or countries were written. Mr. Hutchison writes the course thus, without time or distance, Mala, Bambarra, Shego, Sansanding, Jena, Mashina, Dahlea (a small croom on the lake Dibber,) Kabarra: he adds, cannibals are close to the Joliba, and 30 journies from Timbuctoo, they eat their prisoners: the dead of their own people are put in the Joliba, in wooden coffins.

found the language of Bambarra a sort of corrupted Mandingo; this confirms the numerals repeated to me as the Bambarra:

	Bambarra.	*Mandingo.*
One	Killi	Killin.
Two	Foolla	Foola.
Three	Sabba	Sabba.
Four	Nani	Nani.
Five	Looroo	Looloo.
Six	Wora	Woro.
Seven	Worroola	Oronglo.
Eight	Sagi	Sie.
Nine	Konunto	Konunto.
Ten	Ta	Tang.

From Sego to Sansanding was called one journey, from Sansanding to Jennë three. Jennë was described as on an island of the Niger, the town considerable, and fortified, and with large houses to pray in. I did not understand that it was subject to Timbuctoo; it certainly has a distinct monarch, who was called Malaï Smaera, and the head Moor, Malaï Bacharoo. From Jennë through Dibbir, at the entrance of which is Sanina, to Kabarra or Kabra, the port of Timbuctoo (half a day's walk from it) is a voyage of 20 days. By land, it was only 12 journies, through Mashena (Masina) Farrimabbie, Jimballa (the Jinbala of Mr. Park, which they persisted was not on an island of the Niger, but on the northern bank of it) Taäkim, Assoofoo, Zeddaï, Douraï (probably the Downie in Major Rennell's map) Matarooch, and Makkasoorfoo, probably the Soorka's, whom Mr. Park mentioned as inhabiting the northern bank of the river between Jinnie and Timbuctoo: he also writes that it is 12 journies by land from Jinnie to Timbuctoo. The horizontal distance from Jennë to Jimballa, on Major Rennell's map is about 100 B. miles, and thence to Timbuctoo 90 more. Now

12 journies at 18 miles, give but a horizontal distance of 144 B. miles, wherefore. I should think the northern bank of the lake Dibbir, is not so high as it has been hitherto drawn, and the path so distant as not to be deflected by any curve of the lake. Timbuctoo was described as a large city, but inferior to Houssa, and not comparable with Bornoo. The Moorish influence was said to be powerful, but not superior. A small river goes nearly round the town, overflowing in the rains, and obliging the people of the suburbs to move to an eminence in the centre of the town; where the King lives. This is, probably, the smaller river described by Sidi Hamet as close to the town. Leo says, when the Niger rises, the waters flow through certain canals to the city. There were very few muskets to be seen; the King, a Moorish Negro called Billabahada, had a few double barrelled guns, which were only fired at customs, and gunpowder was almost as valuable as gold. The two latter circumstances, besides the name of the river, were all that I recognised in their reports confirming the description given by Adams, which I conceive to be as inadequate as those collected by Mr. Jackson are extravagant.* The three last Kings before Billa, were Osamana, Dawoolloo, and Abass. Mr. Jackson says there was a King Woollo reigning in 1800, and a Moor who had come from Timbuctoo to Coomassie ten years ago, did not

* The following sentence in the description of Leo, conveys an idea of the decline or decay of the city. " Cujus domus omnes in tuguriola cretacea stramineis tectis *sunt mutatœ*." Yet immediately after we receive the contrary impression on reading " Visitur · tamen elegantissimum quoddam templum cujus murus ex lapidibus atque calce vivo est fabricatus: deinde et palacium quoddam regium quodam Granato viro artificissimo con-ditum. Frequentissimæ hic sunt artificum mercatorum præcipuè autem telæ atque gossypii textorum officinæ; huc mercatores Barbari pannum ex Europa adferunt." In the Description de l'Afrique en Flamand, published about a century and a half after-wards, the author seems to be aware of the advanced decline or decay of Timbuctoo. ." Les maisons étoient autrefois fort sumptueuses, mais elles ne sont maintenant que de bois enduites de terre grasse et couvertes de paille."

know King Woollo (Adams's King) was dead, as he was reigning at the time he left Timbuctoo. Abass probably had a short reign like Saï Apokoo the second. This Moor also said that Woollo's favourite wife (called by Adams, Fatima) was named Fatooma Allizato. The editor of Adams shews that the name of Fatima, affords in itself no proof that its possessor was Moorish, or even a Mohammedan woman. I think it is probably derived from a numeral, for it answers to five in the numerals of Garangi (a country described to be northwards of Jennë) which are

One	-	-	Kerriminna.
Two	-		Ferriminna.
Three	-		Sowaninna.
Four	-		Firrima.
Five	-		Fahtima.
Six	-	-	Tata.
Seven	-		Manninia.
Eight	-		Pirima.
Nine	-		Missirima.
Ten	-	-	Guahee.

Numerals are frequently added to names in Ashantee.

Perhaps the old ms. which I purchased with difficulty from a Jennë Moor, will recompense the translator by a fuller account, but I fear religion only is the subject. It contains thirteen pages, with some marginal notes in a different hand. I should have observed, that, generally speaking, I found the Moors very cautious in their accounts, declining to speak unless they were positive, and frequently referring doubtful points to others whom they knew to be better acquainted with them. I did not succeed in procuring the numerals of Timbuctoo, but the language is different from that of Houssa, as the words opposed to those recollected by Adams will shew :

	Timbuctoo.		Houssa.
Man	Jungo		Motoo.
Woman	Jumpsa		Motee.
Camel	So		Rakoomee.
Dog	Killab		Karree.
Cow	Fallee		Saneä.
House	Dah		Garree.
Water	Boca		Looa.
Tree	Carna		Leeseeä.
Gold	Or		Jennarreä.
A Moor	Seckar		Bibay.

From Timbuctoo * to Houssa is 20 journies; the three first through a woody country, and over the branch of the Niger to Azibbie, the frontier town. Houssa was said to be the largest city north or south of the Quolla, except Bornoo; the Moorish influence to have been established there beyond memory, and the King's name Serragkee. Cabi is not the name of the kingdom, but of a large dependent town and district on the Niger. Mallowa, or Marrowa, as the Negroes pronounce it, (for they seemed invariably to substitute r for the l of the Moors, as Quorra for Quolla)†

---

* " All the country from where the Joliba discharges itself into the Quolla is subject to the Sultan Malisimiel. What makes the Sultan of Timbuctoo so much talked of, is his being near the water side; but his master, the Sultan of Malisimiel considers him merely as a deputy or governor. The four greatest monarchs known on the banks of the Quolla, are Baharnoo, Santambool, Malisimiel, and Malla." W. H.　Malla is Mallowa.

† The Chaymas substitute r for l, a substitution that arises from a defect of pronunciation, common in every zone. The substitution of r for l characterizes, for example, the Bashmouric dialect of the Coptic language. It is thus that the Caribbees of the Oroonoko have been transformed into Galibi, in French Guiana, by confounding r with l, and softening the c. The Tamanach has made choraro (solalo) of the Spanish word soldado." Humboldt's personal narrative, book iii. chap. 9.

is the next extensive in its limits to Bornoo. It is, no doubt, the kingdom of Mellè, misplaced by Leo, and reported to Cadamosto in 1455, as 30 journies beyond Timbuctoo. Major Rennell observes, " we should naturally look for it on the eastward of Timbuctoo," and it has only been placed south eastward, and south of the Niger, because Edrisi has a city called Malel thereabouts, though he calls the name of the kingdom of which it is the capital Lamlam, which Hartman would reconcile by supposing it to be a transposition of Malel, certainly a forced conjecture.* A large town called Mahalaba is the nearest I have found to Malel, to be noticed on the route from Dagwumba to the Niger.† In speaking of all fortified cities, the negroes of Mallowa invariably prefixed Berinnë or Brinnë to the name, as an indication that they were so; this was always the case in mentioning Houssa, Cabi, Cassina, Katinna, &c. &c. I shall place the numerals of Cassina, as written by Mr. Lucas after the Shereef Imhammed, to the right of those of Houssa or Mallowa, from their close affinity, perhaps identity; for this language is spoken far eastward, and the Shereef, as we shall presently see, was rather inaccurate in his recollection of the numerals of Bornoo.

One	-	-	Daia	-	Déiyah.
Two	-	-	Beeyoo	-	Beeyou.
Three	-	-	Okoo	-	Okoo.
Four	-		Odoo	-	Foodoo.
Five	-	-	Beä	-	Beat.

* The position of Mellè is further confirmed in Dapper " Le Roi de *Tombut* prend le nom d'Empereur de *Melli*." This title seems to have been transferred to the King of Houssa from the decline of Timbuctoo, to which the aggrandisement of the former city is to be attributed.

† The King residing in Houssa is the King of Malla; he has seven tributary Kings. W. H.

Six	-	-	Seddah	-	Sheedah.
Seven		-	Becquay	-	Bookai.
Eight	-	-	Tacquass	-	Takoos.
Nine	-	-	Tarra	-	Tarrah.
Ten	-	-	Gwoma	-	Goumah.

Two large lakes were described close to the northward of Houssa, one called Balahar Soudan, and the other Girrigi Marragasee. Calculating the 20 journies from Timbuctoo at 18 miles each, supposing two-thirds to be made good on the horizontal distance (equal to 212 g. miles) and the course N. E., I have placed Houssa, 18° 59′ N. and 3° 59′ E. This agrees pretty well with the account of its being 17 journies from the Niger, or Quolla, which give 306 B. miles, and the horizontal distance 176 g. miles. Houssa has hitherto been laid down about 2 journies N. of the Niger. I have an impression that the city of Houssa will be found to lay about E. N. E. of Timbuctoo, of course nearer the Gambaroo, which runs through its dominions, and thus account for the reports of its being situated upon the Niger. Leo certainly meant Mallowa and the Gambaroo, when he wrote, " Melli regio quæ extendit se ad flumen quoddam quod ex Nilo (i. e. Nigro) effluit trecenta millia passuum," adding, " regnum opulentissimum, maximè artificum et mercatorum copia, frequentia templa, sacerdotes et populus qui Nigritas omnes civilitate antecedunt :" which they certainly appear to do : see a few of their articles for the British Museum. May not the Maurali of Ptolemy be the Melli of Leo, and the modern Mallowa or Marrowa ? his large adjunct to the Niger to the south indicates the two rivers. Major Rennell seems to have expected the present discovery, when he writes (commenting on Mr. Park's report that Houssa was 30 journies by land from Tombuctoo, and 45 by water) " Possibly it may be that Houssa is situated on a different river from that which passes by Tombuctoo (the Joliba,) but which may be an adjunct of it, and may run into it in the quarter of Tombuctoo." In Dapper's translation of the Description De l'Afrique du Flamand, 1686, I find " Cette contreé (Melli) s'etend environ cent lieües *le long d'un bras* du Niger."

Tarrabaleese, 50 journies westward of north, was much spoken of from the number of its market places. This must be Tripoli, the Arabic corruption of which is Trabŏlis. The Moors gave me a route to Tunis or Toonis, but I cannot recognise any name in Major Rennell's map, (which I could not procure until my return,) unless Sabbai be Sebba, and Mookanassa Mourzouk, in Fezzan. There is also another route eastward which I cannot trace. See Appendix.

From Kabarra the Quolla, continuing its course southward of east, passed by Uzzalin, Googara,* Koolmanna, Gauw, Tokogirri, (perhaps the Tokrur of Edrisi and Gatterer) Askeä, Zabirmë, and Cabi to Yaoora, which I imagine to be the Youri of Major Rennell's map.† De Lisle places a kingdom, Yaouree, south of the Niger. It is a very celebrated ferry, occurring in a variety of routes from the north of the Quolla to Ashantee, spoken of always as westward of Cassina, and with little variation as 25 journies from Timbuctoo. Now as the Moors called it one day's journey from Sego to Sansanding, and Mr. Park made it scarcely more, I will assume this as the rule to calculate the distance from Timbuctoo to Yaooree, and afterwards consider its place according to the routes from Dagwumba, through it, to Cassina. Twenty five journies from Timbuctoo would place Yaoora about 70 miles above

---

* I did not hear of the Gotoijegee, Carmasse, or Gourmon of Amadi Fatouma; it is clear that he was not very correct in names. I never once heard Silla called Sellee, Dibbie, Sibbie, or Kabra, Rakbarra.

† The Jennë Moor notices between Kabarra and Cabi, Gauw (a great kingdom) Quoülla, Askeä, Zabirma. Ptolemy has a city called Geua on the Gir.

the Berrisa in Major Rennell's map, but this makes the horizontal distance from Yaoora to Dagwumba about 850 B. miles, and therefore too great for 42 journies, the greatest number allowed in the routes from Dagwumba to Yaoora.

I would not presume to investigate after Major Rennell, it would be absurd in me to expect to throw any new interest into the discussion, but by making clear the accounts I collected ; to do which I must decline the course of the Niger from Cabi (Mr. Horneman writes it flows southward from Haoussa) even to a junction with the Bahr Kulla. For, placing Yaoora in 13° 30′ N. and 8° 30′ E. in conformity with its distance from Timbuctoo and a declining course to the Kulla, the horizontal distance to Yahndi, the capital of Dagwumba, will be 600 B. miles : now 42 journies, the greatest number allowed by the travellers, at 20 miles each, (rejecting one third, as heretofore, lost in the windings of the path) give the horizontal distance at 560 B. miles. This is certainly an additional argument to the similarity of the names Quolla and Kulla, for the identity of these rivers ; but not so strong a one as that the routes both of Moors and Negroes, allow but 40 journies from Dagwumba to the point of crossing the Niger for Houssa. The course to this point was described by the Moors as a little to the eastward of north : now 40 journies on a N. N. E. course, by the former rule, places this ferry 15° 1′ N. and 3° 33′ E. agreeing very well with our previous position of Houssa, and proving that the course of the Niger must decline considerably, for more than two extra journies would otherwise be required for the north eastward route from Dagwumba to Yaoora. Major Rennell only writes that the course of the Niger is *probably* to Wangara. Mr. Ledyard, in his comparatively minute description of that country, (which I shall notice in the route to Bornoo) says nothing of its bordering on the Niger. Major Rennell, in the construction of the geography of Mr. Horneman's report, writes, " M. D'Anville also had an idea, and so describes it in his map of Africa, 1749 (possibly from actual information,) that the Niger declined to the south beyond Gana, so that the termination of it in the lake Semegonda was $3\frac{1}{2}$ degrees of latitude to the south of Gana." There is a kingdom called Kulla as well as a river, and there is also a kingdom Quollaraba: raba being probably no more than an adjunct equal to the prefix dar, and signifying a kingdom. Mr. Dupuis, in his notes on Adams, says of an intelligent Negro, " his account was chiefly curious from his description of a nation which he called Gallo or *Quallo*, which conveyed to me an idea of a people, more advanced in the arts, and wealthier than any that I had previously heard of: within three days journey of the capital was a large lake or river which communicated with the Wed Nile." The commended arguments of the Quarterly Review, (which I have never had the advantage of reading,) must be in a great degree auxiliary, in arguing, to support the Congo hypothesis, a course of the Niger equally declined with that which I have followed for the identity of the Quolla and Kulla. The junction of the Quolla with the Bahr Abiad, or Nil, as the Moors called it, cannot be more descriptively expressed, according to every account I received, than in the words of Mr. Horneman. " Some days past I spoke to a man who had seen Mr. Brown in Darfoor, he gave me some information respecting the countries he travelled through, and told me that the communication of the Niger with the Nile was not to be doubted, but that this communication before the rainy season was very little."*

* The Jennë Moor told Mr. Hutchison, " the Quolla was the largest river in the world, and about 5 miles wide, having a very rocky channel, the banks on both sides very high, and rugged: in many parts canoes often take a day to cross, from the dangerous whirlpools, and sudden squalls; at other places the stream runs with great

We will pursue the course of the Quolla from Yaoora (where I should judge from description it must be about 3 miles wide) before we apply the routes northward of it.* One journey eastward of Yaoora, (sometimes called Yawooree by the Negroes,) it passed Nooffie, doubtless the Nyffe of Mr. Horneman and others, and which De Lisle has written Nouffy : 3 journies thence it passed Boussa, which Amadi Fatouma reported, as it was to me also (see Diary) as the place of Mr. Park's death, but I could hear nothing of the rock and door. Boussa is not in Major Rennell's map, but I observed Bousa in the map of De Lisle before alluded to ; it is probably the Berrisa of Edrisi. Twelve journies thence it passed Atagara, but, previously, Hoomee, and Rakkah.† Southward of the latter, they described an inland country called Koofee, possibly Kosie, a country I shall presently introduce, as visited by a mulatto, behind 'Lagos. Thirty journies from Atagara, it flowed through the kingdom of Quollaraba,‡ which thus falls precisely where

rapidity. The houses in its environs are either terraced or shingled, as thatch cannot resist the frequent high winds."

* The Jennë Moor has placed Gangë as an island in the Quolla just below Bousa. This must be the Gongoo of Imhammed, and Ben Ali, south of Cassina. Mr. Lucas writes " the width of the Niger is such, that even at the island of Gongoo, where the ferrymen reside, the sound of the loudest voice from the northern shore is scarcely heard."

† The Jennë Moor traces the course from Yaoora, thus : Boussa, Gangë, Wawa, Noofa, Quollaliffa, Atagara ; the only difference being the position of the latter place, possibly an error of mine, as the name Atagara was not noticed in the charts I made the Moors draw, but only in the more particular enumerations of the countries the Quolla passed ; the names of which I minuted from their utterance, and afterwards attached their remarks as interpreted to me.

‡ The Jennë Moor calls this Quolla liffa. Mr. Hutchison, who has a servant, a native of it, describes it as a very powerful kingdom, as the Shereef Brahima described it to me, and as was the impression of Mr. Dupuis. Mr. H. adds, on Negro and Moorish authority, " it is to the King of Quallowliffa that the country in which Canna, Dall, and

Major Rennell has laid down the kingdom of Kulla. Six journies thence it passed Mafeegoodoo, and 13 journies beyond, the lake Cadee or Caudee. This I should consider to be the Cauga of Edrisi, which Major Rennell has identified with the Fittri of Mr. Brown, for into this the second large branch of the Niger, or the river Gambaroo, is said to run; but it is considerably too much to the southward for the Cauga in Major Rennell's map, being, according to the accounts of the Moors, only 3 journies northward of the Quolla: yet Edrisi writes " besides a river of the name of Nile or Neel *passes by* Kauga." What inclines me to think the Cauga may be more distant from Bornoo the capital, though not from the frontier of that kingdom, (15 journies being the number reported to me as well as to Mr. Brown) is, that the Negroes of that city were not so well acquainted with this lake as the Moors. My sketch in the map, of course, represents the sketches and descriptions of the natives. They described the Cadee or Caudee as an immense water, like a small sea, frequently overflowing the neighbouring country, and sometimes so convulsed as to throw up large quantities of fish and other contents; meaning, in short, a volcanic lake. The Moors called it also the Bahr el Noä, having a tradition that the waters of the deluge retired to, and were absorbed in it. A very high mountain was spoken of, at an equal distance between the Caudee and the Quolla.* Twelve journies

Yum Yum, where cannibals are, is subject." Mr. Horneman mentions Yem Yems cannibals south of Kano 10 days; and the account is further confirmed in my subsequent geographical sketch of the interior of Gaboon. Mr. Horneman's information that the Niger flowed towards the Egyptian Nile through the land of the Heathens, which Mr. Park quoted as an argument for the Congo hypothesis, doubtless referred to these cannibals

* " At times the water of this lake is hot, and it boils and bubbles with a great noise, often overflowing the surrounding country. The bones of fish thrown up by the volcano are so numerous, that the Arabs mix them in the swish of their houses. There are a

from Caudce, the Quolla received the river Sharee from northward, which, I imagine, if not the Misselad, may be a river deriving its name from the Abu Shareb of Major Rennell's map. The Quolla was said to pass to the southward of Bagarrimee, (the Baghermee of Mr. Brown.) Kalafarradoo, (I cannot find any name nearer to this than the Courourfa of De Lisle, and Kororfa, said in Mr. Beaufoy's MSS. to be W. of Begarmee). Foör (Darfur, according to Mr. Brown, means the kingdom of Foör) and lastly to skirt Waddaï, the Waddey of Mr. Horneman, who wrote that it was east of Begharmee, and west of Darfoor ; but, as it was reported to me east of Darfoor, by every person, and as Mr. Brown did not hear of it to adjust its position, I have placed it so.*

The junction with the Nile having taken place, as Mr. Horneman before reported, south of Darfoor, they continued the course to a large country called Soonar,† indisputably the kingdom of Sennaar. Hence to Massar,‡ or Egypt, they did not always agree themselves in the various names, nor can I recognise any on the map, unless their Shewa Abenhassa be Bennassa, Minsoor, Misur, Gammeacha, Gammazie ; Sooess, Sohaig ; Kaheea, Kahoul ; Zaragoo, Nayazoogoo ; and their Lamabalara, in the country of

great many islets in the lake, which is so extensive, that they cannot see the end. Between it and the Quolla rises a very high hill, from the top of which is an extensive view ; it is a day's journey from the water on either side. The Arabs eat black rice, corn, and sweet beans, called Tummer." W. H.

* The Jennë Moor has also placed it E. of Foor. Mr. Hutchison writes the course, after him, from Atagara, thus : " Maffagoodoo, Sharee, Lake Chadee, Phorr (beginning of Arabs) " Wadie." Mr. Horneman writes " A great part of the people of Wadey, together with their King, are Arabs."

† Mr. Hutchison has written it Sooänar.

‡ " Cairo is still called, in the figurative language of the East, Misr, without an equal ; Misr, the mistress of the world." Quarterly Review. Mr. Hutchison writes, that the Moors told him it was so called after Misraim, who settled there.

Egypt, the Bahr be la ma of Mr. Horneman ; of the latter there can be no doubt.*

My friend, the Shereef Brahima had, as well as some others, been to Mecca and Medina. I place great reliance on this man's information (invariably confirmed by the Negroes) from his caution and diffidence, and my experience of his character; for he was ultimately a valuable friend to the Mission : he was the only Moor who dared to refuse to be present at human sacrifices. The MS. No. 2. is his writing, and professedly the route from Dagwumba through Bornoo to Massar,† it consists of six pages well written. This would have been a valuable man to have engaged to travel through the interior, for he was capable of making circumstantial minutes, and I think he might have been engaged to do so by a moderate Fort pay. The Moors talk much of the King of

---

* The following, in the left hand column, are the places or countries as written by Mr. Hutchison, after the Jennë Moor, agreeing with those the Moors reported to me.

Shuewa - - - -	Shewa Abenassa.
Swiss - - - -	Sooess.
Zall - - - -	Zaloo.
Machazoogee - - -	Machawazoo.
Tabarbass, cultivation, volcano from the Quolla two days, two days to the top, - -	} Tabarrabass.
Askanderee - - - -	Askandaraia or Sakunderree.

The latter place is Alexandria. The Moors called the Mediterranean Sea to me by two names, Baharlë Malee, and Sabbaha Bahoori. Mr. Hutchison writes it Baramela or Bahermale, and adds, " Seven rivers from Africa turn their course to it, but only two reach the shores, of which the Nile is one. The rush of the waters of the Nile when they meet the sea, is so great, that the waves are driven into the air with great force, and retire like waves against a rock. The Red Sea, they say, assumes various colours at different periods from seven streams pouring their course into it, salt water and fresh, red, blue, yellow, &c."

† " Half of the inhabitants of Massar are white, and half black ; they have a Fort and Governor." W. H.

Santambool, * as a powerful monarch and formidable to the Christians.

It will excite surprise that I heard nothing of Wangara,† as was the case with Mr. Brown, not even after I had, contrary to my general custom, submitted the name: but I heard very much spontaneously of Oongooroo. Mr. Horneman called Wangara, Ungura, and De Lisle, Ouangara, we shall find it in the route from Yaoora to Bornoo or Barranoo. Bornoo was described to me about northeast from Yaoora, which agrees very well with Major Rennell's position, established beyond all contradiction short of an observation, but, the horizontal distance, (lowering the place of Yaoora as I have done) thence to Bornoo would be upwards of 1000 B. miles, whereas they described it to be but 51 journies, which allowing 20 miles to each, as the country was said to be much more favourable to travelling, and the path more direct than that we came, would give but an horizontal distance of 680 B. miles. Mr. Horneman heard that Bornu was but 15 journies from Kassina; I was told 33 if walked, 19 if rode. Major Rennell has made the distance about 30 journies, considering the 15 journies applicable to the western boundaries of the empire, and not to the capital.

We will now return to Yahndi and proceed northwards to Houssa. Nineteen journies from Yahndi is Matchaquawdie, six beyond is Goorooma, 10 thence Dolooë, subject to Goorooma, and only five journies from the Quolla, described as about two miles wide there. When Amadi Fatouma mentioned that he passed

---

* Stambool is the Arabic pronunciation of the familiar or vulgar name of Constantinople, the etymology of which is ιϛαμαι πολιν.

† Mr. Hutchison writes, " Wangara is the name of a region comprehending Mosee Kong, and other neighbouring countries south of the Niger (if not some to the north of it) but Oongooroo is the name of the country laying between Cassina and Bornoo.)" Mr. Park has *Wangeera* in the route from Sego to the coast of Guinea.

Gourouma, I should suppose he meant this kingdom of Goorooma, Dolooë, as subject to it, being probably included under that name. I must impress, however, that this northern route from Dagwumba to the Niger, being, with that from Kong to Jennë, the only ones unauthenticated, otherwise than by cross examination, I do not report them with the same confidence, which I do the others. Two journies from the northern bank of the Quolla is Gamhadi, to which three large towns belong, Dogondaghi, Toodonkassalee, and Toompasseä, and numerous dependent crooms. There were three routes from Gamhadi, the first northward to Houssa 15 journies, passing the large river Gambaroo the ninth, between which and Houssa is a district called Zessa. The second route is to Katinnee, a city and state of the Mallowa kingdom, one month from the Quolla. On this route the Gambaroo is crossed the tenth day, and Sowhoondë, Souoola, (perhaps Sala) Quattara-quassce, Doorooma, Soroo, Zabbakou, Dinka, Doochingamza, and Dammisamia were mentioned as large towns on the route. The third route was through the Fillanee country, (doubtless the Fullan* of Ben Ali) which had been frequently at war with Mallowa, to the kingdom of Kallaghee, 14 journies from the Quolla, the Gambaroo being passed the tenth. The numerals of Kallaghee are

One	-	-	Gadee.
Two	-		Sillil.
Three	-		Quan
Four	-		Foolloo.
Five	-		Vydee.
Six	-	-	Zoodoo.
Seven	-		Etkassa.

* " The dress of the people of Fullan (a country to the west of Kassina) resembles the cloth of which the plaids of the Scotch Highlanders are made." Ben Ali.

Eight	-	Shiddowka.
Nine	-	Woollaä.
Ten	- -	Woma.

A country called Barrabadi was described eastward of Mallowa, between it and Bornoo; its numerals corresponded with those of Bornoo.

We will now return again to Dagwumba, and follow the route thence, over the Quolla, through Yaoora to Bornoo. Gamba we have already described as five journies north eastward of Yahndi, thence two journies, over a high mountain called Yerim, and across a river running southwards (which the Moors called Mory, but which it would seem is the continuation of the Karhala) is Gooroosie, four journies thence Zoogoo, probably the Zeggo of Major Rennell's map; 10 farther the kingdom of Barragoo. De Lisle has placed his kingdom of Bourgou thereabouts. North-westward of Barragoo is Koomba, the Kombah of Major Rennell's map. The position of this kingdom is pretty well ascertained, because those who came from it, described Goorooma as its northern neighbour, and Barragoo to be the first kingdom passed through in their journies to the coast below Whydah. Eight journies from Barragoo is Toombeä, three beyond is Goodoobirree. A river running to the Quolla (as it was said, but more probably from it) called Leeäsa, flows close to the eastward of this path, and is crossed, going from Goodoobirree southwards, to a large king-dom called Yariba by the Moors, but Yarba more generally by the natives. Major Rennell has drawn a river communicating with the Niger close to Youri, so has De Lisle. This river Leeäsa is the only one I heard of, answering in the least degree to that of Sidi Hamet, but Wassana was a name unknown. Aquallie is the frontier town of Yariba, one journey from Goodoobirree, and one from Bootee, second only to the capital, Katanga, four journies beyond it. Yariba was described to be about 24 journies, through Hio, (its immediate neighbour) from Arătakassee or Alătakassee, which we shall hereafter recognise in Ardra: this determines its position pretty well.* Dahomey was said to be tributary to Yariba, as well as to Hio, which I have an impression is also tributary to Hio. From Hio to Daliomey is seven journies. The military are despotic in Hio, they always intercept the new King on his way to the palace, and demand his naming some neighbouring country for their invasion and plunder, before they confirm him. The King before the present, had named Dahomey, but after three years neglect of the fulfilment, he ordered the army against a northern neighbour. The army went, wasted and pillaged the country, but when within a day's march of the capital on their return, they sent deputies to enjoin his abdication, as inevitable to a falsehood to them; he was obstinate; they arrived and cut off his head. The numerals of Hio are

One - -	Innee.
Two -	Eygee.
Three -	Etta.
Four -	Ernee.
Five - -	Aroon.
Six - -	Effa.
Seven -	Eggay.
Eight -	Eggo.
Nine -	Essun.
Ten - -	Eywaw.

* Mr. Hutchison sends me this route, as given him by the Jennë Moor, thus, (supposing me not to have heard of Yariba) " from Goodaberry, over Lasa small water to Quolla, at Boussa; few hours walk to Yaraba; 28 days from Dahomey:" he adds, " recollect that the King of Dahomey is tributary to the King of Yaraba, who is the same in that quarter, as the King of Ashantee is here."

The Hio man, who gave me the above numerals, spoke of the Apaccas as a more powerful northern neighbour, but I never heard of them from any other person.

Yariba must certainly be the Yarba of Imhammed, though he described it as 18 or 20 journies from Gonjah towards the N.W., for he is likely to have been incorrect in this, because we have proved him to be so, in stating, that Ashantee was the capital of Tonouwah, which appears to be a district or town of Dagwumba, the people of which kingdom are by no means warlike as he represented them, nor have they any notion of taming the elephant: he reported that Calanshee was a dependency of Ashantee, whereas no Ashantee knows the name; that Gonjah was 46 journies from the coast, when it is but 30. Major Rennell reasonably conceived the Yarba of Imhammed to be the Yarra of De Lisle, at the back of Sierra Leone, but as this country is not preserved in his own map, I presume it cannot be of much consequence, politically or commercially, whereas Yariba, indisputably eastward of Kong, is always announced to enquirers, both by Moors and Negroes, as a very powerful, and much frequented kingdom. Another argument is, that all the Moors I saw at Coomassie, were almost ignorant of the countries westward, only speaking of those their enquiries for the source of the Quolla had made known to them : indeed, I did not see one who had travelled westward, or south westward of Bambarra, but our Accra linguist told me that he had recognised a Moor at the Rio Pongos, whom he had seen in Coomassie (when sent there on the eve of the second Ashantee invasion) who told him that he had been two months travelling from Kong, and crossed a very large river. Imhammed's Affow (if not Taffoo, or the Inta country) I conceive to be Afflou, a town and district of the Krepee or Kerrapay country, and a short walk from the sea by Quitta, westward of Yarba, as he says, but more than eight journies.

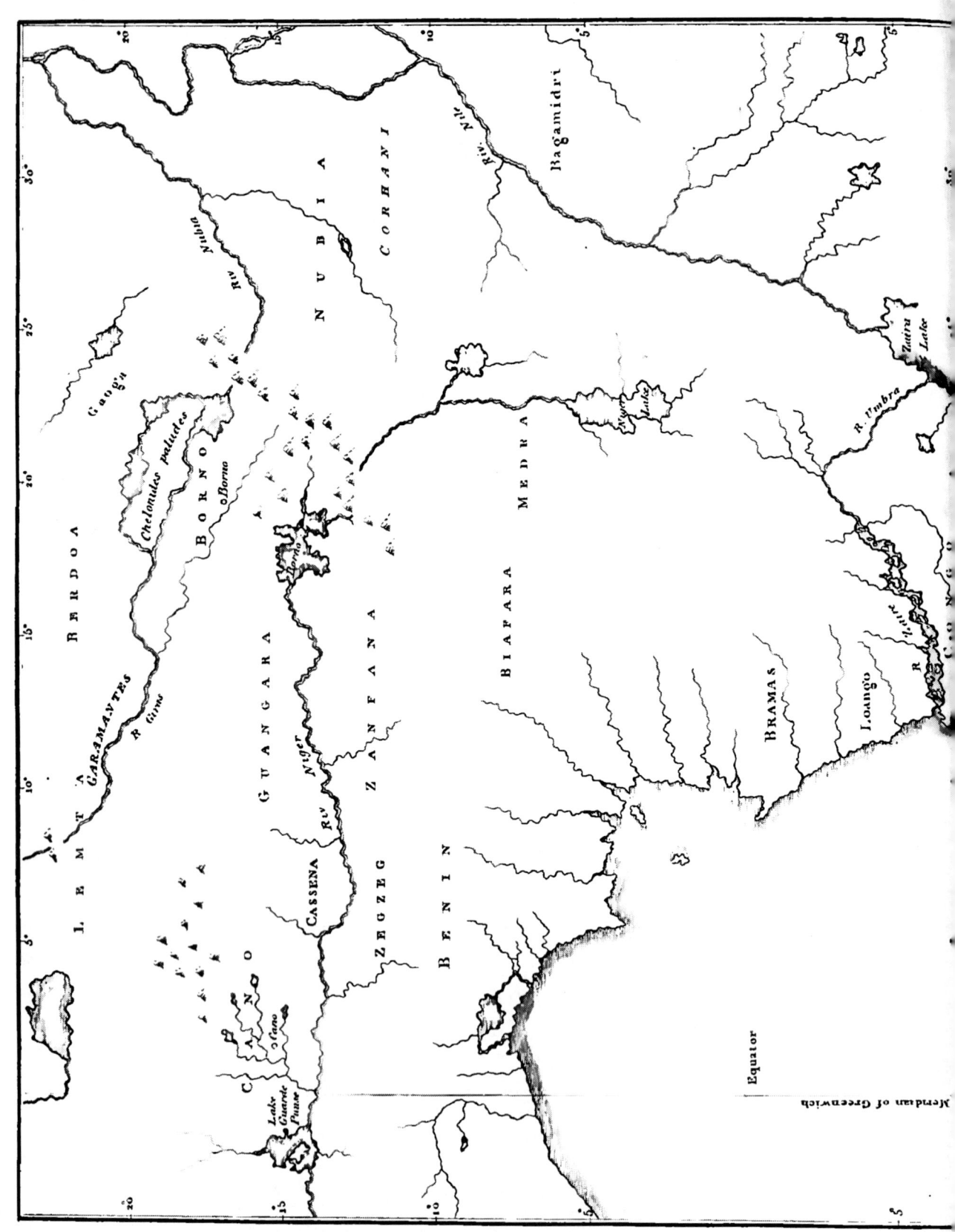

The Kerrapay country, which is extensive and independent, will be described, in proceeding from Cape Coast Castle, along the coast, eastward.

To return to the route from Yahndi to Yaoora, three journies from Goodoobirree towards the Quolla through Gillimakafoo, Garagaroogee, and Paänghee, is the large city of Kaiama, and four beyond it, through Mahalaba, (the nearest name to the Malel of Edrisi,) Marramoo, and across the small river Wooroo, (running to the Quolla) is the city of Wauwaw,* three journies from the Quolla. Ten journies from the northern bank, through Yaoora, and skirting the eastern limits of Zamfara, is Goobirree, so called by the Moors, and Goobur by the Negroes.† Mr. Beaufoy learned that Gubur was to the south of Wangara, and De Lisle writes it Goubour. Thence to Kassina, having crossed the large river Gambaroo, is eight journies. Eighteen journies, calculated at 18 miles each on a N. E. course, from the altered position of Yaoora, would place Kassina in 15° 43′ N. and 10° 43′ E., instead of 16° N. and 11° 45′ E. Mr. Lucas learned that Kassina was five journies from the Niger, or about 100 miles from that water, which it is likely to be from the upper branch or the Gambaroo, which river skirting Kanoo, and Oongooroo, (or Wangara,) before it descends to the lake Cadee, (though I could not prove satisfactorily that it did so,) would account for Edrisi's placing Kano, and Wangara, on the Niger.‡ From Kassina to Dawoorra is six

---

* The Jennë Moor gave this route thus : Wawa to Kiama, a great kingdom, 3 days ; close to the eastward a desert ; 1 day Garagroogee ; 1 day Wala ; 1 day Goodaberry.

† " Guber est à cent lieuës de Gago vers l'Orient, et en est separé par un desert inhabitable à quatorze ou quinze lieuës du Niger. Cette contrée est entre de hautes montagnes, et toute pleine de villages ; celui où le Prince tient sa Cour a quelque mille maisons." Dapper.

‡ I shall adjoin an outline of the great river in one of the maps of Dapper's Descrip-

journies: this must be the Daura of Mr. Horneman, though in the drawing of the Marrabut it is placed north of Kano. From Dawoorra to Kanoo is four journies. D'Anville placed it 90 miles to the N. E. of Kassina, and in the drawing just alluded to, it is placed inland northward of the Niger. The only authority for supporting Edrisi's position of it, is what Mr. Matra was told at Marocco. The Moor who informed Mr. Beaufoy that boats went with the stream to Ghincä, (the Gano or Kano of Major Rennell) placed Jinnie between it and Houssa, so gross an inaccuracy as to justify our doubting him on the other point. The Ginea of Leo more probably meant Jennë, and he seems to write of that navigation as a distinct one from that to Melli eastward.* From Kanoo, through the large towns Madagee and Adagia, to Oongooroo is nine journies, but seven on a joma or camel, "Est iter octo dierum versus orientem" (Edrisi.) From Oongooroo to Barranoo is 15 journies on foot according to the Moors, nine on horseback according to the Negroes, by route No. 12. Bornoo or Barranoo was spoken of as the first empire in Africa,† the King's name, according to the Moors, was Baba Alloo, but the Negroes called him Massinnama.‡ Kassina, and the intermediate countries on

tion de l'Afrique, traduit du Flamand, because the book is very scarce, and I do not remember to have seen the Niger, the Gir, or the Congo so laid down in any other.

* The removal of Cano from the banks of the Niger agreeable with every report I received, is supported by Dapper. " A cent soixante et dix lieuës d'Agadez et à deux cent du Niger on trouve ce royaume (Guber), au milieu du quel est la ville de Cano fermée de murailles de bois et de pierre, et qui a des maisons bâties de même."

† " The Mahometans of Senaar number Bornoo amongst the four most powerful monarchies of the world; the other three are Turkey, Persia, and Abyssinia: the sovereign of Bornoo is more powerful than the Emperor of Morocco." Lucas.

‡ Ce royame, qu'on croit avoir été la demeure des Garamantes, est une vaste Province au levant de Gangara, qui s'étend vers l'Orient l'espace de cent soixante dix lieuës et est éloignée du Niger de cinquante.

the route, were subject to him with many others. One district belonging to Bornoo was named Panaroo, and the vassal King or governor of it, Yandee Kooma. A small river, called Gaboöa* by the Negroes, ran southwards near Bornoo, and six journies eastward from it, close to Aweeac, a large one Zerrookoo Keroboobee. Mr. Horneman writes, the Wad el Gazel is not a river, but a large and fertile valley. The Negroes of Bornoo were well acquainted with Baghermee. Imhammed's recollection of the numerals of Bornoo must have been very imperfect, for I have written them at least half a dozen times, both from Moorish and Negro inhabitants, and my spelling agreed with that of another person present. They are

			Imhammed's.
One	-	Leskar	Lakkah.
Two	-	Ahndee	Endee.
Three	-	Yaskar	Nieskoo.
Four	-	Deegah	Dekoo.
Five	-	Oöogoo	Okoo.
Six	-	Araskoo	Araskoo.
Seven	-	Tooloor	Naskoo.
Eight	-	Woskoo	Tallóre.
Nine	-	Likkar	L'ilkar.
Ten	-	Meeägoo	Meikoo.

Ben Ali said the language of the common people of Bornoo had a strong resemblance to that of the neighbouring Negroes. Mr. Lucas writes that no less than 30 languages are spoken in these dominions. The following are the numerals of Maïha, one month to the north-eastward, subject to Bornoo, and the King's name Smaï Doonama.

* Mr. Hutchison heard of another river near Bornoo called Koomoodoo gaiguina: he could not hear of the Wad el Gazel.

One	- -	Lagen.
Two	-	Indë.
Three	-	Eäska.
Four	-	Daäger.
Five	- -	Ohoo.
Six	-	Araska.
Seven	--	Tooloor.
Eight	-	Weska.
Nine	- -	Likar.
Ten	- -	Inagoon.

The Negroes called Kanem, Kandem; were well acquainted with Doomboo, and spoke much of the kingdom of Asben.

We will now return to Cape Coast Castle, and seek the best descriptive authorities, in aid of the observations which have been made by the Commissioners and others, for the maritime geography from the river Assinee to Lagos.

The latitude and longitude of Cape Coast (called by the natives Igwa, and in the Affettoo district) according to Messrs. Ludlam and Dawes, the Government Commissioners who surveyed the coast in 1810, is 5° 6′ N. and 1° 51′ W. Elmina, the native name of which is Addïna, is about seven miles to windward of Cape Coast. Twelve miles from Elmina is Commenda, an English fort, the town is called by the natives Akatayki, the Dutch fort was destroyed in the American war. Nine miles thence is Chama, or Assĕma, at the mouth of the Boosempra. Six hours pull up the river, is an island, where Attobra, one of the Warsaw caboceers, who supplies the Dutch with canoes, is building a large house to retire to; four hours above which is his croom. Colonel Starrenberg was pulled three days up the river in a canoe; his progress was much impeded by rocks, and at length arrested by a large cataract, which, being considered a powerful fetish by the natives, the canoe-men dared not to approach. Nine miles from Chama, where the Dutch have a fort called Sebastian, is Succondee, the first town in the Ahanta country. The English fort was destroyed by the French in the American war, but there is a settlement house. The Dutch fort is called Orange. Four miles from Succondee is Taccorary, and a Dutch fort. Nine miles beyond is Boutrie where the Dutch have a fort, formerly belonging to the Brandenburgh Company. Three miles from Boutrie is Dix-Cove, or Nfooma, and in the interval Boossooä, the capital of Ahanta, which is divided into three districts, Amanfoo, Adoom, and Poho. The first is about one journey (through Geämma) behind Boossooa, and one from the river Ancobra, the caboceer is of the next consequence to the King, whose power and means are extremely limited. The two latter districts are not more than half a journey behind Taccorary. The small river running into the sea at Boutrie, rises in the Adoom district, which is said to abound in gold, but the pits have not been worked for many years, from their fear of the Warsaws. Amanfee also abounds in very fine gold, which is generally found in quartz, and is ground upon stones arranged under large sheds for the purpose. In a respectable periodical publication of the last year, I observe, the King of Ashantee called King of Ahanta, Inta, or Ashantee; this is one of the many proofs of the indiscriminate ideas of that monarch before the Mission. Eighteen miles from Dix-Cove passing Achooma and Accoda, (where the Dutch have a fort, and which is close to Cape Three Points) are the ruins of Hollandia, formerly belonging to the Brandenburgh Company, and called Fort Royal Fredericksburg. Sixteen miles farther is Axim, where the Dutch fort Anthony, their Vice Presidency, is situated. The people of Axim speak a dialect of the Ahanta. About two miles westward is the mouth of the Ancobra, so called by the Portuguese from its windings, the

native name is Seënna.   Col. Starrenberg, who went up the river
as far as the ruins of Elisa Carthago, the extreme navigable point,
for any but a very small canoe, says, he cannot form any accurate
idea of the distance, but supposes it was about 20 Dutch miles
and the course N. E.   Meredith says 50 English: he was very
careless and incorrect in writing, " the French built a fort on the
right bank of this river, and· at about 50 miles from its mouth;
where they had a great gold trade, that soon excited the jealousy
of the Dutch, who expelled them.   The Dutch however did not
long enjoy this acquisition, for the chief got embroiled with the
natives, and betook himself to the desperate remedy of blowing up
the fort."   Elisa Carthago was built by the Dutch governor Ruig-
haven, who died, as appears by his tomb stone at Elmina, before
1700.   The French never had any but a small factory, almost at
the mouth of the river, and the Dutch officer in charge of Elisa
Carthago had enjoyed a good trade many years before the cupidity of the natives reduced him to the act of despair, related by
Bosman, and still recorded by the natives, who narrated it to Col.
Starrenberg.   The following is from the Latin translation of Dr.
Reynhaut : " The chief of Elisa Carthago being at variance with
the natives, who invested the fort, and finding he could not resist
them any longer" (for as the story goes, he had been reduced to
fire pieces of rock gold from the want of bullets) " feigned to treat
with them, and invited them for that purpose into the hall of the
fort, under which he had placed several barrels of gunpowder, and
a small boy with a match, ordering him to apply it directly he
stamped his foot on the floor of the hall above.   This he did, after
reproaching the natives with their cupidity, and they were all
blown up together.   One of the servants of the fort had just before
contrived to effect his escape with most of the papers."   In
navigating from the mouth of the Ancobra or Seënna to Elisa

Carthago, the following towns, on the banks, are passed, Boasso, Tarbo, Marmeresse, Ejujan, Tetchbrouw, Gura, Barnesoe, Uromanio, Afamkan, and Aduwa. Gura is a small state, the people of which speak the same language as those of Axim. From Aduwa there are three grand roads, one to the Aowin country, one to the Dankara, and one to Asankarie, a considerable town in Warsaw. From Aduwa to Dankara numerous small crooms are passed through, and the first large one of the latter country is Kenkoomabaraso, only three journies from Coomassie. The people of Dankara come to Axim to trade. From Aduwa to Aowin the first considerable town is Taqua. The Warsaw country is governed by four caboceers, independent of each other, of whose relation and power, the best idea I can give, is by comparing it with that of the tyrants Geron and Theron, who ruled at the same time in Sicily. Intiffa, the richest caboceer, and whose power extends the farthest, resides at Abbradie, one short journey from Elmina. Cudjo Miensa (Miensa is the numeral three) is his principal counsellor, and will succeed him. Nerbehin was formerly the residence of Quashee Jacon, another independent caboceer, but of Intiffa's family; he was driven from thence by Esson Cudjo, who now rules there: he fled to Samcow (situated about one day's journey on the frontier of Warsaw, behind Succondee) of which Musoe, a slave of his, has raised himself to be the caboceer, and now protects his master until Esson Cudjoe's death. Attobra, another independent caboceer, lives at Dabroadie, on the Boosempra. The greatest breadth of the Warsaw country is supposed to be 60 B. miles, and the greatest length 100 or 120. About 28 miles from the Ancobra, begins the kingdom of Amanaheä, in which the English fort Apollonia is situated: it extends about 100 miles along the coast, but not more than 20 in-land. The various numerals of the coast will be submitted in an essay on the Fantee language.

F f

Barely four miles eastward of Cape Coast is Moree, and the Dutch fort Nassau. Six miles from Moree is Annamaboe, the most complete fortification in the country; five miles thence Cormantine, the first fort possessed by the English, and built by them about the middle of the seventeenth century. It was taken afterwards by the Dutch, and being stormed, was almost destroyed by the Ashantee army, before it attacked Annamaboe: the position is very commanding. Tantumquerry, a small English fort, is about 18 miles from Cormantine, (crossing the small river Amissa, an hour's walk in-land from which is Mankasim, the capital of the Braffoe district of Fantee) the natives call the town Tuam. Eight miles from Tantum is the town of Apam, where is a Dutch fort and a small river. Eight miles from Apam is Simpah or Winnebah. The people of Simpah are Fantees, but their language is called Affoottoo. They are in the district of Agoona. About nine miles from Simpah is the Dutch fort Berracoe, the natives call the town Seniah. Attah of Akim laid a contribution on this fort in March 1811. About 27 miles from Berracoe is Accra, or Inkran, once subject to Aquamboo, which people, according to Isert, formerly drove them to Popo. Meredith fully describes Accra and the environs, but he does not mention that according to the natives the Portuguese settled here first, (Isert writes in 1452) and exercising the greatest cruelties and enormities, were extirpated by the Accras (their town was then situated a little behind the present), who executed the governor and his countrymen, on a spot whence they still take the earth to rub a new born child, in commemoration of the event. ·Accra, according to the observations of the Commissioners, is in 5° 20′ N. and 10′ W. Mr. Meredith, after quoting this observation, placed it in his outline of the coast in 58′ E. Between two and three miles from the English fort, is Christiansburg Castle, the Danish head-quarters.

We will follow* Isert in his route from Accra to the Volta, as he travelled it several times. " Two miles from Christiansburg is Labbodee, where there was formerly a fort: this is the residence of the grand fetish, and the Bishop. Two miles to Pessin, two to Temmen, where the Dutch had a small fort, abandoned in 1781, two (leaving Nimboe a little in the bush) to Ponee, a deserted Dutch fort, now a Dutch factory; two miles thence (crossing a brakke streek or low land, up to the shoulders in the rains, and 300 fathoms broad, sometimes called Ponee river) are great and small Pram Pram, where the English have a small fort or fortified factory. Two long miles thence is Friedensbourg fort at Ningo, the people of which speak a different language called Adampee, (the name given to their country,) a mixture of Ashantee, Kerrapee, and Accra; it is a republic." Behind Adampee is the Crobo mountain, the people of which, though but a few hundreds, have hitherto baffled the Ashantees, by leaving their croom at the bottom of the mountain, which is of great height, rugged, accessible but by one narrow path, and with springs of water on the top, whence they roll down upon their enemies, the large stones and fragments of rock which abound. " From Adampee I went in one day to

* I observe, in a modern publication, Dr. Isert's described as a second visit to Africa, under the auspices of the Danish government, encouraged by his reports to attempt colonization in Aquapim, and that he died from anxiety and exertion. This was not the case, it was his first and only visit, the Danes never attempted colonization, and he embarked for the West Indies as I have before stated. Having read the above, however, I wrote to Dr. Reynhaut, who translated some passages from the Dutch into Latin for me, and the following is an extract from his letter in reply. " Quod attinet Iserti in Africam reditum, ibique ejus obitum, ficta hæc est fama. Verum est juxta Quitam post victoriam in Augnacos populos reportatam, Danos arcem condidisse, cui nomen insigniverunt Prinzenstein; sed nullæ culturæ incubuerunt, nec colonias struxerunt, nec minus falsum est umquam Isertum in Africæ littoræ inferiora regis jussu rediisse, colonias extruendi gratia, nam præter opus Botanicum quod Floræ Guinensis titulo occurrit, nullum aliud de illo scriptum existit."

Addah, 12 miles. Two and a half from Ningo is a croom called Laï, the inhabitants of which have removed, some to Addah, some to Ningo: the English had a factory here, long gone to ruin. One mile west of the Volta, there was formerly a croom called Foutchi." Reckoning four English miles to one Danish or Dutch, Addah would be 96 miles from Christiansburg, but Meredith makes it but 67, therefore we will take the medium and call it 87. From the Volta to Cape St. Paul's is five leagues by sea, according to Dalzel, and 15 miles by land, according to Norris's map of Dahomey and its environs. Quitta, about 12 miles from it (according to Norris) by the observation made in H. M. S. Argo in 1802, is in 5° 45′ N. and 1° 29′ 30″ E. by chronometer. Accra lies, according to the Commissioners, in 10′ W. Taking the medium between Isert and Meredith, Christiansburg Castle, about three miles eastward of the English fort, is 87 from Addah, but as that place is six miles from the mouth of the Volta, we will call it 81: allowing one mile for the breadth of the river and 18 miles for the difference of longitude between it and Quitta, (according to Norris,) the distance from English Accra to Quitta will be 103 B. miles, which being equal to 89 geographical miles, place Quitta in 1° 19′ E. instead of 1° 29′ 30″ as by the observation of the Argo, and that supposing the whole distance to be made good horizontally, which is impossible. Wherefore I should think Isert, who had travelled it, was more likely to be correct in making the distance from Christiansburg to Addah 96 miles, than Meredith in calling it 67.

Norris's observation, placing Cape St. Paul's in 5° 52′ N., I conceive to be incorrect, as that of the Argo must be preferred, which places Quitta in 5° 42′ N., instead of 6° 2′ N., as in Norris's map. This should not have escaped Mr. Dalzel's notice in the "New Sailing Directions," where both observations are cited in the same page, without any remark on the inconsistency, for Quitta and not St. Paul's, is thus made the Cape or western limit of the Bight, the eastern side of which is called the Bight of Benin, I regret, amongst other disadvantages, that of not having the opportunity to consult the chart of Mr. Demayne (the master of H. M. S. Amelia) which is said to be more accurate than any other.*

Quitta is included in an independent state of Kerrapay, called Agwoona, which extends thence along the coast to the Volta; the towns from that river to Quitta are Attoko, Terrobee, Footee, Agwoona, Whiëe, and Tegbay. Agwoona lays half a mile from the shore, and about 15 miles from the Volta. The inhabitants of all the other towns are obliged by the law to bury their dead in Agwoona, the capital; the caboceer of which is supreme over the others, but not absolute. Between Quitta and Popo, lay the Kerrapay towns Egbiffeemee, to which several of the Quittas have retired, Edjenowah, Oöoglooboöe, and Afflou or Afflahoo, a little way from the beach. These towns are governed by caboceers, independent of each other, as well as of Agwoona; and in the last a mixture of Adampë and Kerrapay is spoken, accounted for by the emigration of a large body of the former people. Another independent state of Kerrapay is Tettaytokoo, 2 journies behind Popo; the King is said to be despotic, and the capital composed of circular houses. There is also another smaller interior state, governed by a

* Since I have been at sea I have drawn the maritime part of my map again, and laid down the Forts and other points according to the observations quoted in Norrie, (4th edition, 1816,) which agree so very nearly with those of the Commissioners in the two instances cited, that I conclude he has been allowed to copy the whole series from their papers, which I believe have never been published. Even in Dr. Mackay's valuable publication, Cape Coast Castle is laid 1° 23' too much to the eastward. I presume too that the observations made by H. M. S. Amelia, are part of those quoted by Norrie, although the Argo's observations of the longitude of Quitta and Whydah are not confirmed. I observe a small error which makes 1' 28" N. and 7' 24" E. the difference between Kormantine and Annamaboe, the former is only 5 miles eastward of the latter.

caboceer called Quaminagah. Tadoo, however, is allowed to be the largest kingdom of Kerrapay, 6 journies behind Popo, (which the Fantees call Inshan, but the natives Taun or Taum) described as a large town; and the Accra language is spoken there as well as the Kerrapay, in consequence of the temporary emigration of the former people in 1680. The Kerrapay numerals are

One - -	Eddee.
Two -	Effee.
Three -	Eltong.
Four -	Ennay.
Five - -	Altong.
Six - -	Adday.
Seven -	Adrinnee.
Eight -	Ennee.
Nine -	Indee.
Ten -	Owoo.

The Negroes of this country are of a much more daring and desperate character than their neighbours, and were always the most severely treated in the slave ships. Mr. Meredith, who writes it Crepee, placed it west of the Volta.

Whydah, according to an observation of the Argo, is 6° 14′ N. 2° 31′ E. I do not recollect Dalzel to have mentioned that Anotto is produced in the neighbourhood of Whydah. I am not certain whether it is by the Bixa orellana; but the shrub at Whydah may be classed under Polyandria Monogynia. Lambe made it 200 miles from Whydah beach to Abomey; Norris 112, Dalzel 96. By Mr. Norris's own account of his journey, not more than 20 hours were occupied in travelling, which at 4 miles an hour, the greatest pace which I think the hammock men can average, would make the distance 80 miles. An officer in this service went to Dahomey, without hurrying, in 3 days; and considers a dispatch would reach it in 2 : he thinks it can scarcely be 70 miles; but calling it 80 as above, and supposing 54, two thirds, to be the horizontal distance made good, equal to almost 47 G. miles, Abomey would lay in 7° 12′ N. Yet Mr. Dalzel writes it lays in about 7° 59′ N. : Whydah being in about 6° 25′ in the map affixed to his history; this requires 108 B. miles to be made good on the horizontal distance, whereas he calls that of the whole journey but 96, and Mr. Norris, who drew the map, 112. The public were certainly indebted to Mr. Dalzel for the History of Dahomey, but it was his duty, as an intelligent and considerate man, to correct such an error as this ; and if the author of the preface had reflected, he would not have written,'' The map, is that of Mr. Norris, with a few additions, which for the places on the coast, and the position of Abomey, is near enough to the truth.'' Mr. Dalzel should have corrected a greater error in this map, the course of the Lagos river, for altering which I shall presently quote his own authority in addition to others.

An officer in this service, who resided at Lagos three years, and is the only European resident who has survived of those who have made the attempt, enables me to correct the following errors. The Pelican bank is much smaller than it appears on the charts ; the Doo island (which lays N. W. and not N. of Lagos town) where the natives go to make fetish, is not more than one mile in circumference ; and there is no river of that name. The beach over which the Portuguese and French (who never cross the bar, where there are 3 fathoms water) transport their goods to the canoes, is not more than 100 yards wide, instead of one mile. In Norris's map prefixed to Dalzel's History, the Lagos river-is made to cross the path to Dahomey near Torë. In the Sailing Directions for the Coast of Africa, to which Mr. Dalzel was the chief contributor, and who revised the work, we find, '' River Lagos is the mouth not only of the river of that name, which runs to the *eastward from Ardrah,*" &c. and the river Mr. Norris crossed near Torë, which he calls pretty deep and rapid, but with a bridge over it, is by the account of other gentlemen, officers in this service, who have been to Dahomey, no more than a marsh.   The gentleman before mentioned to have resided three years in Lagos, informs me the grand branch of that river flows from the northward of the island, where the pretended river Doo is placed, he found it so wide on entering it, that being in the middle, where there are 10 fathoms water, he could scarcely see the land on either side.   The current is impetuous, and floating islands, and large masses of alluvial matter come down with such force, in the rainy season, as to trip vessels from their anchors in the English road. De Lisle makes the Lagos river flowing from the N., and the French are allowed to be much better acquainted with this part of the coast. That called the West river in Norris's map, is only a creek ; and what he calls the Lagos river, and draws running close to Bădaggry, Ardrah, and passing Torë, is the Western river. Bădaggry is not more than 5 or 7 miles from the beach, instead of 15, and the tide only ebbs and flows so far.   Ardrah is from 25 to 30 miles from the beach, instead of 18; and the river is crossed at about one-third of the distance from the sea : this is what we call Porto Novo, for there is not more than beachmen's huts on the shore opposite the anchorage. The natives call Ardrah Aratakassee, or Allatakassee, and the country Essaäm, or the great. The river continues its course not more than 100 yards from the sea, at Whydah, and proceeds equally close (indeed frequently the ridge between them is covered with water) until passing Quitta, it falls into the Volta near the mouth.

The above mentioned gentleman proves the informant of Adams's editor incorrect, in stating that the Houssa traders were constantly to be met with at Lagos, previous to the abolition of the slave trade, for it has always been the policy of Kosie, a kingdom on the eastern bank of the river, and about 60 miles inland from the mouth, to prevent all intercourse between the traders of the interior, and those of Lagos, to secure to themselves the exorbitant profits they made as the brokers or medium. The Europeans who traded at Lagos, once meditated forcing a passage up the river in armed boats, and a vessel of 18 guns was got over the bar, and anchored close to Lagos town ; but the project was abandoned as too perilous. Sometime afterwards the King of Kosie desired a European might visit him, to gratify his curiosity, and that of his people ; but no one being willing, a mulatto, named Peter Brown, was dressed up and sent. This man, being now at Cape Coast, I have questioned. Several armed men were sent to conduct him, and relays of canoe men sufficient to continue brisk pulling ; which they did from the evening till the next day, before he left the river to proceed by land ; it was still very wide, and more than 4 fathoms deep ; considerably, for aught he knew, for the bamboo poles of that length, with which the natives push the canoe forward, when they get close enough to the banks to do so, would not touch the bottom in the middle. Relays of hammock men then carried him at a brisk pace until evening, when he reached Kosie, which he described as a town of great extent, and the buildings to resemble those in the drawings of Coomassie. The King gave orders that the crowd should not intrude themselves into his house, treated him very handsomely, and dismissed him after three days. He only heard the people of Kosie speak of two great nations, the Hios, and the Awissees.

The gentleman before mentioned has an impression, from all the enquiries he recollects to have made, of the slaves of the interior, that the merchants convey them by water the greater part of the way ; and their reports were strengthened by his having an opportunity of seeing canoes brought from Kosie to Lagos, and purchased from the slave merchants of the interior. They were very superior in size and convenience to those of the coast, were covered in, with a distinct apartment for the trader and his wives, and would hold a hundred slaves. I never heard any slaves speak of being brought any part of the way by water, but I have not seen any who were brought to Kosie or Lagos.

The Karhala is the only large river likely to communicate with, or to form that of Lagos; possibly the Karhala might run to the large lake in Hio, which Snelgrave says (from the information of the Portuguese mulatto he found at Abomey) " is the fountain of several large rivers which empty themselves into the Bay of Guinea." The Lagos river may flow from this lake, but this is mere conjecture. The gentleman to whom I am indebted, places the Mahees north of Dahomey, instead of north-west as in Norris's map, which is allowed to be far from discriminate in the interior parts, in the preface to Dalzel's History, and this is also more probable, because about nine years ago, the King of Hio entirely conquered the Mahees, and upwards of 20,000 of them were brought for sale to Lagos.

The Joös, inconsiderately reported to Adams's editor as being, with the Anagoos and Mahees, the principal nations on the journey to the Niger, and nearer to the coast, avoiding Dahomey, are probably the Jaboos, who are about 40 miles westward of Kosie, and not behind Cradoo, as in Norris's map. They are celebrated for the cloths of their name, of which the Portuguese have shipped such large quantities. The Anagoos, or Nagoos, are the north westward neighbours of Dahomey.

The extent of Fantee is corrected from the conjectural enlargement of it by Mr. Meredith, and, with that of Ashantee, Akim, Assin, Warsaw, Ahanta, &c. &c. is sufficiently distinct in the present map. A more enlarged, and particular map of Fantee, &c. would not be interesting to the public, but as it might be desirable to geographers, I shall keep it in view as a duty, and, at some future time, endeavor to add to the observations of latitude and longitude which have been already made on the coast.

I may not conclude without acknowledging the guidance, and assistance, which Major Rennell's previous investigations have afforded me; without impressing, that had not some sketches of the interior been collected by the industry of the emissaries of the African Association, and afterwards connected and formed into a general outline, blended with the feeble lights of the ancients, my enquiries would neither have been excited or directed ; and this present small contribution to our slender knowledge would have perished an embryo. When I reflect on the creative researches of the genius of D'Anville, and the acumen and erudition of Major Rennell, it is my greatest anxiety to make my deference in investigation, as manifest as the public duty which exacted the involuntary presumption ; and I cannot conclude more appropriately, than by addressing the latter in the expressive lines of Virgil:

" Nec calamis solum æquiparas sed voce magistrum
Fortunate—tu nunc eris alter ab illo.
Nos tamen hæc quocunque modo tibi nostra vicissim
Dicemus."

CHAPTER II.

History.

To speak of the death of a former king, the Ashantees imagine to affect the life of the present equally with enquiring who would be his successor; and superstition and policy strengthening this impression, it is made capital by the law, to converse either of the one or the other. The inability of the natives to compute time, and the comparatively recent establishment of the Moors, may be pleaded as additional apologies for the imperfect history I have collected.

According to a common tradition, which I never heard contradicted but once, the Ashantees emigrated from a country nearer the water side, and subjecting the western Intas, and two lesser powers, founded the present kingdom. These people being comparatively advanced in several arts, the Ashantees necessarily adopted a portion of their language with the various novelties; which probably created the limited radical difference between their language and that of the Fantees; for I could not find, after taking the greatest pains, more than 200 words unknown to the latter. The weights of the Inta country, in particular, were adopted with their names, by the conquerors, without the least alteration

The tradition, scanty in itself, is very cautiously adverted to, the government politically undermining every monument which perpetuates their intrusion, or records the distinct origins of their subjects : but, from the little I could collect, it appeared to have been an emigration of numerous enterprising or discontented families, to whom the parent state afterwards became subject. I am inclined to think, (the account of their coming from a country nearer the sea being too general for conjecture to revolt from,) that they emigrated from the eastward of south, where the territory admitted to be Ashantee proper is remote, compared with its extent southward, or westward of south, and the former consequence of Doompassie, and the towns eastward of it, support this ; yet, the very few natives who pretended to any opinion on the subject, had an impression, that their ancestors emigrated from the neighbourhood of a small river, Ainshue, behind Winnebah : a croom called Coomadie is to be found there, but there is nothing else to countenance the report.

The Ashantee, Fantee, Warsaw, Akim, Assin, and Aquapim languages are indisputably dialects of the same root ; their identity is even more striking than that of the dialects of the ancient Greek : now the Fantees and Warsaws both cherish a tradition, which exists also in many Ahanta families, that they were pressed from the interior to the water side by the successful ambition of a remote power ; whence it may be concluded, that the Ashantee emigration we are now considering, was posterior to a more important movement of the whole people, corresponding with that of their neighbours. I will not dilate upon this secondary subject by referring to internal evidence, there is nothing to recompense either the investigation or the perusal.

One curious evidence however may be added of the former identity of the Ashantee, Warsaw, Fantee, Akim, Assin, Aquamboe, and part of the Ahanta nations ; which is a tradition that the whole of these people were originally comprehended in twelve tribes or families ; the Aquonna, Abrootoo, Abbradi, Essonna,

Annŏna, Yoko, Intchwa, Abadie, Appiadie, Tchweedam, Agoona, and Doomina; in which they class themselves still, without any regard to national distinction. For instance, Ashantees, Warsaws, Akims, Ahantas, or men of any of the nations before mentioned will severally declare, that they belong to the Annŏna family; other individuals of the different countries, that they are of the Tchweedam family; and when this is announced on meeting, they salute each other as brothers. The King of Ashantee is of the Annŏna family, so was our Accra and one of the Fantee linguists; Amanquateä is of the Essonna family. The Aquonna, Essonna, Intchwa, and Tchweedam, are the four patriarchal families, and preside over the intermediate ones, which are considered as the younger branches. I have taken some pains to acquire the etymology of these words, but with imperfect success; it requires much labour and patience, both to make a native comprehend, and to be comprehended by him. Quonna is a buffalo, an animal forbade to be eaten by that family. Abrootoo signifies a corn stalk, and Abbradi a plantain. Annŏna is a parrot, but it is also said to be a characteristic of forbearance and patience. Esso is a bush cat, forbidden food to that family. Yoko is the red earth used to paint the lower parts of the houses in the interior. Intchwa is a dog, much relished by native epicures, and therefore a serious privation. Appiadie signifies a servant race. Etchwee is a panther, frequently eaten in the interior, and therefore not unnecessarily forbidden. Agoona signifies a place where palm oil is collected. These are all the etymologies in which the natives agree. Regarding these families as primæval institutions, I leave the subject to the conjectures of others, merely submitting, that the four patriarchal families, the Buffalo, the Bush Cat, the Panther, and the Dog, appear to record the first race of men living on hunting; the Dog family, probably, first training that animal to assist in the chase. The introduction of planting and agriculture, seems marked in the age of their immediate descendents, the Corn stalk and Plantain branches. The origin and improvement of architecture in the Red earth; and of commerce, probably, in the Palm oil: indeed, the natives have included the Portuguese, the first foreign traders they knew, in that family, alleging, that their long and more intimate intercourse with the blacks, has made the present race a mixture of the African and Portuguese. The Servant race reminds us of the curse of Canaan. This resembles a Jewish institution, but the people of Accra alone practise circumcision, and they speak a language, as will be shewn, radically distinct, yet not to be assimilated to the Intā, to which nation they are referred by the Fantees, merely because it is the nearest which practises circumcision. Accra is a European corruption of the word Inkran, which means an ant, and they say the name was either given or assumed on account of their numbers; this must have been before their wars with the Aquamboes.

When Adokoo, chief of the Braffoes, a Fantee nation, consulted the venerable fetish men of the sanctuary, near Sooprooroo, on the Ashantee war, they answered, that nothing could be more offensive to the fetish, than the Fantees preventing the peaceable intercourse of their inland neighbours with the water side, because they were formerly all one family.

- The conduct of the later emigration of the Ashantees is ascribed to Saï Tootoo, who, assisted by other leading men of the party, and encouraged by superstitious omens, founded Coomassie, and was presented with the stool, or made King, from his superior qualifications. This account is supported by the mixed nature of the government, founded on equality and obligation, and the existence of a law, exempting the direct descendants of any of Saï Tootoo's peers and assistants, (in whom the Aristocracy originated) from capital punishment.

The Dwabin monarchy is said to have been founded at the same time by Boitinnë, who was of the same family as Saï Tootoo, being the sons of sisters. Boitinnë and his party, took possession of Dwabin, the largest of the aboriginal towns, (leaving Saï Tootoo to build Coomassie) whence it seems his followers were the more powerful; indeed I have heard it confessed by a few Ashantees, that Dwabin had formerly the pre-eminence, though they have always been firm allies in war, and equal sharers in spoil and conquest. This common interest, preserved uninterrupted more than a century, by two rising powers, close to each other, with the view of a more rapid aggrandisement, and their firm discretion in making many serious disagreements subservient to the policy, is one of the few circumstances worth considering in a history composed of wars and successions. I do not think there is such an instance in our heptarchy, nor do I recollect any other in history, but that of Chalcis and Eretria.

Bakkee, who died, as I have related,* about a year ago, was the son of Saï Apokoo, the second king, and an infant at the breast at the time of his father's death; he was a very old man when he incurred the present King's displeasure, which supports the report of the Moors, that the kingdom has been founded about 110 years. Bosman and Barbot mention the Ashantees, as just heard of by Europeans, about the year 1700, which confirms this account. The anxiety of the Ashantee government for daily records, immediately on the establishment of the Moors, who were only visitors until the present reign, acknowledges the perplexities and deficiencies of their early history too candidly, to leave any encouragement to the researches of strangers. Records beyond half a century are not to be found in the archives either of Cape Coast, or Christiansburg Castles, so that the chronology can only be founded on that of the Moors, and circumstances.

* See Diary.

The Ashantee government concentred the mass of its original force, and making the chiefs resident in Coomassie and the few large towns they built in its neighbourhood, with titular dignities, conciliated those whom they subdued by continuing them in their governments, and checked them by exacting their frequent attendance at festivals, politically instituted. Military command seems to have been the sole prerogative of Saï Tootoo; his judicial and legislative power being controlled by the chiefs or aristocracy much more than at present, who, as in the Teutonic governments, directed the common business of the state, only consulting a general assembly on extraordinary occasions.

Saï Tootoo defeated the Akims and Assins, subjected the Tufel country, and subdued many small states in the neighbourhood. He also conquered Dankara, the King of which, Intim Dakarey, was so considerable a trader in slaves, that the Dutch Governor General paid him a monthly note from his own purse, and assisted him with two or three small cannons, and a few Europeans, on the eve of the Ashantee invasion: the former are now placed as trophies in Coomassie, at the top of the street in which the Mission was quartered. Booroom was subjugated soon after.

Saï Tootoo did not live to see all the streets of Coomassie completed, for war being declared against Atoä, a district between Akim and Assin, he invaded that country. The chief of the Atoas, unable to face such a power, dexterously insinuated his small force through the forest, until he reached the rear of the Ashantee army, which the King was following leisurely with a guard of a few hundred men, all of whom were destroyed by the Atoäs, who shot the King in his hammock. This happening near a place called Cormantee, (razed to the ground in vengeance,) and on a Saturday, the most solemn oath of the Ashantees, is " by Saturday and Cormantee;" (" Mïminda Cormantee;") and no enterprise has since been undertaken on that day of the week.

1720. Saï Apokoo, brother of Saï Tootoo, was next placed on the stool. Had there been no brother, the sister's son would have been the heir; this extraordinary rule of succession, excluding all children but those of a sister, is founded on the argument, that if the wives of the sons are faithless, the blood of the family is entirely lost in the offspring, but should the daughters deceive their husbands, it is still preserved.

Saï Apokoo finished the building of Coomassie, and exchanged compliments with the King of Dahomey, since which there has been no intercourse; the latter, probably, as a despotic monarch, did not wish to give his people any opportunity of contemplating the greater freedom of the Ashantee government.

Saï is the family name of the present race of Kings, some of their relatives bearing it as well. Innăna is also the cognomen of the Kings of Dagwumba.

Apokoo invading the kingdom of Gaman, Abo, the King, fled to Kong, whither the Ashantee army pursued him. The King of Kong politically compelled Abo to meet his enemies on the frontier, least they might disturb a neutral kingdom. Abo being defeated, purchased a peace by presenting large sums of gold to the various chiefs, and consenting to an annual tribute. Apokoo next subjected Takima, whence the Fantees are said to have emigrated, and forced a second emigration of the people to Gomawa, at the back of Winnebah. He dispossessed the Akims of the English, Dutch, and Danish Accra notes.* The mortifying destruction of European records, confines me to the report of the more intelligent natives on the subject of these notes, who declare, that the people of Accra being deprived of them by the fraud of the Akims, when they were assisted by them against the Aquamboes, the Akims were in their turn obliged to yield them to their conquerors the Ashantees.

* See the explanatory list of words and the early dispatches in the First Part.

Tribute being demanded from the neighbouring kingdom of Dagwumba, a war ensued, and its troops were defeated. The King of Dagwumba, convinced that his former reliance on a superior population was vain, from the military genius of the Ashantees, and the commercial disposition of his own people, dispirited from their want of fire arms,* prudently invited a peace, before a more decisive defeat left him no dignity, and his enemies no moderation for treating. As it was, they still respected his resources, and were content to secure him as a tributary, rather than exhaust their forces in his subjugation, in the infancy of their kingdom. A triumph in policy was in the view of the King of Dagwumba, equivalent to the small diminution of personal dignity; and at the expense of an inconsiderable tribute, he established a commercial intercourse, which, his markets being regularly supplied from the interior, was both an advantage and a security to him, from the great convenience to his warlike neighbours, whose superstition assenting to his great reputation for making saphies, and for augury, would not only augment his revenue, but insure him superior respect as a tributary. Intā had previously become tributary.

I should have mentioned, that every subject state was placed under the immediate care of some Ashantee chief, generally resident in the capital, who seldom visited it but to receive the tribute from the native ruler, for whose conduct he was in a reasonable degree responsible. Thus Quatchi Quofie has now the care of

---

* Fire arms are unknown to such of the nations on the south of the Niger as the Shereef has visited; and the reason which he assigns for it is, that the Kings in the neighbourhood of the coast, persuaded that if these powerful instruments of war should reach the possession of the populous inland states, their own independence would be lost, have strictly prohibited, and by the wisdom of their measures, have effectually prevented this dangerous merchandise from passing beyond the limits of their dominions. Lucas.

Dankara, Odumata of Soota, Apokoo of Aquamboe, Oöosa Quantabisa of Daboia, &c. &c. Their policy, in short, not only in this particular, but in many others, seems to have been closely similar to that of the Persians, as described by Herodotus.

Boitinnë, the founder of Dwabin, died in this reign.

1741. Saï Apokoo was succeeded by his brother Saï Aquissi. I could not learn any particular exploits of his, excepting that he preserved the subjection of the states previously reduced. The King of Akim, in his time, (the last who had the power of governing without consulting the pynins or elders) desiring to go to war with his neighbours, was obliged to obtain permission from the Ashantee government, which he did by the promise of sending them half the spoil; but, gaining little or nothing, he did not do so. He soon afterwards heard of Aquissi's intention, to demand his head; and knowing that King's word was irrevocable, he summoned his ministers, and desired to sacrifice his life for the quiet of his people: his ministers insisted on sharing his fate; and a barrel of powder being brought for each to sit on, they drank a large quantity of rum, and blew themselves up with the fire from their pipes. Dr. Isert also heard of this in Akim.

1753. Aquissi was succeeded by Saï Cudjo. The Aristocracy was retrenched and conciliated by this monarch, who raised his favourite captains to the vacant stools,* uniting three or four in one, and swearing that their lives should be equally sacred, (see p. 4,) to anticipate any doubts of his fidelity to the constitution.

Saï Cudjo defeating the Warsaws and Assins more decisively than his predecessors, first compelled them to acknowledge their fealty to Ashantee. He also subjected Aquamboe, and Aquapim,

---

* "To succeed to the stool," does not mean to the seat in the council, but is the common expression for succeeding to a property even in private life. The same stool, or seat descends through many generations.

quelled several revolts of other countries, and was esteemed a very great captain. The grandfather of Amanquateä Atooa, conquered Sawee, killing the king Boomancumma; and Bakkee, soon afterwards, subjugated Moinseä. In this reign Quama, king of Dwabin, died.

1785. Saï Quamina succeeded his grandfather Saï Cudjo, at a very early age. The Akims revolted soon after his accession, under Ofoosoo, their most active ruler for many years: he engaged several smaller states in alliance, and defeated the Ashantees repeatedly; at length the treachery of his followers procured Quatchi Quofie, the Ashantee general, his head; with which he returned to Coomassie, the country having again submitted. The fame of Ofoosoo made Quatchi Quofie so vain of this achievement, that he had a figure of him made, with which his umbrella is still crowned, and before which he dances with every insulting gesture and vaunt, when he arrives on the ground at the various ceremonies. The present king has frequently been heard to say, that it was a great pity this old man did not know better, for the Akim caboceers generally attended his summons with alacrity and good will; but the sight of the insulted effigy of their favourite leader, disgusted them, and excited their revolt. These brave people have risen from their dependence at least eight times.

The government finding a pretext to invade Banda, the King Odrasee vigorously opposed the Ashantee army; but at length, seeing he must inevitably fall into their hands, to prevent his head being found, which circumstance he knew would sorely disquiet the enemy,* and solace his own people, ordered, just before he

---

* On the death of the late King of Amanaheä, two competitors for the stool appeared, one called Suikee or Suiquah; the other's name I am ignorant of. Both collected their slaves and adherents, and fought. Suikee was obliged to fly, and hide himself in the bush; but the people being dissatisfied with the conqueror, Suikee re-appeared against

killed himself, a woman to be sacrificed, and the abdomen being ripped, his head to be sewn up within it, and her body afterwards to be buried in the heap of the slain. It was discovered by bribes, and is now on one of the King's great drums. Soota was also subjugated in this reign, occupying the army under Odumata ten years, during which period he was not allowed to see Coomassie. Odumata afterwards subdued Coranza, the larger part of his army being Gaman auxiliaries.

Saï Quamina raised Apokoo to the stool of Assimadoo, to whom he had been a servant, in exclusion of the family.

The Danish Governor-General, meditating the punishment of the Popos, applied to Saï Quamina for 5000 Ashantee auxiliaries; the request was granted, but while the troops were on their march down, the Governor died, and his successor prudently paid 250 ounces of gold, (alleged to have been advanced by the King for their subsistence on their march to Christiansburg Castle) rather than involve himself in the expenses and troubles of such an alliance.

1798. Saï Quamina had remained twelve months on a visit at Dwabin, deaf to the remonstrances of various deputations urging

the town. When his rival was reduced beyond all hope, he threw all his gold, which filled several jars, into the lake; and then collecting his wives and the different branches of his family, went with them into a remote part of the bush, and cut all their throats, with the exception of one son, whom he reserved to assist him in burying the bodies. He then made this son swear on his fetish, to kill and bury him, and never to discover where the bodies were laid: the son fulfilled the oath, and returned to Apollonia, but I am not certain what became of him. After Suikee had seated himself firmly on the stool, he by some means discovered where the bodies were concealed; he caused them to be dug up, and taken to Apollonia town; he then ranged them in a sitting posture, in a row along the beach, with stakes to extend their arms, and support their heads: this horrid spectacle was exhibited until even their bones had perished. One of Suikee's first acts after his accession, was to consecrate his hiding place in the bush, making it death, or a heavy fine, for any one to swear by Suikee's bush, and not to keep the oath.

his return, and infatuated beyond recovery by the arts of his mistress, Gyawä, the daughter of the King ; when it was formally
announced to him, that if he was not present at the approaching
Yam custom, he would be deprived of the stool. It is said, that
his woman refused to accompany him to Coomassie, either dreading the resentment of his mother, a woman of violent passions, and
great ambition, or, which is more probable, influenced by her
father to mingle this repugnance with her blandishments, to acce-
lerate the ruin of Saï Quamina, which he was not without hopes
might lead to his own aggrandisement. The form of the dethrone-
ment is interesting. Appia Danqua, whose power seems to have
been equal to that of mayor of the palace, repaired to the King's
mother with the chief captains, and deliberately recounting the
offences of her son, commanded her to remonstrate with him, as
the daughter of their old king, and the parent to whom he owed
his elevation. The mother, who no doubt had assisted in the
private council, affecting to bewail her own misfortune and her
son's disgrace, confessed, with seeming reluctance, that her remonstrances had already been despised, that the king had even
attempted her life, and begged them to raise her second son, Saï
Apokoo, to the stool the elder had forfeited. This was complied
with, and they sent Saï Quamina a few of his women and slaves,
desiring him to retire into the bush and build himself a croom, and
on his death; which happened soon after, as it was said, from the
poignancy of his feelings, they made the greatest custom for him
which had ever been known. The sable Cleopatra died soon after
him. It was whispered, that those he had formerly injured incessantly insulting him in his retirement, even to abusing his wives
before his face, he had a private interview with the present King,
communicated several schemes of conquests, invoked him to distrust, and, if possible, to punish those who had forsaken him, and

implored death; which was inflicted (as the blood of the royal family could not be shed, and as he could not be privately drowned in the sacred river) by fixing his feet on the ground, bending his body backwards with a prop in the small of his back, and suspending several large teeth of ivory from a noose around his neck, which, hanging from the prop, strangled him.

1799. Saï Apokoo did not live more than a few weeks after being elevated to the stool, and was succeeded by his brother Saï Tootoo Quamina, the present King, who must then have been about seventeen years of age. On this occasion, the general assembly of the captains, jealous of the aristocracy, and desirous of making a favourable impression on the young King, insisted that the remaining members of it, should propitiate the reign, by publicly disclaiming their exemption from capital punishment.

The invasion of the Fantee kingdom in 1807 was the first important military act of the present reign, the circumstances and origin of which, being pretty accurately described by Mr. Meredith, in the extract in the Appendix, I need not repeat. Whilst the invasion was meditating, Baba, now the chief of the Moors, presented himself to solicit an asylum in Coomassie, having been driven from Gamba by the rapacity of the King, his near relative; and professing solely to desire the recovery of a large property with held from him, to make the King of Ashantee the heir to it. The King promised he would oblige the King of Gamba to do him justice, on his return from the Fantee war, if Baba and his companions were fortunate in their prayers and charms for his success. The King of Gamba did not think proper to resist the demand afterwards made through the Ashantee government.

1807. Coonadua, the King's mother, was left regent during his absence; this woman was a second Messalina, and many young aptains who refused to intrigue with her, from fear or disgust, ave been ultimately the victims of her artifice and vengeance.

Yaboquorra, the King of Dwabin, died in this interval, and was ucceeded by his grandson, Boitinnë Quama, now about twenty ears of age.

1811. Attah, caboceer or King of Akim, had followed the King the first Fantee war, and behaved well. Apokoo being sent on n expedition against the Fantees of Winnebah and Berracoo, ttah received orders to join him with his contingency; instead of hich, he sent a message to Apokoo, before he passed the Boompra river, refusing to join him, and advising him not to attempt pass through his country. Apokoo reported this immediately the King, who, as is usual, sent to Attah to enquire if he had id so. He confessed that he had, without hesitation, adding, at the King treated him like a slave, in incessantly summoning im to attend his wars, and besides, that he never could forget that aï Cudjo had cut off his grandfather's head, and that he would ght with Apokoo whenever he came. Soon afterwards, Quamina uma, (the father of Becqua, captain of Danish Accra,) and one f the King's sons, returning to Coomassie with a large quantity of old collected to make custom for the King's mother, Attah intercepted, robbed, and murdered them and their party, with the xception of one, whom he desired to tell the King that this act ould convince him he was in earnest, and determined to go to ar with him. Apokoo was immediately ordered to proceed gainst Attah, who had engaged Quaw Saffätchee as a party in the evolt, who was weary of the same laborious vassalage. When pokoo entered the Akim country, Attah was for attacking him mmediately, and at sun rise, but Quaw impressing his doubts of eir succeeding against the superior warfare of the Ashantees, egged him to stop until three o'clock, when the Ashantees

generally ate and slept, and when they might be better able to
retreat if worsted, as the enemy never pursued in the dusk. The
attack was a surprise, but the fight continued obstinate and unde-
cided until night, when Apokoo found he had lost so many men,
that he immediately dispatched a messenger to summon the Accras
to his aid, as vassals to the King. His messenger reached Accra
the next day, and that people joined him on the following, on
which the enemy retreated precipitately; Attah to windward, and
Quaw to Adda. Apokoo followed the latter, who having escaped
him after a tedious watchfulness, Apokoo, believing the Danish
governor, Mr. Flindt, to have connived, made him his prisoner,
and kept him with the army, which soon afterwards encamped in
Aquapim, five months, during which time he was treated with
kindness and respect, but his ransom amounted to nearly £400.
Apokoo was soon after ordered back to Coomassie. He told me
he brought the bell of Adda fort as a trophy.

Appia Danqua had been sent, at the same time with Apokoo,
with 6000 men against the Fantee states which were disposed to
the revolters. He defeated them at Apam, and took Baffoo the
Annamaboe caboceer prisoner, but whilst his army was before
Tantum, intelligence of the approach of Attah, who had retreated
from Apokoo, but whose name was as redoubtable as his disposition was rapacious, subdued his firmness, and under the plea of
prudence, hurried him back to the interior.

The path was afterwards shut for two years, through the vigilance,
and from the terror of Cudjo Cooma, who had been elected to the
stool of Akim, six months after the death of Attah, whose immediate successor (Quawko Ashantee) tyrannized so cruelly during
that period, that he was commanded by the people to kill himself,
and could only obtain the indulgence of a week's respite, which he
spent in singing and dancing, in fact in making his own custom.

Quaw Saffatchee had also leagued with the Fantees who attacked the Accra town, but were repulsed. The King suddenly determined to open the path to receive the arrears of pay due from the Forts, and sent Amanqua Abiniowa with an army of 20,000 1814. men, charging him to offer no violence nor commit hostility, unless provoked by attack, but to receive the submission of the Akims and Aquapims, and merely to exact a fine to seal it. Appia Danqua was sent at the same time with a smaller army to the back of Winnebah and Tantum, to intercept the revolters if they fled to windward. Abiniowa proceeded to Aguiasso, one day's march from Aquapim, unmolested, when one of his foraging parties was attacked by Cudjo Cooma and seven men killed. A general engagement took place the next morning, and after six hours fighting the Ashantees were victorious, and sent a jaw-bone and a slave to each of the Accra towns. Amanqua then marched to Accra to receive the King's pay, and remained nearly twelve months in its neighbourhood. He then returned to Aquapim, where, after some time, he received a message from the King, with a large quantity of gold, advising him that he must not see his face again unless he brought the heads of Cudjo and Quaw. Amanqua did not immediately communicate this message to his captains, but ordered them to deposit their equipage and property in Accra, and then, making a large custom for three days, to propitiate the enterprise, he took fetish with all his captains that they would never return to Coomassie without the heads.

1816. Appia Danqua had died in Assin in the interim, and was succeeded by his brother Appia Nanu, under whom Bakkee was the second in command. The King hearing nothing of his progress, and his indolence being reported to him, sent orders to Amanqua to join him, which he did at Essecooma, reproaching him for his cowardice. Soon after this, the skirmish at the salt pond near Cape Coast took place, the detachment was principally of Assins, and commanded by Quasheemanqua. Yokokroko soon afterwards joined the combined army, (which had marched to Abra,) with a few hundred men destined to attack Commenda.

Not long after the palaver was settled at Cape Coast, and the army again divided, Cudjo Cooma was killed by a party of Appia Nanu's at Insoom or Incoom near Essecooma; upon which, Appia, instead of marching to join Amanqua as had been concerted, returned to Coomassie, where he was coldly received, but not accused until the 12th of July last (see Diary). Adoo Danqua, the brother of Quaw Saffätchee, came to the Accras and concerted the delivering of him up, as he had tired him out with his wanderings. The Ashantees agreed to prevail on the King to give him the stool if he did. A few Accras and a few Ashantees accompanied him, and when he came near where his brother was hid, one day's journey from Accra, he placed an ambush, and sitting down, expostulated with him, and recommended him to kill himself; but Quaw would not, alleging that he should eventually wear out the King's patience in pursuing him; on this Adoo rose, and a shot was immediately fired at Quaw, who was brought down and rose again four times, exclaiming that his brother was his murderer, who reflected the reproach on his own obstinacy. The body was brought to Accra, and his head sent to Coomassie, and it is now a trophy at Bantama or the back town. Amanqua then returned to Coomassie, and arrived about six months before the Mission.

The Aowins, to anticipate the ambitious views of the Ashantee government, lately sent an embassy with offers of service and tribute, but the amount of the latter has not yet been decided.

The King had sent to demand the royal stool of Buntooko or Gaman which was thickly plated and embossed with gold; it was given up by Adinkara, the King, from fear; his sister, a woman of masculine spirit and talent, and the soul of the government, being absent. On her return, she reproached her brother severely, and ordered a solid gold stool to be made to replace it. That being also demanded, as the right of the superior, with a large gold ornament in the shape of an elephant, dug out from some ruins, the sister, receiving the ambassadors, replied, that the King should not have either, and added, impressing it with more force than delicacy, that her brother and she must change sexes, for she was most proper for a King, and would fight to the last rather than be so constantly despoiled. The King of Ashantee sent word that she was fit to be a king's sister, and a strong woman, and he would give her twelve months to prepare for war. Several embassies have been sent however to negotiate; two during our stay, the latter, it was said, with an offer of 400 Bendas, (£3200.) but the aristocracy were obstinate, and urged to the King, that his other tributaries would laugh at him, if he did not get the King of Gaman's head. The small pox was raging in Buntooko.

It is clear, that the King of Ashantee contemplates the reduction of the King of Dwabin from an independent ally to a tributary. We witnessed one circumstance to the point. A messenger being sent to require gold of Dwabin, the King of which is a very weak young man, a captain of the royal family replied, that there was no war on foot to require gold, and as it could only be for the individual benefit of Ashantee, the government must be reminded that Dwabin had formerly exacted gold, and was not now to be subjected to imposition, because the right had been yielded from respect to the sister kingdom. This being reported to the King, he suppressed his anger, and sent a gold headed sword, with other marks of dignity and favour to this man, who, to his surprise, refused them, alleging, that the honours he already possessed at

home became him better. The King still temporised. Some
months after, at the full assembly convened for the proclamation
of the treaty with the British Government, the mother of the King
of Dwabin, who acts as regent, and over whom Saï is known to
have much influence, suddenly, and no doubt at his instance,
accused this captain of plotting to deprive her son of the stool.
The accusation was supported by others, who prayed the King to
judge the palaver. The King of Dwabin sat with the greatest
indifference. The accused made an animated appeal to the assembly, and Saï affected to support him vehemently, and ordered
the linguists to give him chalk, or acquit him. The man thanking
him very earnestly, Adoosee was desired to tell him, that his ill-will
to the King of Ashantee had been reported in a very aggravated
manner; but as it was no longer believed, he was only required to
take fetish, that he liked the King, and would do him all the good
he could; this done, the man received several marks of favour and
bounty.

Saï Tootoo is considered to take better care of the treasury than
any of his predecessors : he cautiously extends his prerogative, and
takes every opportunity of increasing the number of secondary
captains, by dignifying the young men brought up about his
person, and still retaining them in his immediate service.

Saï Acotoo, the King's brother, and the heir to the stool, appeared to me very inferior in ability; but the Ashantees say
otherwise.

The King's private character is amiable; the children of his
brothers share the fondness and indulgence which endear him to
his own, and his few moments of recreation are the liveliest of
theirs. The circumstances connected with the various instances
which we witnessed of his generosity to others, justify me in
ascribing it to the benevolence of his disposition. His admiration

of ingenious rather than splendid novelty, has frequently imposed
the appearance of a covetousness, scarcely culpable from his reve-
rence for invention, and the amazement its extent excited. To
present him with the trifles which attracted his notice when he
visited us, offended him, he told us we must only answer his questions, and let him examine them; to make dashes on the occasion
of a private visit, was to vitiate the motive of the condescension,
which could not be repeated unless we paid more respect to his
dignity and friendship. The King is certainly capricious, and his
liberality of mind is stained by prejudices against individuals which
he confesses to be unaccountable; and to several of the principal
actors in his brother's deposition, (which, desirous to extend his
prerogative, he would tacitly censure,) he has been unjustly severe.
His humanity is frequently superior to his superstition and policy,
he offended Quatchi Quofie, one of the four, by limiting the
human sacrifices at his mother's funeral, and resisted all the impor-
tunities, founded on precedent, for the allowance of a greater
number. He dismissed us twice with apologies for not proceeding
to business, confessing, the first time, that he had been unusually
irritated just after he sent for us, and had not recovered his calm-
ness; the latter, that some agreeable news had induced him to
drink more than fitted him to hear great palavers like ours. In
his judicial administration, a lie always aggravated the punishment,
and truth generally extenuated, and sometimes atoned of itself for
the offence: he invariably anticipated the temerity of perjury,
where convicting evidence was to be opposed to the accused.
The King's manners are a happy mixture of dignity and affability,
they engage rather than encourage, and his general deportment is
conciliating though repressive. He speaks well, and more logically
than most of his council, who are diffuse, but his superior talent is
marked in the shrewd questions by which he fathoms a design or

a narrative. He excels in courtesy, is wisely inquisitive, and candid in his comparisons : war, legislature, and mechanism, were his favourite topics in our private conversations. The great, but natural fault of the King is his ambition; I do not think it has ever proved superior to the pledge of his honour, but it certainly has, and that frequently, to his sense of justice, which is repressed rather than impaired by it. This sketch of his character being narrowed to my own knowledge, will be assisted by the following history of Agay, the second linguist.

Agay, when a boy, carried salt from Aquoomo to Coomassie for sale; he was afterwards taken into the service of Aquootoo, caboceer of that place, against whom the government had instituted a palaver, but wrongfully. Agay accompanied the caboceer when he was sent for to Coomassie for judgment. After the King's messengers had spoken, misrepresenting the case in preference to confessing the King to be in the wrong, and the caboceer was confused, this boy suddenly rose, and said, to use the words of the narrators, " King, you have people to wash you, to feed you, to serve you, but you have no people to speak the truth to you, and tell you when God does not like your palaver." The assembly cried out unanimously, that the boy might be hurried away and his head taken off; but the King said, " No! let him finish;" and Agay is said to have spoken three hours, and to have disclosed and argued the palaver to the King's conviction, and his master's acquittal. He was retained to attend the King, but treated with no particular distinction. A serious palaver occurring between two principal men, it was debated before the council, who were at a loss to decide, but inclined to the man whom the King doubted; judgment was suspended. In the interim the King sent Agay, privately, to the house of each, to hear their palavers in turn, tête-à-tête; he did so, and when the King asked him who he thought was right, he confirmed his impression. " Now," said the King, " I know you have a good head." Agay was then made a Linguist, and presented with a house, wives, slaves, and gold. Sometime afterwards, the King confessing a prejudice against a wealthy captain, his linguists, always inclined to support him, said, " If you wish to take his stool from him, we will make the palaver;" but Agay sprung up, exclaiming, " No, King! that is not good; that man never did you any wrong, you know all the gold of your subjects is your's at their death, but if you get all now, strangers will go away and say, only the King has gold, and that will not be good, but let them say the King has gold, all his captains have gold, and all his people have gold, then your country will look handsome, and the bush people fear you." For this the King made him second linguist, and much increased his property. When Amanqua had the command of the army against Cudjo Cooma, the King asked him which linguist he would take, he replied, Adoosee or Otee; the King said, no! I will give you this boy, he has the best head for hard palavers. Amanqua urged that he was too young, the King told him he was a fool to say so. He then made Amanqua take fetish with him to report the merits of Agay faithfully, who distinguished himself so much, that he is always employed in difficult foreign palavers.

The manners of the higher orders of captains, always dignified, are courteous and hospitable in private, though haughty and abrupt in public. I believe them to be jealous rather than tenacious of their honour, and their sophistry is as ingenious as their maxims are prepossessing. They consider that war alone affords an exertion or display of ability, and they esteem the ambition of their King as his greatest virtue. They have no idea of the aggrandisement of a state by civil policy alone. They are candid in acknowledging their defeats, and just to the prowess of their enemies, but they possess little humanity, and are very avaricious and oppressive. They listen to superstition with the most childish credulity, but they only cultivate it for the preservation of life and the indulgence of passion; beyond this, the Moors could never advance their enquiries; they are neither curious nor anxious about a future state, pretending to it from rank and achievement rather than domestic virtue; and believing, if the latter were outraged, the solemnities and sacrifices of their funeral customs would purchase their repose. · Indeed, licensed as they are by the zealous conflicts of rival superstitions, (Moorish and Pagan,) their lives are moderate and benevolent to what might be expected, and merit more than our excuses.

The lower order of people are ungrateful, insolent, and licentious. The King repeatedly said, he believed them to be the worst people existing, except the Fantees, and not comparable with many of their inland neighbours. Perhaps we should agree with Voltaire, " Je crois qu'il faut plutôt juger d'une puissante nation par ceux qui sont à la tête, que par la populace."*

* The principal districts of Fantee, are, the Affettoo, the Braffoo, and the Essecoomah; Cape Coast is in the former. The Dey of Affettoo (a title probably introduced by the Portuguese) was formerly supreme in Fantee, so far as summoning the other kings and caboceers at pleasure, prescribing their political conduct, and being appealed to and sentencing in all cases of life and death, wherever or by whomsoever the crime may have been committed; witchcraft excepted. Upwards of a century ago the small pox almost depopulated Affettoo, then the largest town and capital of all Fantee, (it is about 10 miles inland from Cape Coast,) and all the immediate heirs to the stool being cut off, the supremacy was transferred to Mankasim. The present Dey, however, preserves a spiritual authority over the other kings and caboceers, and is esteemed as the superior fetish man; when they desire rain, for instance, they apply to him to procure it, and they look to him solely for their chronology, which he preserves by knotting strings. Mankasim then became the capital and largest town of Fantee, but it was almost destroyed by the Ashantees in their first invasion of 1807. Any Fantee caboceer who did not attend the summons of the King of Mankasim, was suspended by him, and after-

wards displaced by the diet. Adoo, the last King of the Braffoos, despoiling all his sub-jects of their most valuable property, and countenancing the individuals of his family in the same assumption and violation, without any regard to persons; they were all seized, on his death, by a simultaneous rising of the people, and sold off the coast as slaves, to get rid of the race. Adookoo, one of the leading men, was then called to the care of the stool, with the title of caboceer only, it being still considered as an interregnum, but he exercised the same supremacy and privileges which the King had done, and was acknow-ledged by the whole country. During his retreat and wanderings in the bush, after several defeats by the Ashantees, the Fantee towns have assumed many political and judicial rights before centered in Mankasim; but Adookoo is now expected to summon them all, and re-establish the ancient order of things, which they deem too sacred to think of resisting. It was not the Braffoos, or the whole people of that district, who had the privilege of living abroad at the public expense, and who took whatever they pleased of the property of others, as Mr. Meredith has stated; but the state officers of that district called Brofoos, who acquired that name from the hide in which the tobacco is rolled, being formed into a seat peculiar to them, never using a wooden stool. They were the executors, and not the organs of the law, and always sat to the right and left of Adookoo, but had no voice. The number was twelve, and the dignity immemorially hereditary in as many families. These men were allowed to take whatever they pleased at home and abroad, but since Adookoo's misfortunes, and inability to support them, they have been content to beg for their tithes in the large towns, and only exercise their rapacity in the small crooms of their own district.

CHAPTER III.

Constitution and Laws.

THE King, the Aristocracy, now reduced to four, and the Assembly of Captains,* are the three estates of the Ashantee government.

The constitution requires or admits an interference of the Aristocracy in all *foreign* politics, extending even to a veto on the King's decision; but they watch rather than share the *domestic* administration, generally influencing it by their opinion, but never appearing to control it from authority; and their opinions on civil questions, are submitted with a deference, directly in contrast to their bold declarations on subjects of war or tribute, which amount to injunction.

The Ashantees advocated this constitution by the argument, that the interference of the Aristocracy in all foreign politics, makes the nation more formidable to its enemies, who feel they cannot provoke with impunity, where there are so many guardians of the military glory; who, by insisting on a war, become responsible in a great degree for the issue, and pledge an energy and exertion, in

* It has been shewn in the history, that the Aristocracy was originally formed of the peers and associates of Sai Tootoo the founder of the monarchy, who owed his elevation not to his superior rank, but to his superior endowments and address. The Aristocracy has been gradually retrenched since Saï Cudjo pointed out the way.

comparison with which, such as could be excited by a despotic monarch, must be deemed disinterested. They added, that an almost independent administration of the King, was better calculated for the domestic government, because the decrees of a monarch have naturally more force with the people, (over whom his power is unlimited) and, further, that a civil power in the Aristocracy could not be reconciled to the Assembly of Captains, to whom the former estate was already sufficiently invidious for the health of the constitution.

In exercising his judical authority, the King always retired in private with the Aristocracy to hear their opinions, to encourage their candor without diminishing his majesty in the eye of the people; and in using his legislative prerogative, he was said always to give them a private opportunity of defending the old law, rather than of objecting to the new; though, from the same state policy, the latter was announced to the Aristocracy as well as to the Assembly of Captains, before the people, as the sudden and arbitrary pleasure of the King.

The general Assembly of the Caboceers and Captains, is summoned merely to give publicity to the will of the King and Aristocracy, and to provide for its observance; unless on state emergencies, or unprecedented occasions, such as the Treaty with the British Government. The following anecdote, related to me by many Ashantees, will illustrate the freedom of their constitution.

A son of the King's quarrelling with a son of Amanquateä's, (one of the four) told him, that in comparison with himself, he was the son of a slave; this being reported to Amanquateä, he sent a party of his soldiers, who pulled down the house of the King's son and seized his person. The King hearing of it sent to Amanquateä, and learning the particulars, interceded for his son, and redeemed his head for 20 periguins of gold.

The most original feature of their law, that of succession, has been mentioned in the History, with the argument on which it is founded: it is universally binding; the course is, the brother, the sister's son, the son, the chief vassal or slave to the stool. In the Fantee country, the principal slave succeeds to the exclusion of the son, who only inherits his mother's property, frequently considerable, and inherited from her family independently of her husband: the daughters share a small part of the fetish or ornamental gold, which is much alloyed with silver.

The sisters of the King may marry or intrigue with whom they please, provided he be an eminently strong or personable man; that the heirs of the stool may be, at least, personably superior to the generality of their countrymen.

The King is heir to the gold of every subject, from the highest to the lowest; the fetish gold and the cloths are generally presented by him to the successor to the stool, from which the slaves and other property of the deceased are inseparable. The King contributes to the funeral custom to validate his claim, and usually bestows ten periguins of the dust gold on the successor, (if of a rich man,) who is in all cases liable for the debts of the deceased, though the amount is generally made good to him sooner or later, if he has influence with those about the King, or recommends himself to his notice personally. This law is sometimes anticipated, by a father presenting his children with large sums of gold just before his death. Boiteëm, the father of Otee, one of the King's linguists, is known to have done so, but the son discovers his wealth very deliberately.

The gold buried with members of the royal family, and afterwards deposited with their bones in the fetish house at Bantama, is sacred; and cannot be used, but to redeem the capital from the hands of an enemy, or in extreme national distress; and even then, the King must avoid the sight of it, if he would avoid the fatal vengeance of the fetish or deity.

If a slave seeks refuge from an ally or tributary, he is restored; if from an unconnected power, he is received as a free subject.

The tributary state which distinguishes itself in suppressing the revolt of another, is rewarded by privileges at the expense of the offending power: thus if a subject of the former kills a subject of the latter, the price of a slave only can be recovered, instead of the fine otherwise attached to the death of a freeman; and the damages for other injuries are reduced in proportion.

If the subjects of any tributary do not like the decision of their ruler, according to the laws of their own country, they may appeal to the King, and claim decision by the law of Ashantee. The commission allowed to the collectors of tribute or fine, is two periguins out of ten.

The direct descendants of the noble families who assisted the enterprise of Saï Tootoo, the founder of the kingdom, are not subject to capital punishment, but can only be despoiled. There are now but four remaining, Ananqui, Assafee, (see Diary,) and two others, all beggars.

We were present at the promulgation of the following law: " All persons sent on the King's business shall no longer seize provisions in any country, whether tributary or otherwise, in his name; but requiring food, shall offer a fair price for the first they meet with, if this is refused, they shall then demand one meal, and one meal only, in the King's name, and proceed. This extends to all messengers sent by the head captains, whose servants, as well as the King's, have been long in the habit of extorting goods from traders, and tobacco and provisions in the market place, in the names of their masters, which they shall do no longer without incurring the same penalty which is attached to the former part of this law, 110 periguins." The form of making this law, was, the linguists with their insignia advanced and announced it to each of the four members of the Aristocracy, then to the whole assembly; afterwards Cudjo Appăni, the chief crier, proclaimed it to the people, who shouted their thanks; his fee from the King was ten ackies, from the people twenty. This attachment of the penalty to the law (the chief merit of Zaleucus) manifests some advancement in polity, in securing the accused against arbitary judgment.*

The caboceers of Soota, Marmpon, Becqua, and Kokofoo, the four large towns built by the Ashantees at the same time with Coomassie, have several palatine privileges; they have an independent treasury, though subject to the demands of the government and a judicial power, with the reserve of an appeal to the King. They celebrate their own yam custom after they have attended that at Coomassie, at which all dependents and tributaries must be present, and which seems to have been instituted like the Panathenæa of Theseus, to unite such various nations by a common festival. These four caboceers, only, are allowed, with the King, to stud their sandals with gold.

The blood of the son of a King, or of any of the royal family cannot be shed; but when guilty of a crime of magnitude, they are drowned in the river Dah, by a particular captain, named Cudjo Samfani.

If a man swears on the King's head, that another must kill him, which is understood to be invoking the King's death if he does not, the other man must do so, or forfeit the whole of his property, and generally his life. This very frequently occurs, for the blacks

* By the laws of Ahanta, which are peculiar, if any subject or sojourner is in urgent want of provisions, he may seize the first he meets with, paying the owner the prices which have been fixed by the caboceers: this is similar to the law of Lycurgus. At the Contoom or annual Harvest Custom, the Ahantas revise their laws, as Solon enjoined the Athenians to do, annulling some and adding others.

in their ardor for revenge, do not regard sacrificing their own lives to bring a palaver on their murderer, which their families are sure to do.

To be convicted of cowardice is death.

A subject may clear any part of the bush for building a croom, or making a plantation, without paying any thing to the King as lord of the soil; but he must pay a small sum to the possessor of the nearest croom or plantation, through which his path runs.

The government has no power to direct the traders to any particular market, though it interdicts the commerce with any power which may have offended it.

All the King's linguists take fetish to be true to each other, and to report faithfully.

If any subject picks up gold dropped in the market place, it is death, being collected only by order of the government on emergencies; see Revenue.

Theft of the King's property, or intrigue with the female attendants of the royal family, or habitual incontinence, is punished by emasculation; but crim. con. with the wife of a man who has been so punished, is death: being considered an aggravated contempt of law.

Interest of money is 33⅓ per cent. for every forty days, which is accompanied after the first period by a dash of liquor. When the patience of the creditor is exhausted, he seizes the debtor, or even any of his family, as slaves, and they can only be redeemed by the payment. This barbarous law was nearly the same in Athens.*

In almost all charges of treason, the life of the accuser is at risk as well as that of the accused, and is forfeited on the acquittal of

* In Ahanta, all old debts must be paid within six weeks from the commencement of the Contoom or Harvest Custom. The creditor can panyar or seize not only the family, but the townsmen of the debtor.

L l

the latter. I understood this, from the best authorities, to be in-indispensible as a check on the palavers; envy, spleen, or covetous-ness would otherwise accumulate.

The accuser is never discovered or confronted to the accused, nor the evidence revealed, until the latter has fully replied to the charge, as outlined by the King's linguists.

Palavers are frequently allowed to sleep even for years, as in the Fantee country, to make the damages sued for, the heavier: for instance, if a man stole a hen twelve months before, the value of the broods and eggs it would have produced, on a fair average, in the interval, would be shrewdly calculated, and sued for.* State palavers are also allowed to sleep for years, but that is to impose the confidence on the accused that the principal witnesses are dead, and the impression is artfully assisted by the policy of the council. The witnesses against Appia Nanu, who had reported his haughty message to the King, had not been seen for nearly twelve months before they burst before him on the day of his trial, having been sent into the bush on the most distant frontier.

No man is punished for killing his own slave, but he is for the murder of his wife or child.† If he kills the slave of another, he must pay the value. If a great man kills his equal in rank, he is generally allowed to die by his own hands: the death of an inferior is generally compensated by a fine to the family, equal to seven slaves.‡

---

* The Ahanta laws do not allow of these protracted palavers, and only award the in-trinsic value of the articles stolen or destroyed. If a man robs a plantation of a yam, he must pay the owner a tokoo of gold, and take two more. In Fantee the pettiest theft frequently entails slavery.

† In the kingdom of Amanaheä or Apollonia, the tenth child is always buried alive.

‡ A person accidentally killing another in Ahanta, pays 5 oz. of gold to the family, and defrays the burial customs. In the case of murder, it is 20 oz. of gold and a slave; or, he and his family become the slaves of the family of the deceased. If a man dashes

If a person brings a frivolous palaver against another, he must give an entertainment to the family and friends of the acquitted.

If an aggry bead is broken in a scuffle, seven slaves are to be paid to the owner.

Trifling thefts are generally punished by the exposure of the party in various parts of the town, whilst the act is published ; but more serious thefts cannot be visited on the guilty by any but his family, who are bound to compensate the accuser, and punish their relative or not as they think fit ; they may even put him or her to death, if the injury is serious, or the crime repeated or habitual.

If a man cohabits with a woman without the house, or in the bush, they are both the slaves of the first person who discovers them ; but redeemable by their families.

It is forbidden, as it was by Lycurgus, to praise the beauty of another man's wife, being intrigue by implication.

A captain generally gives a periguin to the family on taking a wife, a poor man two ackies : the damages for intrigue in the former case are ten periguins ; in the latter, one ackie and a half, and a pot of palm wine.

---

himself to the fetish on the head of another, the other must redeem him. If a man kills himself on the head of another, the other must kill himself also, or pay 20 oz. to the family : in Fantee the sum is indefinitely great : this is frequently resorted to, when there is no other prospect of revenge.

Adumissa, an extraordinarily beautiful red skinned woman of Cape Coast, possessed numerous admirers, but rejected them all. One of them, in despair, shot himself on her head close to her house. The family demanding satisfaction ; to save her relations from a ruinous palaver, she resolved to shoot herself in expiation. She accordingly assembled her friends and relatives from various parts of the country, and sitting, richly dressed, killed herself in their presence with golden bullets. After the body had been exposed in state, it was buried with a profusion of cloths and gold. The beautiful Adumissa is still eulogised, and her favourite patterned cloth bears her name amongst the natives.

If a woman involves herself in a palaver, she involves her family, but not her husband.

None but a captain can sell his wife, and he, only, if her family are unable to redeem her by the repayment of the marriage fee.

The property of the wife is distinct, and independent of the husband, though the King is the heir to it.

None but a captain can put his wife to death for infidelity, and even then he is expected to accept a liberal offer of gold from the family, for her redemption. To intrigue with a wife of the King's is death.

If the family of a woman are able and willing, on her report of her dislike to her husband, or his ill-treatment of her, to tender him the marriage fee, he must accept it, and the woman returns to her family, but may not marry again.

If a husband is not heard of by his wife for three years, she may marry again, and if the first husband returns, the claim of the second is the better; but all the children of the after marriage are considered the property of the first husband, and may be pawned by him.

Those accused of witchcraft, or having a devil, are tortured to death.

The good treatment of slaves is in some degree provided for, by the liberty they have of dashing or transferring themselves to any freeman; whom they enjoin to make them his property by invoking his death if he does not; an imperative appeal.

CHAPTER IV.

Superstitions.

T H E Negro tradition of the book and the calabash, cited by St. Pierre, is familiar to every native of these parts, and seems the source of their religious opinions. Impressed that the blind avarice of their forefathers inclined all the favour of the supreme God to white men, they believe themselves to have been committed to the mediating care of subordinate deities, necessarily as inferior to the primary, as they are to Europeans.

As the Ashantee manner of relating this tradition differs a little from that of the Fantee, I will repeat it, on the authority of Odumata and other principal men. In the beginning of the world, God created three white and three black men, with the same number of women; he resolved, that they might not afterwards complain, to give them their choice of good and evil. A large box or calabash was set on the ground, with a piece of paper, scaled up, on one side of it. God gave the black men the first choice, who took the box, expecting it contained every thing, but, on opening it, there appeared only a piece of gold, a piece of iron, and several other metals, of which they did not know the use. The white men opening the paper, it told them every thing. God left the blacks in the bush, but conducted the whites to the water side, (for this happened in Africa) communicated with them every night, and taught them to build a small ship which carried them to another country, whence they returned after a long period, with various merchandise to barter with the blacks, who might have been the superior people.

With this imaginary alienation from the God of the universe, not a shade of despondency is associated ; they consider that it diminishes their comforts and their endowments on earth, but that futurity is a dull and torpid state to the majority of mankind.

Their fetishes or subordinate deities, are supposed to inhabit particular rivers, woods, and mountains, as the imaginary deities of the Celts. They are venerated in proportion as their predictions (always equivocal) chance to be realized. The present favourite fetish of Ashantee is that of the river Tando. Cobee, a river in Dankara, and Odentee on the Adirree, are two of the others.

The kings, caboceers, and the higher class, are believed to dwell with the superior Deity after death, enjoying an eternal renewal of the state and luxury they possessed on earth. It is with this impression, that they kill a certain number of both sexes at the funeral customs, to accompany the deceased, to announce his distinction, and to administer to his pleasures.

The spirits of the inferior classes are believed to inhabit the houses of the fetish, in a state of torpid indolence, which recompenses them for the drudgery of their lives, and which is truly congenial to the feelings of the Negro. Those of superior wisdom and experience, are said to be endued with foresight after death, and to be appointed to observe the lives, and advise the good of those mortals who acknowledge the fetish ; their state corresponding, in short, with that of the first race of men after death, as described by Hesiod. Those whose enormities nullify the mediation of the funeral custom, or, whom neglect or circumstances might have deprived of it, are doomed, in the imagination of others, to haunt the gloom of the forest, stealing occasionally to their former abodes in rare but lingering visits. Those who have neglected the custom, or funeral rites of their family, are thought to be accursed and troubled by their spirits.

There are two orders of fetishmen. The first class dwell with the fetish,* who has a small round house, built generally at a distance from the town. They question the oracle respecting the future fortune of a state or an individual, convey its advice, and enjoin the attention of the *audible* spirits of those, any member of their family would question respecting property or domestic circumstances :

"Auditur tumulo et vox reddita fertur ad aures." Æn. vi.

The inferior class pursue their various occupations in society, assist in customs and superstitious ceremonies, and are applied to as fortune tellers or conjurors are in Europe ; especially in cases of theft; when, from a secret system of espionage, and a reluctance, frequently amounting to a refusal to discover the culprit, or to do

---

* At Nanampong (Nanan means a grand-father) near Mankasim, in the Braffoo country, there is a deep dell, inhabited by a number of aged fetish men, whom the Fantees believe to be immortal, and to have lived there beyond all memory, in close converse with the fetish, and ignorant of the world but by intuition. The spirits of the aged and wise are believed to dwell amongst them, and their prophecies and advice are revered as emanations from the fetish. Adookoo, the chief of the Braffoos, used sometimes to consult them in person, but generally through his head fetishman, and the Fantees now attribute the successes of the Ashantees, and their own defeats and misfortunes, to the disregard of what the oracle enjoined ; for, whilst it was obeyed, they say the country always prospered ; and, indeed, from the instances which have been reported to me, the responses appear to have directed a just and prudent policy, highly conducive to the welfare of Fantee. This dell is so impervious, and yet so capacious, that many hundred Fantees were secreted there, during the Ashantee invasions, which these priests had predicted. The house or temple of the principal fetish of the Ahanta country, called Checquoo, is at Apremmadoo, about four miles up the Takaradee river : upwards of fifty superior priests are resident there.

more than replace the property whence it was taken, they are generally successful. The magical ceremony consists in knotting, confusing, and dividing behind the back, several strings and shreds of leather. They are also frequently applied to by slippery wives, to work charms to keep their husbands in ignorance of a projected intrigue, which they affect to do.

The primary dignity is hereditary in families, as the priesthood was in Egypt, celibacy not being enjoined; their property is also hereditary, and they possess other immunities. The latter order is frequently augmented by those, who declare that the fetish has suddenly seized, or come upon them, and who, after inflicting great severities on themselves, in the manner of the convulsionists, are ultimately acknowledged. The fetish women, generally pre-ferred for medical aid, as they possess a thorough knowledge of barks and herbs, deleterious and sanative, closely resemble the second class of Druidesses as described, I think by Mela: they seem licensed prostitutes, before and after marriage.

The present state of these people referring them to a comparison with the nations of ancient Europe,* the close resemblance of many points of their superstition to relative particulars recorded of Greece and Gaul, recalls the following reflection of an eminent writer. " The truth is, there is hardly any thing more surprising in the history of mankind, than the similitude, or rather identity, of the opinions, institutions, and manners of all these orders of ancient priests, though they lived under such different climates, and at so great a distance from one another, without inter-course or communication. This amounts to a demonstration, that

* " And here I cannot but remark, that those accounts, when compared, shew how little manners and minds improve in Africa, and how long, and how much society has been there at a stand:—Jobson saw, in 1620, exactly what Park saw in 1798." Sir W. Young.

all these opinions and institutions flowed originally from one fountain."

Half the offerings to the fetish, are pretended to be thrown into the river, the other half belongs to the priests. The King's offering is generally ten ounces, and three or four slaves : that of a poor subject about four ackies. Children are frequently vowed to the service of the fetish before their birth. A slave flying to the temple, may dash or devote himself to the fetish ; but, by paying a fee of two ounces of gold and four sheep, any person shuts the door of the fetish house against all his run away slaves.*

Every family has a variety of domestic fetishes, furnished by the priests, and answering to the Penates of the Romans ; some are wooden figures, others of arbitrary shapes and materials ; they receive offerings and libations at the yam custom, but are not brought out of the house.†

* A slave dashing or devoting himself to Checquoo, the great fetish of Ahanta, is never redeemed ; the impression of the superior power of that fetish being so awful, that the proprietor of the slave, would believe the death of all his family inevitable, were he to redeem him from the sanctuary.

† The different states of the water side revere different animals as fetish : the hyæna is esteemed so at Accra, the alligator at Dix Cove and Annamaboe, and vultures universally ; and with more apparent reason, as they consume all the offal of the neighbourhood, and thus contribute to its health and cleanliness. A black man killing a hyæna at Accra, would incur a serious penalty. A European is obliged to pay a case of neat rum and one piece of white baft, in which the head of the animal is wrapped, and afterwards buried by the natives. Almost every resident on the coast, can speak to the imitative powers of the hyæna, which Pliny has been ridiculed for reporting. In a fresh water pond at Dix Cove, there is an alligator, about twelve feet long, which always appears on the bank, at the call of the fetish men, who then throw it a white fowl. In a modern natural history, I read, " in this part of the world (Africa) also, as well as at Siam, the crocodile makes an object of savage pomp, near the palaces of their monarchs. Philips informs us, that at Sabi, on the slave coast, there are two pools of water near the royal palace, where crocodiles are bred as we breed carp in our ponds in Europe." I never heard of any royal

In Ashantee there is not a common fetish day, as on the coast.* Different families solemnize different days of the week, by wearing white cloths, abstaining from palm wine and labour, as they do the day of the week on which they were born, which is in fact their second fetish day. The King's family keep Tuesday as their fetish day. Odumata's, Friday. Saturday was the King's birth day, when, as well as on his fetish day, he always sat on a stool placed before his chair as a foot stool would be. Some families never eat beef, others abstain from pork. Fowls and beef are the fetish of the King's family, and consequently never eaten by it.

The Ashantees have their Fasti and Nefasti, or lucky and unlucky days, as the Romans had.† The former consecrated by some good fortune, the latter condemned from some national calamity, as Saturday, for instance, from the defeat and death of Saï Tootoo. They are also otherwise marked than by the week; for I was told, that our month of September contained fewer bad days than any other, and was besides deemed auspicious to travelling:

Ipsa dies alios alio dedit ordine Luna
Felices operum - - - -
- - - - nona fugæ melior.   Geor. i.

I have known Ashantees thirty days coming with dispatches from Cape Coast Castle to Coomassie, in August; and in September, to have arrived in twelve.

If the successor to a stool, or any rich inheritance is a child, they grind aggry beads into a powder, and rub him with it daily,

palaces, or of Sabi (probably Assaboo) on the Slave Coast; the alligator of Dix Cove may possibly be alluded to.

* Tuesday is the common fetish day on the coast, when they neither fish or work in their plantations.
†   Ille et nefasto te posuit die.   Hor. 12, 13.
Romani pariter quosdam atros et nefastos habuere, eo quod in iis clades acceperant; - - -

after washing, believing that it hastens his growth and maturity. When any one denies a theft, an aggry bead is placed in a small vessel, with some water, the person holding it puts his right foot against the right foot of the accused, who invokes the power of the bead to kill him if he is guilty, and then takes it into his mouth with a little of the water, the rest being thrown on the ground, and crossed as he repeats the invocation : their superstition is generally superior to their resolution. I shall be expected to notice these aggry beads.

The natives invariably declare that the aggry beads are found in the Dankara, Akim, Warsaw, Ahanta, and Fantee countries, the greater number in the former, being the richer in gold ; they say they are directed to dig for them by a spiral vapour issuing from the ground, and that they rarely lay near the surface : the finder is said to be sure of a series of good fortune. The plain aggry beads are blue, yellow, green, or a dull red, the variegated consist of every colour and shade. The Fantees prefer the plain yellow bead, the Amanaheäns the blue and yellow, for which they will give double the weight in gold ; those of inferior beauty frequently fetch a large price, from having been worn by some royal or eminent character. Dr. Leyden, who writes, " the aigris is a stone of a greenish blue colour, supposed to be a species of jasper, small perforated pieces of which, valued at their weight in gold, are used for money," (which I never heard of,) rather describes the popo bead ; though that is semi-transparent, (of a bright blue,) resembling carnelian, (which is frequently found in these countries) and said to be obtained in the same manner as the aggry bead. Isert writes, " they are a sort of coral, with inlaid work : the art of making beads is entirely lost, or was never known in these parts : it is not improbable, that in the golden age of Egypt, she had communication with the Gold Coast ; indeed, it has been thought, and perhaps not without some reason, that the Gold Coast is the Ophir of Solomon."

The variegated strata of the aggry beads are so firmly united, and so imperceptibly blended, that the perfection seems superior to art: some resemble mosaic work, the surfaces of others are covered with flowers and regular patterns, so very minute, and the shades so delicately softened one into the other, and into the ground of the bead, that nothing but the finest touch of the pencil could equal them. The agatized parts disclose flowers and patterns, deep in the body of the bead, and thin shafts, of opaque colours, running from the centre to the surface. The natives pretend that imitations are made in the country, which they call boiled beads, alleging that they are broken aggry beads ground into powder, and boiled together, and that they know them because they are heavier; but this I find to be mere conjecture among themselves, unsupported by any thing like observation or discovery. The natives believe that by burying the aggry beads in sand they not only grow but breed.*

* The coloring matter of the blue beads has been proved, by experiment, to be iron; that of the yellow, without doubt, is lead and antimony, with a trifling quantity of copper, though not essential to the production of the color. The generality of these beads appear to be produced from clays colored in thin layers, afterwards twisted together into a spiral form, and then cut across: also from different colored clays raked together without blending. How the flowers and delicate patterns, in the body and on the surface of the rarer beads, have been produced, cannot be so well explained. Besides the suite deposited in the British Museum, I had the pleasure of presenting one of the most interesting kind to Baron Humboldt; and I have also sent one to Sir Richard Hoare, as it seemed to correspond so closely with the bead which he found in one of the barrows, and describes, as follows, in his History of Wiltshire. The notion of the rare virtues of the Glain Neidyr, as well as of the continued good fortune of the finder, accords exactly with the African superstitions. " A large glass bead, of the same imperfect petrefaction as the pully beads, and resembling also, in matter, the little figures that are found with the mummies in Egypt, and are to be seen in the British Museum. This

To return to the superstitions of the Ashantees: when they drink, they spill a little of the liquor on the ground as an offering

very curious bead has two circular lines of opaque sky blue and white, which seem to represent a serpent entwined round a centre, which is perforated. This was certainly one of the Glain Neidyr of the Britons, derived from glain, which is pure and holy, and neidyr a snake. Under the word glain, Mr. Owen, in his Welsh Dictionary, has given the following article: " The Glain neidyr, transparent stones, or adder stones, were worn by the different orders of the bards, each having its appropriate color. There is no certainty that they were worn from superstition originally ; perhaps that was the circumstance which gave rise to it. Whatever might have been the cause, the *notion of their rare virtues was universal* in all places where the Bardic religion was taught. It may still be questioned whether they are the production of nature or art." The beads which are the present object of my attention, are thus noticed by Bishop Gibson in his improved edition of Camden's Britannia. " In most parts of Wales, and throughout all Scotland, and in Cornwall, we find it a common opinion of the vulgar, that about Midsummer eve (although in the time they do not all agree,) it is usual for snakes to meet in companies ; and that by joining heads together, and hissing, a kind of bubble is formed like a ring, about the head of one of them, which the rest, by continual hissing blow on till it comes off at the tail; and then it immediately hardens, and resembles a glass ring, *which whoever finds (as some old women and children are persuaded) shall prosper in all their undertakings.* The rings which they suppose to be thus generated are called Gleinu Nadroedh, i. e. Gemmæ Anguinum, whereof I have seen at several places about twenty or thirty. They are small glass annulets, commonly about half as wide as our finger rings, but much thicker ; of a green color, usually, though some of them are blue, and others curiously waved with blue, red, and white. I have also seen two or three earthen rings of this kind, but glazed with blue, and adorned with transverse streaks in furrows on the outside. There seems to be some connection between the Glein Neidyr of the Britons, and the Ovum Anguinum mentioned by Pliny,* as being held in veneration by the Druids of Gaul, and to the formation of which he gives nearly the same origin. They were probably worn as an insigne, or mark of distinction, and

---

* Præterea est ovorum genus in magna Galliarum fama, omissum Græcis. Angues innumeri æstate convoluti, salivis faucium, corporumque spumis artifici complexu glomerantur, anguinum appellantur. Druidæ sibilis id dicunt in sublime jactari, sagoque oportere intercipi ne tellurem attingat. Profugere raptorem equo. Serpentes enim insequi donec arceant amnis alicujus interventu. Experimentum ejus esse si contra aquas fluitet vel auro cinctum Insigne Druidis. Ad victorias litium ac regum aditus maxime. laudat. Plinii Hist. Natural. L. 29. c. 3.

to the fetish; and on rising from their chairs or stools, their attendants instantly lay them on their sides, to prevent the devil (whom they represent to be white) from slipping into their master's places.

suspended around the neck, as the perforation is not sufficiently large to admit the finger."

The bead engraved in Tumulus No. 9, resembles closely a coarse sort of bead, still manufactured in Syria, brought over by Dr. Meryon. The glass globes dug up in Lincolnshire, and presented by Sir Joseph Banks to the British Museum, are very like a distinct sort of aggry bead, dug by the natives even more rarely than the others, but not larger than a moderate sized apple: they are more opaque than the other beads, and the ground or body is generally black, speckled confusedly with red, white, and yellow.

Aggry is the generic, not the abstract name; '*awynnce*' is *bead*, but aggry is an exotic word no native can explain. When first I heard of similar beads having been lately dug in India, I associated for an instant the expectation that it might have been in the neighbourhood of Agra, and thus have thrown some light on the name; but it appears they were found in Malabar. I am indebted for the following account of this interesting discovery to a gentleman lately returned from India. " The bead you sent me is more like those I saw in India, than any I have seen before; but it is thicker and shorter; neither does the material of which it is formed exactly agree with those in India, which appear to be of a red glass, very like red carnelian (such, however, are frequent among the Aggry beads) with white lines of enamel, inlaid, at it were, in the body of the bead. I gave these to a friend in India, who promised to send them to the Asiatic Society in Calcutta. The circles of stone in which these beads have been found, abound most in Malabar, in the neighbourhood of Calicut; but I have seen them in other parts of India, and I am of opinion that they might be traced throughout the whole of the southern peninsula. They are formed of large masses of rough stones, placed round in irregular circles, some of very large extent, some of smaller: they appear so much like natural rocks, that most persons would pass them unobserved. Several of these circles about three years since were excavated, in the vicinity of Calicut, and in the centre of each of them we found, at the depth of about five feet, a large earthen jar of the same shape as those found in Wiltshire, as near as we could judge, for it was broken to pieces: it was about four or five feet deep, its mouth in general closed with a square piece of granite: the beads were found at the bottom of these jars with some pieces of iron, apparently parts of swords and spears. There was an iron javelin found in one of these places, tolerably perfect: it was about five feet long, with a large iron knob at one end of it. In the centre of one of the circles we came to a flight of seven steps, which led

But the most surprising superstition of the Ashantees, is their confidence in the fetishes or saphies they purchase so extravagantly from the Moors, believing firmly that they make them invulnerable and invincible in war, paralyse the hand of the enemy, shiver their weapons, divert the course of balls, render both sexes prolific, and avert all evils but sickness, (which they can only assuage,) and natural death. The King gave to the King of Dagwumba, for the fetish or war coat of Apokoo, the value of thirty slaves; for Odunata's, twenty; for Adoo Quamina's, thirteen; for Akimpon's, twelve; for Akimponteä's, nine; and for those of greater captains in proportion. The generals being always in the rear of the army

o a cave excavated in the rock; it measured 11 feet in diameter, and 7 feet in its highest part; the entrance to it was a square opening of about 18 inches, which was closed up by an immense block of granite. We found in this place a great number of earthen pots of very curious shape; in one of these there were the remains of bones, which appeared to have been but imperfectly calcined; in several of the larger jars there were the husks of rice, which dropped into dust immediately they were opened. We found here also an iron tripod, and a very curious stone, somewhat similar to what the Indians now use for grinding their curry powder on. The large stones forming the circles were set upright and capped with still larger ones. They are not of granite, but of the stone of the country in which they are situated; they are of different sizes; I have seen some of them 10 or 12 feet high, and the large stone on the top from 10 to 12 feet in diameter, or perhaps more. Coimbatore is a district situated between the Coromandel and Malabar coasts; it is bounded on the east by the river Cavery, on the banks of which the tumuli are in general situated. In some, a few silver coins have been found, of a square figure, with characters on them, which none of the most learned Bramins have been as yet able to make out; it is in these also that remains of very large swords, &c. have been found. The Roman coins to the number of upwards of 90 were all of gold, and Nero's; each of them had a cut or slit in it. They were not found in one of these barrows, but were discovered in a garden by one of the natives when digging: they were in a small copper pot. Pandu Kuri literally means Pandu's caves or holes. Pandu is a very celebrated personage in the Hindoo Mythology, and a great warrior; it is common in India to ascribe to him all great works of antiquity; this term therefore only shews that those places are very ancient, and that the present inhabitants are quite ignorant of their origin.

are pretty sure to escape, a circumstance much in favour of the
Moors. The drawing of Adoo Quamina will convey the best idea
of this dress, which has been described before, in our entrée; it is
so weighty that old Odumata could scarcely move in his. Janne-
quin, who visited Mandingo in 1637, describes exactly the same
sort of dress as worn by the chiefs of that country, and adds,
" their bodies are so encumbered with these defences, that they
are often unable to mount on horseback without assistance." For
a small fetish of about six lines, sewn in a case of red cloth, which
the King presented to our Accra linguist, Baba charged and received six ackies. The man valued the gift highly; he had expended two pieces of cloth and a quantity of rum in fetish, at
Accra, before he joined the Mission; but for which, he told me,
he was convinced the Ashantees would have managed to poison
him: yet, he was one of the most sensible natives I ever conversed
with. A sheet of paper would support an inferior Moor in Coomassie for a month. Several of the Ashantee captains offered
seriously to let us fire at them; in short, their confidence in these
fetishes is almost as incredible, as the despondency and panic
imposed on their southern and western enemies by the recollection
of them: they impel the Ashantees, fearless and headlong, to the
most daring enterprises, they dispirit their adversaries, almost to
the neglect of an interposition of fortune in their favour. The
Ashantees believe that the constant prayers of the Moors, who
have persuaded them that they converse with the Deity, invigorate
themselves, and gradually waste the spirit and strength of their
enemies. This faith is not less impulsive than that which achieved
the Arabian conquests.

Neither the Ashantees or their neighbours have any tradition of
a deluge, nor does Catcott, the only writer I recollect to have read
on its universality, report any Negro tradition, though he submits

hat of the American tribes, with those of the other nations of the
orld. The Moors told me, that the waters of the deluge retired
), and were absorbed in the lake Caudi or Caughi, which they
lso called Bahar Noohoo, or the sea of Noah.

Amongst other observations, I recollect the Moors to have said,
iat Moses spoke like God, that Abraham was the friend of God,
iat Jesus was a spirit of God, but that Mahomet was the best
eloved of God. They added, that there were four books written
y the inspiration of God, at different times. Moses wrote Tau-
itoo; David, Zaboura; Jesus, Lingheel; and Mahomet, Al
:oran. Lightning, they said, was occasioned by God waving his
and to direct the courses of his angels. One Moor was a great
tymologist; he told me, that Mahomet rushing between two
rmies, who were fighting, exclaimed to one party, " Toorek!
'oorek!" (leave off! leave off!) and that those people were thence-
irward called Turks. I questioned them concerning the origin of
ations; they told me, that Japhet was the most active in covering
ie nakedness of his father, which Ham discovered, and thence the
ibjection of black men the descendants of Ham, to Europeans
ie descendants of Japhet. Shem, from whom they were them-
:lves descended, they said, was neither so good or so bad as his
rothers, and therefore his children enjoyed a medium of endow-
ient and favour. They augured from the sacrifice of sheep, with
hich the King supplied them abundantly, and, excepting those
ho had made a pilgrimage to Mecca, (of which they told us
onderful tales) did not hesitate mingling the superstitions of the
atives with their own, either for their profit or safety. They were
ilerably expert in slight of hand tricks.

CHAPTER V.

Customs.

T ʜ ᴇ Yam Custom is annual, just at the maturity of that vegetable, which is planted in December, and not eaten until the conclusion of the custom, the early part of September. All the caboceers and captains, and the majority of the tributaries, are enjoined to attend, none being excused, but such as the Kings of Inta, and Dagwumba, (who send deputations of their principal caboceers,) and those who have been dispatched elsewhere on public business. If a chief or caboceer has offended, or if his fidelity be suspected, he is seldom accused or punished until the Yam Custom, which they attend frequently unconscious, and always uncertain of what may be laid to their charge. The Yam Custom is like the Saturnalia; neither theft, intrigue, or assault are punishable during the continuance, but the grossest liberty prevails, and each sex abandons itself to its passions.

On Friday the 5th of September, the number, splendor, and variety of arrivals, thronging from the different paths, was as astonishing as entertaining; but there was an alloy in the gratification, for the principal caboceers sacrificed a slave at each quarter of the town, on their entré.

In the afternoon of Saturday, the King received all the caboceers and captains in the large area, where the Dankara canons are-

Engraved by R. Havell & Son.

placed. The scene was marked with all the splendor of our own entré, and many additional novelties. The crush in the distance was awful and distressing. All the heads of the kings and caboceers whose kingdoms had been conquered, from Saï Tootoo to the present reign, with those of the chiefs who had been executed for subsequent revolts, were displayed by two parties of executioners, each upwards of a hundred, who passed in an impassioned dance, some with the most irresistible grimace, some with the most frightful gesture: they clashed their knives on the skulls, in which sprigs of thyme were inserted, to keep the spirits from troubling the King. I never felt so grateful for being born in a civilized country. Firing and drinking palm wine were the only divertissemens to the ceremony of the caboceers presenting themselves to the King; they were announced, and passed all round the circle saluting every umbrella: their bands preceded; we reckoned above forty drums in that of the King of Dwabin. The effect of the splendor, the tumult, and the musquetry, was afterwards heightened by torch light. We left the ground at 10 o'clock; the umbrellas were crowded even in the distant streets, the town was covered like a large fair, the broken sounds of distant horns and drums filled up the momentary pauses of the firing which encircled us: the uproar continued until four in the morning, just before which the King retired. I have attempted a drawing, (No. 2.) it is by no means adequate, yet more so than description could be.

On the left side of the drawing is a group of captains dancing and firing, as described in our entré. Immediately above the encircling soldiery, is a young caboceer under his umbrella, borne on the shoulders of his chief slave; he salutes as he passes along, and is preceded and surrounded by boys (with elephants tails, feathers, &c.) and his captains, who, lifting their swords in the air, halloo out the deeds of his fore-fathers; his stool is borne close to

him; ornamented with a large brass bell. Above is the fanciful
standard of a chief, who is preceded and followed by numerous
attendants; he is supported round the waist by a confidential
slave, and one wrist is so heavily laden with gold, that it is supported
on the head of a small boy; with the other hand he is saluting a
seated caboceer, sawing the air by a motion from the wrist. His
umbrella is sprung up and down to increase the breeze, and large
grass fans are also playing; his handsomest slave girl follows, bearing on her head a small red leather trunk, full of gold ornaments,
and rich cloths; behind are soldiers and drummers, who throw
their white-washed drums in the air, and catch them again, with
much agility and grimace, as they walk along. Boys are in the
front, bearing elephants tails, fly flappers, &c. and his captains
with uplifted swords, are hastening forward the musicians and
soldiers. Amongst the latter is the stool, so stained with blood that
it is thought decent to cover it with red silk. Behind the musicians
is Odumata, coming round to join the procession in his state hammock lined with red taffeta, and smoking under his umbrella, at
the top of which is a stuffed leopard. In the area below is an
unfortunate victim, tortured in the manner described in the entré,
and two of the King's messengers clearing the way for him. The
King's four linguists are seen next; two, Otee and Quancum, are
seated in conversation under an umbrella; the chief, Adoosey, is
swearing a royal messenger, (to fetch an absent caboceer,) by
putting a gold handled sword between his teeth, whilst Agay
delivers the charge, and exhorts him to be resolute. The criers,
all deformed and with monkey skin caps, are seated in the front.
Under the next umbrella is the royal stool, thickly cased in gold.
Gold pipes, fans of ostrich wing feathers, captains seated with gold
swords, wolves heads and snakes as large as life of the same metal,
depending from the handles, girls bearing silver bowls, body

guards, &c. &c. are mingled together till we come to the King, seated in a chair of ebony and gold, and dressed much in the same way as described at the first interview. He is holding up his two fingers to receive the oath of the captain to the right, who, pointing to a distant country, vows to conquer it. On the right and left of the state umbrella are the flags of Great Britain, Holland, and Denmark. A group of painted figures are dancing up to the King, in the most extravagant attitudes, beating time with their long knives on the skulls stuck full of thyme. On the right of the King is the eunuch, who superintends the group of small boys, the children of the nobility, waving elephants tails, (spangled with gold,) feathers, &c.: behind him is the above mentioned captain and other chiefs dressed as in the left end of the drawing. Musicians, seated and standing, are playing on instruments cased or plated with gold. The officers of the Mission are next seen, their linguists in front, their soldiers, servants, and flag behind, at the back of whom is placed the King's state hammock, under its own umbrella. Adjoining the officers is old Quatchie Quofie and his followers; at the top of his umbrella is stuck a small black wooden image, with a bunch of rusty hair on the head, intending to represent the famous Akim caboceer who was killed by him; vain of the action, he is seen according to his usual custom, dancing before and deriding his fallen enemy, whilst his captains bawl out the deed, and halloo their acclamations. The manner of drinking palm wine is exhibited in the next group, a boy kneels beneath with a second bowl to catch the droppings, (it being a great luxury to suffer the liquor to run over the beard,) whilst the horns flourish, and the captains halloo the strong names. The Moors are easily distinguished by their caps, and preposterous turbans. One is blessing a Dagwumba caboceer, who is passing on horseback, (the animal covered with fetishes and bells,) escorted by his men in tunics, bearing lances, and his musicians with rude violins, distinct from the sanko. The back of the whole assembly is lined with royal soldiers, and the commoner ones are ranged in front, with here and there a captain and a group of musicians, who, some with an old cocked hat, some with a soldier's jacket, &c. &c. afford a ludicrous appearance. This description will be rendered more illustrative of the drawing, by referring to that of our entré.

The next morning the King ordered a large quantity of rum to be poured into brass pans, in various parts of the town; the crowd pressing around, and drinking like hogs; freemen and slaves, women and children, striking, kicking, and trampling each other under foot, pushed head foremost into the pans, and spilling much more than they drank. In less than an hour, excepting the principal men, not a sober person was to be seen, parties of four reeling and rolling under the weight of another, whom they affected to be carrying home; strings of women covered with red paint, hand in hand, falling down like rows of cards; the commonest mechanics and slaves furiously declaiming on state palavers; the most discordant music, the most obscene songs, children of both sexes prostrate in insensibility. All wore their handsomest cloths, which they trailed after them to a great length, in a drunken emulation of extravagance and dirtiness.*

Towards evening the populace grew sober again, the strange caboceers displayed their equipages in every direction, and at five

* The description of the siege of Pondicherry in Voltaire occurred to me; it will assist the imagination of the reader: " De grands magasins de liqueurs fortes y entretenaient l'ivrognerie et tous les maux dont elle est le germe. C'est une situation qu'il faut avoir vue. Les travaux, les gardes de la tranchée étaient faits par des hommes ivres - - - - - - - - - - De-là les scènes les plus honteuses et les plus destructives de la subordination et de la discipline. On a vu des officiers se colleter avec des soldats et mille autres actions infâmes, dont le détail, renfermé dans les bornes de la vérité la plus exacte, paraîtrait une exagération monstreuse."

o'clock there was a procession from the palace to the south end of the town and back; the King and the dignitaries were carried in their hammocks, and passed through a continued blaze of musketry: the crush was dreadful. The next day (Monday) was occupied in state palavers, and on Tuesday the diet broke up, and most of the caboceers took leave.

About a hundred persons, mostly culprits reserved, are generally sacrificed, in different quarters of the town, at this custom. Several slaves were also sacrificed at Bantama, over the large brass pan, their blood mingling with the various vegetable and animal matter within, (fresh and putrefied,) to complete the charm, and produce invincible fetish. All the chiefs kill several slaves, that their blood may flow into the hole from whence the new yam is taken. Those who cannot afford to kill slaves, take the head of one already sacrificed and place it on the hole.*

The royal gold ornaments are melted down every Yam Custom, and fashioned into new patterns, as novel as possible This is a piece of state policy very imposing on the populace, and the tribatary chiefs who pay but an annual visit.

About ten days after the custom, the whole of the royal houshold eat new yam for the first time, in the market place, the King attending. The next day he and the captains set off for Sarrasoo before sun rise, to perform their annual ablutions in the river Dah. Almost all the inhabitants follow him, and the capital appears

---

* In Ahanta, at the Contoom or Harvest custom, each family erects its rude altar, composed of four sticks driven in the ground, and twigs laid across the top; the whole is then covered with fresh pulled leaves. A hog, a sheep, a goat, or a fowl is killed, according to the means of the family, and the most delicate parts laid on the altar, a mixture is made of eggs, palm oil, palm wine, the blood of the animal slain, and other ingredients, and also dedicated to the fetish, in small pots placed on the altar. In a few days these altars become so offensive as to render it disagreeable to pass them, but they are never removed.

deserted; the succeeding day the King washes in the marsh at the south-east end of the town, the captains lining the streets leading to it on both sides. He is attended by his suite, but he laves the water with his own hands over himself, his chairs, stools, gold and silver plate, and the various articles of furniture used especially by him. Several brass pans are covered with white cloth, with various fetish under them. About twenty sheep are dipped, (one sheep and one goat only are sacrificed at the time,) to be killed in the palace in the afternoon, that their blood may be poured on the stools and door posts. All the doors, windows, and arcades of the palace, are plentifully besmeared with a mixture of eggs, and palm oil; as also the stools of the different tribes and families. After the ceremony of washing is over, the principal captains precede the King to the palace, where, contrary to usual custom, none but those of the first rank are allowed to enter, to see the procession pass. The King's fetish men walk first, with attendants holding basins of sacred water, which they sprinkle plentifully over the chiefs with branches,* the more superstitious running to have a little poured on their heads, and even on their tongues. The King and his attendants all wear white cloths on this occasion. Three white lambs are led before him, intended for sacrifice at his bed chamber. All his wives, follow, with a guard of archers.

Another national custom is the Adaï, by the number of which the Ashantees appear to reckon their year, which began, I could not understand why, on the first of October. The common people pretend, or believe, that the time for repeating the Adaï, is marked by the falling of a fruit like a gourd, from a tree called Brebretim, and which generally takes place in about twenty days from its first appearance, all the birds and beasts in the neighbourhood crying

---

* " Idem ter socios purâ circumtulit undâ,
    Spargens rore levi et ramo felicis olivæ."   Æn. vi

out simultaneously. They further pretend, that from the fruit of this tree spring various kinds of vegetables. This account of the tree, known in Warsaw as well, is peculiar to Ashantee. The customs are alternately called the great and little Adaï, the former taking place always on a Sunday, the latter on a Wednesday; and it appeared to me, from calculation, that there were six weeks between each great Adaï, and six between each little one, so that the custom was generally held every twenty-one days.

The large drum which stands at the entrance of the palace, adorned with skulls and thigh bones, is struck with great force at sun set the preceding day, as a signal; the whole of the establishment of the palace shout, and their shout is echoed by the people throughout the town. Music and firing generally beguile the night. The next morning the King goes to the fetish house, (Himma,) opposite the palace, and offers several sheep; the blood of this sacrifice is poured on the gold stool, to which extraordinary virtues are ascribed, being considered the palladium of the kingdom: the deposition of Saï Quamina was protracted from his having it in his possession at Dwabin. The caboceers and captains, many coming from towns two or three days distant, begin to march to the large yard of the palace about sun rise, to secure their places. We generally attended between nine and ten, when the King had just seated himself. The first ceremony was penetrating to the King, through the various state officers and attendants, to wish him good morning, at which he slightly inclined his head. The chiefs as they advanced to do so, were supported and followed by a few favourite attendants, who flourished their swords in the air, the gold handles upwards, and the band of each began to play as he left his seat. Young caboceers of five and six years of age, stalked by with interesting vanity. After this the King left his chair, which was turned upside down, and retired a few minutes into the palace.

o o

All the horns flourished as he made his exit and entrée; swords, feathers, elephants tails, were waved rapidly, and the drums beaten with deafening effect. After he was seated, the linguists, preceded by their gold canes and insignia, presented a sheep, a flask of rum, (drank on the ground,) and ten ackies of gold to each superior captain, and somewhat less to the others. Another flourish pro-claimed the dispensation of the King's bounty. Five or six men then rose; and chaunted his deeds and titles for about ten minutes. I regret exceedingly that this chaunt was not noted, it was so harmonious. I observed them put something between their teeth before they began. The same tedious form of saluting the King was now repeated to return thanks. Any new law was afterwards promulgated, which occurred but twice during our stay, and the levee broke up on the King's leaving his chair. Not unfrequently the whole took place during heavy rain. It was computed that the King dashed or presented forty pereguins of gold (£400.) every Adaï custom.*

The decease of a person is announced by a discharge of muketry, proportionate to his rank, or the wealth of his family. In an instant you see a crowd of slaves burst from the house, and run towards the bush, flattering themselves that the hindmost, or those surprised in the house, will furnish the human victims for sacrifice, if they can but secrete themselves until the custom is over. The body is then handsomely drest in silk and gold, and laid out on

---

* The Ahanta's divide time into periods of three weeks. The first week is called Adaï, and is termed the good week, in which much work is done; and traders visit the markets more frequently in this week than at any other time, supposing all they do in it must prosper. The second week is Ajamfoe, or the bad week, in which no work or trade is done, the natives believing every thing undertaken in it must fail. The third week is Adim, or the little good week, in which they both work and trade, but not as much as in the Adaï.

the bed, the richest cloths beside it.* One or two slaves are then sacrificed at the door of the house. I shall describe the custom for Quatchie Quofie's mother, which we witnessed August the 2d.; it was by no means a great one, but it will give the most correct idea of these splendid, but barbarous ceremonies. The King, Quatchie Quofie, and Odumata each sacrificed a young girl directly the deceased had breathed her last, that she might not want for attendants until the greater sacrifice was made. The retainers, adherents, and friends of the family then sent contributions of gold, powder, rum, and cloth, to be expended at the custom; the King, as heir, exceeding every quota but that of the nearest relative, who succeeded to the stool and slaves. The King also sent a sum of gold, and some rich cloths to be buried with the deceased, in the basket or coffin. I could not learn the various sums of gold dust with sufficient accuracy to note them, but the following were the quantities of powder presented on the occasion:

Quatchie Quofie - -	20 oz. (of gold) kegs.
King - - - -	4
King's brother - - -	2
Amanquateä - - -	2
Odumata - - -	2
Apokoo - - -	1
Otee - - - -	1
Yapensoo - - -	1
Amanqua Abiniowa (the nephew)	2
(Name illegible) - -	1
Adoosey - - -	1
Jessinting - - -	1
Saphoo - - - -	1
Ooshoo - - -	1
Inferior retainers - -	4
	44 nearly 12 barrels.

* --- Tum membra toro defleta reponunt,
Purpureasque super vestes, velamina nota,
Conjiciunt ; Æn. vi.

In Fantee they dress the body richly, and usually prop it erect in a chair, exposing it

The inferior retainers of Quatchie Quofie gave four ackies of gold, and eight fathoms of cloth each. I was told these contributions were unusually small, from the command of the King that the greatest economy should be observed in every expenditure of powder, on account of the approaching war.

We walked to Assafoo about twelve o'clock; the vultures were hovering around two headless trunks, scarcely cold. Several troops of women, from fifty to a hundred in each, were dancing by in movements resembling skaiting, lauding and bewailing the deceased in the most dismal, yet not discordant strains; audible, from the vast number, at a considerable distance. Other troops carried the rich cloths and silks of the deceased on their heads, in shining brass pans, twisted and stuffed into crosses, cones, globes, and a fanciful variety of shapes only to be imagined, and imposing at a small distance the appearance of rude deities. The faces, arms, and breasts of these women were profusely daubed with red earth, in horrid emulation of those who had succeeded in besmearing themselves with the blood of the victims. The crowd was overbearing; horns, drums, and muskets, yells, groans, and screeches invaded our hearing with as many horrors as were crowded on our sight. Now and then a victim was hurried by, generally dragged or run along at full speed; the uncouth dress, and the exulting countenances of those who surrounded him, likening them to as many fiends. I observed apathy, more frequently than despair or emotion, in the looks of the victims. The chiefs and captains were arriving in all directions, announced by the firing of muskets, and the peculiar flourishes of their horns, many of which were by this time familiar to us; they were then habited plainly as warriors,

until it is dangerous to do so any longer: they bury it in their house, with as many gold ornaments as they can afford to dedicate. The men called the town drummers are only allowed to die standing, and when expiring are snatched up, and supported in that posture. In Ahanta they frequently exhibit the body chalked all over.

and were soon lost to our sight in the crowd. As old Odumata passed in his hammock, he bade us observe him well when he passed again: this prepared us in a small degree. Presently the King's arrival in the market place was announced, the crowd rolled towards it impetuously, but the soldiery hacked on all sides indiscriminately, and formed a passage for the procession. Quatchie Quofie hurried by, plunging from side to side like a Bacchanal, drunk with the adulation of his bellowing supporters; his attitudes were responsive to the horror and barbarism of the exultations which inspired them. The victims, with large knives driven through their cheeks, eyed him with indifference; he them with a savage joy, bordering on phrenzy: insults were aggravated on the one, flattery lavished on the other. Our disgust was beguiled for an instant by surprise. The chiefs who had just before passed us in their swarthy cloths, and the dark gloomy habits of war, now followed Quatchie Quofie, glistening in all the splendor of their fetish dresses: (see drawing, No. I.) the sprightly variety of their movements ill accorded with the ceremony. Old Odumata's vest was covered with fetish, cased invariably in gold or silver. A variety of extraordinary ornament and novel insignia, courted and reflected the sun in every direction. It was like a splendid pantomime after a Gothic tragedy.

We followed to the market place. The King, and the chiefs not immediately connected with Quatchie Quofie, were seated under their canopies, with the usual insignia and retinue, and lined about the half of a circle, apparently half a mile in circumference; the soldiery completed it, their respective chiefs situated amongst them. Thirteen victims, surrounded by their executioners, whose black shaggy caps and vests gave them the appearance of bears rather than men, were pressed together by the crowd to the left of the King. The troops of women, before described, paraded without the circle, vociferating the dirge. Rum and palm wine were flowing copiously, horns and drums were exerted even to frenzy. In an instant there was a burst of musketry near the King, and it spread and continued incessantly, around the circle, for upwards of an hour. The soldiers kept their stations, but the chiefs, after firing, bounded once round the area with the gesture and extravagance of madmen; their panting followers enveloping them in flags, occasionally firing in all the attitudes of a scaramouch, and incessantly bellowing the strong names of their exulting chief, whose musket they snatched from his hands directly he had fired. An old hag, described as the head fetish woman of the family, screamed and plunged about in the midst of the fire as if in the greatest agonies. The greater the chief the heavier the charge of powder he is allowed to fire; the heaviest charge recollected, was that fired by the King on the death of his sister, 18 ackies, or an ounce avoirdupoise. Their blunderbusses and long guns were almost all braced closely with the cordage of the country; they were generally supported by their attendants whilst they fired, several did not appear to recover it for nearly a minute; Odumata's old frame seemed shaken almost to dissolution. Many made a point of collecting near us, just within the circle, and firing as close as possible to startle us; the frequent bursting of their muskets made this rather alarming as well as disagreeable. The firing abated, they drank freely from the bowls of palm wine, religiously pouring a small quantity on the ground before they raised them to their lips.*

*   " Hic duo rite mero libans carchesia Baccho
                " Fundit humi.   Æn. v.

            " Οἶνον δ'ἐκ δεπάων χαμάδις χέον, οὐδέ τις ἔτλη
            " Πρὶν πιέειν, πρὶν λεῖψαι ὑπερμενέϊ Κρονίωνι." Ομηρ. η.

The Ashantees do so not only on solemn occasions, but invariably; and it would seem that the Greeks did, from the following words of Hecuba to Hector,

The principal females of the family, many of them very hand-some, and of elegant figures, came forward to dance; dressed, generally, in yellow silk, with a silver knife hung by a chain round their necks; one with a gold, another with a silver horn; a few were dressed as fetish women; an umbrella was held over the grand daughter as she danced. The Ashantees dance incomparably better than the people of the water side, indeed elegantly; the sexes do not dance separately, as in Fantee, but the man encir-cles the woman with a piece of silk which he generally flirts in his right hand, supports her round the waist, receives her elbows in the palms of his hands, and a variety of figures approximating, with the time and movement, very closely to the waltz.

A dash of sheep and rum was exchanged between the King and Quatchie Quofie, and the drums announced the sacrifice of the victims. All the chiefs first visited them in turn; I was not near enough to distinguish wherefore. The executioners wrangled and struggled for the office, and the indifference with which the first poor creature looked on, in the torture he was from the knife passed through his cheeks, was remarkable: the nearest executioner snatched the sword from the others, the right hand of the victim was then lopped off, he was thrown down, and his head was sawed rather than cut off; it was cruelly prolonged, I will not say wilfully. Twelve more were dragged forward, but we forced our way through the crowd, and retired to our quarters. Other sacrifices, princi-pally female, were made in the bush where the body was buried. It is usual to " wet the grave" with the blood of a freeman of respectability. All the retainers of the family being present, and the heads of all the victims deposited in the bottom of the grave,

" Ἀλλὰ μέν', ὄφρα κέ τοι μελιηδέα οἶνον ἐνείκω,
Ὡς σπείσῃς Διῒ πατρὶ καὶ ἄλλοις ἀθανάτοισι
Πρῶτον· ἔπειτα δέ κ'αὐτὸς ὀνήσεαι, αἴ κε πίῃσθα· " Ομηρ, ζ.

several are unsuspectingly called on in a hurry to assist in placing the coffin or basket, and just as it rests on the heads or skulls, a slave from behind stuns one of these freemen by a violent blow, followed by a deep gash in the back part of the neck, and he is rolled in on the top of the body, and the grave instantly filled up. A sort of carnival, varied by firing, drinking, singing, and dancing, was kept up in Assafoo for several days; the chiefs generally visiting it every evening, or sending their linguists with a dash of palm wine or rum to Quatchie Quofie; and I was given to understand, that, but for the approaching war and the necessary economy of powder, there would have been eight great customs instead of one, for this woman, one weekly, the King himself firing at the last. The last day, all the females in any way connected with the family (who are not allowed to eat for three days after the death, though they may drink as much palm wine as they please,) paraded round the town, singing a compliment and thanks to all those who had assisted in making the custom.

On the death of a King, all the Customs which have been made for the subjects who have died during his reign, must be simulta-neously repeated by the families, (the human sacrifices as well as the carousals and pageantry) to amplify that for the monarch, which is also solemnised, independently, but at the same time, in every excess of extravagance and barbarity. The brothers, sons, and nephews of the King, affecting temporary insanity, burst forth with their muskets, and fire promiscously amongst the crowd; even a man of rank, if they meet him, is their victim, nor is their murder of him or any other, on such an occasion, visited or prevented; the scene can scarcely be imagined. Few persons of rank dare to stir from their houses for the first two or three days, but religiously drive forth all their vassals and slaves, as the most acceptable composition of their own absence. The King's Ocras, who will be mentioned presently, are all murdered on his tomb, to the number of a hundred or more, and women in abundance. I was assured by several, that the custom for Saï Quamina, was repeated weekly for three months, and that two hundred slaves were sacrificed, and 25 barrels of powder fired, each time. But the custom for the King's mother, the regent of the kingdom during the invasion of Fantee, is most celebrated. The King of himself devoted 3000 victims, (upwards of 2000 of whom were Fantee prisoners) and 25 barrels of powder.* Dwabin, Kokoofoo, Becqua, Soota, and Marmpong, furnished 100 victims, and 20 barrels of powder, each, and most of the smaller towns 10 victims, and two barrels of powder, each. The Kings, and Kings only, are buried in the cemetery at Bantama, and the sacred gold buried with them ; (see Laws ;) their bones are afterwards deposited in a building there, opposite to which is the largest brass pan I ever saw, (for sacrifices,) being about five feet in diameter, with four small lions on the edge. Here human sacrifices are frequent and ordinary, to water the graves of the Kings. The bodies of chiefs are frequently carried about with the army, to keep them for interment at home, and eminent revolters or enemies also, to be exposed in the capital. Boiteäm, (the father of Otee the fourth linguist,) who accompanied the army of Abiniowa in his political capacity, dying at Akrofroom in Aquapim, during the campaign, his body was kept with the army two months before it arrived at Coomassie. I could not get any information on their treatment of the corpse, beyond their invariable reply that they smoked it well over a slow fire.

The laws of Ashantee allow the King 3333 wives, which number is carefully kept up, to enable him to present women to those who

---

* Suetonius tells us that Augustus sacrificed 300 of the principal citizens of Perusia, to the manes of his uncle Julius. We read in Prevost, that 64080 persons were sacrificed, with aggravated barbarity, in the dedication of a temple in Mexico.

distinguish themselves, but never exceeded, being in their eyes a mystical one. Many of these reside in a secluded part of the King's croom, or country residence, at Barramang; a greater number in a croom, at the back of the palace, immediately in the marsh; and the remainder in two streets of the capital. Many, probably, the King has never seen. The streets as well as the croom, are inhabited by them exclusively, and never approached but by the King's messengers, or their female relatives, who only communicate with them at the entrances, which are closed at each end with bamboo doors, where there is always a guard. If the King *consaws* or marries an infant at the breast, which is not unfrequent, she is thenceforth confined to the house, and rigorously secluded from the sight of any but the female part of her family. The King has seldom more than six wives resident with him in the palace. On the occasion of signing the treaty, as explained in the public letter, about 300 were assembled, and none but the King's Chamberlain, and the deputies of the parts of the government, were allowed to be present: they were addressed through their own linguist, a very decrepid old man; many of them were very handsome, and their figures exquisite. When they go out, which is seldom, they are encircled and preceded by troops of small boys with thongs or whips of elephants hide, who lash every one severely who does not quit their path for another, or jump into the bush with his hands before his eyes; and sometimes the offenders are heavily fined besides. The scrambling their approach occasioned, in the more public parts of the city, was very diverting; captains, caboceers, slaves, and children tumbling one over another. I was told what it cost the King daily to support them, but it has escaped me; they are said to live as daintily as himself. None but the chief eunuch, an immense creature, is allowed to bear a message to the King when in the seraglio of the palace.

It has been mentioned before, that the King's sisters are not only countenanced in intrigue, with any handsome subject, but they are allowed to choose any eminently so, (however inferior otherwise,) as a husband; who is presently advised by the King of his good fortune; thus they consider they provide for a personal superiority in their monarchs. But if the royal bride dies before the husband, unless his rank be originally elevated, he is expected to kill himself on the occasion, and also if the only male child dies: if he hesitates, he is peremptorily reminded that as either are his superiors, to whom he is to be considered as a slave, so he must attend them wherever they go; and when a male child is born, the father does it homage and acknowledges his vassalage in the most abject manner.

The Ocra's are distinguished by a large circle of gold suspended from the neck; many of them are favourite slaves, many, commoners who have distinguished themselves, and who are glad to stake their lives on the King's, to be kept free from palavers and supported by his bounty, which they are entirely; some few are relatives and men of rank. All of the two former classes, excepting only the two or three individuals known to have been entrusted with the King's state secrets, are sacrificed on his tomb. The royal messengers, and others of the suite have been described in the processions; they are sometimes fed in the palace, but they have a free seat at the table of every subject.

The King has a troop of small boys, who carry the fetish bows and arrows, and are licensed plunderers; they are so sly and nimble, that it is very diverting to watch them in the market place, which they infest every morning. Whatever they can carry off is fair game, and cannot be required or recovered; but the loser, if he can catch them before they arrive at the palace, may beat them as severely as he pleases, short of mortal injury; however, they bear it as obdurately as young Spartans. Sometimes one party trips up a person with a load of provisions, whilst another scrambles them up: the anxious alarm of the market people, sitting with sticks in their hands, and the comic archness of these boys threading the crowd in all directions, is indescribable. Some of the earliest European travellers in Abyssinia met with a similar troop of royal plunderers, and I believe suffered from them; our property was always respected by them, but they used to entertain themselves with mimicking our common expressions and our actions, which they did inimitably: whilst sketching, they buzzed about me like musquitoes. The Ashantees are without exception the most surprising mimics I have ever heard. I have known a captain, called Adoo Quamina, repeat a sentence after I had finished it, of at least a dozen words, which he knew nothing about, and had not heard before. The King has a sort of buffoon, whose movements were as irresistibly comic as those of Grimaldi.

The King appeared to have nearly a hundred negroes of different colors, through the shades of red and pink to white; they were collected for state, but were generally disgusting objects, diseased and emaciated; they always seemed as if going to shed their skins, and their eyes blinked in the light, as if it was not their element.

About twenty pots of white soup, and twenty pots of black (made with palm nuts) are cooked daily at the palace, (besides those for the consumption of the household,) for visitors of consequence, and a periguin of gold is given daily to Yokokroko, the chamberlain, for palm wine. This would have appeared too large a sum, had I not witnessed the vast consumption and waste of it; for the vigour of an Ashantee being estimated by the measure of the draught he can drink off; nearly half is generally spilt over his beard, which it is his greatest pride and luxury to draw through his fingers when wet. The King was very proud of the superior length of his beard. A large quantity of palm wine is dashed to the retinues of all the captains attending in the course of the day; much is expended in the almost daily ceremony of drinking it in state in the market place; and our party was always well provided for in the course of the evening. The palm wine at the palace was seldom good, but a zest was excited by the exquisite polish of the plate in which it was served. Apokoo, Odumata, and others, sent us some daily that was excellent.

It is to be observed that the King's weights are one third heavier than the current weights of the country; and all the gold expended in provision being weighed out in the former, and laid out in the latter, the difference enriches the chamberlain, cook, and chief domestic officers of the palace, as it is thought derogatory to a King avowedly to pay his subjects for their services. In the same manner the linguists derive the greater part of their incomes, (their influence being occasionally purchased,) for all the dashes or presents of gold the King makes in the year, are weighed out by the royal weights, and re-weighed by them in the current ones. The law allows a debtor to recover of a reluctant or tardy creditor, in the King's weights, besides the interest, (noticed in the laws,) if he is esteemed enough by Apokoo the treasurer, to be trusted with them; or rather, if he can afford to bribe him, or engages to share the profit with him.

After a subject is executed for crime, the body and head are carried out of town by some of the King's slaves, appointed for that purpose, and thrown where the wild beasts may devour them; but if the deceased be of any consequence, some of his friends conceal themselves near where they know the body will be carried, and purchase it, and the right of burial, of these domestics, generally for eight ackies. There are a number of fine large sheep, decorated with bells and other ornaments, about the palace. If any person gets into an ordinary palaver, and wishes the King's interference in his favor, he goes to the captain who has the charge of these sheep, pays him 20 ackies for one, and sends or takes it to the King, as a dash, who commits it again to the care of the captain.

When the King sends an ambassador, he enriches the splendor of his suite and attire as much as possible; sometimes provides it entirely; but it is all surrendered on the return, (except the additional wives) and forms a sort of public state wardrobe. The King's system of espionage is much spoken of (for its address and infallibility) by Apokoo and others, who abet it. A shrewd but mean boy is attached to, or follows the embassy, (sometimes with a trader,) in the commonest capacity and meanest attire; and he is instructed to collect every report, as he passes, and to watch the motions of the embassy as closely as possible. As the extortions of these deputies are always loudly and publicly complained of by the injured inhabitants of the dependent or tributary crooms they pass through, (perhaps being aware they will reach the King's ears,) the particulars are easily acquired. The messengers who were sent with our first dispatches to Cape Coast, excusing the length of the time, (forty days) by alleging that it was found necessary to collect a session of the Fantee caboceers at Paintree; the King replied, " You tell me a lie; you fined a captain there four ounces for breaking an Ashantee law, and you waited to procure and expend the gold, not intending it should be known." The men instantly confessed, and were put in irons; one was the brother of Yokokroko, who paid six ounces for his release, after several days.

When the King spits, the boys with the elephants tails sedulously wipe it up, or cover it with sand; when he sneezes, every person present touches, or lays the two first fingers across the forehead and breast, as the Moors did when they pronounced a blessing, and the Ashantees, invariably, to propitiate one. These troops of boys who carry the elephants tails, are the sons of men of rank and confidence ; for whenever the King dignifies a deserving subject, with what may be termed nobility, he exchanges some of his own sons or nephews, (from eight to fourteen years of age,) for those of the individual, who maintains them, and for whom they perform the same offices, as his own and others do for the King. Thus the present King (the short reign of his brother Saï Apokoo being unanticipated) carried an elephants tail before Apokoo, whose kindness and indulgence to the child secured the preference of the monarch.

It is a frequent practice of the King's, to consign sums of gold to the care of rising captains, without requiring them from them for two or three years, at the end of which time he expects the captain not only to restore the principal, but to prove that he has acquired sufficient of his own, from the use of it, to support the greater dignity the King would confer on him. If he has not, his talent is thought too mean for further elevation. Should he have no good traders amongst his dependents, (for if he has there is no difficulty) usury and worse resources are countenanced, and thought more creditable than a failure, ascribed to want of talent rather than to a regard of principle.

The fees to the King's household on a captain being raised to a stool, are generally eight ounces. I saw two instances of the King paying them himself; the individuals, very suddenly elevated for extraordinary courage, being too poor to do so. They were immediately dispatched to collect tributes, the per centage on which, (see Laws,) and the douceurs, which may be judged of by the amount provided for them in the settlement of the Commenda palaver, would possess them of a good sum to begin with.

The interference of Amanquateä, Quatchie Quofie, Odumata, and Apokoo, is purchased at a most extravagant rate by offenders, whether foreigners or subjects; it is irresistible with the King; Apokoo is generally preferred; minor influence is purchased in proportion. No subject can sit in public with a cushion on his stool, unless it has been presented to him by the King, or one of the four, who, as well as all the other superior captains, receive a periguin of gold for every oath the King exacts of them.

During the minority, or the earlier part of the reign of a monarch, the linguists and oldest counsellors visit him betimes every morning, and repeat, in turn, all the great deeds of his ancestors. The greatest deference seemed to be paid to aged experience or wisdom.

Apokoo is the keeper of the royal treasury, and has the care of all the tributes, which are deposited, separately, in a large apartment of the palace, of which he only has the key. Numerous and various as the sums are, he disposes of them by a local association which is said to be infallible with him, for the Moorish secretary, (who resided some time at Hio,) only records the greater political events. Apokoo holds a sort of exchequer court at his own house daily, (when he is attended by two of the King's linguists, and various state insignia,) to decide all cases affecting tribute or revenue, and the appeal to the King is seldom resorted to. He generally reclined on his lofty bed, (of accumulated cushions, and covered with a large rich cloth or piece of silk,) with two or three of his handsomest wives near him, whilst the pleadings were going forward. He was always much gratified when I attended, and rose to seat me beside him. I observed that all calculations were made, explained, and recorded, by cowries. In one instance, after being convinced by a variety of evidence that a public debtor was unable to pay gold, he commuted sixteen ounces of gold, for twenty men slaves. Several captains, who were his followers, attended this court daily with large suites, and it was not only a crowded, but frequently a splendid scene. Before the footoorh or treasury bag is unlocked by the weigher, though it be by the King's order, Apokoo must strike it with his hand in sanction.

In all public trials, the charges are preferred, in outline, against the criminal by the King's linguists, and he is always heard fully, and obliged to commit or exculpate himself on every point, and to take the various primary oaths, before the witnesses are confronted with him; of whom he is kept as ignorant as possible until the moment of their appearance. The oaths, sometimes four or five, are progressive, generally beginning by the King's foot, or some arbitrary form, and are, apparently, not considereda wful or decisive; such perjuries being commutable by fine. But when the oath, " by the King's father," is administered, every one looks serious, and if, " by Cormantee and Saturday " (see History) is resorted to, there is a gloomy silence; but this is seldom ventured, if the witnesses, (hurried in with a sort of stage effect between that and the former oaths,) confound or perplex the accused.

There are various ways of taking fetish; the two I observed, were, licking a white fowl twice or thrice, and drinking a nauseous vegetable juice without coughing: it was administered by the linguists out of a brass pan in a folded leaf of the plant. If the accused is cleared, he comes forward, and is marked with white chalk by the linguists, after which he bows to, and thanks all the great men in the council. Taking doom is the infallible test, when they consider the case to be too doubtful for human decision. The bark of that tree is put into a large calabash with water, so as to make a strong infusion; it is stirred up whilst the suspected parties sip in turn. It operates, instantaneously and convulsively, as a most violent emetic and purge; those who sip first may recover, and the dregs are frequently left designedly for the obnoxious.*

The criers, upwards of a hundred, who always attend the linguists, are all deformed or maimed, to make them more conspicuous; they wear a monkey skin cap, with a gold plate in front, and the tail hanging down behind. Their common exclamations are, Tehoo! Tehing! Odiddee! Be silent! Be quiet! Pray hear! and these are so incessantly uttered, that they are themselves the only interruption. Several less interesting peculiarities are represented in the drawings of the Yam Custom, and associated with other subjects.

A general is appointed to the command of an army by receiving a gold handled sword of the King's from his hand, (who strikes him gently with it three times on the head,) swearing to return it encrusted with the blood of his conquered enemies. One of the King's linguists always accompanies an army of any consequence, to whom all the politics of the war are entrusted, and whose talent and intelligence in negotiating, are expected to mature the fruits of the military genius of the general, and to reimburse the expense of the war by heavy fines and contributions. The Ashantees are as superior in discipline as in courage to the people of the water side, though their discipline is limited to the following precautions. They never pursue when it is near sun set; the general is always in the rear; the secondary captains lead the soldiers on, whilst those in command, with a few chosen individuals, urge them forward from the rear with their heavy swords, and cut any man down who retreats until the case is desperate. The first object of

---

* In the Warsaw country there is said to be a more dreadful poison called Sabë: if it is thrown upon the skin, it is absorbed by the pores, and has nearly the same instantaneous mortal effect as when given internally.

the Ashantee in close fight, is, to fire and spring upon the throat of his enemy ; to advance every time he fires he feels to be imperative, if his commander thinks it possible, who would, otherwise, if he escaped death in the action, inflict it on him directly it was over. It is one of the sentences of the most popular song in Coomassie, " if I fight I die, if I run away I die, better I go on and die." They are as the antient Spaniards have been described, " prodiga gens animæ et properare facillima mortem." The general has his umbrella spread in the rear, and, besides his guard, has several extra muskets ready loaded for those soldiers who may be driven to him in case of reverse. His band plays all the time, and in his assumed contempt for the enemy, it is the etiquette for him to divert himself at some game, whilst the heads of the slain of any rank in the hostile army are sent to him to put his foot on. When the result of an important action is expected, even with an anxiety by no means sanguine, and the messengers are known to be near the capital, the King is always seated in public, with his golden worra board before him, playing with some dignitary ; and thus receives the news, to impress the people with confidence by his affected indifference to victory or defeat, when superstition had revealed and fated inevitable success ultimately

All the superior captains have peculiar flourishes or strains for their horns, adapted to short sentences, which are always recognised, and will be repeated on enquiry by any Ashantee you may meet walking in the streets, though the horns are not only out of sight, but at a distance to be scarcely audible. These flourishes are of a strong and distinct character. The King's horns uttered, " I pass all Kings in the world." Apokoo's, " Ashantees, do you do right now?" Gimma's, " Whilst I live no harm can come." Bundahenna's, " I am a great King's son." Amanqua's, " No one dares trouble me." This will be further noticed in the chapter on

Music. These peculiar flourishes are more particularly for their government in action, for all the soldiery, indeed I might say all the women and children, being familiar with every flourish, the positions of the various chiefs are judged of when they cannot be seen; whether they are advancing, falling back, or attempting to flank the enemy by penetrating the woods, is known, and the movements of all the others become co-operative, as much as possible. The King's horns go to the market place every night, as near to midnight as they can judge, and flourish a very peculiar strain, which was rendered to me, " King Saï thanks all his captains and all his people for to-day."

Several of the hearts of the enemy are cut out by the fetish men who follow the army, and the blood and small pieces being mixed, (with much ceremony and incantation,) with various consecrated herbs, all those who have never killed an enemy before eat a portion, for it is believed that if they did not, their vigor and courage would be secretly wasted by the haunting spirit of the deceased. It was said that the King and all the dignitaries partook of the heart of any celebrated enemy; this was only whispered; that they wore the smaller joints, bones, and the teeth of the slain monarchs was evident as well as boasted. One man was pointed out to me, as always eating the heart of the enemy he killed with his own hand. The number of an army is ascertained or preserved in cowries or coin by Apokoo. When a successful general returns, he waits about two days at a short distance from the capital, to receive the King's compliments, and to collect all the splendor possible for his entrée, to encourage the army and infatuate the people. The most famous generals are distinguished by the addition of warlike names, more terrific than glorious, as they designate their manner of destroying their prisoners. Apokoo was called Aboäwassa, because he was in the habit of cutting off their arms.

Appia, Sheäboo, as he beats their heads in pieces with a stone. Amanqua, Abiniowa, as he cuts off their legs.

The army is prohibited during the active parts of a campaign, from all food but meal, which each man carries in a small bag at his side, and mixes in his hands with the first water he comes to; this, they allege, is to prevent cooking fires from betraying their position, or anticipating a surprise. In the intervals, (for this meal is seldom eaten more than once a day,) they chew the boossee or gooroo nut. This meal is very nourishing and soon satisfies; we tried it on our march down. Ashantee spies have been stationed three and four days in the high trees overlooking Cape Coast Castle, with no other supply than this meal and a little water, before the army has shewn itself. There is always a distinct body of recruits with the army, to dispatch those with their knives whom the musket has only wounded, and they are all expected to return well armed from despoiling the enemy, or they are not esteemed of promise, and dismissed to some servile occupation. I could not find that they had any idea of fortifications, though undoubtedly common to the large cities on the Niger.

It is the invariable policy of Ashantee to make the contingency of the power last subdued, the revolters recently quelled, or the allies last accepted, the van of their army throughout the campaign, and very frequently there are no Ashantees but captains with the army; but it is composed entirely of tributaries and allies. Thus Odumata subdued Banda with an army of Gamans. In the Ashantee body of the army, which is always that of reserve, the youngest or last made captain marches and engages first, and the others follow seriatim, until Odumata precedes Quatchie Quofie, Amanqua follows him, and Apokoo precedes the King. Were the country generally open, I have no doubt, necessity and their military genius would have suggested greater arrangement and compactness in their movement, which is nevertheless very orderly. Two divisions of an army are rarely allowed to go the same path, lest, being in want of supplies, the neighbourhood should prove inadequate. Aboidwee, our house master, (see correspondence on the Ashantee suicide) who has 1700 retainers, always precedes the King's or Apokoo's division, (which will exclusively occupy the Banda path in the invasion of Gaman) to raise a bamboo house for the King's reception when he comes up.

Infants are frequently married to infants, for the connection of families; and infants are as frequently wedded by adults and elderly men. The ceremony is to send the smaller piece of cloth, worn around the middle, to the infant, and a handsome dash of gold to the mother, as her care then ceases to be a duty, but becomes a service performed to the husband, who also sends frequent presents for the support of the child. Apokoo told me it was a good plan for a man to adopt who wished to get gold, for as the circumstance was seldom generally known, the most innocent freedom when the girl became ten or eleven years old, grounded a palaver against the individual, though he might consider he was but fondling a child, and be wholly ignorant of her marriage. I afterwards understood from several others, that this view was the leading motive.*

It frequently happens, when the family of the wife is too powerful for the husband to venture to put her to death for intrigue, that he takes off her nose as a stigma and punishment, and makes her the wife of one of his slaves. A wife who betrays a secret is sure to lose her upper lip, and, if discovered listening to a private conversation of her husband's, an ear. Women so maimed are to be met

---

* On the Coast, the bride's character is very notoriously published, for part of the husband's present to her family being a flask of rum, and that not sent until the next day; whether it is brimful, or somewhat wanting, indicates her virginity, or early frailty.

with in all parts of the town. Prostitutes are numerous and countenanced. No Ashantee forces his daughter to become the wife of the man he wishes, but he instantly disclaims her support and protection on her refusal, and would persecute the mother if she afforded it; thus abandoned, they have no resource but prostitution. During the menses, the women of the capital retire to the plantations or crooms in the bush.*

In visiting, the chief always gives his principal slaves a few sips of the liquor offered to him, not for security, for it is more frequently after than before he has drank, but as a mark of his favour. He will frequently give his daughter in marriage to a confidential slave, but where there are a few thus distinguished and indulged, (apparently as a political check upon a heterogeneous populace,) there are thousands barely existing.

Their principal games are Worra† (see drawing, No. 10.) which I could not understand, and Drafts, which both Moors and Negroes play well and constantly. Their method resembles the Polish, they take and move backwards and forwards, and a king has the bishop's move in chess. They have another game, for which a board is perforated like a cribbage board, but in numerous oblique lines, traversing each other in all directions, and each composed of three holes for pegs; the players begin at the same instant, with an equal number of pegs, and he who inserts or completes a line first, in spite of the baulks of his adversary, takes a peg from him, until the stock of either is exhausted.

* The women of Ahanta, on the same occasion, are prohibited from entering any inhabited place; and if they attempt to go into a house, are heavily fined or punished. If the family is respectable, they generally erect a temporary shed to shelter her; the poorer class are forced to endure the inclemencies of the weather without any retreat.

† This game is said to be played in Syria also.

CHAPTER VI.

Architecture, Arts, and Manufactures.

THE construction of the ornamental architecture of Coomassie reminded me forcibly of the ingenious essay of Sir James Hall, (in the Edinburgh Philosophical Transactions,) tracing the Gothic order to an architectural imitation of wicker work. The drawings will serve to shew the various and uncommon character of their architectural ornaments, adopted from those of interior countries, and, confessedly, in no degree originating with themselves.

In building a house, a mould was made for receiving the swish or clay, by two rows of stakes and wattle work, placed at a distance equal to the intended thickness of the wall; as two mud walls were raised at convenient distances, to receive the plum pudding stone which formed the walls of the vitrified fortresses in Scotland. The interval was then filled up with a gravelly clay, mixed with water, with which the outward surface of the frame or stake work was also thickly plastered, so as to impose the appearance of an entire thick mud wall. The houses had all gable ends, and three thick poles were joined to each; one from the highest point, forming the ridge of the roof, and one on each side, from the base of the triangular part of the gable; these supported a frame work of bamboo, over which an interwoven thatch of palm leaves was laid, and tied with the runners of trees, first to the large poles running from gable to gable, and afterwards, (within,) to the interlacing of the bamboo frame work, which was painted black and polished, so as to look much better than any rude cieling would, of which they have no idea; a small part appears in the houses in the drawing of Adoom-street (No. 9.) The pillars, which assist to support the roof, and form the proscenium or open front, (which none but captains are allowed to have to their houses) were thick poles, afterwards squared with a plastering of swish. The steps and raised floor of these rooms were clay and stone, with a thick layer of red earth, which abounds in the neighbourhood, and these were washed and painted daily, with an infusion of the same earth in water; it has all the appearance of red ochre, and from the abundance of iron ore in the neighbourhood, I do not doubt it is.

The walls still soft, they formed moulds or frame works of the patterns in delicate slips of cane, connected by grass. The two first slips (one end of each being inserted in the soft wall) projected the relief, commonly mezzo: the interstices were then filled up with the plaster, and assumed the appearance depicted. The poles or pillars were sometimes encircled by twists of cane, intersecting each other, which, being filled up with thin plaster, resembled the lozenge and cable ornaments of the Anglo-Norman order; the quatre-foil was very common, and by no means rude, from the symmetrical bend of the cane which formed it. I saw a few pillars, (after they had been squared with the plaster) with numerous slips of cane pressed perpendicularly on to the wet surface, which being covered again with a very thin coat of plaster, closely resembled fluting. When they formed a large arch, they inserted one end of a thick piece of cane in the wet clay of the floor or base, and bending the other over, inserted it in the same manner; the enta-blature was filled up with wattle work plastered over. Arcades and piazzas were common. A white wash, very frequently renewed,

was made from a clay in the neighbourhood. Of course the
plastering is very frail, and in the relief frequently discloses the
edges of the cane, giving however a piquant effect, auxiliary to the
ornament. The doors were an entire piece of cotton wood, cut
with great labour out of the stems or buttresses of that tree; battens
variously cut and painted were afterwards nailed across. (See
drawing, No. 5.) So disproportionate was the price of labour to
that of provision, that I gave but two tokoos for a slab of cotton
wood, five feet by three. The locks they use are from Houssa, and
quite original; one will be sent to the British Museum. Where
they raised a first floor, the under room was divided into two by
an intersecting wall, to support the rafters for the upper room,
which were generally covered with a frame work thickly plastered
over with red ochre. I saw but one attempt at flooring with plank,
it was cotton wood shaped entirely with an adze, and looked like
a ship's deck. The windows were open wood work, carved in
fanciful figures and intricate patterns, and painted red; the frames
were frequently cased in gold, about as thick as cartridge paper.

What surprised me most, and is not the least of the many circumstances deciding their great superiority over the generality of
Negroes, was the discovery that every house had its cloacæ, besides
the common ones for the lower orders without the town. They
were generally situated under a small arch way in the most retired
angle of the building, but not unfrequently up stairs, within a
separate room like a small closet, (see drawing No. 3.) where the
large hollow pillar also assists to support the upper story: the
holes are of a small circumference, but dug to a surprising depth,
and boiling water is daily poured down, which effectually prevents
the least offence. The rubbish and offal of each house was burnt
every morning at the back of the street, and they were as nice and
cleanly in their dwellings as in their persons.

Drawing No. 3, is one of the oldest houses in Coomassie, inherited by the unfortunate Bakkee, and part of the quarters of the Mission. Its comparative rudeness is evident.

No. 4, is a more modern part of the same house, being one side of a small area about 15 feet square, allotted to the chief officer of the Embassy. These areas are all distinct, and a house consists of an indefinite number of them, some 36 feet square, with several long courts. In paying a visit to a principal man, the state was to detain us some minutes at the door of each area, as he generally received us in the innermost. The figure is one of the King's body guards, which have been described before. The figures are introduced to shew the proportion of the buildings, and to give some idea of the costume.

No. 5, is the exterior of a bed room of Odumata's, which is one side of an oblong area in a very retired angle of his house, about 25 feet by 8. The cloth suspended to the left of the door on the top of the steps, hides the bloody stools which are in the recess. The small gallery in front of the upper room is only wide enough for one person to walk in. The recess and small room below accommodate confidential slaves. The bed room was very small, about 8 feet square, but being hung round with a variety of gold and silver ornaments, had a very rich appearance. The bed is generally about 5 feet high, and composed entirely of large silk-cotton pillows piled one above another. The King of Gaman, we were assured, had steps of solid gold to ascend to his bed. A man wearing a crier's cap, is playing the sanko.

No. 6, is a perspective view of the entrance area to Apokoo's house; the fourth side is an open fronted building like those on the right and left for attendants to wait in, and for the hearing of palavers. The opposite closed side is a bed room. The figure is playing the bentwa (see Music.)

No. 7, is a part of a piazza, which lines the interior of the wall secluding the palace from the street. The piazza is 200 yards long, and inhabited by captains and other attendants on the King; above is a small gallery. Piles of skulls, and drums ornamented with them, are frequent in this piazza. The figure is a common soldier of Ashantee, his belt ornamented with red shells, and stuck full of knives.

No. 8, is the upper end of the piazza, which is more ornamented, and appropriated to the superior captains; who have each a suite of rooms, marked by the small doors under the piazza. A woman is dancing whilst a man plays the flute and rattle.

No. 9, is a view of part of Adoom-street: each open front denotes the residence of a captain, being used for talking palavers, receiving strangers, observing or superintending customs, and evening recreation. The dwelling is entered by the small door at the side, which generally leads through a narrow passage or court to a large area like No. 6, and thence by various intricate ways to smaller and more retired areas like No. 4 and No. 5. A fetish woman has just quitted the centre house; she has on a white cloth, and various pieces of rich silk are hanging round her girdle, her breasts are confined with a scarf, a fillet encircles her head, in each hand she waves a horse's tail, and she continues yelling and swinging round and round until she is quite stupified. A weaver and loom are on her right, and a market woman under her shed on the left.

No. 10, is the exterior of the King's bed room, being one side of an inner area, about 30 feet square. The stunted silk-cotton and the manchineal tree are fetish or sacred, as are the white and red rags at the top of the pole, and the small brass cups supported by the forked sticks. The colored bags hanging over the round doors (the chequering of which is in rel●) contain Moorish charms. The

PART of a PIAZZA in the PALACE.

No. 7.

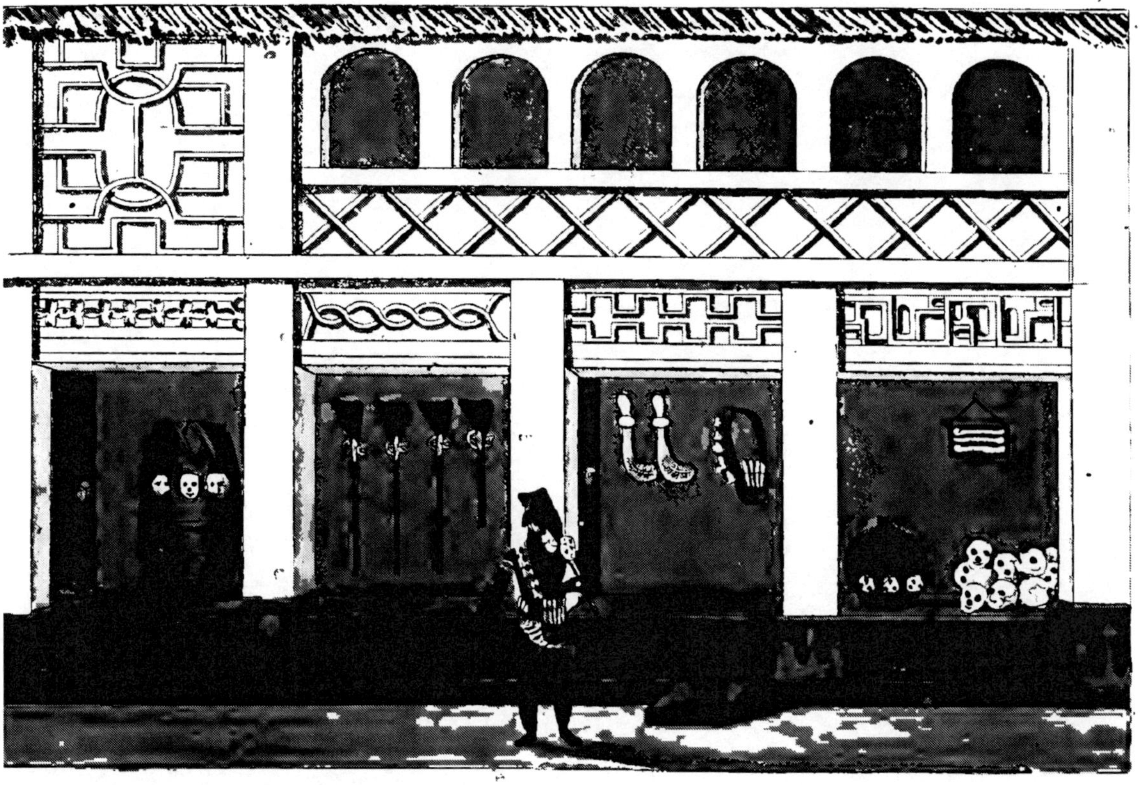

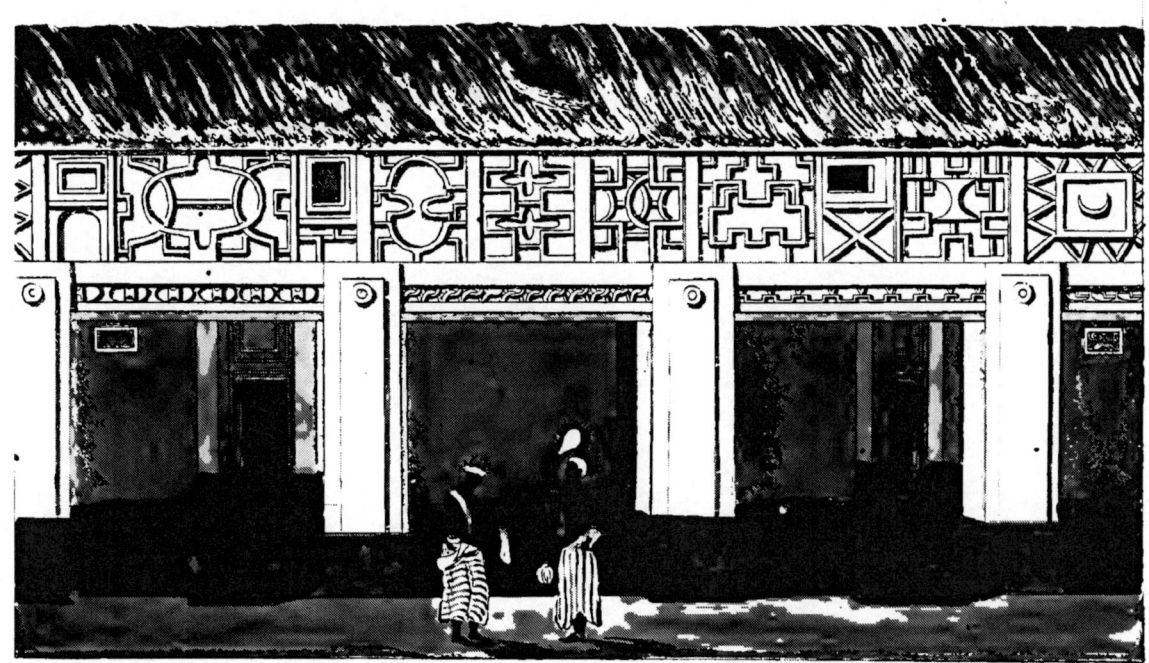

Drawn by T. E. Bowdich Esqr.

No. 8.

PART of a PIAZZA in the PALACE.

Published Decr. 2. 1818, by John Murray, Albemarle Street.

N.º 9.

PART of ADOOM STREET.

THE KING'S SLEEPING ROOM.

carving of the left hand window is cased in silver, of the right hand, in gold. The two men are playing at Worra. The King made frequent enquiries about the architecture of England, of which we gave him some idea by drawings. He was very fond of referring to a project ascribed to Saï Cudjo, and which he declared he would carry into effect directly the Gaman war was over. This was to build a house for his own immediate residence, roofed with brass pans, beaten into flat surfaces, and laid over an ivory frame work appearing within. The windows and the doors to be cased in gold, and the door posts and pillars of ivory. Whether the Moors originated or encouraged this extravagance by the descriptions in their tales, for some of the stories of the Arabian Nights were commonly in their mouths, or whether it was the scheme of his own disposition, prone to magnificence and novelty, the King dwelt ardently on the intention, and by their frequent conversations on the subject, his chiefs appeared scarcely less anxious for the execution than himself. He meditated great improvements and embellishments in his capital, on his return from the war, when it was intended that every captain should be presented with an extraordinary sum out of the public treasury, for adorning or enlarging his house. The ruined streets between Asafoo and Bantama were to be rebuilt, and the six or seven small crooms between Coomassie and Baramang, (the King's country residence,) were to be pulled down, and the inhabitants to occupy a wide street to extend from the city to that croom. This was the darling design of the King; he had already made a sound, broad, and almost direct road, and numerous labourers were continuing to bring it as near as possible to a straight line.

The Ashantee loom is precisely on the same principle as the English; it is worked by strings held between the toes; the web is never more than four inches broad. A weaver is represented in the drawing, No. 3, and a small loom complete is amongst the articles for the British Museum. They use a spindle, and not a distaff, for spinning, holding it in one hand, and twisting the thread, (which has a weight at the end,) with the finger and thumb of the other. The fineness, variety, brilliance, and size of their cloths would astonish, could a more costly one be exhibited; in the absence of which, that for the Museum will doubtless be admired for the two first qualities, and for having precisely the same appearance on both sides. I shall notice in the Chapter on Trade, that the richest silks are unravelled to weave into them. The white cloths, which are principally manufactured in Inta and Dagwumba, they paint for mourning with a mixture of blood and a red dye wood. The patterns are various, and not inelegant, and painted with so much regularity, with a fowl's feather, that they have all the appearance of a coarse print at a distance. I have seen a man paint as fast as I could write. There will be a very fair specimen in the British Museum, the price of painting which was one ackie.

They have two dye woods, a red and a yellow, specimens of which I brought down; they make a green by mixing the latter with their blue dye, in which they excel; it is made from a plant called acassie, certainly not the indigo, which grows plentifully on the Coast. The acassie rises to the height of about two feet, and according to the natives, bears a red flower, but the leaf is not small, fleshy, or soft, nor is it pale or silvery coloured underneath; it is a thin acuminate leaf about five inches long, and three broad, of a dark green.* I regret to add, our best specimens of this plant perished in the disasters of our march, and no drawing was made

* It is a shrub with opposite leaves, no stipules, and having a certain degree of resemblance to *Marsdenia suave-olens* (the indigo of Sumatra) but as the leaves are toothed in the acassie, it probably does not belong even to the same natural order.

ODUMATA'S SLEEPING ROOM. No. 5.

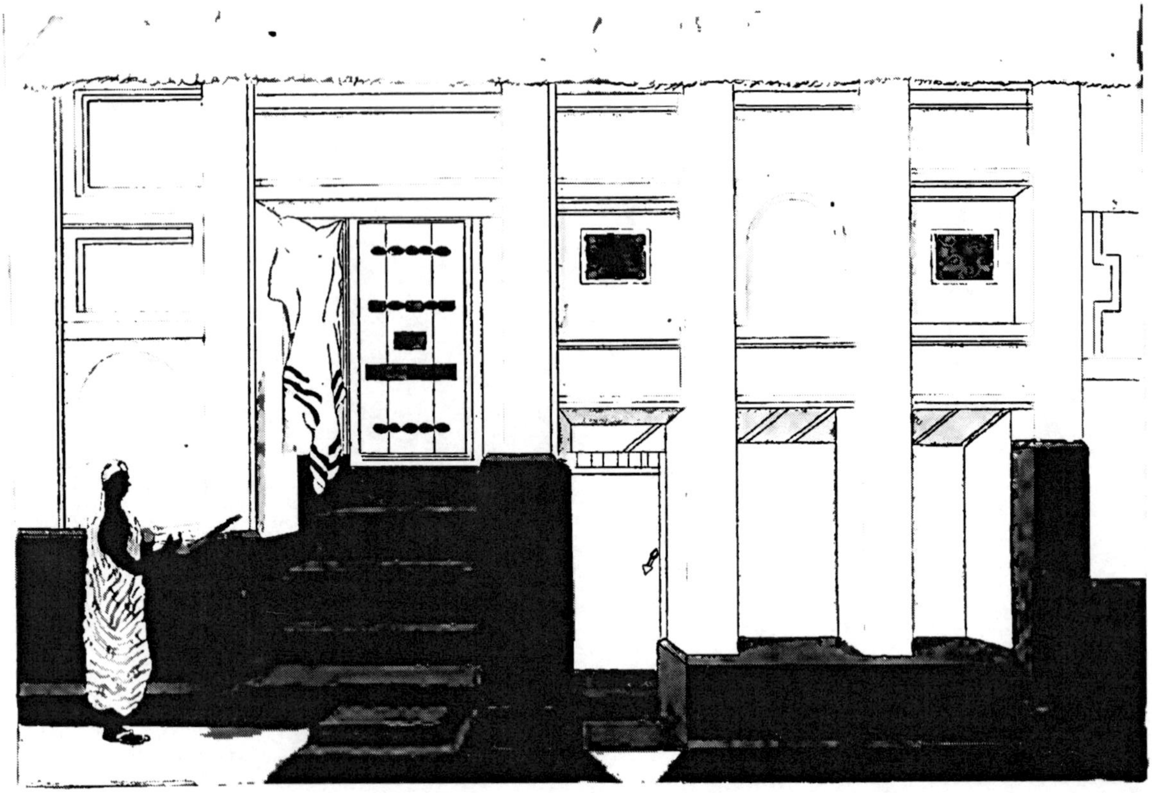

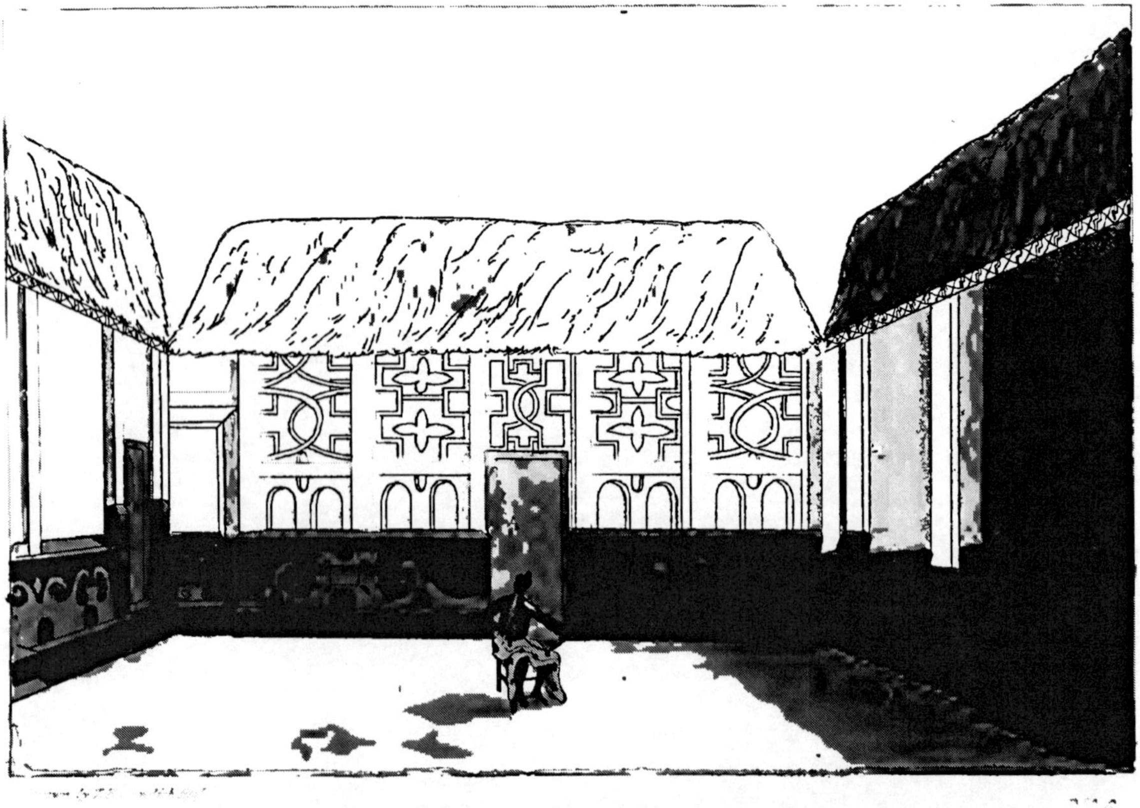

INNER SQUARE of APOOKOOS HOUSE.

PART of the QUARTERS of the MISSION

f it, as it bore no flower in that season; it grows abundantly in
ne woods, and produces a fast and beautiful colour without requir-
ng a mordant. They gather a quantity of the leaves, bruise them
1 a wooden mortar, and spread them out on a mat -to dry, this
nass is kept for use, a proportion of it is put into a pot of water
nd remains six days previous to immersing the thread, which is
eft in six days, drying it once every day in the sun, it is then a
eep lasting blue colour. When a light blue is wished for, the
hread is only allowed to remain in the dye pot three days.

They excel in pottery, as the pipes for the Museum will shew;
hey are rested on the ground when smoked; the clay is very fine,
oolished (after baking) by friction, and the grooves of the patterns
illed up with chalk. They have also a black pottery which admits
of a high polish.

The people of Dagwumba surpass the Ashantees in goldsmith's
vork, though the latter may be esteemed proficients in the art.
The small articles for the Museum, a gold stool, sanko, bell, jaw
oone, and drum, are not such neat specimens as I could wish; the
nan who made them having too much costly work on hand for the
King, to pay our trifles his wonted attention; unfortunately too,
ne was committed to prison before they were quite finished; how-
:ver, they will give an idea. I weighed out nineteen ackies and a
ialf of gold dust for making these articles, one third of an ackie
vas lost in melting, and five was the charge of the goldsmith. We
ost a beautiful silver pipe in the bustle. Bees wax for making the
nodel of the article wanted, is spun out on a smooth block of
vood, by the side of a fire, on which stands a pot of water; a flat
stick is dipped into this, with which the wax is made of a proper
softness; it takes about a quarter of an hour to make enough for a
ring. When the model is finished, it is enclosed in a composition
of wet clay and charcoal, (which being closely pressed around it

forms a mould,) dried in the sun, and having a small cup of the same materials attached to it, (to contain the gold for fusion,) communicating with the model by a small perforation. When the whole model is finished, and the gold carefully enclosed in the cup, it is put in a charcoal fire with the cup undermost. When the gold is supposed to be fused, the cup is turned uppermost, that it may run into the place of the melted wax; when cool the clay is broken, and if the article is not perfect it goes through the whole process again. To give the gold its proper colour, they put a layer of finely ground red ochre, (which they call Inchuma,) all over it, and immerge it in boiling water mixed with the same substance and a little salt; after it has boiled half an hour, it is taken out and thoroughly cleansed from any clay that may adhere to it. Their bellows are imitations of ours, but the sheep skin they use being tied to the wood with leather thongs, the wind escapes through the crevices, therefore when much gold is on the fire they are obliged to use two or three pair at the same time. Their anvils are generally a large stone, or a piece of iron placed on the ground. Their stoves are built of swish (about three or four feet high) in a circular form, and are open about one fifth of the circumference; a hole is made through the closed part level with the ground, for the nozzle of the bellows. Their weights are very neat brass casts of almost every animal, fruit, or vegetable known in the country. The, King's scales, blow pan, boxes, and weights, and even the tongs which hold the cinder to light his pipe, were neatly made of the purest gold that could be manufactured.

Their blacksmith's work is performed with the same sort of forge as the above, but they have no idea of making iron from ore, as their interior neighbours do. Their swords are generally perforated in patterns like fish trowels; frequently they make two blades springing parallel from one handle, which evince very fine workmanship. The needles and castanets will only give some idea of their progress. The iron stone is of a dark red colour, spotted with gray, and intermixed with what had all the appearance of lava, they cut bullets out of it for the army, when lead is scarce. I have brought some arrows of native iron. They have no idea of making a lock like the people of Houssa and Marrowa.

They tan or dress leather in Ashantee, but they do this, and dye it, in a very superior manner in Houssa and Dagwumba; see the sandals and cushion in the British Museum, the former varied and apparently stitched; doubting that there could be such stitching, I undid a part, and discovered that they perforated the surface, and then stuck in the fine shreds of leather. The curious will observe, that the patterns of the stool cushion are all produced by paring the surface. They make their soldiers belts and pouches out of elephant or pig skin, ornamented with red shells. (See drawing, No. 7.)

Of their carpenter's work the stool is a fair specimen, being carved out of a solid piece of a wood called zesso, white, soft, and bearing a high polish; it is first soaked in water. They sell such a stool for about three shillings, in Accra or Fantee it would fetch twenty. The umbrella is even more curious, the bird is cut almost equal to turning, and the whole is so supple that it may be turned inside out. This, only a child's umbrella, is a model of the large canopies I have described in the procession; I gave a piece of cloth value twenty shillings for it. The sanko or guitar is also neatly made, and the chasteness and Etruscan character of the carving is very surprising. The surface of the wood is first charred in the fire, and then carved deep enough to disclose the original white in the stripes or lines of the patterns.

Numbers of workmen are employed in breaking, rounding, and boring the snail shells, as big as a turkey's egg generally, and sometimes as large as a conch. They are first broken into numerous pieces, then chipped round, the size of a sleeve button, and afterwards bored with a bow and iron style fixed in a piece of wood. Lastly they are strung, and extended in rows on a log of wood, and rubbed with a soft and bluish gray stone and water, until they become perfectly round.

Their pine apple thread is very strong, and is made from the fineness of a hair to the thickness of whip cord, it bleaches to a beautiful whiteness, and would answer for sewing any strong material, but, when muslin is stitched with it, it is liable to be cut from the harshness. The women frequently join their cloths, and ornament their handkerchiefs with a zigzag pattern, worked with unravelled silks of different colours. The fetish case is a specimen of their needle work, in the manner of chain stitch.

CHAPTER VII.

Climate, Population, Revenue, City, Market, &c.

T ʜ ᴇ climate will be best judged of by the account of the thermometer (from May to February) in the Appendix. During the first two months, May and June, it rained about one third of the time, throughout July and August it rained nearly half, and abrupt tornadoes were frequent in the evening, just after sun set, ushered in by a strong wind from the south-west. The heaviest rains were from the latter end of September to the beginning of November, they fell even in more impetuous torrents than are witnessed on the coast.* The influence of the harmattan was described as very powerful. Generally speaking, from the elevation of Ashantee, (unfortunately we had no barometer,) it was much cooler in Coomassie than at Cape Coast; indeed, from four to six in the morning, there was a severity of cold unknown on the coast.

I can only calculate the population of the kingdom of Ashantee, small in itself, from its military force, of which the following is the most moderate of the estimates I received.

---

* At Cape Coast in 1815 there was scarcely any rain fell in its season, from May to August. In 1816, the rains were heavy, but no fogs succeeded. In 1817, there was but little rain, but a protracted succession of slight fogs. The climate has been observed, by old residents, to alter as unaccountably within these few years as that of Europe.

Coomassie district (extending to the northern frontier)	60,000
Dwabin ditto - - - - -	35,000
Marmpon ditto - - - - -	15,000
Soota ditto - - - - -	15,000
Kokoofoo ditto - - - - -	15,000
Becqua ditto - - - - -	12,000
Adiabin ditto (between Coomassie and the lake) -	12,000
Aphwagwiasee ditto - - - -	10,000
Daniasce ditto (southwards of Coomassie) -	8,000
Koontarasie ditto (on the lake) - - -	8,000
Gamasie ditto - - - - -	8,000
Amafoo ditto - - - - -	6,000
	204,000

This appears an extravagant force, until we recollect that it is probably one fifth of the whole population.* The Romans when they were a nation of warriors, which these people are, raised a military force equally great in proportion to their population. Barbot heard of the Ashantees losing 50,000 men in two actions, an exaggeration which, nevertheless, serves to argue great military resources. Since the Ashantee invasions, their disposable force has been estimated by old residents in public reports, as upwards of 150,000. From the above particular statement, the population may be estimated at one million, which I believe is little more than half the population of Scotland, the area of which must be more than double that of Ashantee, which certainly does not contain more than 14,000 square miles. Amanquateä, Quatchie Quofie,

* " My friend Mr. Morton Pitt, M. P. has proved, by the enumeration of the inhabitants of a country parish in Dorsetshire, that the men of an age capable of bearing arms are one fourth of the whole community. Mr. Horneman, if I understand him rightly, states the number of actual warriors to be 1500; so that we ought, perhaps, to multiply that number by 5, to get nearer to the total amount of the population." *Major Rennell.*

Odumata, and Apokoo's forces alone amounted to 25,000. The contingencies at command from tributaries, (21 in number) are too indefinite to attempt to detail. Neither Inta or Dagwumba furnish any, the Ashantees pretending to despise their troops too much to use them. The following, which are known to be pretty correct, have generally been the first called into action :

Coranza   10,000
Assin   -   8,000
Takima   -   6,000
Dankara   -   5,000
Warsaw   -   7,000
Booroom   -   12,000
Sawee   -   -   4,000
Akim   -   4,000, before their later destructive revolts 16,000
Aquapim, &c.   1,000

Though polygamy is tolerated to such an excess amongst the higher orders, I do not think, from observation, that the proportion of women to men is two to one. Most of the lower order of free-men have but one wife, and very few of the slaves (the greater proportion of the military force) any. The following calculation is the only one I can think of, and it supports my impression after five months residence.

204,000 Men able to bear arms, about one-fifth of the
                whole population   -   -   -   1,000,000
101,000 Or one-fourth, children under ten years of age
                as found in Great Britain.
 50,000 Boys above that age not capable of bearing arms.
  7,000 Or one in about 28 incapacitated by old age or
                accidents, as found in Great Britain.

362,000   Males 362,000
                                                   Females 638,000

The men are very well made, but not so muscular as the Fantees; their countenances are frequently aquiline. The women also are generally handsomer than those of Fantee, but it is only amongst the higher orders that beauty is to be found, and amongst them, free from all labour or hardship, I have not only seen the finest figures, (which the case of their costume and habits may account for,) but, in many instances, regular Grecian features, with brilliant eyes set rather obliquely in the head. Beauty in a Negress must be genuine, since complexion prejudices instead of imposes, and the European adjudges it to the features only, which appeared in this class to be Indian rather than African; nor is it surprising, when we recollect that they are selected from, or are the daughters of the handsomest slaves or captives; or are expressly chosen by their interior neighbours, to compose part of their tribute to the King of Ashantee, who retains but a small proportion.

Both men and women are particularly cleanly in their persons, the latter washing themselves, and the former being washed by them daily on rising, from head to foot, with warm water and Portuguese soap, using afterwards the vegetable grease or butter, which is a fine cosmetic. Their cloths, which are beetled, are always scrupulously clean. The lowest orders are generally dirty. Occasionally, small delicate patterns in green or white paint are traced on their cheeks and temples. The Moorish negresses darken the edges of their eye lids with lead reduced to a fine powder. The ore was brought from Mallowa and is very rich. The powder is moistened a little, and kept in small boxes, like bodkin cases with a bulb at the end, and prettily covered with cow's hair, within which is a metal stylus to apply the powder, as the women of India do antimony for this purpose. Top-cloths are generally worn, and not by the higher order only as in Fantee. They are commonly of a coarse silk bought at Dagwumba. They wear little or no antiffoo, a sort of cushion projecting from just below the small of the back in the Fantee women, by the size of which, frequently preposterous, and at all times unsightly, their rank, or the number of their children is known. The bosoms of girls of thirteen and fourteen are frequently models, but the young women sedulously destroy this beauty for what is considered a greater, wearing a broad band tight across their breasts, until ceasing to be globular they project conically. Their heads are shaved in fanciful elaborate patterns, having as intricate an appearance as a rich carpet.

The food of the higher orders is principally soup of dried fish, fowls, beef, or mutton, (according to the fetish,) and ground nuts stewed in blood. The poorer class make their soups of dried deer, monkeys flesh, and frequently of the pelts of skins. Yams, plantains, and foofoos, (see the kouskous of Mr. Park) are commonly eaten, and they do not make cankey of their corn, (a coarser sort of kouskous not cleared from the husk) as the Fantees do, but they roast it on the stalk, and when young the flavour closely resembles that of green peas. Besides palm wine they drink Pittō, made from dried corn, which I think must have been the beer Lieutenant Martyn relished so much, for it is quite as pleasant as a brisk small ale. They are forbidden eggs by the fetish, and cannot be persuaded to taste milk, which is only drank by the Moors. Their stews and white soups are excellent, and my companions reported their black soups (made with palm oil) to be equally so.

I cannot pretend to calculate the variable revenue of Ashantee, nor indeed to report its optional sources ; I noted a few particulars.

1. The dust gold of all deceased and disgraced subjects. Boieäm, the father of Otee, left five jars (said to hold about four gallons each) and two flasks. On Appia Nanu's disgrace three jars were seized.

2.   A tax in gold upon all slaves purchased for the coast.*
Customs paid in gold by all traders returning from the coast,
levied near Ansa in Assin.

3.   A tax on the elephant hunters.

4.   The small pits in Soko, which with the washings were reported to yield, sometimes 2,000 ounces per month, at others not
more than 700.

5.   The daily washings throughout Dankara, and the hills dividing Akim and Assin ; very rich in gold.

6.   A tax on every chief increasing the number of his gold
ornaments. Apokoo paid 20 periguins to the King on melting 100.

7. The soil of the market place (see Laws) has been washed but
twice during the present reign.   I was told it produced about 800
ounces of gold each time.   During our stay a heavy rain washed
down a large quantity, which was replaced and carefully covered
with the soil, by the Captain in charge of the market place.   It
was very easily seen after rain.

The tributes of the various nations they had subdued, were in
some instances fixed, but more frequently indefinite, being proportioned to the exigencies of the year ; indeed from various conversations with Apokoo and others, and my own observations during
state palavers, it appeared that the necessities and the designs of
the Ashantee government were the superior considerations, and the
rule in levying tribute every where.   I made the following memoranda.

Inta and Dagwumba never pay in gold, which though plentiful
from commerce, is not found there, cowries being the circulating
medium. Their capitals and all their large towns send the following
tribute annually, and the smaller in proportion.

* Issert mentions this being levied in Akim and other tributary states.

500 Slaves.

200 Cows.

400 Sheep.

400 Cotton cloths.

200 Ditto and silk.

Takima a smaller proportion of the same kind.

Coranza is generally excused, from fidelity, and a long series of military services.

Sawee   -   -   -   200 periguins annually.

Moinseän   -   -   50 bendas ditto.

Gaman had paid, (besides all

   large pieces of rock gold,)   100 periguins ditto.

Akim, Assin, Warsaw, Aowin, &c. &c. were taxed indefinitely by crooms.

Coomassie is built upon the side of a large rocky hill of iron stone. It is insulated by a marsh close to the town northwards, and but a narrow stream; half a mile distant from it N.W., and 60 yards broad; close to it N.E., E., S.E., and S., and about 100, 20, 70, and 50 yards broad at these points. In many parts depth after heavy rains was five feet, and commonly two. The marsh contains many springs, and supplies the town with water, but the exhalation covers the city with a thick fog morning and evening, and engenders dysentery, with which the natives of the coast who accompanied us were almost immediately attacked, as well as the officers. It is a little extraordinary that we never saw a musquito in Ashantee. I could find none but birds eye views of the city, which were uninteresting, presenting nothing but the thatch of the houses; it was encircled by a beautiful forest, which required more time than I could spare, and a more expressive pencil to pourtray. Coomassie is an oblong of nearly four miles in circumference, not including the suburbs of Assafoo nor

T t

Bantama, (the back town,) half a mile distant, and formerly connected by streets with the city, as is evident from the numerous ruins of houses on the path. The slaughter of constant warfare, and the extinction or removal of several ill affected chiefs with their adherents, account for this even in a rising state. The ruins in the interval to Bantama were indeed accounted for by Amanquatĕä (who holds his court there, as Quatchie Quofie does at Assafoo) informing us, that almost all the Ashantees killed before Annamaboe (about 2000 by the most moderate computation) belonged to him, as it was his division which marched along the beach from Cormantine, exposed to the cannon of the fort. Four of the principal streets are half a mile long, and from 50 to 100 yards wide. I observed them building one, and a line was stretched on each side to make it regular. The streets were all named, and a superior captain in charge of each; ours for instance, was Aperremsoo, big gun or cannon street, because those taken when Dankara was conquered, were placed on a mound at the top of it, near Adoo Quamina's house. The area in which we had our first audience was called Daëbrim, the great market, in distinction to a lower street called Gwaba, or the small market. The street above where we lived was called Osamarandiduüm, meaning literally, " with 1000 mukets you could not fight those who live there." One street was named after Odumata, and there was another near it, whose title I forget, but it was equal to prison street. The palace was situated in a long and wide street running through the middle of the town, from which it was shut out by a high wall, terminating at each end at the marsh, where it was discontinued, that being a sufficient boundary. It included Odumata's and the King's brothers residences, and two or three small streets, (besides the several areas and piazzas,) for the King's relief and recreation when the superstitions of the country confine him to the palace. I reckoned twenty

Ichnographical Sketch of COOMASSIE, with the principal Streets and the Situations of remarkable Houses.

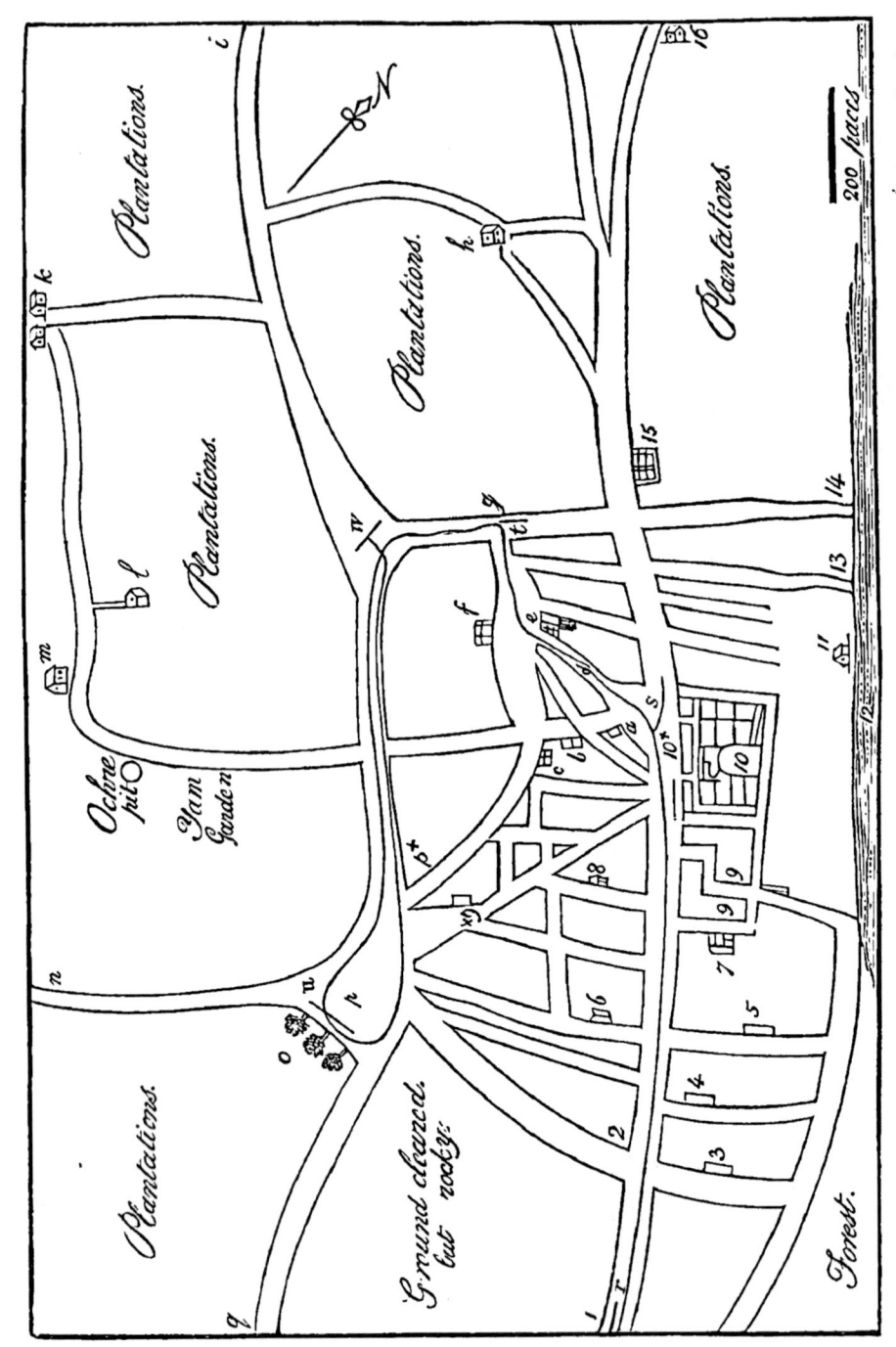

T. E. Bowdich, 1817.

1. Entrance from Fantee and Assin.
2. Agwabu or the small market.
3. King's eldest Sister's house.
4. —— Goldsmith's ditto.
5. Appia Nanu's ditto.
6. Otee's (3d Linguist) ditto.
7. Odumata's (1 of the 4) ditto.
8. King's youngest Sister's ditto.
9. Adoom Street.
9.* Baba's house and the Crumbos (Moors) Street.
10.* Abuogywa or place of execution.

10. Palace.
11. King's wives Croom.
12. Marsh.
13. Entrance from Dwabin.
14. —— Barramang.
15. King of Dwabin's temporary Court.
16. King's Blacksmith's Croom.
a. Himun or the King's fetish temple.
b. Apokoo's (1 of the 4) house.
c. Adooee's (chief linguist.)
d. Apircunsoo Street.

e*. Abridwee's house, the quarters of the Embassy.
f. Adoo Quamina's (chief Captain) house.
g. Osarramandidoum Street.
h. King's Umbrella maker's Croom.
i. Entrance to the high street of Bantama.
k. Croom.
l. Ditto.
m. Ditto.
n. Long irregular suburb, and road to Dankara.
o. Sammonpome or the Spirit Grove.

p. Adooebrim, the large market place.
p.* Small Market.
q. High Street of Assafoo.
—— Course of the procession of the Embassy on its entré.
r. Halted to witness the war dance.
s. Halted to pass the baggage and presents.
t. Halted to witness the human sacrifice.
u. Presented to the King and Chiefs.
u*. Seated to see them march home.

200 Acres

seven streets in all, which I have laid down in a ground plan of the town. The small grove at the back of the large market place was called Sammonpomë or the spirit-house, because the trunks of all the human victims were thrown into it. The bloody tracks, daily renewed, shewed the various directions they had been dragged from, and the number of vultures on the trees indicated the extent of the recent sacrifice; the stench was insupportable, and the visits of panthers nightly. Several trees were individually scattered about the town for the recreation of the inhabitants of those quarters, and small circular elevations of two steps, the lower about 20 feet in circumference, like the bases of the old market crosses in England, were raised in the middle of several streets, on which the King's chair was placed when he went to drink palm wine there, his attendants encircling him.

The Ashantees persisted that the population of Coomassie, when collected, was upwards of 100,000. I think it likely to be much greater than that of Sego, (which Mr. Park reported as 30,000,) from the extended masses of crowd I observed on festivals, when the plantations of the environs are almost wholly deserted. I compared them in my recollection with the crowds I have seen collected in the secondary cities of England, on similar occasions of public curiosity; the only criterion, as I had not time to finish reckoning the number of houses. I say when collected, because the higher class could not support their numerous followers, or the lower their large families, in the city, and therefore employed them in plantations, (in which small crooms were situated,) generally within two or three miles of the capital, where their labours not only feed themselves, but supply the wants of the chief, his family, and more immediate suite. The middling orders station their slaves for the same purpose, and also to collect fruits and vegetables for sale, and when their children become numerous, a part are generally sent to be supported by these slaves in the bush. Perhaps the average resident population of Coomassie is not more than from 12 to 15,000.

The markets were held daily from about eight o'clock in the morning until sun set. The larger contains about sixty stalls or sheds, (a small square frame covered with cotton cloth with a pole from the centre, stuck into the ground, see drawing, No. 9.) besides throngs of inferior venders, seated in all directions. Amongst the articles for sale, were beef, (to us about 8d. per lb.) and mutton, cut in small pieces for soup, wild hog, deer, and monkey's flesh, fowls, pelts of skins; yams, plantains, corn, sugar-cane, rice, encruma, (a mucilaginous vegetable, richer than asparagus, which it resembles,) peppers, vegetable butter; oranges, papaws, pine apples, (not equal to those on the coast,) bananas; salt and dried fish from the coast; large snails smoke dried, and stuck in rows on small sticks in the form of herring bone; eggs for fetish; pittō, palm wine, rum; pipes, beads, looking-glasses, sandals, silk, cotton cloth, powder, small pillows, white and blue cotton thread, calabashes, &c. &c. See Chapter on Trade.

The following are the comparative prices of the markets of Coomassie and Yahndi, the capital of Dagwumba:

	Coomassie.	Yahndi.
A fat bullock - -	£.6 0 0 -	- £.1 0 0
A sheep , - - -	0 15 0 -	- 0 4 0
A fowl - -	0 1 8	- 0 0 5
A horse - - -	24 0 0 -	- 8 0 0
Yams - - -	0 0 8 for two	- 0 0 8 for ten.

The surprising exorbitance of the former is to be accounted for by the abundance of gold, yet labour and manufacture was moderately purchased. In Mallowa, provision is dearer than in Dagwumba, but the articles of trade much cheaper; they manufacture very little cloth, the Moorish traders supplying it so abundantly. The cattle we saw in Ashantee were as large as the English, unlike those on the coast, which resemble the Jersey. The sheep are hairy in Ashantee, but woolly in Dagwumba, an open country, where they manufacture a coarse blanket. The horses in Dagwumba are generally small, some were described to be 15 hands high, but these were never parted with, and the Ashantees did not desire them, for I never saw but one who rode fearlessly. The horses I saw were like half bred galloways, their legs lathy, with a wiry hair about the fetlock, only requiring to be pulled. Their heads were large; dun and mouse colours were said to be common; they were never shod, and their hoofs consequently in the eye of the European, though not in nature, disproportionate; they were fed on guinea grass, occasionally mixed with salt, and sal-ammoniac was frequently dissolved in the water. The saddles were Moorish, of red leather, and cumbersome; the bridles of twisted black leather thongs, and brass links, with a whip at the end; the bit severe, with a large ring hanging from the middle, and slipped over the under jaw instead of a curb chain; the stirrups were like large blow pans, and hung very short. Some of the Moors rode on bullocks, with a ring through the nose.

The extent and order of the Ashantee plantations surprised us, yet I do not think they were adequate to the population; in a military government they were not likely to be so. Their neatness and method have been already noticed in our route up. They use no implement but the hoe. They have two crops of corn a year, plant their yams at Christmas, and dig them early in September. The latter plantations had much the appearance of a hop garden well fenced in, and regularly planted in lines, with a broad walk around, and a hut at each wicker gate, where a slave and his family resided to protect the plantation.

All the fruits mentioned as sold in the market grew in spontaneous abundance, as did the sugar cane: the oranges were of a large size and exquisite flavour. I believe this fruit has hitherto been considered indigenous to India only. We saw no cocoa nut trees, nor was that fruit in the market. Mr. Park's route was through a very different country.* In the marshy ground, a large species of fern is very abundant, there are four varieties of it; in shady places that have been cultivated, various tribes of urtica; and the leontodon grows abundantly to the north of Coomassie. The miraculous berry, which gives acids the flavour of sweets, making limes taste like honey, is common.† The castor oil, (ricinus communis) rises to a large tree, I have only seen it as a bush about three feet high on the coast; and the wild fig is abundant, though neither of them are used by the natives. The cotton plant is very plentiful, but little cultivated. The only use to which they apply the silk cotton, is to the stuffing of cushions and pillows.‡ Mr.

* " It is observable, however, that although many species of the edible roots which grow in the West India islands, are found in Africa, yet I never saw, in any part of my journey, either the sugar cane, the coffee, or the cocoa tree; nor could I learn, on inquiry, that they were known to the natives. The pine apple, and the thousand other delicious fruits, which the industry of civilized man (improving the bounties of nature,) has brought to such great perfection in the tropical climates of America, are here equally unknown. I observed, indeed, a few orange and banana trees, near the mouth of the Gambia; but whether they were indigenous, or were formerly planted there by some of the white traders, I could not positively learn. I suspect that they were originally introduced by the Portuguese." Park's First Mission.

† The curious fruit mentioned in the introduction, and to which I have given the name of oxyglycus, I find was known to Des Marchais, who describes it as a little red fruit, which, being chewed, gives a sweet taste to the most sour or bitter things. Dalzel's Dahomey.

‡ Cotton of the cotton tree (or *silk* cotton) *Bombax Pentandrium Lin.* This cotton is not made into thread, but is used for making pillows and beds. It is also, from its catching fire so easily, commonly put into tinder boxes, and employed in the preparation of fire works. Ainslie's Materia Medica of Hindostan.

Park observed the tobacco-plant, which grows luxuriantly in Inta and Dagwumba, and is called toah. The visitors from those countries recognised it in a botanical work. They first dry the leaves in the sun, then, having rubbed them well between their hands, mix them with water into oval masses, as will be seen; it is further noticed in the Trade Report.

Lions are numerous on the northern frontiers of Inta, elephants (assoon, F. A. soorer, B.*) are remarkably numerous in Kong, but they are also found in Ashantee, with wild hogs (yambo, F. A.) hyænas (patacoo, F. A. boofooree, B.,) cows (anantwee, F. A. B.,) sheep (ygwan, F. A. tsan, B.,) goats (apunkie, F. A. terrie, B.,) deer (wonsan, F. A. B.,) antelopes (ettwan, F. A. B.,) dogs (boddum, etcha, F. tweä, A. opooree, B.,) approximating to the Danish, cats (agramwaw, F. A. B.,) extremely sharp visaged and long necked, Gennet cats (essoor, F. A. B.,) pangolins (appra, F. A. aypra, B.,) alligators (dankim, F A. B.,) &c. &c. &c. The rhinoceros (năree) is found in Boroom, and the hippopotamus (shonsa, A. tchoosooree, B.) in the Odirree river.

The Ashantees say, that an animal called sissah or sissirree, will attack every other however superior in size. The Fantees who had never seen it, had imbibed a tremendous idea of it, from the stories in their own country. I doubt its being so formidable to all other animals, for the skin I saw was not more than three feet long, and the legs short, it resembled that of a boar, but the natives said it was between a pig and a goat. I enquired of the people of Inta and Dagwumba if they had ever heard of a unicorn; one replied, yes! in the white man's country. It is extraordinary that the gnoo, (antelope gnu,) which is found behind the Cape of Good

* F. A. affixed to assoon, denote that to be the native name in the Fantee and Ashantee languages, as B. represents Boroom.

Hope, is known in Inta by the same name.* Where the beds were not an accumulation of cushions, the skin of the gnoo was nailed to a large wooden frame, raised on legs about a foot from the ground, and stretched as we would sacking. It was a revered custom that no virgin of either sex should sleep on this kind of bed. Another animal, called otrum, was described by the inhabitants of the eastern frontier as having one very long horn on one side of the head and a short one on the other; it is much larger than the gnoo. We met with a spotted animal of the cat kind (gahin, F. A. B.,) very common, and allied to the leopard or panther, but whether referable to either of those species, or to be considered as distinct, we could not determine, owing to the very vague and unsatisfactory character by which naturalists have attempted to distinguish them, the kind and number of the rows of spots; which we have observed in individuals of the same decided species, to present almost an infinity of variation.

The vulture (pittay, F. A. epraykee, B.,) which I have before mentioned to be venerated by the natives, for the same reason which the Egyptians venerated the Vulturus Percnopterus, is the Vulturus Monachus, figured by Le Vaillant. Green pigeons (assam) are found, and crows with a white ring round their necks, probably the corvus scapularis figured by Le Vaillant. There were several small birds of beautiful plumage, which sung melodiously; two in particular, the one like a blackbird, and the other of the same colour as the English thrush, but larger. Also a variety of parrots beautifully spangled with different colours. M. Cuvier was misinformed when he wrote (Regne animal, tom. i. p. 108) " Macaque est le nom générique des singes à la côte de Guinée." The name is unknown there as well as in the interior.

* C'est probablement lui qui a donné lieu à leur *catoblepas*. Voyez Pline, lib. 8, c. 32, et Ælien, lib. 7, c. 5, Cuvier. The gnoo is almost always *looking down*.

Dokoo is the generic name. The Simia Diana (effoor, F. A. B.,) which has the most beautiful skin of any monkey, is found in Ashantee as well as in Warsaw. All the natives agree that they do not know of any monkies which dare to attack men, but the akonëson, which they describe as small, and always seen in troops.

Snakes (aboïtinnee, F. A. ewaw, B.,) green, and of all colours; scorpions, lizards, &c. &c. were found as on the coast, with a curious variety of beetles, and the most beautiful butterflies. A few specimens preserved in spirits will be sent to the British Museum,* as the best apology for my ignorance rather than neglect of natural history.

* See Dr. Leach's notice in the Appendix.

CHAPTER VIII.

Trade.

THE currency of Ashantee is gold dust, that of Inta, Dagwumba, Gaman, and Kong, cowries. Mr. Lucas writes, " to the merchants of Fezzan who travel to the southern states of the Negroes, the purchase of gold, which the dominions of several, and especially those of Degombah, abundantly afford, is always the first object of commercial acquisition." I could not learn that any gold was dug or collected in Dagwumba, though considerable quantities are imported, from its extensive commerce. Sixteen ackies make an ounce or newemeën, 36 a benda, 40 a periguin: eight tokoos (a small berry) are reckoned to the ackie, but it will not weigh more than seven: there are eight distinct names for quantities of gold dust from one to eight ackies. Five strings or 200 cowries are equal to a tokoo, as at Accra. The clearest manner of shewing the articles, prices, and profits of the Ashantee, Inta, and Dagwumba markets, will be by a table with remarks; substituting, for the greater convenience, English monies calculated at the currency of gold here, which is £4. the oz.

Articles.	Cape Coast.				Coomassie.					Sallagha and Yahndi.				
	£.	s.	d.	Quantity.	£.	s.	d.	Quantity.	Profit. per Cent.	£.	s.	d.	Quantity.	Profit.
Silk, India	4	..	..	per Piece.	..	5	..	1 span.	175	..	..	..	....	......
—— Fezzan	..	..	..	....	2	..	..	1 fathom.	100	1	..	..	1 fathom.	......
Sarstracunda	1	10	..	....	..	2	6	1 span.	400	..	..	..	....	......
Glasgow Dane	1	10	..	....	..	5	..	1 hdkchf.	75	..	..	..	....	......
Romal	1	..	..	....	1	5	..	piece.	20	..	..	..	....	......
Guinea Stuff	..	10	..	....	..	15	..	....	33	..	..	..	....	......
Silesia	..	10	..	....	..	15	..	....	33	..	..	..	....	......
Dagwumba white Cotton	..	..	..	....	..	5	..	sq. yard.	100	..	2	6	sq. yard.	......
Rum	..	10	..	Gallon.	..	..	7½	dram.	400	..	..	..	....	......
Tobacco, Portuguese ..	6	..	..	Roll.	10	..	..	roll.	75	..	..	..	....	......
							7½	span.	..					
—————— Inta	..	..	..	....	..	2	6	lb.	150	..	..	..	lb.	......
Gunpowder	4	..	..	¼ Barrel.	..	..	7½	1 charge.	400	..	..	..	....	......
Iron	1	..	..	Bar.	1	15	..	bar.	75	3	..	..	bar.	200
Lead	..	10	..	....	..	..	7½	½ inch.	75	..	..	..	....	......
Flints	..	5	..	100	..	..	¼	each.	600	..	..	..	....	......
Spanish Dollar	..	5	..	ea.	..	5	..	....	..	..	..	..	....	......
Sandals	..	..	..	....	..	10	..	pair.	100	..	5	..	pair.	......
Cushions	..	..	..	....	1	..	..	ea.	100	..	10	..	ea.	......
Narrowa Locks	..	..	..	....	..	5	..	....	100	..	2	6	....	......

(*a*) The red taffetas (11 yards in each piece) are unravelled by the Ashantees, and wove into the cloths of their own manufacture: they unravel a few of the fancy silks, but these are generally bought for wear, though they prefer those from Fezzan for that purpose, because the colours are more shewy. Coarse thick scarves are also brought from the interior, equal in substance to a double wove ribbon. One ackie a span was the price in the public market, where it was retailed in these small quantities, for the convenience of the weavers, who did not require, or could not afford to purchase more: the price of a piece was uncertain, as the person who could purchase so much, generally sent a trusty servant to the foreign market, and seldom bought of the traders but when they were necessitated to sell at little more than prime cost. The richest silks, I saw, were worn by the Moors, who had bought them at Yahndi and Houssa.* Reckoning nine inches to a span, there are eight spans in a fathom, which is the Ashantee measure; but the fathom of Inta and Dagwumba, contains only six spans. Even if the Ashantee traders give twenty shillings a fathom, in barter of boossee, salt, rum, iron, &c.; it is considerably

* Since my return to England I have seen some silk brought from Aleppo, and manufactured there, precisely resembling these, which were frequently enriched by gold threads interwoven.

Most of the slaves in Coomassie, were sent as part of the annual tribute of Inta, Dagwumba, and their neighbours, to Ashantee;

cheaper to them than ours, considering that they get 100 per cent. on it at Coomassie. Mr. Lucas mentions " silk wrought and unwrought amongst the articles exported from Fezzan to Kassina. Apokoo and several others related to me, that Saï Cudjo bought a piece of silk at Yahndi, so very fine, that although it could be compressed between two hands, it was nevertheless larger than any cloth I had seen the present King wear, and his appeared monstrous. Apokoo added, that six slaves were paid for it, which would have produced £160. at the water side.

(*b*) This is a highly glazed British cotton of bright red stripes with a bar of white: it is bought solely for the red stripe, (as there is no red dye nearer than Marrowa) which they weave into their own cloths, throwing away the white. There are 280 inches in a piece. A cloth of Ashantee manufacture will be sent to the British Museum, and, I expect, the size, fineness, and variety will surprise.

(*c*) This is also a highly glazed British cotton of more colours, and in handkerchiefs; ten of which are in a 30*s*. piece.

(*d*) This is an unglazed India cotton, not much in demand, and yielding the least profit. The Manchester cotton called Tom Coffee is preferred.

(*e*) This is India cotton unglazed, for all of which there is, in proportion, but a small demand. The Ashantees invariably prefer cloths of the Dagwumba, or their own manufacture, and we rarely saw any others worn in Coomassie.

(*f*) These are white cottons, six yards in a piece, but narrow, they are bought for fetish cloths; but the next article, the white cotton cloth of Dagwumba, is preferred, a piece of which, painted, will be sent to the British Museum.

(*g*) These are the wholesale and retail prices at Coomassie, the average length of a roll is 42 fathoms.

(*h*) Powder is retailed for customs or festivals: those who purchase it for war, or can afford a ¼ barrel, send to the water side for it. A ¼ barrel contains 25 lbs. and the Ashantee charge weighs 16 ackies, equal to ¼ of an ounce avoirdupoise.

(*i*) This was owing to their brisk intercourse with the Spanish and Portuguese slave ships, a dollar generally fetches two ackies or 10*s*. Mr. Park writes, from £1. 5*s*. to £2. 10*s*. at Sansanding.

(*k*) Sandals and a cushion will be sent to the British Museum. In Marrowa they decoct a good red dye from a tree called mossarātee.

The reason green ells are purchased by the Warsaws only, is, that they must be the wedding garment of the females of that country: if they are fast colours, and will not change to a blue with lime-juice, they will not look at them

very many were kidnapped, and for the few who were bought, I was assured by several respectable Ashantees, 2000 cowries, or 1 basket of Boossee was the greatest price given ; so full were the markets of the interior. I have brought some pods of the Boossee ; it is astringent, and the natives chew it to excite a flow of saliva, and allay the sensation of hunger. The* Boossee must be the Gooroo nut, which Mr. Lucas describes as one of the articles of trade between Fezzan, Kassina, Bornoo, and the states south of the Niger. He writes, " Gooroo nuts, which are brought from the Negro states on the south of the Niger, and which are principally valued for the pleasant bitter that they communicate to any liquor in which they are infused," and again " a species of nut—which is much valued in the kingdoms to the north of the Niger, and which is called Gooroo. It grows on a large and broad leafed tree, that bears a pod of about 18 inches in length, in which are inclosed a number of nuts that varies from 7 to 9. Their colour is a yellowish green ; their size is that of a chesnut, which they also resemble, in being covered by a husk of a similar thickness, and their taste, which is described as a pleasant bitter, is so grateful to those who are accustomed to its use, and so important as a corrective to the unplatable or unwholesome waters of Fezzan, and of the other kingdoms that border on the vast Zahara, as to be deemed of importance to the happiness of life. They are purchased at the rate of 12s. for 100 pods."

Sal ammonia is found abundantly in Dagwumba : in the Ashantee market, a lump the size of a duck's egg, was sold for 2s. : they grind it to mix with their snuff, (of which they take large quantities,) as it gives it a pungency agreeable to them. They also dissolve it in the water they give to their cattle, and sometimes drink it themselves for pains in the bowels. The Tamool prac-

* Sterculia acuminata *Palis de Beauvais Flore d'Oware*, 1. *p.* 41. *tab.* 24.

titioners in the East Indies suppose it to be a useful remedy in certain female obstructions, and morbid uterine enlargements. Mr. Lucas writes. "No commercial value appears to be annexed to the fleeces which the numerous flocks of the Negro kingdoms afford; for the cotton manufacture, which, the Shereef says, is established among the tribes to the south of the Niger, seems to be the only species of weaving that is known among them." In Dagwumba, however, they manufacture a coarse kind of blanket from sheep's wool. There is a white grease, which has long been called Ashantee grease by the natives on the coast, who supposed it to be produced in that country. They use it daily to anoint their skins, which otherwise become coarse and unhealthy. The Ashantees purchase it from the interior, and make a great profit by it: it is a vegetable butter, decocted from a tree, called Timkeëä: it is doubtless the Shea butter of Mr. Park.* Mr. Lucas mentions, " small Turkey and plain Mesurata carpets," among the articles exported from Fezzan to Kassina: a small carpet fetches 2 oz. of gold at Coomassie. The Ashantees procure most of their ivory from Kong, where they give 8 ackies, or 40s. in barter, for a very large tooth.

" The preference of the Ashantees for the Dagwumba and Inta markets, for silk and cloth, results not merely from their having been so long accustomed to them, but because they admit of a barter trade. The Boossee or Gooroo nut, salt, (which is easily procured, and affords an extravagant profit,) and small quantities of the European commodities, rum, and iron,† yield them those articles of comfort and luxury, which they can only purchase with gold and ivory from the settlements on the coast. Gold they are

---

* See Sketch of Gaboon.

† Though iron is manufactured in Dagwumba, that from Europe is preferred for finer purposes. The former is an imperfect steel containing a mechanical mixture of unreduced ore.

ill desirous of hoarding; even those less covetous than is generally
their nature, that they may be prepared for the purchase of guns
and powder to a large extent, on any sudden war, and thus ingra-
tiate themselves with the king and the government. Were the
Ashantees a commercial people, they might be the brokers between the interior and Europeans, or, purchasing supplies more
adequate to the demands of their neighbours for European commodities, which would be bought with avidity, realize large properties. But they have no idea of buying more of the various
articles than will supply themselves; and leave a small residue to
barter for the cloth, silk, and tobacco in the Inta and Dagwumba
markets. They are as little commercial as the Romans were in
their infancy, and their government would repress rather than
countenance the inclination, (believing no state can be aggrandized
but by conquest,) lest their genius for war might be enervated by
it, and lest, either from the merchants increasing to a body too
formidable for their wishes to be resisted, or too artful from their
experience to be detected, they might sacrifice the national honour
and ambition to their avarice, and furnishing Inta, Dagwumba, or
any of their more powerful neighbours (who have yielded to circumstances rather than force) with guns and powder (which are
never allowed to be exported from Ashantee,*) break the spell of
their conquests, and undermine their power. The chiefs are fed
bountifully by the labours of their slaves, and sharing large sums
of the revenue, (the fines their oppression has imposed on other

* " Fire arms are unknown to such of the nations on the south of the Niger as the
Shereef has visited ; and the reason which he assigns for it is, that the kings in the neighbourhood of the coast, persuaded that if these powerful instruments of war should reach
the possession of the populous inland states, their own independence would be lost, have
strictly prohibited, and by the wisdom of their measures have effectually prevented this
dangerous merchandize from passing beyond the limits of their dominions."   Lucas

governments,) with incalculable fees for corruption or interference, refine upon the splendor of equipage even to satiety, and still possess a large surplus of income daily accumulating. Were they to encourage commerce, pomp, the idol of which they are most jealous, would soon cease to be their prerogative, because it would be attainable by others ; the traders growing wealthy, would vie with them ; and for their own security, stimulated by reflections they have now too little at risk to originate, they would unite to repress the arbitrary power of the Aristocracy ; and even if they did not, inevitably (as the chiefs conceive) divert the people's genius for war.

It will occur that even to furnish the necessities or luxuries of the Ashantees alone, in cloth, silk, &c. would, considering the extent of the kingdom, considerably augment the returns of our commerce in this part of the world ; and therefore it would be well to wean them, gradually, from the markets of the interior, by inducing their cultivation of cotton, which grows abundantly, is of a superior quality, and which, offered in quantities, in addition to the ivory, would lessen the balance of trade now in our favor, and by enabling them, in some degree to purchase with produce instead of gold dust, remove the present comparative disadvantage in trading with Europeans entirely. This occurred to me, and I explained the view not only to the king, but to the more enterprising and reflecting natives : but they had no idea of a quantity, and immediately concluded cotton to be so desirable to us, that 40 or 50 lbs. would be received in barter for twenty times its value; and they required one tokoo and a half per lb. for it, (say one shilling,) even in gold, and on the spot. When I urged that they must clear the ground, form plantations, and superintend the labours of their slaves; they replied, that the Boossee or Gooroo nut grew spontaneously, and required no labour, that salt was brought to their frontier by poorer nations, and sold for little with-

ʹout the trouble of fetching it; and these articles, with the value, their prevention of all intercourse but their own with the water side nations, attached to a little rum and iron in the interior, fur-ʹ nished them with silks and cotton cloths at a much easier rate, pattern and quality.

A serious disadvantage opposed to the English trade, is that the Ashantees will purchase no tobacco but the Portuguese, and that eagerly even at 2 oz. of gold the roll. Of this, (the Portuguese and Spanish slave ships regularly calling at Elmina,) the Dutch Gover- nor-General is enabled to obtain frequent supplies, in exchange for canoes, two of which, though they cost him comparatively nothing, fetch 32 rolls of tobacco; and the General has sometimes received 80 oz. of gold a day from the Ashantees for tobacco only. If they cannot have this tobacco, they will content themselves with that grown in the interior, of which I have brought a sample. A pre- ference for the Dutch has long been natural to the Ashantees, from an earlier though limited intercourse with them, and from the natural impression, that the English settling amongst their enemies, the Fantees, have encouraged and assisted their provocations and resistance. With this bias in his favor, though the Dutch market, destitute of supplies, had not been visited for many years, the talent of General Daendels, " callidum quicquid placuit," would no doubt have again raised it to a level with the English, cæteris paribus; and his unlimited importation of powder and guns in the first place, with the still more valuable supplies of Portuguese tobacco he receives at present, as superior advantages, have, of course, possessed the Dutch market of superior inducements.

It is to be lamented, the indifference of the Dutch and Danes to their settlements here, being evident from their neglect and re- duction of them, that the British government did not take advan- tage of the disregard, and add them to their own. Elmina is a much finer position for head quarters than Cape Coast; the Dutch fort at Succondee, the best point for the Warsaw trade, and where we have but a house, is strong, admirably situated, and might be put in good condition for £1000. in addition to which, Axim, near the mouth of the Ancobra, would be the only fort to windward worth keeping; and the Danish head quarters, Christiansburg Castle at Accra, with their fort at Adda, (to secure the navigation of the Volta,) would have answered every purpose and view to leeward. One system could then have been acted upon towards the natives, the commerce, confined to the English, would have grown from wholesome regulations, which no other settlers could counteract by selfishness, jealousy, or by facilitating the illegitimate trade we would crush; and the benevolent views of the British government for the improvement and civilization of the natives, would not be defeated by those, who, holding their private interest superior to views in which their own government has evinced no interest, militate against them by fostering suspicions to bar our progress in the interior, and by indulging those habits and customs of the natives, which it must be our first step to correct and divert.

In addition to the obstacles which the inconsistent and selfish conduct of the different European powers towards the natives presents to intercourse and civilization, the continuance of the slave trade under the Spanish flag, is one more serious: no one can imagine the stubborn impediment it was to our negotiations at Ashantee, where the native emissaries from these slave ships arrived not long after us. It not only injures the British commerce here, almost to annihilation, but, slaving being the natural trade of the natives, because it is the most indolent and the most lucrative, the opposition, which is insinuated and believed to proceed from the English alone, conveys a disagreeable impression of us to the interior, as inauspicious to our intercourse and progress, as the even partial continuance of such a trade is to legitimate commerce and civilization. One thousand slaves left Ashantee for two Spanish schooners or Americans under that flag, to our knowledge, during our residence there, doubtless the whole number was much greater; since our return it must have been very considerable, for the slave trade was never more brisk than it is at this moment under the cloak of the Spanish flag, and great risk has been incurred, in consequence, of offending our new friend and formidable neighbour the King of Ashantee, from the firm resistance of his strong intreaties to the Governor in Chief, to allow the return of a powerful mulatto slave trader to Cape Coast town, whence he had been expelled under the present government, as the most daring promoter of that commerce. It is a great pity, in the infancy of our intercourse with this great interior power, that there should have been occasion either for the request or refusal; which there would not have been had the slave trade been abolished, instead of crippled, at the expense, probably, of our own interests and views in the interior, and, which is worse, of the happiness and improvement of the natives. For it is certainly our duty, because it is the most acceptable and the only efficient acknowledgment we can make of the superior blessings and endowments by which we are so indulgently distinguished from these nations, to extend the influence and the participation, both by enterprise and policy, even if our commerce may not be benefitted; and if we gain no other recompense than the satisfaction of our own minds in the ameliorated condition of others, and the opportunity we have made to ourselves of exemplifying our own gratitude.* Whilst one slave

* The dissuasion from barbarities of which millions are now the victims, as the descriptions of the customs of Ashantee and the interior have shewn, and the interests of science, render this duty more imperious. It has been well observed, " apologies for our

ship is allowed to visit this coast, the great convenience and the great profits of the trade will recur, and be perpetuated amongst the Ashantees; they will linger in the hope of its entire renewal, and view the English invidiously, as the enemies to what they conceive to be their only natural commerce; this is another advantage to the Dutch, added to the inherent bias in their favour; and, from the reception and facilities which slave ships meet with at Elmina, our odium is aggravated instead of being participated. " Delenda est Carthago."

present ignorance of every thing that regards geography, &c. might be pleaded by mercantile speculators, but can have little weight with those who have the interests of science at heart, or the national honour and fame, which are intimately connected with those interests. It was not with a view to any immediate commercial advantages, that this liberal encouragement for the discovery of the north-west passage was held out, but with the same expanded objects that sent Cook in search of a southern continent."

Voltaire's remark on India is now only applicable to Africa, " Plusieurs y ont fait des fortunes immenses, peu se sont appliqués à connoître ce pays." I would even recommend indulging the wish of the King of Dahomey to renew and perpetuate his connection with the English, not indeed by resuming the fort, that would be a useless expense, as there is no trade but in ivory, but by establishing a Residency at his capital, the most frugal method of collecting the various accounts of the interior of that neighbourhood for geographical investigators, besides supplying the naturalist. Geographical discoveries in Africa have long been ardently emulated between England and France, and they have stimulated a generous rivalry of investigation between the men of science of both countries. An Englishman first penetrating to the Niger, and determining its course at the moment a learned investigator of the other kingdom had concluded it to be a contrary one, was one of those rational and illustrious triumphs which adorn the historical pages of a nation much more than those of war; for the gratification and the benefit is shared by both, and such successes cease to be invidious when the interests of science are thus mutually at heart. The following immortal tribute from a classic of a rival nation, should stimulate us to challenge as illustrious a record of intellectual research,

- - - - " monumentum ære perennius,
Regalique situ pyramidum altius;"

by a correspondent pursuit of intelligence in Africa.

" Un Anglais, détruit tout ce vain amas d'erreurs dont sont remplies nos histoires des Indes, et confirme ce que le petit nombre d'hommes instruits en a pensé." Voltaire.

Let us suppose this irreconcilable obstacle to be annihilated, as no doubt it will be, and resume our reflections on a commercial intercourse with the interior. The people of Inta and Dagwumba, being commercial rather than warlike, the object, deliberately to be obtained, is an intercourse with them, which would in fact be an intercourse with the interior as far as Timbuctoo and Houssa northwards, and Cassina, if not to Bornoo, eastwards. The wealth, civilization, and commerce of Dagwumba, Mr. Lucas has before reported. Now, in effecting such an intercourse through the Ashantees, who are indisputably the greatest and the rising power of western Africa, and who, having acquired their present extent of influence and command in little more than a century, may be expected to aggrandize their empire considerably; in seeking this connection through them, there are these adverse circumstances, their policy, their jealousy, and their inaptitude to commerce. It has been suggested to the King, and urged with all the address of General Daendels, to open a path to the interior through his kingdom, and to receive a duty or tax on all the merchandize transported, which would afford him a certain and considerable addition to his revenue; but even this appeal to the avarice of the Ashantee government has had no influence. It would be dangerous as well as impolitic to offend the King of Ashantee at any time, with the present garrisons of the forts, madness; and though his influence through that of Dagwumba, which is at his command, would extend to the Niger, yet, I think our anxiety to explore so far should be suppressed for two or three years, until he is satisfied that commerce and not ambition is the impulse. But in the interim, it would be desirable gradually to approach Inta and Dagwumba, by establishing a settlement up the Volta, which has been shewn to run close to Sallagha, the grand emporium of Inta, and is navigable within four days of it; and possibly might be made so even nearer. The Danes would no doubt relinquish their claim to the navigation of the Volta, for it is a doubtful one. ' Dalzel writes, " the Danes claim the exclusive navigation of the Volta, which is disputed by the English, who have a settlement near it, called Loy." The great prices the Ashantees get for rum, iron, &c. from the people of Inta and Dagwumba, and. the avidity with which they purchase their small supplies, leave no doubt of the eagerness with which they would resort to our market; and the silks they ' obtain from Fezzan being dearer than our own, I should think we could induce a preference. Our Manchester cloth and cotton manufactures would be novel and useful to them, as those I saw wore vests and tunics. But here I must observe, that whenever our commerce with the interior may be established, the returns of it, in my opinion, will fall short of the general idea and expectation.

The King of Ashantee viewing our settlements on the Volta, would, I have no doubt, be reconciled by our undertaking to sell neither guns or powder to any but his own people; a measure due to humanity as well as policy, for the preponderance of one great nation is auspicious to the civilization as well as the tranquillity of Africa; but for that, the slaughter of the human species would be incalculable; there would be a constant warfare between the numerous states, naturally querulous, and our passage to the interior would be impossible, not only on that account, but because there would be no powerful monarch to recommend or protect us. If the King of Ashantee were not satisfied with our new settlement confining the trade of guns and powder to himself, he would certainly be repressed by the alarming reflection, that it was at our discretion, (depending on his behaviour,) to supply Inta and Dagwumba with both, and thus to undermine his empire; for it is well known, and has been confessed, that the greater population of these countries, could they but procure fire-arms, would give them a superiority over the Ashantees, to which their greater civilization seems to entitle them. Our force and establishments should be respectable; not to arrogate or to intrude, but to protect the legitimate commercial views, sanctioned and invited by the voice of less arbitrary powers, and also to make their first impression of the English imposing and preservative. Residencies should be established at these courts, and young men of talent, temper, and discrimination be found to fill them, collecting the geographical and statistical desiderata, and forwarding them to be investigated and digested into one report at head quarters, before they were transmitted to England. One or two intelligent Moors might also be engaged to trade by different routes, and minute the directions, distances, and descriptions of the several places; thus paving the way, and lessening the difficulties of a future Mission to the Niger. If the working of gold mines were also an object, the vicinity of the Ancobra affords a rich field; and a small district might either be purchased of the natives, or they might receive a dividend of the proceeds, which would produce them much more than their present inadequate researches, suppressed by their more powerful neighbours the Warsaws.

The benevolent and politic views of the British Government, would thus, by making use of what we have or might easily get, be more probably, if not more speedily realized, than by the perilous, desultory, and limited enterprises of two or three individuals.

CHAPTER IX.

Language.

T H E hypothesis I have met with, I think in Parsons's Remains of Japhet, that the confusion of languages at Babel was a visitation on the family of Ham only, which spread itself over Africa, is certainly supported (considering the radical affinities which have been traced between the Arabic the Russ and the Greek, the Persian and the German, the Qquichua, or language of the Incas, and the Sanscrit, and many others*) by the variety of languages in Africa which cannot be assimilated in the least degree to each other, and which would, I think, resist the laborious ingenuity of the philologist.

I have heard about half a dozen words in the Fantee, which might be said to be not unlike the same nouns in the Welsh language; and this is the only affinity which has been imagined. Two words only in the Accra language have struck me as assimilating to those of any other, the conjunction " *kay* " (*and*), which

---

* The eastern and western branch of this polar race, the Eskimoes and the Tschougazes, notwithstanding the enormous distance of 800 leagues which separates them, are united by the most intimate analogy of languages. This analogy extends, as has been recently proved in the most evident manner, even to the inhabitants of the north-east of Asia; for the idiom of the Tschouktshes at the mouth of the Anadin has the same roots, as the language of the Eskimoes who inhabit the coast of America opposite to Europe. The Tschouktsches are the Eskimoes of Asia. Humbolt, P. N. v. 3, p. 291.

with a broader sound would answer the corresponding Greek cònjunction καὶ ; and *fai* (*to do,*) pronounced as the perfect participle of the same verb in French, and which is spelled *fai* in the old songs of Richard the first, and the troubadour Faydit. The Fantee word *umpa* (*true, indeed,*) may be imagined to resemble the Greek ἔμπας, which has the same meaning; but it is a solitary instanc e

From Apollonia or Amănăheä to the Volta, about 300 miles, six languages are spoken: the Amanaheä, Ahanta, Fantee, Affoottoo, Accra, and the Adampë. The numerals of which will appear, collaterally with others hitherto unknown, at the end of this chapter.

The Ashantee, in comparison with the Fantee, Warsaw, &c. &c. from its refinement of idiom, oratory being so much more cultivated, may be considered as the Attic amongst the dialects of the Greek, but it owes its superior euphony, striking to any ear, to the characteristics of the Ionic, an abundance of vowel sounds, and a rejection of aspirates :

		Fantee.		*Ashantee.*
Key	-	Sāfie	-	Saphwooa.
Lock	-	Karradacoo		Karradoo.
Night	-	Adayfwa	-	Adagio.
Day	-	Aweeabil	-	Aweeabillee.
Gun	-	Etoorh	-	Oteuh.

Vocabularies of these languages would not be interesting to the public, especially as no affinity can be traced ; and I know not how to acquit myself of every thing like indifference to the curiosity at home, (without the dulness of the subject proving more irksome than a disappointment,) unless I endeavour to give an idea of the philosophy of the languages,* and submit their progress, collaterally

---

* " I am aware that languages are much more strongly characterised by their structure and grammatical forms, than by the analogy of their sounds and of their roots; and that

Y y

with that of the arts and manners. The genius of the Accra language differing the most essentially from that of the Ashantee or Fantee, examples from both will be instanced for illustration. I have principally consulted two gentlemen, natives of the country, but educated in Europe: the one resident between forty and fifty years; the other, who has a respectable knowledge of the grammar of the English and French languages, returned from England about ten years back, and both are as fluent as the Negroes in the Fantee and Accra, the latter being their vernacular tongue.

Impressed with the ingenious hypothesis of the learned author of the Diversions of Purley, my first care has been to investigate the particles of the Fantee and Accra, considering the languages of uncivilised people, to be least advanced or removed from the

their analogy of sounds is sometimes so disfigured in the different dialects of the same tongue, as not to be distinguishable; for the tribes into which a nation is divided, often designate the same objects by words altogether heterogeneous. Hence it follows, that we are asily mistaken, if, neglecting the study of the inflexions, and consulting only the roots, for instance the words which designate the moon, sky, water, and earth, we decide on the absolute difference of two idioms from the simple want of resemblance in sounds." Humboldt's Personal Narrative, vol. iii. p. 251.

I am gratified to find, since my return to England, and consequent perusal of the Congo publication, that my investigations of these languages have happened to be consonant with the instructions of Mr. Marsden in his letter to Captain Tuckey, as appears from the following extract. " Where a longer residence admits of freer intercourse, and a means of acquiring a more perfect knowledge of the language, it will be desirable, besides attempting to fill up the larger vocabulary, that pains should be taken to examine its grammatical structure, and to ascertain, for instance, how the nominative and subjunctive words in a sentence are placed with respect to the verb; how the adjective with regard to the substantive; how plurals and degrees of comparison are formed; whether there is any kind of inflexion or variation of syllables of the same word, according to its position in the sentence and connection with other words; whether the pronouns personal vary according to the rank or sex of the person addressing or person addressed; and whether they are incorporated with the verb; and to observe any other peculiarities of idiom, that the language may present; noting the degree of softness, harshness, indis-

primeval simplicity, to which Mr. Horne Tooke's system refers. I found, however, both the Accra and Fantee languages more complete than I expected in conjunctions, and seldom using verbs instead of them, which I presumed they might do. Yet I have no doubt, their half dozen of conjunctions, if examined etymologically by a person thoroughly conversant in the languages, might be traced, and shewn to be the contracted imperatives of the most recurrent verbs, as Mr. Tooke has proved those of our own language to be. Neither the Accra or Fantee have conjunctions answering to each of ours; the distinction between many is neither comprehensible or necessary to them. I will submit their conjunctions, with those investigated in the first volume of the Diversions of Purley.

Fantee.			*Accra.*
Onee -	- and	-	- Kay
Sey -	- { if unless	-	Kedgee
Emphee -	{ still but	-	- Shee
Interah -	{ because since	- -	Nooyĕwon Nunnë
Namoo -	{ notwithstanding though	-	Nemoolay
Anna -	{ otherwise or	- -	Noollay

tinctness, intonation, guttural sounds, and the prevalence or deficiency of any particular letters of the alphabet, as we should term them, such as R and F. The extent of country over which a language is understood to prevail should also be a subject of investigation; and, by what others it is bounded on every side. Also, whether there may not be a correct language of communication between nations, whose proper languages are distinct." I think the very frequent use of *q* is one distinguishing character of African languages: the *r* and *f* are very frequent, the latter especially: the former as a liquid is

There are no adverbs in either language. There are but two in our own which may not be expressed by a verb or an adnoun, *still* and *since;* and these they express by the conjunctions *but* and *because.* " I intreated, but (still) he would not," " because (since) it is so," as the Latins frequently used prepositions for the Greek adverbs. Indeed *since* is expressible by a verb, being derived according to Mr. Tooke from the Saxon *sithan,* seeing that. They express the adverb *much* by the adjective *many; ago* by a verb, " *it passes* ten years;" *almost* by the verb *it wants,* " *it wants* to rain;" and *when* by a noun, " *the time* I was there," coincident with Jones's derivation of ὅτε.* *Nooyĕwon,* (*because*) in Accra, is literally, "*for the sake of.*" *Intērah,* the corresponding word in Fantee, " on the head of," (*tirree is* head) thus, they would say, " I do this on your head," or because you told me. Lest, which is considered by Mr. Horne Tooke to be the past participle of the Saxon verb *leyan,* to dismiss, is not to be found either in the Accra or Fantee : in the former they would say, " *Menkaw hauh ebbēbărădi,*" " do not go there, you fall down;" and in the latter, " *Kaiheah djai nee oheäbwayshee,*" " do not go there, and (or for) you fall down." The use of the noun for the adverb is frequent in Demosthenes, (" εςι δικαιος εχειν," " he justly deserves ") and can only be accounted for in a prose writer, who does not need poetical licenses, as an archaism, disused generally, through invention or refinement. The term adverb is not a just indication of the origin of that part of speech, for, although they are derived from verbs as well as nouns,

---

frequently substituted for *l*, as I have illustrated in the Chapter on Geography. Their pronunciation of *z* approximates to that of the *aspro z* of the Italians. I hope to have leisure and opportunity hereafter for paying this subject more attention. I have not yet had time to make sufficient progress in German to read Vater's Mithridatis, which will no doubt assist my observations.

* From the Hebrew עתה, ote, *time,* has flowed ὅτε, *when;* which τ, π, οπ, being prefixed, becomes τοτε, ποτε, ὁποτε."

yet, in our own language, as well as in the Greek, following Mr. Horne Tooke, the greater number are derived from nouns: and those (of which there are some in the Greek) which may be indifferently derived from a noun, or a verb, may be referred to the former; because, many of the adnouns from which adverbs are derived in the Greek, have been pointed out as disused; and therefore the verbs from which adverbs are exclusively derived, are likely to be derived themselves from obsolete adnouns, which cannot be recalled; for it has been philosophically advanced, that originally there could have been but one sort of words, that is, nouns, or the names of the objects of our sensations and ideas.*

I consider the absence of adverbs, participles, and prepositions, certainly the least indispensible parts of speech, and favouring copiousness rather than energy, to be a proof of the almost genuine, or primeval simplicity of the Accra and Fantee languages, which have not advanced or altered; even in the small degree of their arts or manners; for these have only been ameliorated by commercial intercourse with strangers, who not understanding their language could not have suggested improvements, and from whose languages, they being equally unintelligible, amendments could not have been copied. We find Portuguese nouns, and nouns only, adopted in the Fantee; and that, of necessity, as Saxon nouns were adopted in the Welsh or Celtic, because they had no words to designate novelties they had never before seen or heard of; and, therefore, they called them as those did who introduced them. These primitive languages being, nevertheless, thoroughly adequate to oratory

---

* " Every verb consists of a pronoun, expressing an agent, and of a noun, or the substitute of a noun, expressing an object. Thus, οινος and εγω joined and abbreviated is οινοω; and this term would be sufficient to express *I drink wine,* though originally it meant only *wine I;* association supplying to the speaker and the person addressed the intermediate notion *of drinking.*" Jones.

as well as the commoner purposes of speech, is a strong proof that language was revealed, as Johnson, Blair, Warburton, and others have maintained, and that it was not the fruit of human invention or industry, as Lucretius, Horace, and most of the antients imagined.

Neither the Accra or Fantee distinguish genders, the name of the person, or the context, is the only explication; they have not even a third person feminine, but one pronoun serves for *he, she, it.*

The Accra has a definite and indefinite article, but both are affixed to the noun, as " *minna nooleh,*" I saw the man; " *minna nookoo,*" I saw a man. The indefinite article " *koo*" is the contraction of numeral one, " *ekoo,*" so that I saw a man, is literally " I saw man one." *An* is simply another form of the numeral one, still used in North Britain under the form ane; and in the French, the numeral and the article corresponding to one, are the same. The Fantee, like the Greek, has no indefinite article, or according to Mr. Harris's expression, on which Mr. Horne Tooke is so pleasant, " supplies it by a negation of the definite," which is " *noo,*" affixed, as " *mehoon nimpanoo,*" I saw the man.*

* The word *caboccer* (*chief,*) which I have used in the correspondence, history, and other parts of this work, as the only title familiar to Europeans, (being always substituted, even by native interpreters for the vernacular,) was of course introduced by the Portuguese, and consequently unknown in the interior. It is applied to a chief who has the charge or government of a town, (*croom.*) Such however are indiscriminately called *ōhen* or *king*, in Fantee. Throughout Ashantee the monarch only is called *ōhennie* or *king*, and the chiefs who have the care or government of the towns of his dominions, *sāf'ĕhen*. *Sāfie* or *saphwooa*, means *key*, and the last syllable of the compound, *hen*, is evidently an abbreviation of *ōhennie*. *Safie*, a *charm*, is without doubt identical in a figurative sense with *sāfee, key;* and should, on consideration, be spelt as such, and not *saphie* as I have generally written it hitherto. A Moor is called *Crambo* by the Negroes of the interior, which bears the same interpretation as *Pongheme*, a Spaniard, in the Tamanack, i. e. *a man clothed.*

In the Accra, the plural is formed by inflection, epenthesis, paragoge, and apocope : these changes are almost peculiar in every noun ; the more frequent inflections are, ai, ay, and ee.

	Singular.	Plural.
A woman	yeo	yeay.
A box	adikka	adikkai.
A stone	teh	tai.
Ground	shepong	shepongee.
A hyæna	krang	krangee.
A father	tchay	tchaymë.
A liar	amallalo	amallaloi.
A gun	toon	tween.
A vessel	lelen	ledgenë.
A man	noon	nhal.
A house	tchoon	tchuë.

In the Fantee the plural number is distinguished by the prefix *en*, though generally, if they can, (in a glance whilst speaking) discover the number of objects, they use a numeral with the noun singular ; or, if they cannot be so precise in the instant, they substitute *many* to mark an indefinite number. The Chinese also, are said to drop their plural adjunct " *min*," when there is another word of plurality attached to the noun.

Neither language has prepositions, and of course peraphrasis is generally resorted to : conjunctions are sometimes substituted, as *and* for *with* ; occasionally verbs, as " the King *to give* his captain," for *to his captain ;* and, sometimes, they are presumed from the tone or the context. Mr. Horne Tooke, who values prepositions very much, has traced all but five, of our own language, to nouns and verbs ; and of these five, three have since been traced to nouns and a numeral ; so that *out* and *off*, only, are unaccounted for. Jones, in his Greek Grammar, writes, " the roots of prepositions are nouns and verbs," and, accordingly, he derives απο from the Hebrew, *ab*, a stem, περι from the Arabic *pera*, eminence, υπερ from the Hebrew *aber*, sky, or the Persian *ober*, a cloud: the inseparable prepositions had been traced to nouns and verbs long before.

Degrees of comparison are not expressed by adjectives or adverbs, in either language: but, for he is richer than˙ he, the Accras would say, " *eh phay leh ne;* " the Fantees, " *aw tchen adee*," he *passes him* (in) things: neither language has an adjective answering to rich or wealthy, but " *ne*," and " *adee*," in both, corsespond exactly in meaning and use with the *res* of the Latins: the superlative would be expressed by " *he passes all*." The antient idiom of comparison, antecedent to the general use of inflections or adverbs, was probably similar, judging from the following, and many other sentences in the Greek, " Παρ᾽ ἑαυτὸν μηδένα ἐπιτήδειον ἡγεῖτο, he thought no body fitter than himself;" " πλείονος δόξης παρὰ Μωσῆν ἠξίωται, Heb. xiii. he was counted of more glory, or more glorious than Moses." Here παρα, so frequently expressing comparison, being derived from the verb περαω, *to pass*, is identical with the Accra and Fantee expression.

I observed before that the Accra and Fantee have no adjective answering to rich, they are also deficient in many others, which they supply by a second substantive in the same manner. This idiom is found in the Greek, " Το σωμα της ταπεινωσεως ἡμων, our humiliated body, the body of our humiliation;" Αἱρεσεις απωλειας. destructive heresies, &c. &c." and it is said to be both a Hebrew and Celtic idiom; primeval languages, and the latter, I presume, as rude as those we are investigating.

In the Accra, the personal pronouns are

I	- -	me
thou	-	boh
he, she, it		lheh

we - - whah
you - nnheay
they - - amăy

Me is generally reduplicate before verbs, as " *me me yay*," I eat. *Boh* before verbs generally suffers aphæresis as " *oh yay*," thou eatest, but sometimes not, as " *boh fai*," thou doest: this is also the case with *lheh* as " *heh yay*, *lheh fai*." *Me* is added, as *met* in Latin, to make these pronouns compound. In Fantee the personal pronouns are

I - - me
thou - awaw
he, she, it narra
we - yarra
you - awoo
they - warra;

the latter is used as a possessive pronoun also; *woodde* is affixed to make them compound; they are irregularly contracted before verbs. Considering these barbarous languages of primitive simplicity, and recollecting the original and philosophical deduction of pronouns from verbs, by the Greek professor of Glasgow, as εγω or εγων (which is the more ancient) from λεγων, ipse from επω, I particularly enquired for verbs resembling their pronouns; but, after a long and diligent recollection, neither of my authorities could furnish me with any to the point. It is curious to observe, that the *me* represents the pronoun I, in both these rude languages,* as it does, though not in the nominative case, in most other primitive languages, and in the modern ones derived from them: it would seem to be the natural and involuntary expression for that pronoun.

There is only an active voice in the Accra or Fantee; the pas-

* It is also found in the Empoönga, and other African languages.

sive is expressed by a circumlocution, as he loves, or they love me, for I am loved, &c.* It appears erroneous to consider the infinitive mood as the root of the verb, when it has a separable or distinguishing termination, and *mong* is as distinctly the verbalizing adjunct in the Accra language, as *ere* or *are* in the Latin, εω in Greek, or *an* in the Anglo-Saxon. If we consider the imperative as the divested fundamental form of the verb, it is still difficult in these languages to get at the root, for the use of the infinitive for the imperative, occasional in the Greek, is, in the Accra, so general, that for some time I thought it unexceptionable, and that it had not the two moods.

The Accra has the neuter verb *to be* in the present, perfect, and future tenses, but in the perfect, it is irregular.

I am   I have been   I shall be
meyeh   metay   mahyeh

The Fantee only has it in the present, " *oh yea*, he is." It is remarkable that even the linguists of our forts, who speak English fluently, never understand or use our neuter verb *to be,* but substitute *live* for it, and that, whether they speak of animate or inanimate things; a servant would say, " your keys live in your pocket."

The imperative mood has a present tense complete in each language.

They express the potential mood by adding auxiliary verbs, such as our can, may, &c., have been shewn to be derived from.

The termination of the infinitive in the Accra is generally *mong,*

---

* " The distinction of active and passive is not essential to verbs. In the infancy of language, it was in all probability not known; in Hebrew, the difference but imperfectly exists, and in the early periods of it, possibly did not exist at all. In Arabic, the only distinction which obtains, arises from the vowel points, a late invention compared with the antiquity of that language. And in our own tongue the names of active and passive would have remained unknown, if they had not been learnt in Latin." Jones.

which is rejected in conjugating. In the Fantee it is not distinguished from the first person present, or root. The use of the infinitive mood, even in Accra, is very circumscribed, for it is not found even in the most natural case when two verbs come together, as I want to eat, for which they say, " *metōn meyay*," I want I eat. The infinitive is generally used for the imperative in the Accra, but, otherwise, it only occurs in an idiom almost peculiar to that language, for instance, for are you walking now, they say,

" *Neo*mong oh *neo* neh,"

" To walk are you walking now."

For I am straightening it,

" *Jadjumong* me *jadjio* leh."

" To straighten I am straightening it."

Verbs are invariably used thus, interrogatively, and, generally, in replies. I said almost peculiar, because I think this pleonasm is identified in the Greek idiom, " Ουχι μενον σοι εμενε. Remaining, did it not remain to thee."

The Accra has the present, imperfect, perfect, and future tenses: the imperfect and future being distinguished by the prefixes *bleh* and *ah*, the one before, the other after the pronoun.

" me yāyne.   bleh me yayne.   me yăy.   m'ahye."

I eat it.   I was eating it.   I eat.   I will eat.

But the imperfect tense is never used, unless a sentence precedes it, as

" Bennay heh bă bleh me yay."

" When he came I was eating."

Otherwise, they use the perfect for the imperfect, never replying to a question even, in the latter. The perfect is only distinguished ·from the present by being pronounced short. These explicative particles, *bleh* and *ah*, would, no doubt, be found to be remnants of verbs of appropriate signification, as the *ai* of the French future is derived from *avoir*, were any philologist sufficiently acquainted with the languages to investigate them. *Ne*, signifying it or thing, is adjoined to many verbs, frequently in the present tense only, like the explicative particle *en* conjugated with " *aller*."

The Fantee has a present, perfect, and pluperfect: as " me dedee," I eat, " me adee," I have eaten, " me waya dedee," I had eat. It has no future, yet the time is marked precisely, by adding *soon*, *to-morrow*, &c. to the present.

Neither language has participles; for, I see him coming, the Accras would say, according to their idiom,

" Minnā eh ba'lheh."

" I see his coming."

Ba being a noun, with the definite article *lheh* affixed. The Fantees would say,

" Mehoon deh orraba."

" I see that he comes."

Many verbs in the Accra language are conjugated like reflectives, though they are not so in their nature, as

" Me nakoo me fai lheh

I   not   I did it, for I did not do it.

In the Accra, *ko*, the contraction of *nakoo*, (not,) is added to verbs as a negative, as " *meyayko*," I did not eat; yet, in some instances, they have distinct verbs to express the negative of the action, as " *mahttay*," I will go, " *meyang*," I will not go.

The Fantee prefixes *neën*, not, as " *me dedee*," I eat, " *me neën dedee*," I do not eat; and they have also, apparently, distinct negative verbs, as " *me becko*," I go, " *me'nkoko*," I do not go.

The Accra resembles the Greek in the nice distinctions of some of its verbs and nouns.

Gnăghmong   -   -   To salute in the morning.
Cotaghmong   -   To roll up.

Balbaghtoomong	- -	To draw towards
Tehtemong	- - -	To gather up
Kakow	- - -	The tooth ache *(nanyong* a tooth)
Kodjomong	- - -	To talk a palaver
Song	- - - -	To work as a smith ⎫ neechoomong
Ghnāmong	- - - -	mechanic ⎰ to work
Ninnamong	- - -	To separate weeds from earth

The Accra and Fantee interjections are generally parts of sentences, as, Mr. Horne Tooke has shewn most of our own to be: "*minnannako*," what do I see now, "*me ä whoo!*" I die, "*mädja!*" oh my father, equally responsive to grief, joy, or surprise; and used as involuntarily, and as frequently as the two syllables *boh, hah,* which answer to our *oh,* and *ah,* and which, of course, cannot be called words. An Ashantee striking his foot against a stone, or any thing in his way, exclaims " the thing is mad."

I was surprised to find little, or no inversion in the Accra or Fantee prose*; the substantive precedes the adjective, but there is scarcely any other trace of it: yet, it is one of their poetical licenses, as may be instanced in the following line of a Fantee song;

" Abirrikirri croom ogah odum."

Foreign town fire put in,

for " the foreign town is set on fire." In addition to this inversion, so many peculiar additives, (generally vowels,) and inflexions are allowed, as well as the figures Synæresis, Diæresis, Metathesis,

---

* " He (the savage) would not express himself according to our English order of construction, Give me fruit, but according to the Latin order, Fruit give me, Fructum da mihi, for this plain reason, that his attention was wholly directed towards fruit, the desired object. This was the exciting idea; the object which moved him to speak, and of course would be the first named. Such an arrangement is precisely putting into words the gesture which nature taught the savage to make, before he was acquainted

and Anastrophe, in their poetry, and in their poetry only, (making it unintelligible even to those who can converse fluently with them) that both languages may be said to have a Prosody. From the following song, I imagined the Fantees (for the Accra's are said to possess none but fetish hymns in their own language) to have some idea of rhyme, considering the inversion of the first line as forced, and expressly accommodated to the metre,

Abirrikirri croom ogah odum,

Ocoontinkiï bonoo fum,

Cooroompun,

Coom agwun,

but I have not met with any other instance.

The Ashantees generally use much and vehement gesture, and speak in recitative: their action is exuberant, but graceful; and from the infancy of the language,* nouns and verbs are constantly

---

with words; and therefore it may be depended upon as certain, that he would fall most readily into this arrangement.   -   -   -   -   -   -
We might therefore conclude, à priori, that this would be the order in which things were most commonly arranged at the beginning of language, and accordingly we find, in fact, that in this order words are arranged in most of the antient tongues; as in the Greek and the Latin; and it is also said, in the Russian, the Sclavonic, the Gaelic, and several of the American tongues." Blair.

The arrangement of words in the Chayma is such as is found in every language of both continents, which has preserved a certain air of youth. The object is placed before the verb, the verb before the personal pronoun. The object on which the attention should be principally fixed, precedes all the modifications of that object.

The American would say; " liberty complete love we ;" instead of we love complete liberty; " Thee with happy am I"—instead of I am happy with thee. Humboldt's Personal Narrative, vol. 3, p. 261.

* " In the infancy of language, while words were yet scanty, the most natural way, whereby a writer or speaker might give an additional force to his discourse, was to *repeat* such terms as he wished to render *emphatic*. The more ancient any language is, the more numerous appear the traces of such repetitions; and next to the Hebrew, they

repeated, for force, and distinction, as *one one*, for, *one by one*, or, *each; one tokoo one tokoo*, for, *one tokoo a-piece*. They frequently are obliged to vary the tone, in pronouncing a word which has more than one meaning, as the Chinese do. They have no expression short of you are a liar, and the king was surprised, when I told him we made a great difference between a mistake and a lie; he said the truth was not spoken in either case, and, therefore, it was the same thing; they did not consider the motive but only the fact.

Like the American languages, those of this part of Africa, are full of figures, hyperbolical and picturesque.* One of the kings of the interior, whose territories the Ashantees had long talked of invading, sent forty pots of palm oil to Coomassie, with the message, that, " he feared they could not find their way, so he sent the oil to light them." The Accras instead of good night, say " *wooäu d'tcherrimong*," sleep till the lighting of the world : one of their imprecations against their enemies, is, " may their hiding place be our flute," that is, " our plaything:" when they speak of a man imposing on them, they say, " he turned the backs of our heads into our mouths." Having occasion, whilst at Coomassie, to protest against the conduct of an individual, the king replied, through Adoosce, " The horse comes from the bush, and is a fool, but the man who rides him knows sense, and by and by makes him do what he wishes; you, by yourself, made the horse, who was a

---

form a remarkable feature in the Greek tongue. This $\mu\alpha\omega$ $\mu\alpha\omega$, I desire desire, blended into one word, become $\mu\iota\mu\alpha\omega$, and mean, I greatly desire. $\beta\alpha\omega$ $\beta\alpha\omega$, I walk walk, $\beta\iota$-$\beta\alpha\omega$, I stride, &c. &c. &c. See Jones.

* " The messenger concluded this insulting notification by presenting the king with a pair of iron sandals, at the same time adding, that until such time as Daisy had worn out these sandals in his flight, he should never be secure from the arrows of Bambarra." Park's 1st Mission.

fool, do better the other day, therefore, three of you ought to teach a man, who is not born a fool, and does not come from the bush, to do what you know to be right by and by, though I see he does wrong now." Other instances will appear in their songs.

I shall transfer the imperfect Vocabularies which I formed, and the incidental observations, to the Appendix; as they may not be indulged with so much attention by the generality of readers, as the investigation of the structure.

CHAPTER X.

Music.

THE wild music of these people is scarcely to be brought within the regular rules of harmony,* yet their airs have a sweetness and animation beyond any barbarous compositions I ever heard. Few of their instruments possess much power, but the combination of several frequently produces a surprising effect. The flute is made of a long hollow reed, and has not more than three holes; the tone is low at all times, and when they play in concert they graduate them with such nicety as to produce the common chords. Several instances of thirds occur, especially in one of the annexed airs, played as a funeral dirge; nor is this extraordinary considering it is the most natural interval; the addition of fifths, at the same time, is rare. The natives declare they can converse by means of their flutes, and an old resident at Accra has assured me he has heard these dialogues, and that every sentence was explained to him.

On the Sanko (see Drawing No. 5, and Specimen in the Museum) they display the variety of their musical talents, and the Ashantees are allowed to surpass all others. It consists of a narrow box, the open top of which is covered with alligator, or antelope skin; a bridge is raised on this, over which eight

* " A few melodies in national music have been found incapable of harmony; such as the two first bars of the second part of the Irish tune called The Fair Hair'd Child." Dr. Crotch.

A a

strings are conducted to the end of a long stick, fastened to
the fore part of the box, and thickly notched, and they raise or
depress the strings into these notches as occasion requires. The
upper string assimilates with the tenor C of the piano, and the
lower with the octave above: sometimes they are tuned in Diatonic
succession, but too frequently the intermediate strings are drawn
up at random, producing flats and sharps in every Chromatic
variety, though they are not skilful enough to take advantage of
it. I frequently urged this by trying to convince them they were
not playing the same tune I had heard the day before, but the
answer was invariably, " I pull the same string, it must be the
same tune." The strings are made from the runners of a tree
called Enta, abounding in the forests. All airs on this instrument
are played very quick, and it is barely possible to make even an
experienced player lessen the time, which quick as it is, is kept in
a surprising manner, especially as every tune is loaded with ornament. They have a method of stopping the strings with the finger,
so as to produce a very soft and pleasing effect, like the Meyer
touch of the harp.

The horns form their loudest sounds, and are made of elephant's
tusks, they are generally very large, and, being graduated like the
flutes, their flourishes have a martial and grand effect. It has
been mentioned in the Military Customs of the Ashantees, that
peculiar sentences are immediately recognised by the soldiers,
and people, in the distinct flourishes of the horns of the various
chiefs: the words of some of these sentences are almost expressible
by the notes of the horns; the following, uttered by the horns of a
captain named Gettoä, occurs to me as an instance ·

"O Saï tïntïntóo, ma yūāyïä pa pa."

O Saï great king! I laud thee every where, or exceedingly.
The Bentwa (see Drawing No. 6.) is a stick bent in the form of

a bow, and across it, is fastened a very thin piece of split cane, which is held between the lips at one end, and struck with a small stick; whilst at the other it is occasionally stopped, or rather buffed, by a thick one; on this they play only lively airs, and it owes its various sounds to the lips.

The Mosees, Mallowas, Bournous, and natives from the more remote parts of the interior, play on a rude violin : the body is a calabash, the top is covered with deer skin, and two large holes are cut in it for the sound to escape; the strings, or rather string, is composed of cow's hair, and broad like that of the bow with which they play, which resembles the bow of a violin. Their grimace equals that of an Italian Buffo: they generally accompany themselves with the voice, and increase the humour by a strong nasal sound.

The Oompoochwa is a box, one end of which is left open; two flat bridges are fastened across the top, and five pieces of thin curved stick, scraped very smooth, are attached to them, and (their ends being raised,) are struck with some force by the thumb. I can compare it to nothing but the Staccado nearly deprived of its tone.

The Ashantees have an instrument like a Bagpipe, but the drone is scarcely to be heard.

The rest of the instruments can hardly be called musical, and consist of drums, castanets, gong-gongs, flat sticks, rattles, and even old brass pans.

The Drums (see Drawing No. 7.) are hollow'd trunks of trees, frequently carved with much nicety, mostly open at one end, and of many sizes : those with heads of common skin (that is of any other than Leopard skin) are beaten with sticks in the form of a crotchet rest; the largest are borne on the head of a man, and struck by one or more followers; the smaller are slung round the neck, or stand on the ground; in the latter case they are mostly played with the inside of the fingers, at which the natives are very expert: amongst these drums are some with heads of leopard skin, (looking like vellum,) only sounded by two fingers, which are scraped along, as the middle finger is on the tamborine, but pro- d cing a much louder noise. The gong-gongs are made of hollow pieces of iron, and struck with the same metal. The Castanets are also of iron. The Rattles are hollow gourds, the stalks being left as handles, and contain shells or pebbles, and are frequently covered with a net work of beads; the grimaces with which these are played make them much more entertaining to sight than hearing.

I was fortunate enough to find a rare instance of a native able to play the radical notes of each tune; he is the best player in the country, and I was enabled to collect the airs now offered: with some of the oldest date I have also selected a few of the latest compositions. Their graces are so numerous, some extempore, some transmitted from father to son, that the constant repetition only can distinguish the commencement of the air: sometimes between each beginning they introduce a few chords, sometimes they leave out a bar, sometimes they only return to the middle, so entirely is it left to the fancy of the performer. The observation made on the time of the Sanko may be extended to almost every other instrument, but it is always perfect, and the children will move their heads and limbs, whilst on their mother's backs, in exact unison with the tune which is playing: the contrasts of piano and forte are very well managed.

The singing is almost all recitative, and this is the only part of music in which the women partake; they join in the chorusses, and at the funeral of a female sing the dirge itself; but the frenzy of the moment renders it such a mixture of yells and screeches, that it bids defiance to all notation. The songs of the Canoe men

The oldest ASHANTEE and WARSAW AIR.

Sanko

Nº 1.
Allegro

A very old ASHANTEE AIR.

Sanko

Nº 2.

Aganka oshoom noofa   Ohoibee oshoom noofa   Aganka oshoom noofa
Orphan cries at night _ _ _   cries at night Orphan cries at night

wekirree wekirree oimiyow wekirree   wekirree   wekirree   oimiyow
sad thing sad thing I'm sorry sad thing   sad thing sad thing I'm sorry

When the air is repeated these chords are used as a
prelude and the 1st note of the 1st bar doubled.

WARSAW AIR.

Sanko

Nº 3.
Allegro.

ASHANTEE AIR.

Sanko

Nº 4.
Presto

FANTEE AIR.

Sanko

Nº 5.
Allegro

ASHANTEE AIR.

Sanko

Nº 11.

A FANTEE DIRGE.

Flutes

Nº 12.

Andante

Piano

Fortissimo Drums &c.

Piano

Fortissimo Drums &c.

AN ASHANTEE AIR.

Flutes

Nº 13
Andante

AN ACCRA FETISH HYMN.

Nº 14.

Andante

Afi _ _ naie _ _pwaëe   gnorwoorra afi _ naie _ pwaïe

gnorwoorra   gnorwoorra

gnorwoorra afi _ _ naie _ _pwaïe   gnorwoorra morbee gnorwoorra

gnorwoorra gnorwoorra morbee gnorwoorra

4

A KERRAPEE SONG.

Nº 15.
Andante

Kenneo _ vay nooblou adomevai   Kenneovay nooblou adomevai

noodooloo   a_ domevai   ennoblou Dootoh me po me bloh   a_daŋ_vo l̈ee

FANTEE AIR.   — Oompoochŋa

Nº 16.

FANTEE AIR   Bentwa

Nº 17.
Vivace

ASHANTEE AIR.   Bentwa

Nº 18.
Vivace

MALLOWA AIR.   Violin

Nº 19.
Andantino

MOSEE AIR.   Violin

Nº 20.
Andantino

are peculiar to themselves, and very much resemble the chants used in cathedrals, but as they are all made for the moment, I have not been able to retain any of them.

To have attempted any thing like arrangement, beyond what the annexed airs naturally possess, would have altered them, and destroyed the intention of making them known in their original character. I have not even dared to insert a flat or a sharp.

No. 1. is the oldest air in the whole collection, and common both to Ashantees and Warsaws; I could trace it through four generations, but the answer made to my enquiries will give the best idea of its antiquity; " it was made when the country was made." The key appears to be E minor.

The old and simple air No. 2, is almost spoiled from the quick method of playing it, but when slow it has a melancholy rarely found in African music, and it is one of the very few in which the words are adapted to the tune. I think it is decidedly in the key of C major. The noun aganka, an orphan, is from the verb agan to leave. Oboïbee is a bird that sings only at night, for which I know no other name than the Ashantee. The Warsaw air, No. 3, also in C major, was composed in consequence of a contest between the two principal caboceers of that country, Intiffa and Attobra; one extremely thin and the other very fat; Attobra ran away, and is derided by Intiffa in the following satirical words:

Asoom cōōcōŏrŏŏcōō ŏninny ăgwanny.

Asoom is a dolphin, which, as a beardless creature, is an epithet of the strongest contempt. The literal translation is,

The big dolphin runs away from the small man.

No. 5, which I should conjecture to begin in E minor, and to end in D minor, was occasioned by an English vessel bringing the report of a battle, in which the French were defeated and their town burned. The words are allegorical.

> Abirrikirri croom ogah odum ;
> French   town   fire   put in ;
> Ocoontinkii bonoo fum ;
> Great fighting man, wolf   take you away ;
> Cooroompun coom agwun.
> Cooroompun kills   all goats.

Abirrikirri applies indiscriminately to all nations beyond the sea, as Dunko does to all nations far in the interior. Cooroompun is a very large insect of the genus mantis (soothsayer) frequently met with here, and the natives believe that it kills the sheep and goats by fascination, standing with its eyes fixed on those of the object, and swinging its head and body from side to side without moving its feet, until the animal falls in fits and dies.* Agwun is a noun of multitude, comprehending all the goat kind.

A long tale accompanies No. 6. An Ashantee having been surprised in an intrigue with another man's wife, becomes the slave of the King, and is obliged to follow the army in a campaign against the celebrated Attah, the Akim caboceer mentioned in the history. The Ashantee army having retired, this man either deserted or could not join his division, and after concealing himself some time in the forest, was taken by a party of Attah's, whom he addresses in the following words :

> Eqqwee odin ahi,
> Panther bush here (belongs to)

---

* The power of fascination by the eyes, is believed and dreaded in those parts of Africa as mortal, whether exercised by the fetish priests against men, or by the cooroompun against animals. The idea prevailed in Pliny's time, but it was ascribed to the voice. " In libro quodam Plinii naturalis historiæ legi esse quasdam in terrâ Africâ familias hominum voce atque linguâ effascinantium. Qui si impensiùs fortè laudaverint pulchras arbores, segetes lætiores, infantes amœniores, egregios equos, pecudes pastu, atque cultu optimas, emoriantur repentè hæc omnia." A cooroompun will be found amongst the specimens for the British Museum.

Minăwoo! Minăwoo!

I die! I die!

Me'din adoo croom,

Bush now my croom,

Minăwoo! Minăwoo!

I die! I die!

Babisseäche Minăwoo! Minăwoo!

For woman's sake I die! I die!

Attah m'incomie! Attah m'incomie!

Attah don't kill me! Attah don't kill me!

The man's life, it was added, was preserved when he urged that he understood how to make sandals. The key appears to be E minor.

No. 7, in G major, seems to convey the moral, that riches prompt mankind to wickedness, the word " *makes*" is understood.

No. 9, became a common song in March last in praise of the present Governor in Chief; who, in consequence of the famine occasioned by the preceding invasion from the Ashantees, daily distributed corn to the starving multitude: the words are even more incoherent and figurative than the others, therefore I have not written them, but the meaning to be gathered is, " Poor woman and poor child got no gold to buy kanky ; good white man gives you corn." It will be observed that the air much resembles No. 11, wherefore I suspect it is an alteration, and not a composition; although the key seems to be G major, and it is impossible to attach any key to the latter.

The dirge, No. 12, certainly in the key of C major, has been mentioned before, but here I must add, that in venturing the intervening and concluding bass chord, I merely attempt to describe the castanets, gong-gongs, drums, &c. bursting in after the soft and mellow tones of the flutes ; as if the ear was not to retain a vibration of the sweeter melody.

No. 13, in D minor, is played by only two flutes, and is one of the softest airs I have met with.

No. 14, is an Accra fetish hymn, sung by one man and one woman, or more, at Christmas:

> Afĩnaïē pweë,
>
> The year's ends have met,
>
> Gnōr woorra
>
> Somebody's child
>
> Mŏrbee.
>
> Take blessing.

"Somebody's child," means the child of a person of consequence, reminding us of Hidalgos, "the son of somebody," so applied in Spanish. Its regularity is surprising, and its transition from G major to C major is very harmonious.

No. 15, in G major, is a specimen of the Kerrapee or Kerrapay music, which I have made a point of preserving, as it appeared to me superior even to Ashantee. A young man acknowledges a crime he had attempted to conceal:

> Kennĕövay nooblou adomevai,
>
> Oh pity!   the palaver is spoiled,
>
> Noodooloo adomevai,
>
> It is found, it is spoiled;
>
>> Ēnnŏblou;
>>
>> Think for me;
>
> Dootŏh mĕ pŏ mĕ blōh,
>
> Elders, settle it for me,
>
>> Adăn vō,
>>
>> I am at a loss,
>>
>>> Iëe!
>>>
>>> Oh!

The following is a translation of a long Ashantee song, with little or no air. The men sit together in a line on one side, with their sankos and other instruments; and the women in a line opposite to them. Individuals rise and advance, singing in turn.*

1st Woman. My husband likes me too much,
He is good to me,
But I cannot like him,
So I must listen to my lover.

1st Man. My wife does not please me,
I tire of her now;
So I will please myself with another,
Who is very handsome.

2nd Woman. My lover tempts me with sweet words,
But my husband always does me good,
So I must like him well,
And I must be true to him.

2nd Man. Girl you pass my wife handsome,
But I cannot call you wife;
A wife pleases her husband only,
But when I leave you, you go to others.

* I never heard this sung without its recalling Horace's beautiful little dialogue ode, (9. lib. 3) " Donec gratus eram tibi."

3 B

CHAPTER XI.

Materia Medica and Diseases.

T H E report of the Materia Medica and Botany of Ashantee, was the only one which I was not required to furnish. It was afforded by Mr. Henry Tedlie, assistant surgeon, whose subsequent death has mingled a regret with the recollection of the Embassy, which the recall of my own sufferings, and the family affliction it entailed on me, could never have exacted. The intelligence reached me in England, to correct the pride of success by associating misfortune with it; for the recollection of Mr. Tedlie's social virtues, of his enterprise and ability, makes it a severe one to myself, and to the world. Mr. Tedlie suffered severely from intermitting dysentery during the Mission, but I had hoped it would have been eradicated after his return. He had previously attended the expedition to Candy, and expired at Cape Coast Castle in the 27th year of his age. Throughout the Mission he indulged the feelings of the natives, in his professional capacity, with a patience few could have exerted; whether labouring under sickness himself, or disturbed in the moments of a scanty rest; he awed and conciliated the people by the importance of his cures, and thus contributed to the success of the enterprise.

" During the earlier part of our residence at Coomassie, the season was tolerably favourable to the gathering of plants, but we were then allowed to go out but seldom, and never beyond the town.

Latterly, when better impressions succeeded, and our walks were unrestrained by limits or attendants, the rains not only checked, but generally disappointed my researches, by presenting the subject flowerless, (or in an unfit state for preservation,) and consequently not admitting their classification, as is too evident in the following list of such plants as are used as medicines by the Ashantees.

1. Cutturasuh. (*Chrysanthellum procumbens. Persoon. syn. 2. p. 471, Verbesina mutica Willd.) A small plant, a decoction of which is purgative, before boiling it should be bruised.

2. Adumba, (a species of Ficus.) The bark and fruit are pounded with Mallaguetta pepper and a small plant called awhinteywhinting, boiled in fish soup : two doses in the third month of gestation are said to cause abortion.

3. Koofoobah (Gloriosa superba. Linn.) is bruised with Mallaguetta pepper (lesser cardamom seeds) and applied to the ancle or foot when sprained.

4. Tandoorue (perhaps a Cupania or Trichilia.) The bark is pounded and boiled with Mallaguetta pepper ; used for pain in the belly, and acts as a purgative.

5. Bissey. (Sterculia acuminata. Palis. de Beauvois, Flore d'Oware 1. p. 41. tab. 24.) The fruit is constantly chewed by the Ashantees, especially on a journey ; it is said to prevent hunger and strengthen the stomach and bowels ; has a slight bitter aromatic astringent taste, and causes an increase of the saliva while chewed.

6. Attueh. (Blighia sapida. Hort. Kew. ed. 2. vol. 3, p. 350. Akeesia africana Tussac Flor. des Antilles 66.) A decoction of the bark is said to be anti-venereal. The fruit is eaten.

7. Ricinus Communis Linn. Castor oil nut tree, 30 feet high here, and not a bush as on the coast : not used as medicine by the natives.

---

* I am indebted to Mr. Brown's knowledge for the names and references in the parentheses.

8. Apooder. (*Two species of Leucas, of which one is hardly diffe-rent from L. Martinicensis Hort. Kew. ed. 2. vol. 3, p. 409, the other is perhaps new.*) A mixture of the bruised leaves with lime juice is applied to inflammations.

9. Hooghong. (A species of Urtica) is bruised, mixed with chalk, and drank by pregnant women to correct acidity in the stomach, heartburn, &c.

10. Accocottocotorawah. (*Heliotropium indicum. Linn.*) The juice expressed from this plant is snuffed up the nostrils in cases of severe head-ach. They also inhale the smoke of it into the nose.

11. Crowera (*Acalypha ciliata. Willd. sp. pl.*) is bruised with lesser cardamom seed, and rubbed on the chest and side when pained.

12. Enminim (*a species of Vitis.*) A climbing plant. The juice expressed from the leaves is dropped into the eyes when affected with opthalmia or pain.

13. Secoco. (*Leptanthus?*) A small marshy plant. Is pounded with lime juice and rubbed on the body to cure the crawcraws; a severe and obstinate species of itch.

14. Ammo.—The juice is applied to cuts and bruises.

15. Petey (*possibly a Piper.*) The leaves are pounded and applied as a plaister to inflammatory swellings and boils.

16. Abromotome.—The bruised leaves are used to discuss boils.

17. Yangkompro. (*A syngenesious plant related to Cacalia.*) The pounded leaves are applied to cuts and contusions.

18. Oeduema. (*Musanga cecropioides Br. See Tuckey's Congo, p. 453.*) The hairy sheath or stipule of a large palmated leaved tree; it resembles a skin, is boiled in soup, and used as a powerful emmenagogue.

19. Semeney, (*probably a species of Aneilema.*) The leaves are pounded and applied as a plaister to favour the discharge of boils and collections of pus.

20. Wowwah (*perhaps a Sterculia.*) The inner bark of this tree is scraped fine and mixed with Mallaguetta pepper, and drank for colic and other pains in the belly.

21. Anafranakoo.—The bruised leaves are applied to discuss boils and other inflammatory swelling.

22. Kattacaiben (*Leea sambucina.*) A decoction of the leaves is drank every morning by pregnant women when they experience any uneasiness in the abdomen. The bark of the tree powdered is rubbed on chronic swellings.

23. Aserumbdrue (*a species of Piper related to umbellatum.*) The leaves are used in soup to allay swellings of the belly.

24. Ocisscerce.—The bark of this tree is used to stop the purging in dysentery and diarrhoea.

25. Gingang. (*Paullinia africana Br. See Tuckey's Congo, p. 427.*) The bark of this tree is used internally and externally, mixed with Mallaguetta pepper for pain in the side.

26. Cudeyakoo.—A very small plant. The leaves and stalk pounded are applied to eruptions on the head. A mixture of it with lime juice is applied to the yaws.

27. Affeuah (*unknown*) and Nuinnuerafuh (*Hedysari species.*) A mixture of the bruised leaves of these plants with Mallaguetta pepper, is rubbed on the body and limbs when swelled or pained : a decoction of them, with an addition of the plant Comfany (*Alternantheræ, sp.*) is used internally in the same cases.

28. Adummah. (*Paullinia africana. The same as No. 25.*) A decoction of the bark of this tree, reduced to powder with Mallaguetta pepper, drank once a day, stops the discharge of blood and cures the dysentery.

29. Tointinney (*probably a Menispermum.*) Is chewed with Mallaguetta pepper as a cure for a cough.

30. Apussey. (*A leguminous plant, probably allied to Robinia.*)

The bark of this tree pounded with Mallaguetta pepper is applied to the head in cases of head-ach.

31. Thuquamah.—The bark is pounded and drank in Palm wine, with Mallaguetta pepper, for pain in the belly.

32. Conkknoney, a dark purple coloured Toadstool, the size of a hazel nut, rubbed with Mallaguetta pepper and lime juice, it purges briskly. To stop the purging, a mess of boiled Guinea corn meal and lime juice should be eaten.

33. Suetinney.—(*Brillantaisia owariensis. Palis. de Beauvois Flor. d'Oware,* 2. *p.* 68 *tab.* 100, *fig.* 2.) A decoction of the leaves is drank for pain in the belly.

34. Soominna, (Tetandria Monogynia,) is bruised with lime juice and used to abate cough.

35. Thattha *(Scoparia dulcis. Linn.)*—The expressed juice of this plant is dropped into the ears when pained.

36. Aquey (*Melia Azedarach. Linn.*) A decoction of the leaves of this tree is used with Palm wine as a corroborant.

37. Dammaram (*Mussænda fulgens. nov. spec.*)

The diseases most common in the Ashantee Country are the Lues, Yaws, Itch, Ulcers, Scald-heads, and griping pains in the bowels. Other diseases are occasionally met with, I should suppose in the same proportion that they occur in civilized countries; but I do not know to what cause to assign the prevalence and frequency of one of the most unsightly diseases that can occur in any country: it is an obstinate species of ulcer, or, Noli me tangere, which destroys the nose and upper lip; it attacks women chiefly, although men are not exempt from it; there are more than 100 women in Coomassie who have lost the nose or upper lip from this cause alone: it commences with a small ulcer in the alæ nasi, or upper lip, the size of a split pea, excavated, with the edges ragged and turned inwards, it proceeds by ulcerating under the skin; the bottom of the ulcer is uneven, covered with a foul slough, of a very disagreeable smell, and the discharge is thin, watery, and very irritating: it seldom cicatrices before the alæ nasi and lip are completely destroyed; when it does cease, the skin is puckered and uneven, and has a very disagreeable appearance; the only remedy which the natives use, is an external application of bruised leaves; they seem to let it take its course, without being very anxious about a cure.

Framboesia, the Yaws, is a very frequent disease with the children of the poor and slaves: before the eruption takes place they are severely afflicted with pains in the joints, and along the course of the muscles of the superior and inferior extremities; in young persons, hard, round bony excrescences, the size of a walnut, form on each side of the nose under the eyes. The Natives either are not acquainted with a remedy for this enlargement of the bones, or if they are, they do not put it in practice. I administered alterative doses of calomel and antimonial powder with success, as it stopped the enlargement of the bones and caused them to be absorbed, and relieved the pain in the arms and legs particularly; during the exhibition of the alterative pills, a foul ulcer on the head got well: the natives apply a mixture of the plant Cudey-akoo, with lime juice, to the eruption, but apparently with very little benefit.

Psora, the itch, a very severe species of which, called craw craw, is a frequent disease, and is very contagious; it is most commonly met with in children, few of the Dunko slaves are without it, from their poor diet and extreme dirtiness; they do not seem to experience much uneasiness from it, as they seldom apply any remedy; sometimes they use a rubefaciant, made of a plant called secoco, bruised and mixed with lime juice.

Gonorrhœa is of rare occurrence, two cases came under my care, the patients had never used injections, they drank decoctions of leaves and bark, but could not tell me the plants they used ; one of the ingredients, was a small plant call Cutturasuh, of a purgative nature. The disease is allowed to take its course by the natives, as they are unacquainted with any method to stop it.

Tinea Capitis, the scald head, is a common disease with the poorer sort of Ashantees and slaves, arising from their neglect of cleanliness; the applications which they use to cure it have seldom the desired effect. They apply plaisters of pounded leaves and charcoal, but do not wash the head. In one case, where a boy was placed under my care, he got well in eight days, by having his head very well washed with a brush, soap, and warm water; then a strong infusion of tobacco, applied with a sponge, and when the head was dry, a composition of resinous and mercurial ointment was rubbed on it.

Hydrocele occasionally occurs; they attempt to cure it by frictions of the castor oil nut, burnt and bruised with Mallaguetta pepper, but without any benefit. I drew off the water from one hydrocele, but, from our want of stimulants, could not perform any radical cure. Their applications to Inguinal hernia are equally ineffectual. They never attempt the reduction of umbilical hernia, although some are very large, and the disease very frequent.

When a fracture of the leg or arm happens, the part is rubbed with a soft species of grass and palm oil, and the limb bound up with splints. "If God does not take the patient he recovers in four months," as they say.

I have not seen a single instance of fracture in the Ashantee country. Gun-shot wounds of the extremities, when the bone is fractured, are generally fatal, or, where a large blood vessel is wounded, as they are unacquainted with any method of stopping the hæmorrage; in fact they pay little attention to their wounded men; if they are not able to travel, they are abandoned. One of the King's criers had his thigh dislocated at the hip joint with an anchylosis of the knee; the limb was considerably longer than the other, and the accident must have occurred a long time ago, as he walks very well.

During the time we remained in Coomassie, and from our first entrance into the Ashantee country, I was every day applied to for advice and medicines by those who were afflicted with diseases, of which the number was great, and in the capital more especially, from its very unhealthy situation, being entirely surrounded by an extensive tract of swampy ground, and the natives consequently very subject to dysentery and fever. On first entering the country I was applied to by numbers of patients, many of them miserable objects, from the effects of the venereal disease: to as many of those as applied, during our halt in a town, I gave boxes of pills and strict directions for their use, and told them if they came to Coomassie during my residence there, I would do every thing in my power to cure them. Many availed themselves of my offer, and attended me on my arrival. To those who had ulcers or wounds, I applied the proper dressings, and left with them lint, adhesive plaister, and ointment. Most of them as a mark of their gratitude, sent presents of fowls, fruit, palm oil, wine, &c. to me after I had arrived in the capital. One man in Assiminia, who was nearly in the last stage of existence from a complication of disorders, originating from lues venerea, after I had seen him, sent every week to Coomassie for medicines, and completely recovered. Another in Sarrasoo who had the worst looking ulcers of the inferior extremities, that I have ever seen, did the same, and with the same success. A great many caboceers

3 c

attended me every morning with their slaves and children affected with dropsy, crawcraws, yaws, fever, bowel complaints, &c. and expressed the most unbounded thanks for the medicine and advice they received.

At the King's particular request, I attended his own brother, the heir apparent, who had oedematous feet : by the use of friction, a roller, and an alterative course of calomel, and diuretics, he soon recovered.

The King's uncle, heir to the crown after the brother, was severely tormented with stricture of the urethra; he could only pass urine, drop by drop; three weeks passing the catheter, enabled him to make it in a full stream ; when he immediately requested some powerfully stimulating medicine to correct impotency, which it was not in my power to grant.

The captain whose office it is to drown any of the King's family who have offended, had an ulcer two inches long in the palate bone; when he drank, part of the fluid passed out of his nose, and his speech was very unintelligible; the sides of the opening were scarified, and the granulations touched every third or fourth day with lunar caustic until they united; he got well in one month.

The only unfortunate case I attended, was our guide Quamina Bwa; shortly after we arrived in Coomassie he was attacked with remittent fever; by the use of febrifuge medicines, the cold bath, bark, &c. he recovered, and was able to attend his usual duty of waiting on us, when we visited the king; he went into the country, and I did not see him for six weeks; at the end of that time, he sent for me, and I found him labouring under a severe bilious dysentery, and liver complaint. I was unable to prevent the formation of matter in his liver; it formed a large swelling with distinct fluctuation, and as he hesitated to have it discharged by puncturing with a trochar, it burst internally, and he died. I had one case of cancer of the upper lip, although the disease is said rarely to occur in that part. This case had all the marks of a true cancer; I dressed it every day during the whole time I remained in Coomassie, but the effect flattered and disappointed me by turns.

The most importunate man for medicine, especially of an invigorating kind, in the whole Ashantee country, was old Apokoo, the treasurer and chief favourite. He was afflicted with inguinal hernia: I wrote to Cape Coast for a truss, which I applied, and it gave him immediate relief and satisfaction. He would take the most nauseous drug with pleasure. I generally gave him bark and peppermint water, which he regularly either sent or came for every day, during the two last months of our residence, and earnestly requested me to leave plenty of medicine with Mr. Hutchison, the British resident there. Most of the chief men were very earnest in their solicitations for me to give them stimulating medicines. I always assured them that it was impossible, that the English never used any, and that nothing astonished me more than that they should ask for such things. Their answers were, " they knew that the English had good heads and knew every thing, and must know that too, but I did not wish to give them any."

A List of the Diseases which I have seen in the Ashantee country.

Febris remittens	-	2 cases	Scrophula	-	- many cases
Hepatitis	- -	1	Syphilis	-	- many
Dysenteria mucosa		6	Gonorrhœa -	-	2
Colica -	- -	1	Stricture	-	- 3
Anasarca	- -	3	Cataract	-	- 2
Ascites	- -	3	Staphyloma -	-	5

Ectropium	-	1 case	Umbilical (hernia)	many
Bronchocele	- many		Dracunculus -	7
Cephalagia -	- many		Tinea capitis	- many
Odontalgia -	- 10		Hydrocele -	- many
Ulcers -	- 8		Cancer -	- 1
Framboesia -	- many		Elephantiasis	- 1
Psora -	- many		Lepra -	- 7
Hernia inguinal	- 1			

CHAPTER XII.

Mr. Hutchison's Diary.

Sᴇᴘᴛᴇᴍʙᴇʀ 26. After we left the palace this morning, Apokoo invited me home to take some refreshment. He entered into a long conversation concerning the slave trade: he heard, he said, that an English vessel had arrived at Cape Coast, and had brought out a letter from the King of England to the Governor-in-Chief, ordering a renewal of the slave trade, and asked me, if I had received any letter. I said I had not, but if such a thing had taken place, I thought I should have early accounts. He enquired what were the objections we had to " buy men ?" I told him what I conceived to be proper; he laughed at our ideas, and enquired if the king of Dahomey had not sent a " book four moons ago to Cape Coast, inviting the English to trade again, in his kingdom." I replied there was a message sent, but I could not say exactly in what words, as I was at Dix Cove at the time. " England," he said, " was too fond of fighting, her soldiers were the same as dropping a stone in a pond, they go farther and farther:" at the same time he described an enlarging circle with his hand, and shook his finger and head significantly at me. He was anxious for me to write a " proper book" on the slave trade, many slaves, he told me, had revolted, and joining the Buntokoo standard were to fight against them; there were too many slaves in the country, (an opinion I tacitly acquiesced in), and they wanted to get rid of some of them. There might be a deal of trouble from them; he alone had one slave, who had 1000 followers at arms, and he might trouble them as Cudjo Cooma did, who was a slave of his when he revolted, and whose adherents alone were 10,000, independent of runaways, &c.

In the afternoon the King sent me a ceremonious message, with his compliments, saying he would be glad if I attended him in his customs, &c. when he should sit in public. I replied that I would be happy to do so, as it was the King's wish, except when human sacrifices were offered, but then it would be contrary to my inclinations, my religion, and my instructions.

Shortly after I was told the King was in the market-place drinking palm wine. I went for the first time and took my seat on his left. The King made me a present of a pot of wine, as did several of his chiefs. When he drank, the whole of the music played, while the executioners, holding their swords with their right hands, covered their noses with their left, whilst they sung his victories and titles. About half a dozen small boys stood behind his chair, and finished the whole with a fetish hymn. The King enquired how many servants I had, and several questions of the same kind. After sitting about half an hour the assembly broke up, the King rising first, which is the signal to retire.

Since the mission departed I have not been annoyed by any boys calling after me. After seeing Messrs. Bowdich and Tedlie through the town, on their going away, as I returned home the crowds thanked me as I passed, for staying. I suppose they hardly imagined, when it came to the last, that I would do so: indeed when I returned to my lodgings I found them solitary enough; and, in the night time, three men found their way into the house; one of my servants awakening, shouted out; I struck at one of them with my sword, but missed him: in the morning it

was discovered that he had succeeded in stealing nearly half a sheep,
a quantity of kankey belonging to the boys, and a table knife. I am
not sanguine enough to imagine I shall be long allowed to take my
walks unmolested ; when the novelty of my remaining alone passes
away, they will return to their old insolencies.

Monday 29. Paid Apokoo a visit, and dashed him a razor.
Several people were there talking palavers, and wishing him to
interest the King for them ; among others, an old captain complained heavily of Quamina Bwa, our guide, but since dead, who
he said had stolen a slave from him and sold him during the Fantee
war ; he had unavailingly applied to the family, he therefore
wished it to be brought before the King.

Apokoo complained of head-ach, and one of his women brought
a decoction of herbs, which she poured into a hollow piece of wood
with two tubes, these were inserted in the nostrils, and the liquor
poured in, while the head was held back, and afterwards spit out
by the mouth ; I have seen the same poured into the ear for a like
complaint. He wished me to try a little of it ; I of course declined
it. He called one of his daughter's, and wished me to consaw, or
espouse her ; I told him she was too young ; he said that was
nothing, as he would keep her for me : he added, the Ashantee
custom was, if a great man's wife with child took another man's
fancy, he consawed the child in the womb, and if born a girl, when
she grew up she became his wife ; if a boy, it was his to serve and
attend on him, and he took care of it. Four ounces of gold it
generally cost to consaw a girl. I said he was a rich man ; " true,"
he replied, " but it sometimes costs eight or ten ounces, sometimes
only two." Observing a bow and arrows standing in the room, I
began to amuse myself with shooting them ; he told me these were
only for play, but when they went to fight, they tipped them with
iron, and put a deadly poison on it, which caused almost instant

death; the poison is made from vegetables boiled in a large pot, and the arrows steeped in it. He shewed me the marks of two arrow wounds which he received in battle. He then began to consult his fetish, by a quantity of strings, with various ornaments on one end to denote their good or evil qualities; these were mixed promis- cuously together, and taking them in his right hand, he put them behind his back, and drew out one with his left; this was repeated about 20 times. A wicker basket was then brought on a small stool covered with a silk cloth, in it were two lumps like pin- cushions, made of eggs, palm oil, &c.: he then turned up the bottom of his stool, and making three holes in it with something like a cobler's awl, he drove in three pegs with a stone, muttering to himself all the time, and waving each string round his right ear; an egg was then brought in broken at one end, and placed alter- nately on the lumps in the basket, and crushed on the stool where the pegs were put in: this he did every morning before he went out, to keep him out of bad palavers through the day.

Tuesday 30. This morning Apokoo invited me to take a share of his umbrella, and attend the King, who went to finish his ablu- tions. We walked along through an immense crowd; the streets were lined with the chiefs and their respective suites. We went down to the place where the King washes; a low platform was erected where the stools were laid on their sides. The linguists and officers of the household stood on one side holding gold rods and canes, the fetishmen formed a crescent to the north side. The King performed the ceremony of laving the water over himself, sprink- ling the various articles the same as on Saturday, and the proces- sion concluded as before.

On walking back Apokoo wished to try on one of my gloves, and as usual put it on the wrong hand; his gold castanets pinched him when the glove was on, which made him shout out rather lustily, and stop short, I called out " you stop the King;" " never mind," said he, and his attendants pulled to get the glove off. The King sent to know what occasioned the stoppage, Apokoo held up his hand compressed, exclaiming, " *Gamphnee*," (it hurts me,) and stopped till it was got off.

In the afternoon I called on Odumata, who said he was angry that I had not called before. I told him I came to thank him for allowing a slave boy he has, to do any thing for me; he said I might have him so as I fed him, I replied I would do so. He entered into conversation concerning the power of England over other nations, and the danger of going to sea; he had lived three years at Apollonia when a young man, and had seen many Portuguese, but did not like them, " as they were all wenches!" He seemed pleased that I did not like them either. He wished me to purchase a horse from him for eight ounces, I said I would give him four." " I must not want one, or I would not offer him so," was his reply. I said that I had no place to ride it in, the country being all bush, and the King did not like me to go very far; he replied, they were soon going to fight, and, as I should go with them, it would be better for me to have a horse to ride than to walk. I answered, I should lay hold of some wild boar and gallop it; this observation struck him with astonishment, and stroking down his beard, he asked my servant if he thought I could do so, who replied, if I took it in my head I certainly would. Odumata said the people would think the devil was come among them. This he told me is the last day of the year, according to their calculation, but from what reason I do not know. In the Sarem countries, he told me, they work iron from the stone, and silver, gold, &c. into trinkets, better than in Ashantee. I enquired why they did not make iron here, as they have plenty of ore; his reply was truly African; " why should they do so, when they had plenty of gold to buy it, and could get it so near." I told him of England's resources from her own manufactories; he said it was not good for white men to know so much; if black men knew those things they would all run to England. When I got home I sent him a present of a razor, he sent two messengers to thank me, such is their fashion; and for even the smallest article they return thanks the next day. Odumata enquired why I did not get drunk sometimes, and come to see him then, I told him, were I to get drunk in Ashantee, I ought to have my sword broke over my head, that I had indeed got tipsey the evening before I came away, with my friends, and might perhaps do so when I returned, but not till then. He gave me some palm wine, and looked amazed at my swallowing only half a tumbler full, " he would drink three pots before he went to bed!" (about 15 gallons.)

Wednesday, October 1. The King dictated a letter to the Governor at Cape Coast, stating, that the King of Cape Coast had broken the law by insulting an Ashantee man, who swore, by the King of Ashantee's head, that if the Cape Coast King did not kill him, he must pay 110 periguins of gold to the King. This practice, though it savours of madness, is yet often resorted to for revenge, as it is almost sure to end in the ruin of the other party. The Cape Coast King had threatened, that the Governor would put the Ashantee man in the slave hole till he died, which appeard to irritate the King very much.

The King then enquired if I had any yams at home; I told him I had a few of his last present; he told me he would send more to the house for me, which he did, and gave me $5\frac{1}{2}$ ackies gold; then pressed me to take some gin and water; on his being told that it must be very little, for I was afraid of an attack of spleen and liver, and eat little and walked much, he said that was proper.

Thursday 2. Through this and the afternoon of yesterday I felt very feverish, not being able to get any sleep for the rats at night. I kept my room all day; the King sent a pot of palm wine in the evening. Adoo Quamina called.

Friday 3. Whilst writing letters, Apokoo sent his compliments and would be happy to see me; I went, and he said he was sorry he had not seen me for some days. I told him I was sick the two former days, and to-day was writing to my family how I liked Ashantee; he hoped I would give the King a good name in England. I should tell truth. He enquired if I would like to see his croom (village.) I replied yes! He was going there this evening, and if no palaver came, he would send his people for me in the morning, to carry me. He asked if I was not for one of his daughters, that he might be called my father. He then enquired why I did not wear my hair tied, and let my beard grow; he recollected Colonel Torrane and Mr. White having tails at the siege of Annamaboe, and they looked very handsome. He requested me to show him the skin of my arm, he gazed on it with seeming pleasure, begged I would allow him to touch it; on receiving permission, he rubbed his hand over it, exclaiming "*Papa Taffia*," (very handsome) and repeated his invitation to go to the croom. I took my leave.

As I was going home I met a man white-washed, carrying a vessel covered over with a white cloth: this I have been often told is Tando fetish, but can learn nothing more. Music and a great crowd went with it to Adoo Quamina's house, at the front of which they put it down, and sacrificed a child of Cudjoo Cooma's, the Akim revolter, over it, as an annual sacrifice of the King's.

Saturday 4. Apokoo sent his people for me in the morning, who took me to his croom, about three miles S. W. of Coomassie. The road was in good order, and newly cut on account of my going; his slaves all turned out to see me, many of them never having seen a white man before. Apokoo came to the entrance of the croom, which is small, to meet me, and took me into the place where he lives himself; it is like all country houses here, a square lined with palm leaves and thatched with grass; his own room, raised on the floor, painted with red inchuma or ochre, and at one end of it, his couch raised on wood with plaited palm leaves, and covered with large cotton cushions. Near his head hung three strings of fetish, made of gold, red earth, horn, and bone, in the shape of thigh bones, horns, jaw bones, &c. &c. One side of the square was fitted up with a forge and bellows to work gold; another served as a cooking place, and the fourth for his sons to sleep in. About 11 o'clock he went to one of the side places to eat, that he might not trouble me in his room, as he said. Before he began, small pieces of yam were laid on his fetish; a small table was then set before him, and clean water poured into a brass pan, with which he washed his right hand, and then eat with it:—they are careful not to touch victuals with their left hand. A large pot of yams and another of fish being boiled, he satisfied himself first; the remainder was then divided into as many lots as there were persons to partake; when the door was opened, and about twenty sons and daughters, with their calabashes, received each their mess. He had given my servant two fowls, some fish and yams, and told him to make any thing I could eat; I told him to make a soup of the fowls. When I was eating, Apokoo said he thought I was ashamed, and requested I would let him put down the screen; I told him I dared not eat much through the day, being afraid of sickness. He enquired if I wished to go to sleep, for his couch was at my service. I declined the offer, and he went to sleep himself. Shortly after, four of his wives came from town with a mess for him; he was awaked to know if they were to have admittance, as usual: he ordered them to set down the meat and go away; they pretended to do so, but sat down under one of the sheds, and began to annoy the slaves, but their stifled laughter soon awoke Apokoo, who stretched out his neck, and seeing them, told them in a passion, it was because I was there that they wished to stop, and that they had better be off; they took the hint and made their retreat. He got up to shew me his gold ornaments, which weighed 146 bendas (£1168.) and made his people kindle the forge fire to melt some rock gold to make a fish; but the mould not being perfect, it was spoiled. He enquired if ever I had been in a yam plantation; on my replying in the negative, we went to see one; he asked if I would allow him to ride in my hammock, I gave him leave; it was better than his basket, he said, except that he did not like his legs hanging down. He wished me to dig up a yam; the people brought me a long pointed stick, which is forced into the earth to loosen the yam, afterwards the fibres are cut with a knife. After I had dug up ten, he hoped I would accept of them as a present; yams are set like potatoes in Europe, they are put in the ground about December, so that they are nine months growing to maturity. He said he should not go to Coomassie that night, as he had to decorate his drums with tigers skins, but that he would be in on Tuesday. If I wished to come out and see him before that time he would send people for me, and be glad. I said I should come out some other time, but not so soon. I set off for Coomassie about six o'clock, having spent a very agreeable day.

About seven o'clock the King sent for me; on my going, he would trouble me, he said, to read a book he had that day found in a man's possession. It proved to be a Danish note to the King for three ounces per month, dated August 1, 1811; it seemed as if a seal had been affixed to it, but the impression had disappeared, and it was very much worn. The King said he never knew of it; that an Ashantee captain had received and kept it, but he would enquire about it. His majesty wished me to drink something, I declined it; he hoped I was not sick, I said no, but drinking made my head ach; he hoped I would sleep sound, paid me many compliments that I cannot repeat; enquired of my servant if I was a good master, with other questions of the like nature.

Saturday 11. The King sent for me, and on going to the palace I found them in full council talking palavers. Adoosee was ordering a messenger to go to Quamina Bootaqua, to make him proceed to Cape Coast, and inform the Governor that Payntree had sworn by the King and had broke his oath, Bootaqua having sent word to the King of it; but they did not mention any thing to me. After this, Adoosee informed me, that messengers have gone from Amanfoo, sent by Sam Brue, to complain that the Cape Coast people had come armed against him to kill him. After hearing a long statement of grievances, they told me I must write to the Governor about it; I said I would, at the same time I assured the King that Sam Brue was a slave trader, and not to be tolerated at Cape Coast, his conduct was so infamous; they then called on his messenger to know what reason Sam had to leave Cape Coast; he entered at great length into the grievances experienced by Brue from the Governor in Chief and officers, because he owed eight ounces of gold; I was called in to reply, which I said I could not condescend to do, until I heard from the Governor in Chief, as they had sent messengers to complain to him. Adoosee charged four messengers with what they were to tell the Governor, making them take fetish and other formalities usual only on great occasions, thereby giving the affair an importance it did not merit. The King, on the breaking up of the council, said he would send for me shortly after, to write an account of the affair to the Governor; when I returned home, I did communicate the whole to the Governor, as the King's letters are so hurried.

I heard nothing from the King all day, but at night a Fantee man called on me, who had been taken by the Ashantees in last year's war, and whom I had been trying to liberate by speaking in his behalf to the King, and concerning four ounces of gold that had been taken. The captain concerned in it, to get quit of the palaver, had urged one of his wives to swear the man had lain with her; she accordingly made a formal complaint; the man was put in irons in the bush and only released yesterday morning as they thought to catch the King when he had some palavers pending, which would make him angry; they therefore brought it before the King yesterday morning, thinking he would order the man's head to be cut off; but he told the King that this palaver was brought against him because I had spoken for him; the woman was called, who insisted the man had lain with her, the man denied it, and on being offered fetish he cheerfully took it, and swore by the King to the contrary. The woman would not do so, and the King ordered the irons to be taken from the man, and put on the woman, telling her, she had not looked at the man properly, as it must be some other person.

Tuesday 14. This morning a man was beheaded at the door of the house where I live, by Aboidwee, the house master: it appears, the man in question was brother to a caboceer, and presumptive heir to his property; tired of waiting so long he made fetish incantations, and other ceremonies peculiar to them, to destroy his brother; this coming to the brother's ears, and also, that he had enjoyed one of his wives five times, he complained to the King and requested he would put the offender to death to save his own life; the King complied, and ordered Aboidwee to put the sentence in execution.

Wednesday 15. The Adaï custom. I went as usual with flags, and first received the usual offering of rum, and ten ackies of gold instead of a sheep. I called on Baba, the chief of the Moors, in the afternoon, who said he would teach me Arabic if I would teach him English; I said I would; but I am afraid he is too old for progress. I called on Odumata in my way back, who annoyed me as usual to drink palm wine, although it gives me a head ache. Akotoo, the King's brother, was there, who said he had only seen me four times since the mission went away, and wished me to call on him. The conversation turned on the King's going to war, and his anxiety for me to go and see how they killed their enemies, and he would give me gold to feed me. I was told by a Fantee man, that Sam Brue had procured 200 guns and a quantity of powder for the King, for slaves he had sold to the Spaniards now on the coast.

Friday 17. Deputies from the Warsaw states arrived a few days ago, to settle the differences between them and the Ashantees. It is thought, a fine to the King and future tribute may compromise the matter. Odumata informed me, that the slave ship has 600 slaves on board; and that, through Sam Brue's exertions; he confirmed the report of the guns and powder.

Sunday 19. The heaviest rain, thunder, and lightning I ever saw, and has continued for several days and nights. About 7 o'clock A. M. the King's drums announced his going to the market-place, where all his chiefs went and were drenched with wet till 2 o'clock P. M. when the King sent for rum and palm wine and dismissed them drunk and dirty. On Monday the scene was continued till the slaves had got the house covered in.

Tuesday 21. Agay the linguist returned from Assin, where he had been four months; and brought with him a number of Fantees and their families, as slaves. During the eruption of the Fantees in 1816, many of them ran to the Assin country to try and elude the vigilance of the King, but he heard of it, and sent

Agay to demand them, who, after a long negociation, succeeded. A council was held at Abrassoo on the Barramang road, and the slaves were sent to Barramang to build a new croom for the King.

Sunday, November 2. The King has been busy for the last twelve days making fetish, &c. for the success of the war; the Moors going every morning to the palace for prayer and sacrifice: to day being Adaï custom, I went as usual, and received ten ackies of gold and a flask of rum, the foremost in the assembly, which was numerous.

. Friday 7. A serious palaver has arisen between the King and Adoosee the chief linguist, he having taken a bribe from some person to misrepresent a palaver to the King; this coming to the King's ear, he sent in a fury to Adoosee, who, on being charged with it, thought his life would be the forfeit, and sent an express to Apokoo to come and intercede for him; Apokoo being at his croom, it has been several times talked before the King, but no settlement, has taken place.

Several people have been making application to me to demand them of the King, as belonging to the forts, having been detained as slaves during the Fantee war, and when Winnebah fort was destroyed. They are commonly very old, and of the female sex.

Saturday 8. Adoosee has got his palaver settled by paying twenty ounces of gold, and six or eight sheep to the King; Adoosee's friends alleged that he ought not to pay any thing, because when any palaver comes he settles it at once; but if he is not there, they have to go to council, which in fact is true; but notwithstanding his abilities, and that he takes his seat as usual, the King looks at him with a gloomy eye. The King has been busy making human sacrifices for the success of the war, at Bantama, Assafoo, and Aduma, in the evenings; and the Moors make their offerings of sheep in the palace in the mornings according to the moslem ritual. Though the zealous Christian may lament that the Gospel has not taken place of the fetish, yet the friends of humanity will rejoice that the King favours the Moors, as many lives have been saved that would otherwise have been destroyed at the present crisis. To day a bullock was offered up in the chief market-place, previous to the entrance of the chiefs, caboceers, &c. into the town, to meet in council, and determine on the method of conducting the war: in the afternoon, Boitinnë Quama, King of Dwabin, sent his compliments to me to announce his arrival. Shortly after, the various bands of music declared the arrival of the tributaries, &c.; the King of Ashantee took his seat in the market-place, and received their compliments as they passed before him. About nine o'clock at night Boitinnë, King of Dwabin paid me a private visit, and brought me a present of two curious Gennet cats.

Sunday 9. At day break the firing of guns, music, &c. announced a custom for the husband of the King's sister (the second woman in the kingdom), he having died in the bush on Friday, about 7 o'clock; the King went to the market-place to make custom, and sacrificed two men; several others were killed by various caboceers. In the evening Apokoo and the other captains who are to exhibit their gold, paraded the streets, firing musketry, &c.; the crowd was great. At 8 o'clock, his majesty of Dwabin came with the messengers he sent to Cape Coast to have a suit of clothes, he said two trunks were at his house and he brought a sword to shew me, which the Governor had sent.

Friday 14. Before I got up, I was annoyed with a crowd of captains who began to annoy me for liquor. I ordered them out and desired a boy to keep the door fast. I sent a dash of wine, rum, sugar, soap, butter, and perfumery to the king, who was highly pleased. To all the principal captains, a dash of rum, wine, and sugar, till I had nearly expended my stock : the whole day was a continual annoyance from visitors, troubling me for drink, but as I was resolved to give to those only who were worthy, many of them were disappointed. This week past Apokoo and several of the captains have been making an exhibition of their riches; this is generally done once in life, by those who are in favour with the King, and think themselves free from palavers. It is done by making their gold into various articles of dress for show. Apokoo, who sent for me before his uproar began, shewed me his varieties, weighing upwards of 800 bendas of the finest gold ; among the articles, was a girdle two inches broad. Gold chains for the neck, arms, legs, &c. ornaments for the ancles of all descriptions, consisting of manacles, with keys, bells, chairs, and padlocks. For his numerous family of wives, children, and captains, were armlets and various ornaments. A superb war cap of eagle's feathers, fetishes, Moorish charms, &c. Moorish caps, silk dresses, purses, bags, &c. made of monkey skin. Fans, with ivory handles, made of tiger skin, and decorated with silk. New umbrellas made in fantastical shapes, gold swords and figures of animals, birds, beasts, and fishes of the same metal; his drums, and various instruments of music, were covered with tiger skin, with red belts for hanging them. Ivory arrows and bows, covered with silk and skins, and many other weapons of war or fancy, such as the mind in a like situation would devise. Apokoo was anxious that I should come and see him when out, but from the noise, I judged that they were too turbulent for me to venture without a chance of being insulted.

Saturday 15. Again annoyed by the people wishing for drink. Apokoo called with his retinue to thank me ; for the Governor had given his people a flask of Jamaica rum. He had got three days

to play, as he called it, and was sorry that he' had not seen me.
I told him I had very seldom been out, except when there was no
noise, as the people were so unruly in the evening.

Monday 17. In the afternoon Apokoo sent a message, saying
he was come to the door of the house to play and shew me his
gold, hoping I would come out. I went and found a Moorish
carpet spread, at one end of which I was seated under an umbrella,
while Apokoo and his wives, children, and captains danced by turns
before me. Some of his young wives were dressed with great taste,
a rich silk cloth with a bag made of fine fur, slung over the
shoulder, studded with gold ornaments: on the left shoulder they
held a pistol, and in the right hand a silver bow and arrow.
During the dance, if Apokoo was pleased with them he took the
bow and hung it on some of the ornaments, when she retired from
the dance; this was a strong mark of approbation, if I may judge
from the applause that followed : to some he gave a little gold.
Several times he took from their necks various ornaments which he
placed on my knees and over my left shoulder; this was the
greatest mark of honour he could shew me; and his band played
a tune in praise of England, and of our abilities in settling differences. Many of the captains sent him presents of gold and rum.
I gave him a large flask of wine, which he said pleased him more
than all the others, as it would shew the people I thought him a
good man.

Thursday 20. The Moorish caboceer of Alphia called to day,
requesting I would allow him to bring his brother and nephew who
had arrived, as they wished to see me: on receiving my permission
he sent for them, and as they immediately made their appearance,
they must have been waiting at the door. I shewed them a compass, sand-glass, quadrant, some phosphorus, and several other
things; at the sight of each they bent their heads to the ground,

exclaiming " Allahoo Akabir !" God is great. I gave the caboceer a wax candle, piece of a perfumed soap (which he was going to eat!) a flask of Jamaica rum, and some sugar ; things he had never seen before : he begged to be allowed to touch my hand, and continued calling out Ah! bielane Wasieh! Ah Nasara! Ah white visier! Ah Christian. He said he had a sister whom he would make me a present of, if I would have her. The caboceer of Alphia is brother to the caboceer of Premehinie, east of Ashantee, in the Sarem region, and subject to Saï Tootoo ; it is 14 days journey to Alphia, one day to Brookoom, where the head fetish of that country dwells, and one day more to Crumassia and Sodie, a range of high hills.

1 told him I would buy his horse if he would put a reasonable price on it, and would give him a note to get powder, rum, &c. at the Cape : he said the Ashantees brought rum to Sarem, but they boiled pepper in water and sold it to them ; he never tasted such good adrue (medicine) as mine.

I have been learning Arabic this last month, principally from the Shereef Abraham, who comes from Boussa, where Mungo Park was drowned, and he, as he says, was an eye witness to it; his great sanctity made the King of Ashantee send for him to pray and make sacrifice for the success of the war. The other Moors here look on him with an evil eye, because he will not wear fetishes as they do, and be present at human sacrifice. This place now presents the singular spectacle of a Christian and Mahometan agreeing in two particulars, rejecting fetishes, and absenting themselves from human sacrifices and other abominations : the rest of the people, of whatever country they may be, when the King's horns announce any thing of the kind, strive who will get there first to enjoy the agonies of the victims. The Shereef told me to-day, that the reason he came so seldom to see me, was, that the

King had heard he was teaching me the Koran, but he wished him
not to do so, he did not wish me to know how " to call on God ;"
but, said Abraham, I shall teach you as much as I can, that when
you go to your own country you may give the Moors a good name,
for I told the King you knew Arabic before you saw me, and we
sometimes spake together in that language.   He had a beautiful
copy of the Koran which he intended to leave me, but the King
had told him he must have it, that when any trouble came he might
hold it up to God, and beg his mercy and pardon : but he would
try and get a small one for me.

Saturday 22. This morning a slave belonging to the house master
swore by the King's head that he must kill him to day.   A great
uproar ensued, while they put him in irons, and they got out the
family stools and sacrificed fowls and sheep, pouring the blood on
them to propitiate the wrath of the King from the family.   The
King was then told of it, who said as that was his fetish day he
could not kill a man that day, but to-morrow he would behead him.

It appears he had connection with one of his brother's wives,
who, hearing of it, cautioned him from doing so again, or else he
would tell the King and make him kill him : he was again found
with the woman, and his brother went to the King to complain.
Hearing this, and fearing the torture, he swore by the King that
he must shoot him with eight muskets.   The King on being told
this, said he would put such small shot into the muskets as only to
wound him, and then he should torture him ; hereby fulfilling his
own law, which he considers sacred.

Sunday 23. About 12 o'clock sent for by the King, whom I
found scolding his sister for disobedience in one of her slaves.
After sitting some time talking on indifferent subjects, the King
said he should go to council, about what he was going to say to
me.   Shortly after he sent one of his sons to say his father was

going to eat and wash, if I would be kind enough to return home. I heard that messengers from Elmina had arrived the evening before, and expected to hear of some complaint of breaking the law, as they style it: although I could not reconcile it with an observation I had made; a pair of razors I had presented to the King were invariably sent to me to sharpen, as the King wished to shave with them, when any favourable affair was to be talked, and that morning they came as usual.

I was again sent for, and the King announced in a formal manner his intention of going in person to make war on Adinkara, the King of Buntookoo, and wished me to announce it to the Governor. I therefore wrote a letter of the King's dictating, stating this to the Governor, and requesting him to give on trust 300 oz. kegs, powder, and 300 muskets, and sending to the Governor in Chief six periguins of gold, and to the Governor of Annamaboe four periguins, to purchase a cloth for him, the handsomest they could find, and inviting them to send him a dash and make the town's people do the same, for the prosperity of the war. His Majesty was very lavish in his compliments of the generosity of the English, and their great riches; he then enquired if I was willing to go to fight, I replied certainly, if I could obtain the Governor's permission, I should like it very much: he thanked me very warmly. I heard, on my return to the house, that the Dutch General had sent as a present to the King 60 oz. kegs powder, and the Elmina people 40, which caused this stir.

Monday 24. Sent for again to write the Governor word that the King sent down 30 men to be clothed as soldiers, if the Governor could spare clothes, one of them to be as captain and one a serjeant, with a flag. His Majesty also wished to have arrow root, Port wine, sugar, candles, and a few other things for the campaign. I was then told to write a letter to the Danish Governor in Chief to the same effect, and to ask him for payment of what was due on his note. I foresaw this would make an uproar; and on the note being handed to me to know what was due on it, when I told the King that nothing was on it, he got into the greatest rage I have yet seen him in, with the captain who receives the pay. This man had been sent down to Accra about three months ago, to receive what pay was due, Mr. Bowdich writing to the Danish Governor in Chief to know, for the King's satisfaction, what was sent. On his return, the latter stated that the King's note was paid up to the ensuing Christmas. There being a great deficiency between what was stated in the letter, and what the captain produced, he charged Mr. Bowdich with mis-stating what was in the letter; Quashie Apaintree, the linguist, was sworn on the King's fetish to interpret proper; the Ashantee still insisted, and to clear himself, said the book was *not* paid to Christmas. The King and linguists remembered this, and when they heard that the note was actually paid to the end of the year, every one tried who would be loudest in their accusations against him. Apokoo, who is his chief, was loudest against him, he said he had used him disrespectfully, and never gave him any of the dashes he received; besides he had given the lie to an English officer, and at the same time he cheated the King; he therefore left him to the mercy of his Majesty. The King said he must return him all the gold back he had lent him; and as for the fort at Accra, he might take the pay when he pleased. A hat, certainly a bad one, was brought in, and the King asked me if I thought it worth the price charged for it. I replied I was not a judge, as such hats were not sent out for us; but if I were, I must positively decline interfering in the King's affairs with his servants. By degrees the King worked himself to such a height of passion, that throwing his cloth around him, and hastily rising, he ordered the captain's arrest. The King's sons seized on him, and he stood appalled, as the silver cane fell from his hand. I once thought the King would have committed some extravagance, none of the chiefs daring to rise; Agay at length arose, and in his energetic manner requested that his majesty would recollect I was present. The King ordered his sons to go with the captain to his house, and bring him all the gold they found; he then withdrew, but I heard him storming in his apartments. Shortly after, Odumata's brother came to say, that the chiefs might thank me, as were it not for my sake, every one of them would have been turned out of the palace by the slaves. Agay, who was the only one who followed the King, came to apologise for the abrupt departure of his Majesty: he hoped I would not be offended, and requested I would go home and dine, as it was late, and the King would send for me soon.

Tuesday 25. The King sent for me to write another letter to the Governor, saying he had sent down three pieces of rock gold as a pawn for powder; they were the largest I have yet seen, one of them weighing about 20 ounces. I gave his Majesty a packet of letters to be forwarded to Cape Coast: he rallied me on the size of it, and said he supposed I wrote the Governor and Mr. Bowdich every palaver in town.

To-day the stool of Alphia was declared in abeyance; the son of the caboceer Premehinia having brought a complaint against the caboceer of Alphia, who is brother to the former; his sable highness came on a beautiful Arabian, of a very small size; at the sound of drums and horns he danced and went through various evolutions.

Friday 28. To-day the caboceer of Alphia was deposed, and his brother the caboceer of Premehinia had the stool attached to his other possessions. In the afternoon whilst I was out, the Moorish prince, with a large retinue, called to pay me a visit, I found one

of his attendants sitting at the door with a gold sword, who, on receiving permission, went and told him I was come home; shortly
after he came, and expressed great wonder at all he saw. He
said I had too many silver spoons, and modestly requested I
would give him one or two; his attendant who fanned him thought
so too, as he attempted to steal one, but one of the servants happening to pass, he threw it under the table. I wished him to sell
me his horse, but he said he was too great a man to walk home,
and the ground hurt his feet.

Sunday 30. The King paid me a long visit, he heard, he said,
that my horse had died, and had come to see me least I should
think he forgot me, but he had so much fetish to make, and so
many palavers to settle, that he had little time. The conversation
then turned on the travels of Englishmen, and the white men
drowned in the Quolla (Niger.) I explained to his Majesty the
objects of the expeditions sent from England to the interior of
Africa, and expressed how anxious I was to get Mr. Park's books
and papers for the King of England; his Majesty promised to aid
me in doing so, and before he went away, desired me to point out
to him what I conceived the proper method.

The King then began to talk about my living with him, and if I
liked to do so; he said I was like a king, and wished his people to
treat me with respect, and every one run to see me when I went
out, as they run to see him. I said that some of his people wished
to accuse me of treason for putting buckles in my shoes at the
Adaï custom. The King said that none dared do so, but those
whom he ordered, any other would have their heads cut off: but I
was different, and he knew Englishmen did what was proper. His
majesty took his leave with many expressions of personal attention,
which, whether they were sincere or not, were at least to be
received with politeness.

Monday, December 1. One of the King's nephews came to see me, but was terribly afraid to pass the man in irons who swore on the King, least he should swear that when the King killed him, he must also kill his nephew, which would cost a deal of gold; for such is the sacredness of the law, that in that case the King must do it. I had a key of a door where I could privately let him out, without passing through the courts of the house, by which he gladly made his escape. This man has been no small annoyance, as no person of rank will venture to call on me, least they should be brought into trouble by his swearing on their heads.

Tuesday 2. The King to-day made a present of 10 periguins of gold to the Moors in town for their services, and they were to divide it themselves. This created no small altercation among them; those belonging to the town wished to keep it all, and not give the Shereef Abraham any, who came from the banks of the Niger; as the King had that morning told him he wished him to accompany him to the war, he told them it was of no consequence, as he should not accompany the King unless he was looked on with the same degree of rank as Baba, as, indeed, he was superior from his knowledge, and belonging to Mahomet's family. On this they gave him three periguins, the same that Baba had: all were then pleased with their portion except one, called Aboo, who only had 10 ackies; he consoled himself by making the usual exclamation, " God is great! he never dies, he never sleeps," and said he left the palaver in his hands.

Thursday 4. Apokoo paid me a visit to thank me for some medicine I had given him, being sick after his great custom; he enquired if I heard that Fantee messengers were come to this place, I said no, but I expected them soon to take the King's fetish, as he wished them to do so, previous to his going to war; he then told me that the King heard there were some on the path, and could not think what their message was; I told him they must either be those the Governor was sending up, or Fantees with the King's tribute; on his going away, he requested I would let him out by the door I had the key of, as he also was afraid of the man in irons swearing on his life, and was glad he could avoid passing him.

Friday 5. This was the coldest morning I have felt since I came to Africa, being scarcely able to take breakfast, I was so chilly; the thermometer stood at 65°.

I was desired to write a letter to General Daendels, telling him the King had lost his notes for the Dutch forts, and requesting him to give new ones to Akimpon. The King's father had conquered the Akim chief, who held a note for Dutch Accra; he also conquered the King of Adinkara, who had the Elmina note, both of which were given up to him; he would not take them both in one note as the General wished, but he must have one payable at Elmina and one at Accra. When the King weighed out the gold for his messengers expences, he weighed 10 ackies for me, which I hoped his Majesty would take back, as I did not wish for them, and requested he would not think I wished payment for writing a letter for him. My scruples were laughed at by them all, and the King said "that white men were very singular, as they gave gold or a good dash to any one who did any thing for them, yet they would not take any: he wished to do something like white men, and when any one did any thing for him he gave them something, and he wished me to take this to shew his good will." Odumata, who is the greediest man in Coomassie for gold, whispered, if I did not like it, I might send it to him when I got home. I did not exactly understand him, or I would have offered it to him then with pleasure, to expose his avarice.

The captain who was arrested last week for peculation on Danish

Accra, appeared in his place to day; he had promised Amanquateä and Quatchie Quophie, the two chief captains, a large present if they would settle the affair for him, which they did, and he received the letters to proceed to the fort as usual.

Apokoo having told the King of the inconvenience arising to any chief coming to me, from the culprit in irons being in the way, he was removed to a private part of Apokoo's house, where he could annoy no one, till the Adaï custom, when he is to be beheaded, as the affair cannot be settled without.

Sunday 7. Several of the Moorish caboceers came to take leave, as they were going to-morrow to their own country previous to the war, and were to meet the King on the road when he went, and consequently would not see me again for some time; on my enquiring how long the King was to be absent, they replied, God had told them seven months would finish the war; they enquired if I should like to see them at Cape Coast, as they should come and see me, to which I said I should. After drinking coffee, &c. they took a hurried leave, as one of the King's people came to tell me one of his Majesty's daughters was dead, and shortly after, constant discharges of musketry announced the custom. The King in the afternoon came to the market place close to the house, to make custom with his chiefs. I understood that human sacrifices were to be offered, and walked out to avoid the uproar.

On my way I paid a visit to Baba, who was performing ablution; he said he was going to prayer, but would soon have done, I told him I would sit down till he had finished. Cow hides were spread in rows for the worshippers, in the front was a large hide for Baba. All having taken off their sandals and prostrated themselves with their faces to the east (to Mecca,) the service began by one of them chaunting the usual call to prayer; the chorus of Allahoo Akaber! (God is great) was well performed by the others.

There was something solemn and affecting in it, contrasted with the heavy discharges of musketry and shouts of the populace in the distance, which proclaimed the bloody sacrifice was begun, while the vultures and crows wheeled in mazy circles expecting their usual share of the banquet, and the sun shot his last gleams through the heavy fogs that encircled the town.

As I went home I passed the headless trunks of two female slaves, laying neglected and exposed in the market place, that had been sacrificed, one by the King and one by the deceased's family. The vultures were revelling undisturbed amidst the blood.

I happened to-day to throw down a tumbler of wine and water with my foot, having placed it on the ground, while the Moorish Shereef was with me; he bent his head to Mecca, pronouncing "God is great!" and told me it was my good angel who had done so, for who might tell but there was poison in the cup to destroy me? he said man had always two angels attending him, one on his right hand as his good angel, and one on his left as his evil one; whatever good he did was prompted by the former, and whatever ill by the latter one. I have never found them without a reason for every thing, or a name, except to the mother of Moses, whom they say nobody knows on earth; the Shereef gravely enquired if I knew the name of Aboobaker's father, I assured him I did not; he told me many of the Moors could not tell, but as he was of Mahomet's family he knew more things, and told me it was *Kahābata.*

I heard from the Sarem Moors that they fight with bows and arrows steeped in deadly poison, the least scratch of which is instant death. They gather scorpions tails, snakes heads, and the poisonous parts of any reptile that affects man; this, with several vegetable substances which they would not name, are put in a pot, and set over the fire at sun rise; they boil it all day and must not eat or drink, but stir it about repeating incantations, and shaking a pair of iron castanets, without which, the charm would be incomplete. I saw an old hag at this work on the Bantama road, who would not answer my question as to what she was doing, but made many wry faces, and squint looks, for me to be gone and not spoil her work, and while I stood, she stirred, and muttered, and clattered the castanets with greater fury.

My attention being anxiously turned towards information concerning the Niger and its course, all enquiries end in making the Nile its continuation. An old Moor from Jennë told me, unasked, that while he was at Askanderee (Alexandria) twenty-six years ago he saw a fight at the mouth of the Nile between ships, and one of them was blown up in the air with a terrible exploslon. This must have been the battle fought by Lord Nelson, although there is a mistake in the date of seven years; he surely could not invent such a story. He states also, that returning to Masser (Grand Cairo) the European armies advanced to that place; the first army took every thing they wanted and would not pay: but when the second European and Turkish army got possession of it, they paid for whatever they wanted. All the Moors were ordered to retire to one quarter of the city, and not allowed to mix with the soldiers; this agrees with Sir Robert Wilson's account of the Egyptian campaign. I shewed him a seal I have, of Pompey's pillar, which he said he knew; he had travelled from Jennë to Masser on a joma (camel) and drew me a map of the Quolla and Nile from its source to its emptying itself into the sea at Alexandria. There is one thing that disagrees with Mr. Park's account, they call the Niger Quolla at Jennë, Sansanding, &c. and describe the Jolliba as falling into the Quolla to the east of Timbuctoo. When I told them of the conjectures that the great river of Africa emptied itself into a large lake, they laughed at such an idea, and reasoned so as to put wiser heads to the blush. "God," say they, "made all rivers to run to the sea, you say that small rivers go there: the Quolla is the largest river in the world, and why should it not go there also? Was it to lose itself in the lake, where could the waters go to?" They describe the Quolla as about five miles in breadth, and having a very rocky channel, the banks on both sides very high and rugged; in many places, canoes often take a day to pass a short distance, from the dangerous whirl-pools, and sudden squalls: at other places, the stream runs with great rapidity.

They think the Mediterranean sea to be circular, without mixing with the ocean; seven rivers from Africa turn their course to it, but only two reach the shores, of which the Nile is one. The rush of the waters of the Nile, when they meet the sea is so great, that the waves are driven into the air with great force, and retire like waves against a rock. They call the Mediterranean sea Bahare Mall. The Red sea, say they, assumes various colours at different periods, from seven streams pouring their course into it, red, blue, yellow, &c. Hence they call it Majumaal Bahare, or the confluence of streams. They are very fond of mystical numbers, and often quote seven. The lake Caudie they call Bahare Nohoo, or the water of Noah, from the tradition that the deluge broke out from thence. They describe it as encompassed with rocks, within which is a bed of sand, and then the water. This we may allow to be a little fanciful, as I have seen a map of the earth drawn by Baba, where the world is supposed to be round, and encompassed with a rocky girdle, the sea is supposed to flow between this and the earth, which is placed in the centre. They are not singular in this idea; as all rude nations form the same notions of the globe:

but though we reject, with reason, their foolish notions of many things, it would be no great sign of wisdom to refuse every information from them.

Man is a reasoning animal, and enquires into the nature of things in a rude, as well as in a civilised state; and if he cannot give a just, will at least give a plausible reason for many things.

The Moors say "That the noise people hear, when they stop their ears with their hands, is the rolling of the waters of libation in paradise, where Mahomet purifies all those he saves from hell, before they enter into the state of the blessed.' It is for this reason they perform ablution before they pray; the fire burning other parts of their bodies, while their face, hands, feet, &c. remained untouched, hence Mahomet when he looks for them, knows them from Jews, Christians, &c. They have also a sentence written on their foreheads, " Hooalie Jahanamoo naataka raboo baskafaatee Mahomada roosoola lahee sallee allahoo alahe wasalame."

Inoculation for the small pox is practised in the Moorish countries; they take the matter, and puncture the patient in seven places, both on the arms and legs. The sickness continues but a few days, and rarely any person dies of it. It is also done in Ashantee. Seven is their mystical number.

Monday, December 8. To day the King killed a man on account of his daughter who died yesterday, and to be out of the way, I called on Odumata, whom I found well charged with palm wine: his usual discourse of the greatness of the King and the manner of the Ashantees fighting took up his time: he said that when white men wished to fight, they sent a book to the other party, telling them they would meet them on such a day, but the Ashantees took their enemies by surprise, which shortened their wars. I told him he had repeated the same story about fifty times in two months, and wished to know if the English did so at Annamaboe, where fifteen white men killed thousands of Ashantees; this put him on the fidget, as I knew it would, and he said that it was on him the English fired first, and he fought them without the King's leave, who was angry when he heard that they had returned the fire of the fort; I told him it was a fine excuse to cover their defeat. He enquired if I thought they could not have taken the fort? I told him if they could have done it they would. He said, if the King says we must do any thing, we must do it. I asked him, if the King told them to pull down the moon, if they could do it? He then got up from his chair and began to manoeuvre how he and Apokoo were to have made a breach in Annamaboe fort, to the no small enjoyment of several of his wives, captains, and slaves, who were present; they were to have burned the gates, and with axes to have cut through the walls. He said they had Dutch and Danish flags, which they had taken from forts; why, I enquired, did they not show the English trophies? They had none, he said: and the King had told them, that were he to kill white men from England, he might as well kill all the cocks in the kingdom; the one told the hour, and when to rise in the morning; the other brought them good things from England, and learned them sense; besides, if any of their slaves did ill, they told them they would sell them to the whites, which made them better. I told him black men had the eyes of a thief, the paws of a tiger, and the belly of a hog, for they were never satisfied; he said I was right, for they were now going to war, and would take whatever they could find; he thought 30,000 Ashantees would be killed, but that was nothing. He then locked up his wives because I put evil in their heads, by saying that Englishmen allowed every one a husband. I then took my leave.

Monday 15. Baba, the chief of the Moors, having told me that a Moor was going to Jennë, I took the opportunity of writing a letter to two Europeans who reside there, and, I suppose, belonged to Mungo Park's expedition, seven soldiers being unaccounted for, who were in good health when they were separated from Mr. Park. There are also two white men at Timbuctoo, who have been there several years. The Moors are confident that the letter will reach them, which is much to be desired, as some information may be obtained of that celebrated traveller. Baba came, and the old Moor with him, to whom I delivered the letter; he received it from Baba with much ceremony, and to induce him to forward an answer, I promised him a suitable reward*. The whole of the Moors came in a body with drums, muskets, horns, and all the attendant pomp of chiefs; they had just taken leave of the King, and came to do the same to me. Having remained about

---

* " Mr. Wm. Hutchison, British Resident at Coomassie, the capital of Ashantee, hearing there are two Europeans at Jennë, takes the opportunity of a Moor returning to that place, to write to them. It is earnestly requested, that some information will be sent to Cape Coast Castle, whether or not, those, to whom this is addressed, belonged to the expedition of Captain Mungo Park, or by what means they reached Jennë. As no certain accounts have reached England of the fate of that gentleman and his companions, any particulars will be interesting; also, whether or not the Niger is the river known here by the name of Quolla, Joliba, or any other appellation unknown in Europe. Also, its course, and the opinions among the natives as to its termination, with the names of any towns or countries it may run through. It is also reported that there are two white men at Timbuctoo: should it be possible to render any assistance to either, it will be done from Cape Coast Castle on accounts being received of the certainty of their situation; and the means which may be found to make the Europeans on the Quolla revisit their native country: in the mean time, any information will be anxiously expected, as to the fate of their companions; and whether they have heard of an English expedition, lately arrived at the Niger. Two notices in English and Arabic accompany this, offering a reward for information.

December 9th,

half an hour, and drank some wine, they set out for their journey with noisy clamour.

Sunday 21. Apokoo called and told me he was going to morrow, with the King, to the camp, on the Barramang path, to make fetish, and would return on Wednesday: he seemed to expect that I would say I would go also; but as the King had not sent to me, I did not express any wish. A boy brought some milk covered up, and he lifted the lid to look what it was, some of it touched his fingers, and he sent for water, herbs, and different things to purify his fingers; he said he would give me a present if I would give over drinking milk: I told him if he sent me an ounce of gold daily, I would not do it; he cursed the milk, and the boy for bringing it. Thus many of them are so particular, they will not stay where eggs are, another shuns a fowl, one hates beef, and many mutter a charm if they meet a pig. The Moorish Shereef discovered a piece of pork one day in the boy's room, and made such a noise, that I thought one had struck him, nor would he cease till I ordered it away.

Monday 22. The King, and almost all the captains, set out early this morning, with great bustle for the camp, many sent their compliments previous to going.

Wednesday 24. The King and all the people returned in the evening, and went to the upper market place; where the King seeing me at the door, ordered them to pass down the street to the palace, the chiefs all saluting as they passed. The King, who was the only one that did not walk, made his people halt, and held out his hand to me, which I took, and bade him welcome to his capital; he enquired if I was well, and after he passed, he looked round with a smile and shook his finger at me: I suppose because I did not follow him to the camp. His Majesty afterwards sent his compliments, as did several of the chiefs.

·· Thursday 25. This being Christmas day, I displayed the flag, and paid every attention to it that I possibly could ; many of the chiefs hearing of it, sent their compliments, expecting a present, but of course were disappointed.

·Friday 24. Baba called, and began an oration about Sam Brue, hinting that he should like if I could get Brue, the slave trader, back to Cape Coast.   He was my good friend, I was his friend, the Governor was my friend, Brue was his friend, and a long genealogy fit to puzzle a Scottish or Welch family herald.   I told him no person must interfere in such affairs.   He had that morning received from Brue, powder, guns, and cloth for slaves he had sent down ; he brought me a piece of the cloth to shew me, it was very coarse with large red figures on it.   I told him when he washed it, he would need to take his staff and put on his sandals to hunt after the colours ; he told me he had found that out ; for he had washed a piece, and he could not tell what colour it was: He then began a dissertation on the *good* the slave trade did them, and what changes he had seen since he came here ; he thought God intended to change the power of white men, and give it to the blacks and Moors.   I told him he was going to make Mahomet a liar, as the Alkoran told them that the whites were to have sovereign dominion to the end, because of Noah's sons' behaviour to him when drunk ; and if God was inclined to hide his face from white men, because of any ill they did, I did not think he would transfer it to Africans for any good they had done ; he said I was right, and when they thought wrong the Christians could put them right.   Seeing a Prayer Book on the table, he enquired if that was " Lingeel," the name they give the New Testament ; I replied it was the form of worshipping God in English Churches ; he wished me to read a little of it to him, as he had heard that white men prayed to God so—and muttered in a form, it must be allowed, too often resorted to by lazy clergymen. They conceive to worship God in any other way than chaunting or singing is absurd. I have had more than once to sing (if I may presume to call it so) from the psalms of David, and chaunt the responses of the service, to convince them that there is something more than mere muttering in prayer, were it properly performed, besides describing the organ used in churches to assist the harmony. They have often asked me about the high priest at Rome, and whether or not we had any thing shaped out that we called god. I told them the English abhorred all represen-tations of the Eternal, and that nothing was adequate to represent him. They are very tenacious on this point, and as scrupulous as any Protestant may wish, conceiving it an inexcusable crime to have any thing of the kind. They have many times enquired if we offer any sacrifice to God. I told them that our Scriptures do not allow the shedding of blood of any kind; the last great expiation of the Christians being performed by Jesus when he died on the cross, in commemoration of which, the offering of bread and wine formed the sacrifice. Neither did we pour out libations* before drinking, because any thing poured forth before drinking, or victuals set apart before eating, is an offering to devils.

The Shereef Abraham coming in with one or two more, I en-quired about Solomon's Al Genii, and whether or not they knew any thing of free masonry. I had questioned them several times before, and knew none of them were free masons; they now told me that there was such a sect in Arabia, and conceived them to be magicians, as they controlled the spirits of air. They were much astonished to hear that I was one, and eagerly enquired if I knew about Solomon's seal, the building of the temple, and other matters, which universal belief endows free masons with,—matters, I told

* I have observed some of the Moors who have been a long time in Ashantee pour forth a little of any thing before drinking. It may be remarked, that all the worshippers of the fetish do this, and also set apart some of their victuals before they eat.

them, I might not speak of. They told me they knew we kept some of our genii on a floating island in the sea; if any ships came near it, the genii were instructed to laugh at them, and the island disappeared; with other such stories. One of the boys told them I had a stuff (phosphorus) which they supposed gave me such power; they wished to see it, and laughed at first at the idea of any thing in water producing fire, or that I could confine that element and dare to keep it in a trunk; I put it to the proof, by burning a piece of cloth, paper, and mat, and told them if they were not satisfied they might have some on their skins, but they did not choose it, and called out in wonder, " Houa Kahina iakul naroo malekaneran," " he is a magician and eats fire, he is the King of fire;" be it remembered that this last appellation is peculiar to the devil. The Shereef after thinking some time, enquired if that stuff was not made from the bones of genii? I told him bones were in the composition. He wished to know if we killed genii and took their bones, I told him blood was never shed in England but for great crimes; true, he said, but none could see *us* do so. I told him there was an eye that never sleeps, at which he bent his head, pronouncing " God is great." The Moors then held a conversation in Arabic, by which they settled that I must be in the secrets of Solomon, and the Shereef Abraham related one of the Arabian tales, by which Balkes or Bilkis, Queen of Sheba, is made out to be the child carried away by the dog in one of the stories of that work. Balkis, according to them, adored the sun, and Solomon made her turn and worship God; he commanded the genii to transport her palace from her own country to Jerusalem, and the three palaces he built for her in Arabia Felix had gold mixed with the mortar with which they were formed. They wished to know if I could move a house? I told them, such was the mystery attached to our concerns, that it was difficult to answer them; any thing not concerned with masonry, I might answer; this, they said, was what the people in their country said. Abraham said he was sure the Arabian magicians made use of bones from genii to make fire and control them. It would be a curious circumstance to know that phosphorus, and inoculation, existed in Arabia in the days of its splendour, and continue now; as they are considered as two of the most eminent among modern European discoveries. After they were gone, I called on Odumata, whom I found all talk as usual. He said he knew I wished to take some of the King's sons to Cape Coast for education, but the captains had represented to his Majesty, that they did not wish it. If the King wanted gold, and they had it, they would give it him; and were always ready when he called them, to receive his foot on their necks, and swear to do whatever he wished them, or never to return. The reason he gave, was, that they were afraid of being discovered when they cheated the King, which they made no secret of avowing, and having their heads cut off. I told him he did not like a white man to live here then; yes, he said, they all liked that; but he was sufficient to settle all palavers between the King and the English, without any of the King's people knowing English. He began to boast of the many wives and children he had, more than Englishmen. I told him there was a possibility of an Englishman knowing his father; but no black man could tell his; they were all slaves, and rendered incapable of inheriting their father's property; none of his children need to thank him, he neither could give them any thing while alive, nor leave them any thing when dead, and many of them kept wives, while their slaves enjoyed them. He said I spoke very true, but that I could not show keys with him; he produced two large bunches, and I offered him an ounce of gold if he would shew me a lock for each key; he evaded this: I took them in my hand, and found many of them broken, and various articles of lead and iron to make the bunches large; his people, and some chiefs that were with him, enjoyed his perplexity, if I might judge from their chuckling.

Several of the King's brother's slaves appeared in pursuit of two of their fellows, flogging them with whips; one of the culprits bounding over every obstacle, threw himself at Odumata's feet, which saved him from their flogging; the man who had charge of him appeared, and in a long and animated harangue, with many gestures, stated the trouble he had had from the runaway, and concluded by swearing, the man must be given up to him in the morning to go and work. It is customary for slaves, when they fall under their master's displeasure, to take shelter in some other chief's house, who tries to get them excused.

Saturday 27. The King sent for me, to give me letters which had arrived; and on my opening them, two small packages of gold tumbled out. The King asked, if they were for me or him. I enquired if he expected gold from any one at Cape Coast, he said, no. I told him, it was unlikely gold would be sent to any one but me. The King, turning to his captains, said the Governor was a good man, sending me gold whenever I asked for it, and I eat a great deal of gold. I told him, I never wished a present of gold from any one; what I got was my pay, as Englishmen did not give gold to one another. He intended returning his messengers on Tuesday, as he said, two of them having come up in English uniforms, as the Governor was to fit out thirty at the King's request. His Majesty wished me to taste a bottle of tincture of rhubarb the Governor had sent him; I did so, lest he should think there was something bad in it. I had then to taste some tincture of cinnamon he had received some time ago; I swallowed them with great distaste, as I had felt very unwell the preceding day, and that

3 H

morning, and had taken medicine just before the King sent, and not eaten any breakfast.

In the afternoon Apokoo called; he had heard Adoo Bradie had been on board a ship, and that 400 flags were hoisted to receive him ;* that was the reason, he said, they did nor wish any of the King's people to learn to read and write, they became white men, and saw so many fine things, they never thought of returning to Ashantee.   I told him if it was disagreeable, it would be given over. Every one was pleased, he said, to think any Ashantee great man was well used at Cape Coast; but it turned their heads, not being accustomed to it.   The King would give Adoo Bradie fetish when he came back, and if he told the King lies, the fetish would catch him, and where would be the good?   The English would have all their trouble for nothing.

His Majesty, some years ago, took one of Apokoo's daughters to wife; she is now one of the finest women in Coomassie, and must have been a great beauty.   It was discovered by the chief eunuch that she had intrigued with one of the attendants.   It was told the King that one of his wives had proved false; "let her die instantly," said he in a rage; the slave whispered him " it is Apo- koo's child."   He rose in silence, and went to the harem, and the culprit being sent for, the King turned his head away, while he folded his cloth around him, and lifting the curtain to let her pass, he exclaimed " go, you are free! your father was my father,† he is my friend, and for his sake, I forget you ; when you find any man good enough for you, let me know and I will give him gold." Her father has not allowed her to marry again.

---

* The signals happened to be drying on board H. M. S. Cherub, Captain Wills, then lying in the roads of Cape Coast.

† It will be remembered, that the present King carried an elephant's tail before Apokoo, until he unexpectedly succeeded to the stool.—See page 295.

When any public execution, or sacrifice, is to take place, the ivory horns of the King proclaim at the palace door, " wow! wow! wow!" " death! " death, death, death!" and, as they cut off their heads, the bands play a peculiar strain, till the operation is finished.

The greatest human sacrifice that has been made in Coomassie during my residence, took place on the eve of the Adaï custom early in January. I had a mysterious intimation of it two days before, from a quarter not to be named. My servants being ordered out of the way, I was thus addressed, " Christian, take care and watch over your family; the angel of death has drawn his sword, and will strike on the neck of many Ashantees ; when the drum is struck, on Adaï eve, it will be the death signal of many. Shun the King if you can, but fear not." When the time came to strike the drum, I was sitting thinking on the horrors of the approaching night, and was rather startled at a summons to attend the King. This is the manner he always takes to cut off any captain or person of rank; they are sent for to talk a palaver, and the moment they enter, the slaves lay hold of them, and pinion them, and throw them down ; if they are thought desperate characters, a knife is thrust through their mouth to keep them from swearing the death of any other, when they are charged with their crime, real or supposed, and put to death or torture.

Whilst I was with the King, the officers, whose duty it is to attend at sacrifices, and are in the confidence of the King, came in with their knives, &c. and a message was sent to one chief to say, that the King was going to his mother's house to talk a palaver, and shortly after his Majesty rose, and proceeded thither, ordering the attendants to conduct me out by another door.

This sacrifice was in consequence of the King imagining,

that if he washed the bones of his mother and sisters, who died while he was on the throne, it would propitiate the fetish, and make the war successful. Their bones, were therefore taken from their coffins, and bathed in rum and water with great ceremony; after being wiped with silks, they were rolled in gold dust, and wrapped in strings of rock gold, aggry beads, and other things of the most costly nature. Those who had done any thing to displease the King, were then sent for in succession, and immolated as they entered, " that their blood might water the graves." The whole of the night, the King's executioners traversed the streets, and dragged every one they found to the palace, where they were put in irons: but (which is often the case) some one had disclosed the secret, and almost every one had fled, and the King was disappointed of most of his distinguished victims. Next morning being Adaï custom, which generally brought an immense crowd to the city, every place was silent and forlorn; nothing could be found in the market, and his Majesty proceeded to the morning sacrifice of sheep, &c. attended only by his confidents, and the members of his own family. When I appeared at the usual time, he seemed pleased at my confidence, and remarked that I observed how few captains were present. He appeared agitated and fatigued, and sat a very short time.

As soon as it was dark, the human sacrifices were renewed, and, during the night, the bones of the royal deceased were removed to the sacred tomb at Bantama, to be deposited along with the remains of those who had sat on the throne. The procession was splendid, but not numerous, the chiefs and attendants being dressed in the war costume, with a musket, and preceded by torches; the sacred stools, and all the ornaments used on great occasions, were carried with them; the victims, with their hands tied behind them, and in chains, preceded the bones, whilst at intervals, the songs of death and victory proved their wish to begin the war. The procession returned about three P. M. on Monday, when the King took his seat in the market-place with his small band, and " death! death! death!" was echoed by his horns. He sat with a silver goblet of palm wine in his hand, and when they cut off any head, imitated a dancing motion in his chair; a little before dark, he finished his terrors for that day, by retiring to the palace, and soon after, the chiefs came from their concealment, and paraded the streets, rejoicing that they had escaped death, although a few days might put them in the same fear. I had been attacked by a violent fit of ague in the morning, from having stood so long in the sun the day before while with the King, it being unusually hot. I dared not send out my people to procure any thing, least they should be murdered, and in fact there was nothing in the market to be had: there was not even a drop of water in the house. The sacrifice was continued till the next Adaï custom, seventeen days.

CHAPTER XIII.

Sketch of Gaboon, and its Interior.

T HE River Gabon, or Gaboon, as the English pronounce it, is placed by some, N. 30', E. 8° 42', by others, on the equator and E. 9° 23': the former longitude is certainly the more correct; judging from three reckonings of the vessel in which I visited it; unfortunately, I had not the requisites for an observation. The former latitude also, is, doubtless, the correct one of Cape Clara; for an observation, taken as we were beating in by Round Corner, gave 23' N.; and another, taken about 35 miles up the river, 15' N. From Cape Clara (which is not 'very high land,') to Sandy point, being an oblique line, may be about 25 miles, but the direct width of the mouth of the river, cannot be more than 18. From 22 to 25 miles up the river, lay Parrot and Konig islands, called by the natives Embenee and Dambee; the former (on which ships have been hauled to careen) 1¾ miles in circumference and uninhabited, the latter considerably larger, and having a village on the hill. The natives mentioned the ruins of a Portuguese fort there. Konig island is not more than a mile from Rodney's or Oweëndo point, where there is a large bight; which, with the one opposite, within Eghirrighee point, makes the width of the river nearly thirty miles in this part. From these points it seems to form an inner basin, the greatest width of which, just above Goombena creek, is about twelve miles, judging from shots; for the work of the ship being heavy whilst in the river, and the crew suffering from the climate, (the first mate and carpenter dying,) no assistance could be spared for a survey. There are several large creeks in the river, Goöngway is the most so, and Goombena the second.

These names, being, of themselves, as uninteresting as the list of bearings would be, I shall reserve both the one and the other, with the outline of the river adjusted to them, for the Portfolio of the African Association; and also two or three sketches of the different parts of the river, not worth publishing, but, possibly, useful for the introduction of more accurate observers.*

* I believe no instructions for entering the River Gabon are in print, the following were compiled from the log-book of the Lord Mulgrave, which has been laden in the river the three successive years she has been chartered as a store-ship by the African Committee, and beat into it this time. When standing for the river, from the southward, it is best to give Round Corner a good birth, as a shoal or sand-bank runs off between that and Sandy point, and also in case of being becalmed, as the ground is foul and bad for anchoring. A channel goes in by Sandy point, but it is rarely used but by small vessels. Leave Round Corner about three leagues, and stand over for Cape Clara until you have the river well open, then steer for a bluff point about two miles inside of the Cape, where you will find from eight to ten fathom water. You may stand in, till you are about two miles from the above point, and then steer up the river, keeping the north shore aboard, and steering for the highest land you see, which lies above Quaw Ben's town. In mid-channel, you will find nine fathoms, until you bring Sandy point on a line with Cape Clara bearing S. S. E. You are then in the narrowest part of the channel, which is not more than two or three miles wide, and your greatest soundings will be six fathoms. When you are well inside these bearings you may haul off from the shore at your leisure, and steer for Parrot Island. When athwart of Quaw Ben's town, and about five miles off shore, you will find twelve and thirteen fathoms. In standing up from Quaw Ben's, give Prince Glass's town a good birth, as a shoal runs off to some distance, your soundings will be from seven to nine fathoms; you may anchor on any part of the north side, without danger. Between Konig and Parrot Islands, is very good anchorage in seven fathoms, and a soft, muddy, bottom; thence to Abraham's town, you will have from seven to four fathoms at low water; and small vessels may go a considerable way up the river, for there are three fathoms at Naüngoo or George-Town creek,

About forty-five miles from the mouth, the river forms two arms. The one runs north eastwards, by a point called Ohlombompole by the natives of Gaboon, and Gongoloba by the Shekans or interior people; the entrance is about four miles wide. The other, runs apparently S. S. E. by a point called Quawkaw, and Quanlie by the two nations, and is about two miles broad. It was an inconsiderate observation of Mr. Maxwell's, " If the Niger has a sensible outlet, I have no doubt of its proving the Congo, knowing all the rivers between Cape Palmas and Cape Lopez to be inadequate to the purpose." The Volta may be thought so, but the Lagos certainly cannot, nor the Danger, or Gaboon; and, surely, the rivers del Rey, and Formoso are not; which are thus noticed, within a few pages of Mr. Maxwell's observation, by the judicious Editor of Mr. Park's last mission, " The Rio del Rey and the Formoso, are stated to be of considerable size, being each of them seven or eight miles broad at the mouth; and the supposed Delta, estimated by the line of coast, is much larger than that of the Ganges : consequently, the two streams, if united, must form a river of prodigious magnitude."

There being little prospect of the ship completing her cargo (red wood and ebony) within two months, I determined to divert such a tædium under an insalubrious climate, by investigating and compiling the interior geography, as far as I could from the reports of the slaves, and traders. The most enterprising of the latter, and

about forty-five miles up the river. If you are turning into the river, when you are within the Cape, stand no further off than into five fathoms, for as you close the middle ground, the soundings are very irregular; you may have five fathoms; and, before the next cast, the ship may be ashore. The widest part of the channel, is not more than about $5\frac{1}{2}$ miles, until you are nearly athwart of Quaw Ben's town, when you may stand over to the south side, as you are then inside the bank. There is a very good watering-place at Rodney's point. Ships unacquainted, may anchor off the Cape and wait for the sea breeze, which generally sets in before noon.

the greatest travellers in the interior, living on board the vessel during her loading, I conversed with them constantly, as they spoke good English; and I went on shore twice, passing a night the latter time, to Naängo or George's Town, two miles up the romantic creek of Abaäga, about forty-five miles from the mouth of the river. I found the Governor (so his title was interpreted) a very hospitable and intelligent native, and speaking good English. He had travelled much in the interior, when young, was still very inquisitive for particulars, and produced me a troop of slaves for questioning, which furnished a native of almost every country I could hear of. I saw two young negroes, the sons of native rulers, who spoke and wrote French fluently. The one had been sent to that country for education, and the other in his voyage to England for the same purpose, was taken and carried to France, and generously educated and maintained by the owner of the privateer.* Each remained in France upwards of eight years before they were sent back to Gaboon, and professed to be very anxious to return to it, depicting the native habits not only as uncongenial, but disgusting to them. The Congo hypothesis, the primary stimulus to my enquiries, making geographical particulars the most desirable, I will defer those on other subjects, and submit the compilation of seven weeks investigation and inquiry under the above advantageous circumstances.

The native name of the country of Gaboon, is Empoöngwa; it dos not extend above the branching of the river, or more than forty miles in length; and is about thirty in breadth, including the river, which they call Aroöngo. We will pursue the north-eastern arm first. There is a sand-bank in the middle of the entrance,

* I am sorry to say those whom their parents have been persuaded to entrust to English vessels for the same purpose, have invariably been sold as slaves, in violation of every assurance; an infamy of which the French have never been guilty in a single instance.

and three small islands, Soombëä, Ningahinga, and Ompoöngee, are just beyond it, where the water becomes fresh. About two miles further, is a larger island called Cheēndue, inhabited, and the women of which are constantly employed in fishing for white mullet, being abundant. They dress them with a kind of chocolate, which I shall notice presently. Several large trees grow out of the water, one, eminently high, is directly in the middle of the river; they are called Intinga, or the iron tree. The eastern banks of this arm are inhabited by the Sheekans, who, with all the nations of the interior, are called Boolas by the Gaboons, a term synonymous with Dunko in Ashantee. Adjoining Sheekan are the Jomays, who speak a dialect of the same language. The Sheekans bury their dead within the house, under their beds. The Gaboons prohibit these people from visiting the coast, lest they should deprive them of their profits, as the medium between the interior and shipping, whether for slaves or manufactures.

The Sheekans, like their neighbours, only reckon from 1 to 5, conjoining these numerals afterwards, as Mr. Park has shewn the Feloops and the Jaloffs to do.

One	-	-	-	Ilwawtoe
Two	-	-	-	Ibba
Three	-	-	-	Bittach
Four	-	-	-	Binnay
Five	-	-	-	Bittah
Ten	-	-	-	Ducoom
Twenty	-	-	-	Eboomebba
Hundred	-	-	-	Kama

The source of the north-eastern arm is unknown, it probably flows from the River Danger, called by the natives Moöhnda, which flows very far from the interior; and, though not so wide, is considerably deeper than the Aroöngo or Gabon. There is a creek passing Quaw Ben's town in the River Gabon, which runs inland, within a short distance of the Moöhnda, so that traders proceeding so far by it, carry their canoes over the interval to that river. The Nokos, Apooks, and Komebays, inhabit the lower space between the Rivers Gaboon and Danger.

Having pulled up the N. E. arm for two days and nights, they land, leaving the river about one mile broad; and after two jour-nies, (skirting Sheekan,) reach Samashialee, the capital of the country of Kaylee, (sometimes called Kalay,) and the residence of the King Ohmbay. Samashialee, is described as a considerable town, and Asāko, as the second to it; their houses are all of bam-boo. The Kaylees manufacture iron from the ore, which abounds every where in this part of Africa; but they are very careful not to let the coast people see them do so, as knives, spears, mats, and bamboo cloth, are their articles of barter with them, for brass rods, cottons, and other European commodities. I procured some of the knives and spear heads, of their own iron. The bamboo-cloth has the appearance of coarse brown Holland. Their mats are very fine, and much varied in colors and patterns. It is remark-able, that the latter do not partake at all of their own wild cha-racter, but are of that chaste, simple outline which would be called elegant by civilized nations. These people are cannibals, not only eating their prisoners but their dead, whose bodies are bid for directly the breath is out of them. A father has frequently been seen to eat his own child. Fowls abound in their country, but they never eat them, nor will they goats, which are equally numerous, whilst human flesh is to be had. Salt fetches an enor-mous price. The people of Gaboon would be afraid to venture amongst them, even as traders, but for their musquets, and a strong body of Sheekans, always engaged to accompany them. Their country is mountainous and woody. There are people inhabiting a mountain close to the north-eastward of Kalay, who are said to

see best in the night time, when they travel, and work, sleeping
most of the day, because the light hurts their eyes, which are remarkably brilliant. Ivory is plentiful. The Kaylee seems to be a
dialect of the Sheekan.

One	-	-	-	Woto
Two	-	-	-	Ibba
Three	-	-	-	Battach
Four	-	-	-	Binnay
Five	-	-	-	Bittan
Ten	-	-	-	Dueoom

Northward of Kaylee, two journies, is Imbekee, adjoining the
Moöhnda or Danger. One moon distant, in the same direction,
passing through the countries, Beesoo (three journies from Imbeekee) Aösa, and Hetan, are the larger kingdoms of Badayhee,
and Oongoomo; the King of the latter is Enjukayamoo, and the
capital Mattadee, described as a very large town. The numerals
assimilate to those of Kaylee.

One	⸱	-	-	Woötta
Two	-	-	-	Beeba
Three	-	-	-	Bittach
Four	-	-	-	Binnay
Five	-	-	-	Bitten

Travelling (still northward,) through the small states of Oon-
damee and Bolaykee, in six journies they reach the extensive
countries of Paämway, and Shaybee, which adjoin each other; and
on their northern frontier is Bayhee, through which kingdom the
River Wola or Wole flows; the largest river they had ever seen or
heard of, and running eastward. My friend the Governor, always
impressed on me, that this was the largest river in the world, and
ran, to use his own words, " farther than any one, except God,
knows, farther than Indee; all the great rivers in this country come
from Wole." The Moöhnda, he had always understood in the long
course of his enquiries, to flow from it; but he could not speak so

positively of that, as of the junction of the Ogooawai and the Wole, as he had himself been to a considerable distance up the Ogooawai, which, returning to Gaboon, we shall proceed to. All the nations on this route were said to be cannibals, the Paämways not so voraciously so as the others, because they cultivate a breed of large dogs for their eating; this seems the favourite meat in most parts of Africa.

Those who travel eastward, pull for a day and a half up the right hand or south-eastern arm of the Gaboon or Aroöngo, which arm is formed by the junction of several small streams, about sixty miles from its confluence with the north-eastern arm. Landing about thirty-five miles up it, two and a half journies are occupied in travelling over an uninhabited country, described as savannah, and called Woongawoonga; it is entirely open, and buffaloes are numerous. Here they reach the Ogooäwai, a rapid river, frequently as wide, and, generally, considerably deeper than the Gaboon; and which, as we shall presently see, runs to the Congo, of itself insignificant. One day up the Ogoöawai, is the small kingdom of Adjoomba, consisting but of four towns. One journey beyond, on the Ogooäwai, and north-eastward, is Gaelwa, a kingdom of more importance, its length three journies. The King's name is Roiela, and the capital, a considerable town, Inkanjee: Goondemsie is second to it. Adjoining Gaelwa is Eninga, where the river widens considerably; this country is larger than Adjoomba, very populous, and composed of several small governments. The river winds very much; frequently they save time by carrying their canoes over the peninsulas; they are also opposed by impetuous currents. Hitherto the language is the same as the Empoöngwa or Gaboon. Twenty journies from the frontier of Gaelwa and Eninga, through the small state of Okota, is the kingdom of Asheera; and ten beyond it, that of Okandee, the greatest they know. The King's name is Adoomoo, the capital extensive, and kept particularly clean: their law forbids any native of Okandee to be sold as a slave. None of the nations on the Ogooäwai are cannibals. On the eastern confines of Okandee this river is described to join or flow from the Wōla. The countries between the Moöhnda and Ogooäwai, are called Sappalah, Koomakaimalong, and Okaykay, and described as vast extents of savannah. Deeha was spoken of as a large country in the neighbourhood of the Wōla. I could not make these interior natives, or the people of Gaboon, understand what I meant by a Moor; there are none but pagan negroes throughout. The slaves recently arrived viewed me with affright; they said none in their country would believe there were white men.

I could hear of no great controlling kingdom, like Ashantee, in these parts of the interior, nor do I think any such exists eastward of Yarriba, or other than numerous small states, as far behind Dagwumba and its neighbours in civilization, as they are behind Europeans. The name,* situation, magnitude, and course of the

* Wōla is probably the Empoöngwa corruption of the original name Quolla or Kulla, for, presuming that name to be given to it in the Mallowa or Houssa country,* to denote its being a branch or arm of the great river, dividing into it and the Gambaroo after leaving the lake Dibbir, (Kulla being *child* in the Mallowa,) it doubtless retains the same name in the country known at Gaboon; not only because Mr. Brown first reported the river Kulla (*Bahr Kulla*) and the kingdom (*Dar Kulla*) to be situated thereabouts, but because from the following observation of Mr. Hutchison's, received since I wrote my geographical chapter, it appears, that the language of the kingdom which bears the name of the river, is at least a dialect of the Mallowa language. " I send you the numerals of Quolla liffa, as given me by the servant boy I have got lately, who comes from that country, which is near the cannibals:" see Appendix, Language.

* The Jennë Moors however called it Quolla, which inclined me at first to derive its name from *Killi*, the numeral *one* in the Bambarra, as if to denote it the first or greatest river; as Yahndi, the name of the capital of Dagwumba, implies its pre-eminence; *Yahndi* being *one* in the language of the country.

Wōla, leave little doubt of its being the Kulla or Quolla; though I am not clear that they said there was a country of the name of the river, nor did I recognize the name of any of the countries I had before heard of, as being in its neighbourhood. With those on the northern banks of this large river they did not profess to be acquainted, and those on the southern may be intermediate between the Moöhnda and Ogooawai routes, which diverge from Empoöngwa, the former northward, the latter north-eastward. Forty journies from the Empoöngwa frontier to the Bahr Kulla agree very well with the distance. A strong argument, in addition to the above, for the Wōla and the Quolla being the same river, (recollecting my description of the Paämways, and all the nations on the line of the Moöhnda, as cannibals,) is suggested by the reperusal of the following remarks of Mr. Horneman, and Mr. Hutchison, already quoted in page 202 : " The Yem Yems, cannibals, are south of Kano, ten days," which agrees very well with the lowered course of the Niger, which I have been obliged to lay down. " It is to the King of Quallowliffa that the country in which Canna, Dall, and Yum Yum, where cannibals are, is subject." It is true, that the character only, and not the names of the nations visited from Empoöngwa, can be identified with Mr. Hutchison's Canna, Dall, and Yum Yum; but the Moorish pronunciation, or writing of negro names, especially those only known to them by report, is very incorrect and capricious. To Mr. Horneman, they were called Yem Yems; to Mr. Hutchison, Yum Yums, and sometimes Jum Jums. The names Bapoonoo, Okobella, Banginniga, Oonbamba, and Asango, may possibly be identified hereafter amongst the countries approximating to the Wōla.

We will return to Adjoomba, where the Ogooäwai divides itself; the smaller arm called Assazee runs to Cape Lopez, which is in the kingdom of Oroöngoo; the monarch, Ogoöla, from his power surpassing every other in the neighbourhood of the coast, has acquired the name of Pass-all with the traders who speak English. Between Oroöngoo and Adjoomba is the kingdom of Oongobai. The King's name is Pendanga, and the numerals are,

One	- - - -	Rappeek.
Two	- - - -	Ramboise.
Three	- - - -	Mittasee.
Four	- - - -	Binnay.
Five	- - - -	Bittan.
Six	- - - -	Sambal.
Seven	- - - -	Bittooba.
Eight	- - - -	Bissamen.
Nine	- - - -	Bwoi.
Ten	- - - -	Deëoom.

An intelligent native of this country had fled to Gaboon to avoid execution.

The larger arm of the Ogooäwai, flowing south-eastward, as wide as the Gaboon, through the country of Tanyan, (the western frontier of which is five journies from that of Adjoomba,) runs into the Congo, (which is comparatively small before the confluence,) about ten days pull from the mouth of that river. A very intelligent man who acts as interpreter or trade man to the vessels which frequent the river Gaboon, confirming this account of the slaves and traders, I enquired into the circumstances to which he owed his knowledge. He is the son of the principal trader in Gaboon, called Tom Lawson, who speaks English fluently. Eight years ago, this young man, Wondo, went from Gaboon to the Congo, in the Nimble, Everett master. After the vessel had traded some time, as high up in the river as she might safely venture, the captain sent him and three or four other negroes in a boat with goods, to go up as much higher as they could. His account was, that they passed Evehelee and Cormee, when they came to a fall of water upwards of twenty feet high. A native, who preceded them in his canoe, directed them to enter a small channel to the east, which, by a considerable sweep, avoided it, but the natives, he persisted, both pulled their canoes up, and let them down this fall, by long fibrous roots twisted into cordage, and affixed to the large trees above; frequently, however, the most expert were victims to their intrepidity, generally in the descent; their canoes were made purposely in the shape of a bow. I expressed my doubts, questioned him with seeming indifference, at many different times, on this subject, and requested others to do the same; his account never varied. He was naturally very cautious in what he said, by no means given to the marvellous in recounting his travels, but a corrector of that disposition in others. To the last moment he persisted in this report. Just beyond this fall is the confluence of the Ogooawai and the Congo, which takes place in Tanyan.* From

---

* " The information received here (at Mavoonda) of the upward course of the river, was more distinct than any we have yet had; all the persons we spoke to agreeing tha after ten days in a canoe, we should come to a large sandy island, which makes *two channels, one to the north west, and the other to the north east; that in the latter there is a fall, but that canoes are easily got above it;* that twenty days above the island, the river issues by many small streams from a great marsh or lake of mud." Captain Tuckey's Narrative. In a map, " Regna Congo et Angola," in Dapper's Description de l'Afrique, 1686, a large arm is laid down, about two hundred and fifty miles up the Zaire, running to or coming from the north-east. As this book is scarcely known, there being but one copy in England, it may be interesting to the reader to see a description of the Congo and its source, according to the geographical opinions, a century and a half ago, for 1686 is the date of the translation from the German. Refer first to my copy of a part of one of the many maps in Dapper's work, p. 211. Au midi de cette riviere (Niger) est le Zaire, ou la grande riviere de Congo qui prend sa source de trois lacs, au sentiment de Pigaser. Le premier se nomme Zambre d'où procede le Nil, le second Zaire d'où sortent les rivieres de Lelunde et de Coanze, et le troisième est un lac formé par le Nil. Mais le principal est le Zambre qui est comme le centre d'où les fleuves de nord le Nil, au levant Cuama

3 K

this point he described the latter as gradually dwindling to its source, (not more than six days distant, by Encombë and Eveheea,) so that the Congo owed its magnitude and rapidity entirely to the Ogooawai.* He mentioned a chief named Mangoff, to have been a

et Coavo, au midi Zeila et Manice ou Manhessen, et au couchant la riviere de Zaire, qui par divers bras arrose toute la partie occidentale de l'Afrique, situé au delà de la ligne, les royaumes de Congo, d'Angola, de Monomatapa, de Matamam, de Bagama-diri et d'Agasymba jusqu'au cap de bonne-esperance ; pendant que le Nil, Cuama, Coavo, Zeila, et Manice traversent l'Abyssinie et tous les païs qui sont entre la mer-Rouge et Cuama. L'embouchure de Zaire est à cinq degrez quarante minutes de latitude Meri-dionale. Elle à trois milles de large et se décharge dans l'ocean avec tant d'impetuosité, que l'impression qu'elle donne à la marée, dont elle rend le cours ouëst-nord-ouëst et nord-ouëst au nord se ressent en pleine mer, à douze milles de la côte. Quand on a perdu la terre de vue, on découvre une eau noire, de la verdure, des cannes et des roseaux qui ressemblent à de petites îles, et que la violence de la marée entraine après soi du haut des ecœuils. De sorte qu'à moins d'un vent d'arrière il est fort difficile de resister au courant et d'aller jetter l'ancre dans la rade de Cabo Padron. On ne sauroit remonter ce fleuve plus de vint ou vint cinq lieues au-dessus de son embouchure, à cause des cascades qui sont au milieu de son lit et qui s'élancent du haut des rochers avec tant de bruit qu'on l'entend à deux ou trois lieues de là. Plusieurs ruisseaux se déchargent ou sortent de ce fleuve et arrosent le païs : ce qui est fort commode pour les marchands et les habitans qui peuvent aller commodément d'un village à l'autre sur des canots. Les peuples qui demeurent le long de ces ruisseaux sont des gens de petite taille.

* The following, which Baron Humboldt sketched before me, (and which is only laid down in Walker's Map of the World on the globular projection) is a more extraordinary concatenation of rivers; considering the opposite courses of the Orinoco and Amazon when connected by the Casiquaire, which is more curiously situated than the south eastern branch of the Ogooawai, flowing, through Tanyan, into the Zaire.

principal man in the Congo, and he sung his boat chorus as a specimen of the language, " Malava napa, malava mabootay, ma· bootay." He said, Mangoff lived at Barrima. He spoke of a place called Ohlobe, but I omitted to minute the particulars.

The master of a Liverpool ship, laying in Gaboon river, having visited the Congo annually for many years, I availed myself of an opportunity of conversing with him also. He mentioned Bōma as the principal place of trade, but he did not consider it more than forty miles up the river; it was so called after a chief, whose son has now succeeded him. Binda, a secondary place of trade, he reckoned to be ninety miles from the entrance of the river, on the north side; but there are so many arms or branches there, that it is very difficult to distinguish the Congo itself, which he had always understood to terminate soon afterwards.* The houses he

* " Captain Tuckey could only learn that the paramount Sovereign was named Blindy N'Congo, and resided at a banza named Congo, which was six days journey, in the interior from the ' Tall Trees,' where, by the account of the negroes, the Portuguese had an establishment, and where there were soldiers and white women. This place is no doubt the St. Salvador of the Portuguese. The following is the description in Dapper: La province de Pembo est la plus considerable de tout le royaume dont elle contient la ville capitale, et forme comme le centre. Cette ville porte le nom de banza chez les Ethiopiens, les Portugais la nomment présentement S. Salvador, et Marmol l'appelloit Ambas Congo. Elle est presque au milieu de la province, située sur une roche fort haute, *à 76 lieues de France ou 150 milles de la mer*, au sud-est de la riviere de Zaire, et ombragée de Palmiers, de Tamarins, de Bacoves, de Colas, de Limoniers et d'Orangers. Le côtau sur lequel elle est bâtie est si haut, que de dessus son sommet on porte la vue aussi loin qu'elle se peut étendre, sans qu'aucune montagne l'arrête. Il n'y a point de murailles autour de cette ville, si ce n'est d'un côté de devers le Midi, que le premier roi chrétien donna aux Portugais pour les mettre à couvert des insultes. Il fit aussi fermer de murailles son palais et toutes les maisons royales qui sont aux environs, laissant une place vuide où l'on bâtit ensuite un palais et un cimétiere. La cime de la montagne est occupé par des maisons baties fort près l'une de l'autre : les personnes de qualité en possedent la plus grande partie, et sont des enceintes de bâtimens qui ressemblent à une

described as wretched, and transportable, so that a trader buying one for a trifle, could have it moved to any part of the banks he pleased. Sea horse teeth were to be bought plentifully, they buried them with their dead, dedicating them as the Ashantees do gold, and generally sticking one erect on the grave, as a sort of monument. He spoke very ill of them from his own experience; they had frequently attempted to poison the water on board his vessel. A few months back they cut off a Portuguese vessel, destroyed the crew, and plundered her. I anxiously anticipate the perusal of Captain Tuckey's journal.

Tom Lawson, who has as much, if not more influence than his brother the King, says he would provide an escort headed by his son Wondo, and guarantee the safety of any exploratory party to the river Ogooawai, and five days up it; that is as far as Okota. Two hundred pounds laid out in goods, I think, would defray the

petite ville. Les habitations des personnes du commun sont rangées de file, en diverses ruës, elles sont assez grandes, mais les murailles ne sont que de paille; excepté quelques unes que les Portugais ont faites, dont les murs sont de brique & le toit de chaume. Le palais du roi est aussi grand qu'une ville ordinaire; il est fermé de quatre murailles, celle qui regarde sur le quartier des Portugais est de chaux & de pierre, les autres ne sont que de paille, mais travaillée fort proprement. Les murailles des sales & des chambres sont ornées de tapisseries de paille nattées avec beaucoup d'art. Dans l'enceinte intérieure du Palais, il y a des jardins & des vergers embellis de berceaux & de pavillons fort beaux pour le pais, quoiqu'au fond ce ne soit pas grande chose. Il y a dix ou douze Eglises, la Cathedrale, sept chapelles dans la ville & trois Eglises dans le chateau du Prince. Il y a aussi un couvent de Jesuites, où trois ou quatre de ces Peres sent tous les jours le Catechisme au peuple, & des écoles où l'on enseigne le Latin & le Portugais. Il y a deux fontaines, l'une dans la ruë de St. Jaques & l'autre dans une cour du Palais, qui fournissent abondance d'eau fraîche, sans qu'on se donne la peine de refaire les aqueducs ou de les entretenir. Oûtre cela il y a un bras de la riviere Lelunde, qu'on nomme Vese, qui sort au pié de la montagne, au Levant de la ville; son eau est fort bonne, le peuple en va puiser, & elle sert à arroser & rendre fertiles les campagnes d'alentour. On y a des pourceaux & des chevres; mais peu de moutons & boeufs; on les renferme la nuit dans des parcs qui sont dans la ville près des maisons.

expenses, and presents, en passant, handsomely, and there are many opportunities by which two officers might be sent from Cape Coast to Gaboon for the purpose, and by way of the islands, return to it. A man of war might convey them, and call for them, on her cruise.

Kings are numerous in Gaboon, and scarcely comparable even with the petty caboceers of Fantee. The greatest trader, or the richest man of almost every small village assumes the title, and frequently suffers gross indignities from his subjects, from not having the power to punish them. The King of Naängo seems of acknowledged superiority, and is comparatively respectable, both in means and power; he is known to trading vessels by the name of King George. The brother succeeds before the son. The legislative and judicial power is vested in the Governor, controlled by the King, who may order the death of a man; but, if he assigns no good reason, the offensive party is generally allowed to retire elsewhere. All children share the property of the father in equal portions, except the eldest son, who has about half as much again as any other. If a man kills another, he has a public trial; and, if he cannot justify the act, which it seems he may in many instances, his own death is inevitable. If he kills one of his wives, (his rank is designated by the number,) he pays a fine to her family, who, and not the husband, are involved in all her palavers. The acknowledged heir to a property may bring a palaver against his father, or whoever may be possessor of it, for killing a slave unjustly, or otherwise injuring the property, and oblige him to make good the injury.

A man may not look at, or converse with his mother-in-law, on pain of a heavy, perhaps a ruinous fine; this singular law is founded on the tradition of an incest. It is a common custom to lend their wives to one another; if a man evades a promise of this kind, the Governor awards heavy damages to the plaintiff. If an applicant is refused, and is detected in intrigue, the whole of his property is forfeited to the husband of the woman, who, if it is not speedily delivered, may kill the man, and burn his house. I heard of no law so barbarous or disgusting, as this any where in the interior of the Gold Coast. They assured me they never made human sacrifices.

A man of consequence never drinks before his inferiors, without hiding his face from them, believing that at this moment only, his enemies have the power of imposing a spell on his faculties, in spite of the guardiance of his fetish. When a man dies, the door of his house is kept shut seven days. The whiskers of the men, and the side locks both of them and the women, hang down in narrow braids, sometimes below their shoulders, the ends commonly tipped with small beads, and the front locks are generally braided to project like horns. The women wear a number of thick brass rings (the trade brass rod twisted) round their legs. A woman of consequence has a succession of them from the ancle to the knee, which announce her approach when walking, and jingle when she dances. The female slaves support even the heaviest burdens from a broad band or string around the temples. Like other negroes, different families have different fetish, some will not eat a cock, nor others a hen. I could not discover any distinct ideas of the creation, or of a future life. They believe implicitly in the superior fetish of individuals from Sappalah and other countries in the interior.

Tom Lawson's ' fetish man,' a native of Sappalah, has so thoroughly persuaded his master, by his address and fortuitous circumstances in war, that no bullet can injure him, strike him where it will, (either rebounding, or penetrating to be thrown from the stomach at pleasure) that this old man, who has lived almost the whole of his life in European vessels, always presses every stranger to become equally convinced by firing at him. His son bribed this man to endue him with the same fetish, and eagerly making trial of its virtue, received a musket ball, which fractured the small bone of his arm. The address of the fetish man accounted for this, to the entire satisfaction of every body, by declaring (being the most probable crime he could guess in the emergency) that it was at that instant revealed to him by the offended fetish, that this young man once had a stolen intercourse with his wife at an improper season; it was immediately confessed as a truth, and they are as obstinate believers as ever.

Naängo consists of one street, wide, regular, and clean. The houses are very neatly constructed of bamboo, and afford a ground floor of spacious and ·lofty apartments. They sleep on bedsteads encircled with musquito curtains of bamboo cloth. The manners of the superiors are very pleasing and hospitable, and a European may reside amongst them, not only with safety, but with comfort and dignity. I do not think the old and new town contain 500 inhabitants between them. From the sickness which prevailed on board the vessel, the climate must be very insalubrious. The density of the atmosphere from exhalation was even more oppressive than the heat, which was intense before the setting in of the sea-breeze, and at all times sensibly much greater than I had experienced on the Gold Coast, or in the interior: there was no thermometer on board. The Empoöngwa is the softest negro language I have ever heard, being characterized by the duplication of vowels, separately pronounced. Their numerals are;

One	-	-	-	Hemoödee
Two	-	-	-	Mban
Three	-	-	-	Ntcharoo
Four	-	-	-	Nahee
Five	-	-	-	Nchanee

Six	-	-	-	Oroöba
Seven	-	-	-	Ragginnoömoo
Eight	-	-	-	Ennanakee
Nine	-	-	-	Enogoöm
Ten	-	-	-	Hegoöm

They do not possess a single manufacture, depending for all their comforts and conveniences on the superior ingenuity of their inland neighbours, and the supplies of shipping. They plant but handfuls of corn, and rear a few goats and fowls. Cotton grows spontaneously. They make a good black dye from the mangrove and ebony shavings. They reduce the red wood to a very soft powder, by breaking a soft species of stone, and sprinkling the finest particles of it on a flat piece of red wood, which they rub violently against another flat piece; the mixed powders are then thrown into water, and that of the wood floating on the surface is strained and dried. They rub children with this powder for cutaneous eruptions.

The African Ourang-outan (Pithecus Troglodites) is found here, the one I saw was two feet and a half high, but said to be growing. I offered a fair price for it, considering they are not rare there, and would not give more when I heard of one being already in England. The native name is Inchego: it had the cry, visage, and action of a very old man, and was obedient to the voice of its master; its agony on espying the panther on board was inconceivable.* There is a curious variety of monkeys. The favourite and

* This panther or leopard, was sent to the Governor-in-Chief by the King of Ashantee, and was so perfectly tame as never to be tied up, but strolled at liberty through the apartments, playing with the servants and children. It was presented to the Duchess of York, and died at Exeter 'Change, a short time after it landed, of an inflammation on the lungs. The extraordinary playfulness and good humour of the animal, and the preservation of its health and tameness during a four months voyage, (during the colder

most extraordinary subject of our conversations on natural history, (which I introduce merely to excite enquiry) was the Ingēna, compared with an Ourang-outan, but much exceeding it in size, being generally five feet high, and four across the shoulders; its paw was said to be even more disproportionate than its breadth, and one blow of it to be fatal; it is seen commonly by those who travel to Kaylee, lurking in the bush to destroy passengers, and feeding principally on the wild honey, which abounds. Their death is frequently accelerated by the silliness which characterizes most of their actions: observing men carry heavy burthens through the forest, they tear off the largest branches from the trees, and accumulating a weight (sometimes of elephants teeth,) disproportionate even to their superior strength, emulously hurry with it from one part of the woods to another, with little or no cessation, until the fatigue, and the want of rest and nourishment, exhausts them. Amongst other of their actions, reported without variation by the men, women, and children of Empoöngwa and Sheekan, is that of building a house in rude imitation of the natives, and sleeping outside or on the roof of it; and also of carrying about their infant dead, closely pressed to them, until they drop away in putrefaction.* The larger birds in the creeks were uncommon, if not unknown. Pelicans abounded.

part of which he banquetted sumptuously on dead parrots) made the loss very mortifying.

*The description the natives give of this animal agrees extraordinarily with that of the Quoja Morrou in Dapper.

Les Quojas Morrou, dont on a parlé dans le royaume de Quoja, naissent dans le royaume d'Angola. Comme cet animal tient beaucoup de l'homme, bien des gens ont cru qu'il étoit issu d'un homme & d'un singe, mais les Negres même rejettent cette opinion. Il y a trente ou quarante ans qu'on apporta en Hollande un de ses animaux, dont on fit present à son Altesse le Prince Frederic Henri. Il étoit de la grandeur d'un enfant de trois ans, *mais il avoit bien le double d'épais, étant d'une taille carreé,* fort vigoureux &

Chamelions were plentifully caught, but none lived more than a month on board the vessel, whether fed with flies, or not at all. The changes of those I watched seemed confined to the shades between a very dark, dusky green, and a bright yellow; when placed on any black substance they became the former, and when any thing light approached them, they changed to a bright green, which hue, if the substance was yellow, was interspersed with the most brilliant spots of that colour. · I could not discern that they ever acquired a tinge of blue or red; when at rest in their cage, their color was dark green, mottled with still darker spots.

In my rambles about the environs of Naängo, I formed some idea of the general face of vegetation in Empoöngwa. Being the rainy season, of course it did not possess its usual beauty. The red wood trees abounded, with many which were new to me. The Mangroves clothed the banks of the creeks and river, even growing some yards from the banks in the water, and their lower branches frequently covered with oysters. The palm wine tree was plentiful. Like most parts of Western Africa, the woods were so covered beneath with shrubs and plants, that they seemed im-

agile: *car il levoit des choses fort pesantes & les portoit d'un lieu en un autre.* Le devant de son corps étoit nud, mais le dos étoit couvert de poil noir. Sa face avoit quelque chose d'humain, mais son nez étoit plat & retroussé. Ses oreilles, son sein, et ses mamelles, ses coudes ses mains, le bas de son ventre & ses parties naturelles, ses jambes & ses pieds resembloient parfaitement à ceux d'une femme, parce que c'étoit un animal femelle. *Il se tenoit debout & marchoit souvent tout droit ; il buvoit fort proprement, portant, d'une main le pot à la bouche et le soutenant de l'autre; il se couchoit de même, mettoit sa tête sur un chevet, ajustoit la couverture sur son corps, & à le voir ainsi étendu on l'auroit pris pour un homme.* Aussi les Negres rapportent-ils des choses prodigieuses de cet animal; ils assurent qu'il force des femmes & des filles, *& qu'il ose s'en prendre à des hommes armez.* Et selon toutes les apparences c'est là ce Satyre si celebre chez les Anciens, dont Pline & les poëtes ont tant parlé par oui-dire & sur des rapports incertains.

penetrable. Immense runners, twisting together, dropped from the branches like large cables, generally covered with parasites; sometimes adhering to the parent stem, they became themselves a tree, and at others, shooting across to the branches of neighbouring trees, seemed to connect the forest in a general link. The climbing plants contributed to this entanglement, for, interlacing their tendrils amongst the trees, they enwreathed them in the most beautiful flowers, or dropping in festoons, formed a splendid drapery to the sober green of the canopy: amongst these the convolvolus cairicus was conspicuous, from its extreme variety, the flowers being not only of that beautiful lilac, so much esteemed in England, but of the brightest blue, dark brown, pale yellow, white, pink, buff with a purple eye, and all the shades which an opening flower presents from budding to decay.* I gathered a few specimens of the plants as I walked along, which may be acceptable to botanists. I can only lament that so many circumstances conspired to render my account of them imperfect; the rainy season, my slight knowledge of botany, and the absence of all instruments which might have enabled me to examine the very minute flowers which frequently presented themselves; but I am convinced many new species might be discovered. I will submit a few which were remarkable for their different virtues, and of which drawings or specimens are preserved.

The Cosa Cosa grew upon a tree about ten feet high, the flowers in clusters, but rarely two fully blown at the same moment, the corolla white, tube shaped, but cleft to the bottom, tinged at the top with crimson and yellow; a slightly tinged glutinous petal was fixed within

* " Les Botanistes remarquent même très fréquemment ces accidens de couleurs dans les plantes venues en lieux agrestes. Je n'en citerai qu'un exemple entre mille. Sur les rives sauvages du Volga et du Samara, Pallas a trouvé l'Anemone patens chargé de périanthes tantôt bleus, tantôt blancs, tantôt jaunes."—Mirbel 1ère partie, p. 264.

the corolla, and adhered firmly to it; when separated, I found the two anthera fastened to it, without filaments, and between them laid the style, the stigma having a small hook at the back to fasten it between the two anthera. The juice is used for curing inflammations of the eyes.

The Endaägoo *(Cyperas articulatus. Linn)* had the appearance of a grass, the bulbous root was used as a worm medicine.

The Owallifa was not in blossom, the prickly leaf was applied to swellings when they wished to reduce them by bleeding; flogging the part affected, as boys frequently do their chilblains with holly.

The Edjamba *(a species of Urtica)* bears a multitude of minute green flowers, the leaves wear the appearance of nettles, and when laid on the skin produce blisters.

The Eninda Aboönee *(Leea sambucina)* is an umbelliferous plant, the infusion of which is said to correct nausea.

The Oonkoolankolee *(Aneilema bracteolata. Br.)* bears a very delicate lilac blossom, with only two petals, which fly back and expose the other parts of the flower; the least breath of air will disturb them The natives wash their children with its infusion, if they are backward in walking.

The Econda Boomba (*Bidens*, probably a new species, but too imperfect to be determined) is anti-venereal, as an infusion; the flower resembles the chamomile.

The Shewawono bears a spike with leaves resembling those of Hedysarum. The decoction is said to cure rheumatism

The tobacco grows spontaneously; but I do not consider this so strong a proof of its being indigenous to Africa, as that it grows in Inta. The Portuguese have probably introduced it into Gabcon.

The natives here as well as elsewhere have a number of fetish

·plants; the most remarkable seems the Ewelly welly, (the Ascrumb-drue of Ashantee, a species of Piper related to Umbellatum) the broad leaf of which, when rubbed on a fetish man, is said to render him invisible.

The Eroga, a favourite but violent medicine, is no doubt a fungus, for they describe it as growing on a tree called the Ocamboo, when decaying; they burn it first, and take as much as would lay on a shilling.

The medicine they most prize is the Neoöndoo; a small quantity was spared to me reluctantly. Four nuts grow in a pod on a very large tree of the hardest wood; it is purchased greedily, only growing on the frontier of Empoöngwa, and is used successfully by those afflicted with gravel.

In killing elephants they use two poisons, both of which are the milky juices of the stalks of plants. Inquaw indjoo (a plant belonging to the natural order *Aroidea*, and referable to the Linnean genus *Arum*) bears a hard white berry in a spiral cluster. The Ygwan agwan berries are red, and in perfection at the time that the flowers are budding. These juices are rubbed on the muskets balls, spears, arrows, and knives, and the effect on the elephant is described as almost instantaneous.

They make bird lime from a tree called Epoowa.

Besides the pine apple, the common thread of Africa, they use that of two other plants, the Ezoönee (*Triumfitta elliptica, Nov. Sp.*) and the Naängoo, an *Urtica*, or genus nearly allied to it. The former bears a yellow flower, too minute for my inspection. The top of the latter is surmounted by five or six delicate flower stalks; the blossoms were exceedingly minute, and of a lively green.

The governor of the town brought me two or three very harsh rough leaves, which he said were from the plant Egoögoo (a species of *ficus*) not then in blossom; they are used in planing wood, polishing and cleaning various articles of household furniture, and feel like emery paper. At the same time he gave me what they are very fond of chewing, a delicate little mimosa, (*Abrus precatorius. Linn.*) the taste of which resembles liquorice.

A beautiful red pod, the blossom of which was out of season, contains small black seeds, in taste exactly resembling the cardamom. The natives of this place, and also of the interior, are very fond of them. In Booroom the plant is called Booroomma, and at Gaboon, Entoöndo.

The Caoutchouc is to be met with here; the natives describe it as the product of one tree only,* the olamboo; their method of collecting it is curious. After the incision is made in the tree, whence it oozes like a glutinous milk, they spread it over their arms and breasts with a knife, (having first shaved themselves, that the hair of the skin may not be torn up when it is taken off,) in the form of a plaister. It is either rolled up in balls to play with, or stretched over the heads of drums; they do not seem to apply it to any other use.

They make their torches from the wood (odjoo) of which they form their canoes, the resinous parts are broken in small pieces, and tied closely in very long leaves; the smaller end is fixed to an

---

* " India rubber is obtained from the milky juice of different plants in hot countries. The chief of these are, the Jatropha elastica and Urceola elastica. The juice is applied in successive coatings on a mould of clay, and dried by the fire or in the sun, and when of a sufficient thickness the mould is crushed and the pieces shaken out." Nicholson.

" It has been discovered that caoutchouc is not exclusively the produce of the Heven caoutchouc, but that it is furnished by several other plants. We know it to be obtained in large quantities from the Jatropha elastica of South America, and Dr. Roxburgh has given us a description of an Indian plant (Urceola elastica) which affords a juice that when thickened has all the properties of the caoutchouc. We moreover know that the milky exudations of the Jack tree (Artocarpus integrifolia) the Banyan tree (Ficus Indica) and also that of the Arasum tree (Ficus religiosa) possess nearly similar qualities." Ainslie's Materia Medica of Hindoostan.

upright stick placed in the ground of the apartment; they afford a brilliant light, and the resin, when burning, emits a grateful odour.

The Odica, from which they make a kind of chocolate, is a very high and large tree, bearing an acuminate shining leaf. The nuts, which are white, are contained in a round pod with a bulb at the end, twice as large as a man's fist, green without, and yellow within; the parts surrounding the nuts are squeezed into water, which they sweeten like honey. The kernels are strung and smoke dried, and then beat in water into large masses, having the appearance of coarse chocolate, but the flavour of a rank gross gravy. It might be more palatable otherwise prepared.

The vegetable butter (which certainly belongs to the natural order *Sapoteæ*) brought to the Ashantee market, is here well known by the name of Onoöngoo: it is a large tree, and the nuts are enclosed in a round red pod, containing from four to six: the flower is also red, from description. My servant, a native of Booroom, called the tree Kirrimkoon, and the butter Incoom; the Ashantees call the latter Sarradee; in Mallowa the tree is called Timkeëä. The nut is first boiled, and the oil or butter afterwards expressed; in Booroom and Mallowa it is skimmed from the surface. It tasted quite as good as fresh butter before any salt is added, and we relished the meat fried in it exceedingly. Being the rainy season I could neither get a sight of the flower or the pod of this or the odica, but I procured the nuts and produce of both. The curious may compare this butter with the specimen of the Ashantee grease. Before I understood them to be distinct trees, I concluded the odica and the butter both to be the produce of the cacao-nut, but the butter answers closely to Mr. Park's description of the shea-tolu, though the tree did not resemble the American oak.

The Kolla nut grows on one of those trees which are supposed to sow their own seed; it is round, and the size of an Orleans plum, having a very hard shell, the kernel is white, and, after being exposed to the sun for a few days, becomes even sweeter than a filbert. The natives frequently soak them in salt water for a few weeks, and relish the rank flavour they then acquire. They form the principal food of the lower orders. They have a round orange coloured fruit, called Incheema, the size varies from that of a small cocoa nut to a large one; the capsule is very thick, and when cut yields a milky juice; a number of hard, dark brown seeds, surrounded by a pulp, are found within, the latter only is eaten, and when gathered fresh from the tree, is of a very delicious flavour, not unlike that of a green gage. If the fruit is suffered to fall from the tree, the bruise renders it unwholesome and unpalatable.

Every dark night, Tom Lawson was sure to direct me to look in the direction of what some foolish Europeans had persuaded him must be a diamond mountain. It lays about three days eastward of Empoöngwa in direct distance, but from the fear of the intervening people, he had been obliged to visit it by a circuitous route, which occupied seven days; he lost the pieces he procured, in a skirmish on his return; they illuminated a great circumference. It is considered a powerful fetish, and described as a very high mountain. I must admit, that when there was no moon, a pale but distinct light was invariably reflected from a mountain in that quarter, and from no other.

The red and yellow ochres brought to me, were dug in the neighbourhood of a savannah three journies south-eastward of Empoöngwa, where they insisted there were large pits of strata, not only of red and yellow, but of other colours. They believe, that if a man attempts to carry off different colours at the same time, he is paralyzed on the spot. Gold has never been found in this part of Africa.

EMPOÖNGWA SONG.   Inchambee

Nº 1.
Allegro

EMPOÖNGWA SONG.

Nº 2.
Andantino

Notes sung by the white Negro from Imbeekee.

Nº 3.
Andante

Presto

Andante

long-rapid-recitative

bis

The music of Empoöngwa is, generally, very inferior to that I have before noticed. The enchambee, their only peculiar instrument, resembles the mandolino, but has only five strings, made from the root of the palm tree; the neck consists of five pieces of bamboo, to which the strings are fastened, and, slipping up and down, are easily, but not securely tuned; it is played with both hands; the tones are sweet, but have little power or variety. Long stories are recited to the enchambee in the moon-light evenings, in a sort of recitative; a favourite one, is an account of the arts by which the Sun gained the ascendancy over the Moon, who were first made of coeval power by their common father.

No. 1, (which, I imagine, commences in F major, and ends in G major) is an Empoöngwa air played on the enchambee. I do not know if the inversion of words is common, in their conversation as well as in their songs. A native envies a neighbour, named Enga-ëlla, who has ivory to barter with a vessel.

Amorill injanja   Engaëlla;   impoongee   m'adgillinjanja.
A brass pan he has got Engaëlla; ivory,   I have got none.
Here again we find *me* answers to the personal pronoun I.

No. 2, in G major, is a song in which the men sing the air alone, and the women join in the chorus. It is an old one, and the subject the first appearance of a white man. One verse will be quite enough to satisfy others and exculpate myself. At least half a dozen followed it.

    Ma   bengwoo   ma bengwa   baïa.
A fine strange thing,   A fine strange thing, my mother.
    Deboonga sai   camberwoona   nayennee.
Like the leaf of the fat tree,*   true I say,   so it is.
    Sangwa moochoo,   baïa.
    I make you look to-day,   my mother.

* The vegetable butter.

3 M

Baï yamgwan boonoo.

My mother fears this fetish man.

My patience during a series of dull Empoöngwa songs, was re-compensed by the introduction of a performer, as loathsome as his music was astonishing. It was a white negro from the interior country of Imbeekee; his features betrayed his race, his hair was woolly, and of a sandy colour, with thick eye brows of the same; his eyes small, bright, and of a dark grey; the light seemed to hurt them, and their constant quivering and rolling gave his counte-nance an air of insanity, which was confirmed by the actions of his head, and limbs, and the distortions of his mouth. His stature was middling, and his limbs very small; his skin was dreadfully dis-eased, and where it was free from sores bore the appearance of being thrown on, it hung about him so loose and so shrivelled; his voice was hollow, and his laugh loud, interspersed with African howls. His harp was formed of wood, except that part emitting the sound, which was covered with goat skin, perforated at the bottom. The bow to which the eight strings were fixed, was con-siderably curved, and there was no upright; the figure head, which was well carved, was placed at the top of the body, the strings were twisted round long pegs, which easily turned when they wanted tuning, and, being made of the fibrous roots of palm wine tree, were very tough and not apt to slip. The tone was full, har-monious, and deep. He sat on a low stool, and supporting his harp on his knee and shoulder, proceeded to tune it with great nicety; his hands seemed to wander amongst the strings until he gradually formed a running accompaniment (but with little va-riety) to his extraordinary vociferations. At times, one deep and hollow note burst forth and died away; the sounds of the harp became broken; presently he looked up, pursuing all the actions of a maniac, taking one hand from the strings, to wave it up and down, stretching forth one leg and drawing it up again as if convulsed, lowering the harp on to the other foot, and tossing it up and down. Whilst the one hand continued playing, he rung forth a peal which vibrated on the ear long after it had ceased; he was silent; the running accompaniment served again as a prelude to a loud recitative, uttered with the greatest volubility, and ending with one word, with which he ascended and descended, far beyond the extent of his harp, with the most beautiful precision. Sometimes he became more collected, and a mournful air succeeded the recitative, though without the least connection, and he would again burst out with the whole force of his powerful voice in the notes of the Hallelujah of Handel. To meet with this chorus in the wilds of Africa, and from such a being, had an effect I can scarcely describe, and I was lost in astonishment at the coincidence. There could not be a stronger proof of the nature of Handel, or the powers of the negro.

I naturally enquired if this man was in his senses, and the reply was, that he was always rational but when he played, when he invariably used the same gestures, and evinced the same incoherency. The accompanying notes were caught whilst he was singing; to do more than set them down in their respective lengths, was impossible, and every notation must be far inadequate.

As regards the words, there was such a rhapsody of recitative, of mournful, impetuous, and exhilarated air, wandering through the life of man, throughout the animal and vegetable kingdom for its subjects, without period, without connection, so transient, abrupt, and allegorical, that the Governor of the town could translate a line but occasionally, and I was too much possessed by the music, and the alternate rapture and phrenzy of the perfomer, to minute the half which he communicated. I can only submit the fragments of a melancholy and a descriptive part.

Burst of a man led to execution,

> Yawa yawa wo wo oh
>
> Yawa waï yawa
>
> What have I done? what have I done?

Bewailing the loss of his mother,

> Yawa gooba shangawelladi yaisa
>
> Wo na boo, &c.
>
> My mother dies; who'll cry for me now
>
> When I die? &c.
>
> Pahmbolee gwoongee yayoo, &c.
>
> Which path shall I seek my love?
>
> Hark! I know now,
>
> I hear her snap the dry sticks,
>
> To speak, to call to me.

Jiggledy jiggledy, jiggledy, too too tee too, often invaded or broke off a mournful strain; it was said to be an imitation of the note of a bird, described as the wood-pecker.

Three Portuguese, one French, and two large Spanish ships, visited the river for slaves during our stay, and the master of a Liverpool vessel assured me that he had fallen in with 22 between Gaboon and the Congo. Their grand rendezvous is Mayumba. The Portuguese of St. Thomas's and Prince's islands send small schooner boats to Gaboon for slaves, which are kept after they are transported this short distance, until the coast is clear for shipping them to America. A third large Spanish ship, well armed, entered the river the night before we quitted it, and hurried our exit, for one of that character was committing piracy in the neighbouring rivers. Having suffered from falling into their hands before, I felicitated myself on the escape. We were afterwards chased and boarded by a Spanish armed schooner, with three hundred slaves on board; they only desired provisions.

CHAPTER XIV.

Suggestions for future Missions to the Interior of Africa.

A MISSION to Dagwumba is of the first importance. See Geography, p. 178. The commercial genius and opulence of its people, their disinclination and inaptitude to war, their superior civilization, and the numerous caravans which frequent this emporium, from the most remote parts of the interior, make a treaty of intercourse most desirable, both for commerce and science. But it is more imperiously desirable, or rather this enterprise becomes a duty, from the recollection, that, from this King's proverbial repute for sanctity, if he were persuaded by the deliberate remonstrance of a British Resident, at least to mitigate, if not ultimately to abolish human sacrifices, his example would naturally be followed by the several neighbouring monarchs who make him their oracle.

Mr. Hutchison's courage, his love of enterprise, and his interest in intellectual pursuit, to say nothing of a feeling towards myself, which I cannot but be proud of, would, I am sure, lead him to anticipate my wishes and strengthen my hopes of success, by having him again as a companion; and his diary must have proved, though very imperfectly, compared with a personal acquaintance with him, how well he is qualified for an appointment, so important to the interests of commerce, science, and humanity, by his discretion, zeal, and benevolence.*

A third officer (and a zealous and able successor to Mr. Tedlie has presented himself) should accompany this mission, to proceed under the King of Dagwumba's guarantee and recommendation, which is omnipotent to the Niger, to Wauwaw (on the banks of that river where Mr. Park was buried; for no plea could be less suspicious, than the King of England's natural anxiety to send an officer to the Sultan of Wauwaw, to learn the particulars of Mr. Park's death, and to enquire for his papers, especially as a Moorish emissary passing through Yahndi, was instructed to do so, directly we heard of the circumstance in Ashantee. The officer alluded to (who is a medical man, well acquainted with natural history, and an accurate draftsman) should be content with a sight of the Niger, and remain at Wauwaw collecting and observing, until an exchange of letters with Cape Coast, through the Resident at Yahndi†; when it would be seen how far it might be prudent, (having replaced him at Wauwaw) to allow him to proceed to Cassina, Houssa, or Timbuctoo; that is, if the Sultan of Wauwaw would guarantee his safety, under the same promise of reward previously held out to the King of Dagwumba.

No moment could be more auspicious than the present for this enterprise to Dagwumba, since the King of Ashantee's absence and perplexity in the Gaman war bars his molestation or hindrance; though I have no expectation that he would offer either, were he at liberty, or aware of the occasion: see page 342.

* This gentleman being already superseded by Mr. Dupuis (formerly Vice-consul at Mogadore, and now Consul at Coomassie) is of course at liberty to indulge his disposition for enterprise.

† The King of Dagwumba should be promised additional presents on the receipt at Cape Coast Castle of the first dispatch from the Niger.

If the trade of Dagwumba be so extensive as was invariably reported to us (and to Mr. Lucas at Mesurata on the Mediterranean) it might then become desirable to establish a British market up the Volta; but this is an after consideration. Geographical circumstances are much more in favour of a mission to Dagwumba than they were in that to Ashantee, (besides, that there are no irritating political retrospects to be debated on arrival,) for the Volta or Adirree is navigable from the sea to within eight days march of Yahndi; (see page 176;) even if we do not calculate on the reported junction of the river Laka, which would bring us close to Yahndi.

The presents should all be ingenious novelties, rather than costly apparel, for they are not only more acceptable and more imposing, but, which is very important, much more portable; and would require so few carriers, as to diminish the expense of conveyance as much as the expense of purchase. The negroes have more than anticipated our *portable* displays of splendour, from the pageantry and descriptions of the Moors; and we have had the advantage of witnessing what kind of presents made the most auspicious impression on the King of Dagwumba's powerful neighbour, which were certainly all of the class of ingenious novelty. I should recommend, therefore, a few pieces of tissue and rich silk, with gold thread interwoven, to shew that our manufactures can be accommodated to their taste; see note page 331.

Pieces of worked muslin.
One piece of ditto, worked with gold thread.
Scotch damask.
Palampours, with gold and silver leaf.
Manchester cottons, of rich pattern.
Red, blue, and yellow broad cloth.
Raw silk, of various colours; see page 331.

Of the foregoing, only small quantities as presents to the King and principal Moors, by way of samples of our manufactures.

Two pair of richly cut glass decanters.

A small silver bowl embossed.

A handsome lamp.

A military saddle and bridle, with pistols, &c.

Two musical snuff boxes.

A good bird organ.

Two or three common violins, being the instrument of the country.

Pandean pipes.

Cymbals.

Two bugles.

Kaleidescopes.

An inferior gold repeater for the King.

Two or three common silver watches.

A telescope.

Camera obscura.

Magic lantern.

Microscope.

Pocket compasses.

Boxes of phosphorous matches.

Arabic Bibles, and Arabic literature.

Two or three landscapes, in sympathetic ink.

A port-folio of engravings of English costume and public buildings, with a set of the drawings of this work.

A copying writing apparatus for the chief Moor.

Wax, seals, pencils, Indian rubber.

Two boxes of water colours.

Drawing and writing paper, and vellum.

Razors, scissors, knives.

A handsome double barrelled gun.

Two boxes of carpenters tools.

A small turning lathe.

A small plough.

A made up türban of gold tissue, with a gilt circle for the head, set with false stones, for the chief Moor.

A silk union flag.

An air gun.

Candles and perfumed soap.

Bark, and other medicines.

The officers of the mission should be provided with Troughton's pocket sextant, Dollond's 32 feet telescope, the new barometers, &c. &c.

The Danes having deserted their fort (Adda) at the mouth of the Volta, their government, on being solicited, would surely not only not obstruct, but favour so important a scientific enterprise, and not compel us to reach the river over land, as we could do, by marching through Aquapim and Quaoò. The man of war on the station might convey the mission to the mouth of the Volta, and one of her boats accompany the canoes (which should be brought from Cape Coast) a day or two up the river.

It would be well to be prepared with several impressions of a manifesto (in Arabic,) explanatory and impressive of the legitimate and benevolent views of the British government, as an introduction to the King of Dagwumba, preparatory to our negociation, and also to serve the same purpose at Wauwaw, and to circulate through the interior. Numerous impressions of the certificates circulated in behalf of Major Peddie, should also be circulated, Mr. Ritchie's name being substituted, and the reward for an act of kindness acknowledged in a letter from that gentleman, being made payable (after an authority from Cape Coast) at either of the

3 N

British Residencies, Coomassie, Yahndi, or Dahomey; for as there are many officers to spare at Cape Coast, the expressed wish of the latter monarch should be immediately gratified, and our intercourse renewed by a Residency.   See note, p. 340.

I think all the objects of the Dagwumba mission could be effected in four months; when I should feel impatient to visit the river Gaboon, for the purpose of penetrating to the Ogooawai, and going as far up it as I might with prudence.   See p. 436.   The discovery of so large a river in this situation is very important.

Arrangements could probably be made at Eninga or Okota (p429.) for the guarantee of an after mission to Asheera: also for one from Gaboon to Kaylee; and, which is most important, for the south-eastern navigation (from Adjoomba, p. 431) of the branch of the Ogooawai running through Tanyan into the Congo.

But there is another enterprise which should not be forgotten, the navigation of the Lagos river to the highest point, (p. 224) and a visit to Kosie, (p. 225,) a Residency at which court would doubtless lead to a similar establishment in the powerful and commercial kingdom of Yarriba.   See p. 209.

The Residents at the various courts, who, as I have impressed before, should be young men of acquirement, patience, and address, should receive occasional instructions from head quarters, directing their enquiries and observations to the geographical and scientific desiderata, more peculiarly belonging to or expected from their different neighbourhoods, which would be suggested from the closer study of these subjects by the individual at the head of a department of discovery at head quarters, and also by the scientific Societies in England according to their peculiar pursuits.

The Residents should make quarterly reports, accompanied by specimens of natural history, to be digested into one annual report at head quarters, (with the various geographical improvements and discoveries, adjusted and embodied in one large chart) for forwardance to England.

All Residents and Conductors of Missions, should be provided with small copying apparatuses, so that they might forward their original dispatch, and one duplicate, to Cape Coast, by two different opportunities, always retaining the other copy, in case of accident, or until the receipt were acknowledged.

If it could be afforded, a medical officer should afterwards be added to the more important Residencies, to attach and relieve the natives.

Botanical and Mineralogical excursions, (taking sextants, telescopes, and barometers,) into Ahanta, Aowin, Warsaw, Akim, and Aquapim, small surveys, &c. &c. should be undertaken, ad interim, not only from the smallness of the expense and the great comparative benefit, (as we know nothing of these countries beyond their position,) but to qualify the younger officers (of congenial disposition and acquirement,) for future missions and residencies.

The young men soliciting appointments in England, should be required to make themselves acquainted with the grammar of the Arabic language, and practical astronomy, before they receive their commissions; and one or two intelligent Moors from the interior, should be invited, by a pay, to settle at Cape Coast Castle, to perfect these officers in writing and speaking the language. The Fantee language should also be cultivated, as it is a dialect of the Ashantee.

The soldiers of the settlements should no longer be enlisted from the mulattoes and Fantees of the neighbourhood, making the present paltry force the more inefficient, from local and family attachments, inseparable from human nature, and preventing their acting cordially, if at all, on emergencies for the rescue of human victims, or the punishment of their relatives and townsmen, for insult, or contempt of the British legislation for the abolition of the slave trade, &c. The Negroes captured in the illicit Spanish and Portuguese slave ships, of whom there must be a number unemployed at Sierra Leone, would form the most desirable military force, even preferable to European, which has recently been adopted by the Dutch. These rescued Negroes would possess no attachment, beyond that which the considerate kindness and good conduct of their officers might induce; the climate would be natural to them; and they would prove valuable companions, if not intelligent guides, in future missions to the interior. There should at least be two hundred and fifty of these soldiers at head quarters, (one company being trained as artillery by European serjeants) and fifty at each other settlement, if but two.

The three missions, to Dagwumba, Wauwaw, and Ogooawai, would not cost above a thousand pounds, judiciously expended in England; which is not so much as the annual expense of either of the six paltry out-forts (exclusive of the head quarters, and the vice presidency, which is but 9 miles from Cape Coast, and, since the abolition of the slave trade, an useless and absurd position;) the mere existence of which, although it may excite astonishment, and reflect credit on the mercantile ingenuity and economy of the African Committee, is notoriously a disgraceful caricature on the British name.

Three respectable establishments, one at Cape Coast Castle, one at Accra, (a rich and open country,) and one at Succondee, (if we could not purchase Axim, which commands the navigation of the Ancobra,) with an allowance of a thousand a year for a progress in the interior, (beneficial to commerce, science, and humanity,) would be productive of fame and honour, and probably of wealth, to our nation.

APPENDIX.

APPENDIX. No. I.

Extract from Meredith's Account of the Gold Coast.

Origin and History of the Ashantee War.

THE Assin country lies at the rear of the Fantee, and borders on the Ashantee country. It was divided into two states: the one governed by King Cheboo and Quacoe Apoutay; and the other by King Amoo. Apoutay, although not elevated to the dignity of King, held equal sway with Cheboo; but they were each subordinate to the King of Ashantee. A man of opulence died in Amoo's town; and, as is customary on such occasions, gold and other valuable articles were deposited with the body in the grave. On this occasion, one of Cheboo's people was present, and seeing what was done, watched an opportunity to rob the grave: which he effected, and escaped with the treasure. Amoo his neighbour sought redress of Cheboo and Apoutay, but without success: he then laid the affair before the King of Ashantee; who summoned all the parties before him, gave them an impartial hearing, and awarded in favour of Amoo. Quacoe Apoutay was detained as a hostage until restitution should be made: but he, in a short time, contrived to make his escape, and, when at liberty, refused to accede to the award made by the King of Ashantee. On this Amoo attacked the town in which Cheboo and Apoutay resided, and routed his opponents: after this, at the instigation of the King of Ashantee, the parties met to settle the dispute; but Quacoe Apoutay acting treacherously on the occasion, sent privately to Cheboo for an armed force to support him: and a battle was the consequence, which ended in the death of the man who had committed the theft, and the total defeat of Apoutay and his forces. At this crisis the King of Ashantee, willing to bring about a peace, again interfered. He sent two gold manillas, the one to Amoo, the other to his adversary, directing them to cease all hostilities; to which both parties agreed, and took the manillas. Amoo obeyed the King; but Quacoe Apoutay attacked Amoo, and drove him in his turn from his town. Amoo, indignant at the repeated deceptions of Apoutay, obtained succours, and overthrew his treacherous opponent. The King of Ashantee still anxious to reconcile his neighbours, and unwilling to draw his sword, presented two gold swords and an axe to Amoo, and recommended him to conciliate Quacoe Apoutay, and terminate their quarrels.   Amoo consented to obey the King, but in the mean time was again attacked by his implacable foe, and totally defeated, and lost in the contest the golden sword and hatchet.   His opponent committed ravages wherever he came, killing messengers, and every man who fell into his hands, not sparing even the King of Ashantee's messengers! A war with the King of Ashantee followed hereupon: Quacoe Apoutay and Cheboo dreading his vengeance, fled to the Fantee country: in consequence of which the King sent a message to Acoom, the caboceer or mayor of Assecoomah (a small state tributary to the King of Ashantee,) accompanied by a present of twenty ounces of gold; stating the necessity of his pursuing his enemies to the Fantee country, but giving assurance of the King's pacific disposition towards the Fantees, and that his only object was to get into his possession Cheboo and Apoutay: the Fantees would not interfere, nor allow the Ashantee forces to come into their country. Upon this answer, Appey Dougah,* the King of Ashantee's general, collected, by command of his master, a large force, and gave the enemy battle at Buinka in Fantee; he displayed great gallantry, and defeated the two Kings, in conjunction with the Fantee forces that had joined them.   Next day Cheboo and Apoutay having rallied their forces, and formed a junction with a fresh Fantee force, gave Appey Dougah battle; but were totally defeated, with the loss of many killed and made prisoners: among the latter was Atia,† the caboceer of Abrah, the principal town of Fantee.   A large sum was offered for his ransom, but refused; and he was committed to the care of Acoom, the caboceer of Assecoomah, in whom the King had great confidence; but this person betrayed his trust, and liberated the enemy.   Quacoe Apoutay, baffled at all points, sent to the King of Ashantee to accept his conditions, provided he would discharge his debts on his return home.   To this proposal the King agreed, and, in token of his friendship, sent various presents to Cheboo and Apoutay; who, instead of receiving them with gratitude, beheaded the messengers   This wicked and unprovoked act roused the indignation of the King of Ashantee, and he vowed eternal war against the aggressors.   Acoom (who had been forgiven by the King for his treachery in suffering Atia to escape,) being in possession of a large quantity of provisions, was applied to by the King of Ashantee for a supply, which he with seeming cheerfulness granted: six times he delivered faithfully those that were contracted for, but, the seventh time, he betrayed about one thousand men who had been sent for them, and sold them in March or April, 1806.   In consequence of this conduct Acoom became involved in the war: very shortly afterwards the King of Ashantee defeated him, and made rapid progress with his army towards the

* This should be Appia Dunqua; he was the elder brother of Appia Nanu, an account of whose disgrace is in the Diary.
† This should be Atta.

coast in search of Cheboo and Apoutay. The Fantees opposed his march, but were defeated in every onset; and the Braffoes were nearly extirpated by the Ashantees in their march. The Annamaboes, instigated by the remaining Braffoes, were impudent enough to receive and protect Cheboo and Apoutay; which proved fatal to them. At this period the Governor of Cape Coast Castle, being under some apprehension for the safety of the British settlements, was inclined to send a flag of truce with a message to the King of Ashantee, who was now (May, 1806) at Abrah, and only fifteen or twenty miles from the coast. The Annamaboes (who were consulted on the measure) objected to it, and the design was consequently suspended. The Governor was anxious to know upon what terms the King would consider the British, and wished to become a mediator; but the Annamaboes, who placed a vain dependence on their name and strength, fully expected that the King and his army would be conquered; and that if not the whole, the greater part of the army would fall into their hands; and hence were not disposed to pacific measures, nor would they permit the Governor's messenger to proceed inland. Shortly after this, a division of the Ashantee army made its appearance at Cormantine, and routing the inhabitants from the town, completely destroyed it. The captain of this division contrived to get into the Dutch fort, and having pillaged it of a number of articles, took up his residence there. It was now time to become acquainted with the King's intentions; and for that purpose the Governor of Annamaboe fort sent a messenger with a flag of truce to the commander of this division, intimating a wish to be acquainted with the King's motives for marching an army to the coast, and proposing himself as a mediator. This message, we may suppose, was conveyed to the King; and on the following day three men were observed coming from Cormantine with a white flag dis played, and (Mr. White) the Governor, expected they were the bearers of some agreeable and satisfactory intelligence: in this however he was much disappointed; for the commander of that division of the Ashantee army being in possession of fort Amsterdam, was elated with his success, particularly in getting to the sea side; (a circumstance which inspired him with such joy, that he went to the beach and dipped his sword three times in the sea, some of which he had conveyed to the King as a proof of his success :)— whether those circumstances stimulated him to try the disposition of the English chief, we know not; but the message he sent, imported a degree of haughtiness by no means agreeable to Mr. White, and was to this effect: that when the Governor would send him twenty barrels of gunpowder, and one hundred muskets, he would be told what the King's designs were. To comply with this demand would be acknowledging too much submission, and would doubtless give the King a very indifferent opinion of the British character. Mr. White behaved politely to the people, gave them some refreshment, and told them that he regretted that the King, or their master, did not appear inclined to come to an explanation, or to conciliate matters: that if the King would point out in what manner the Annamaboes had offended, he would use his authority to have satisfaction given: that until he was assured of their having transgressed, or having injured his Majesty, they were entitled to the protection of the fort, if they sought for it: and that, finally, if the King's army should come with any hostile intentions near the fort, it would be fired upon.

After this two or three of the heavy guns were fired with shot, for the purpose of giving them an idea of the destructive power of artillery; and they were preparing to depart, when private information was received, that the flag of truce would be violated in its return, and the men murdered. Whereupon Mr. White and Mr. Wilson (a gentleman not in the service,) escorted them, and left them in safety within a short distance from their quarters. The Governor now anxiously looked for a definitive reply from the King, and every assiduity was used to place things in a defensive position; and the towns-people having heretofore placed a firm reliance on their strength, became alarmed, and were solicitous to be assured of the Governor's protection. Mr. White informed them, that if the King of Ashantee intended to attack the town, he would give them all the assistance and protection in his power; at the same time advised them of the most prudent measures to be employed for their safety and defence. He instructed them, in the first instance, to have strong parties on the look-out, and to guard every avenue leading into the town; and, on the first alarm, or approach of the enemy, to send the old men, women, and children to the fort, where they would be received; and as many as the fort would not accommodate, to come close to the walls, where they would be under the protection of the guns.

At this crisis Mr. White and the inhabitants of the town were ignorant as to the strength of the Ashantee forces, and had but an imperfect idea of the bravery and intrepidity of the men who composed the King's army. It was supposed that the Ashantees partook of the dispositions of the natives on the coast, who in general cannot stand against a regular and determined fire, and often creep into some concealed hole, when cannon or musket shot are heard to whiz among them; or, if the Ashantees were superior, it was little imagined that their courage, or ardour for conquest, would carry them to the very muzzles of the guns, and consequently expose them to inevitable destruction.

About a week had elapsed, and no news from the King; which was no favourable indication of pacific measures. The commander of the division at Cormantine, and who proved to be the King of Dinkara, sent forward a party to ascertain the strength of the town of Annamaboe, and succeeded in gaining possession of a village called Agah, situated upon a point of land about one mile eastward from Annamaboe; whence every movement of the Annamaboes on that side could be observed. This was considered an annoyance, and on the 14th of June a strong body (indeed almost the whole of the town's people) marched out for the purpose of dislodging the Ashantees. The action was clearly seen from the fort. The Annamaboes were received in the most gallant and spirited manner by nearly a third of their force, and for some time the contest was doubtful. The Ashantees fired with more regularity than could be expected, and their muskets were well directed; whereas the Fantees kept up a confused fire without taking aim; they however succeeded, and the Ashantees retreated in excellent order, keeping possession of part of the village which lay concealed in a valley, and where the Annamaboes did not think proper to proceed. The Annamaboes were either too confident of their strong position, or thought too insignificantly of their opponents, to attend to the advice given them by Mr. White; for while they were amused by this small party, the King, with the main body, was vigilant in securing the different passes leading to the town, and was at this time only three miles to the rear of it.

Early on the 15th those who were on the look-out observed the Ashantee army in motion: the alarm was given, and every man who was able to carry a musket, repaired to meet the enemy. As the town was situated at the rear of the fort, and extended some distance inland, no prospect of the contending parties could be obtained; smoke was seen to arise from different parts of the surrounding country, and heavy discharges of musketry were distinctly heard. Alarm and confusion now prevailed throughout the town, and the women, children, and old men, made the best of their way to the fort, the area of which they soon filled, after which the gates were closed. The volleys of musketry were advancing very fast, and the Fantees were retreating in great disorder: one or two great guns were fired over the town with a view to impel terror on the assailants, but they were too much elated with hopes of conquest, and too resolute to be affrighted: about eleven o'clock the musket balls were heard to whistle in every part of the fort, and the Ashantees entered the town in every direction, pursuing the vanquished to the beach, where the slaughter was great.

The Annamaboes conceived, that with the aid of their canoes and their knowledge of swimming, they should be able to escape, but they were pursued too closely by the Ashantees, whose fury appeared to be insatiable; men, women, and children were followed by indiscriminate destruction. During this work of carnage, the Governor was very active with his small garrison to repel the assailants; a twenty-four pounder, that pointed along the beach to the westward, several times discharged grape-shot among them, whereby vast numbers must have fallen: a three-pounder likewise, which flanked the gate on the east side was frequently fired with grape, notwithstanding fresh parties came on much quicker than they could be repelled; and at length they came under the walls for the purpose of carrying away the women who could not be received into the fort. About this period the Governor* was wounded in two places; one ball struck his

---

* Mr. White, who, after an absence of twenty seven years from his native country, expired a few hours after he landed in it.

mouth and carried away four of his teeth, another ball passed through his left arm; and nearly at the same time an officer and two men were wounded, and one man killed.

Things assumed now a more serious and dangerous aspect than was apprehended, and gave the garrison a strong assurance of the disposition of the enemy, who, it was evident, intended to bend his utmost efforts against the fort. The Ashantees were confident that by gaining possession of it, a large booty would be obtained. However, the small number which composed the garrison of Annamaboe at this period, consisting of Governor White, Messieurs Meredith, Swanzy, Smith, and Baines; also four free mulattoes and twenty men, including soldiers, artificers, and servants, were confident of the severity of their situation. The walls being high, and accurately flanked, and the gates sound and well barricadoed; the Governor, from the nature of his wounds, from great debility in consequence of much effusion of blood, being constrained to retire, and the command of the fort having devolved on the senior officer, who perceiving that the cannon in one quarter could not be used with effect, for the enemy fired with such precision as to cut off every man who was exposed at an embrasure, depended solely on the musket; and another man having been killed about noon, and two more wounded:—the garrison was now reduced to the small number of eight, including officers, who could be depended upon, and the Ashantees were using every effort to force the western gate; but were twice repulsed with no small loss. A third time they attempted it, and endeavoured to apply fire to the gate; but the man who brought the materials for that purpose, extinguished the fire by falling a corpse upon it. In all their attempts they were defeated with musketry alone, and notwithstanding that their efforts to gain an entrance into the fort proved ineffectual, the contest was continued till six o'clock. After this cessation, and before total darkness came on, the garrison used all possible energy in repairing injuries, and preparing for the defensive, in case of hostilities being renewed in the night.

On the following day a scene replete with the horrors of war exhibited itself:—heaps of dead and wounded around the walls, and for a mile along the eastern shore, tossed about by a violent surf:—houses unroofed, and others on fire:—the sorrowful countenances of the old men, who sought refuge in the fort; the mournful lamentations of the women, and the pitiable cries of the children, presented a picture of exquisite feeling and of the greatest distress! Of the number the town contained, and which we will calculate to have been at least fifteen thousand souls, we may suppose that two-thirds of that number perished. The fort afforded refuge to about two thousand of every description, and about two hundred escaped to a rock surrounded by the sea, and at pistol-shot from the beach, where they remained unmolested, and notwithstanding the vigilance of the Ashantees, we may suppose that two or three thousand effected their escape. Without going into further enquiry, we may venture to state that eight thousand Fantees were destroyed; and although they were attacked by at least three times their number, yet if they were actuated by one-third of the bravery of their opponents, they would have committed some execution, and doubtless would have checked that intrepidity and ardour which were so pre-eminently conspicuous in their enemy. Their resistance was very feeble; terror seized them at the commencement of the attack, and it impressed them so forcibly, that the sea formed but an indifferent barrier to their precipitate flight.

When the fury of the Ashantees against the Fantees was a little diminished, they turned part of their force against the fort with great coolness and resolution, advancing with shouts expressive of their loyalty and courage, to the very muzzles of the guns. At the east side of the fort, two three pounders, which were well served, destroyed numbers of them with every discharge of grape: but at the west side, the cannon which flanked the gate could not be rendered useful, in consequence of advantages the enemy possessed, and which were not to be found on the opposite quarter, where the musket alone was to be dependended upón: and we have the authority of the gentleman who commanded (after Mr. White was wounded) of stating, that he and another officer (Mr. Swanzy) fired nearly three hundred rounds of ball-cartridge in keeping the gate clear, and protecting those who were under the walls. Mr. Swanzy was so injured with the recoil of his musket, that he could not use his right arm for some days without much pain, and the other officer (Mr. Meredith) was nearly in the same state.

What loss the Ashantees sustained cannot be precisely laid down: the King, prior to his departure from Annamaboe, said, he lost three thousand men: but in that number he probably included those who were carried off by disease. His men however suffered very severely; for their approach was made with such large bodies, that twenty, thirty, or perhaps more, fell with every discharge of grape-shot; and the musket not only killed, but very often wounded at the same time, so close were the enemy.

At this period (the 16th of June,) the fort was in an awkward state,—clompletely blockaded on the land-side, and a very imperfect communication by sea, and only a few weeks provisions for the number it contained; add to which, the effluvia from the dead bodies, which were approaching fast to a putrid state, excited very uneasy apprehensions. These circumstances demanded some extraordinary effort, which the garrison, from its weakness, could not attempt. Every person, from great exertion and constant exposure to a vertical sun on the 15th, and from solicitude and want of rest, was much fatigued. Nevertheless things wore a more promising appearance; whenever plunder was attempted, which now and then was the case, it met with resistance. There was not, however, any desire manifested by the Ashantees to renew hostilities, and every motion indicated a wish for peace. The garrison too was very desirous of such an event, but did not wish to be the first to yield, or to offer any terms without orders from the chief-governor. The King, from his late successes, had a high opinion of his power and the bravery of his army. On the other hand the small garrison, notwithstanding its reduced state, had no mean opinion of itself, and wished to confirm in his Majesty an idea of the superior skill of Europeans.

The Governor at Cape Coast was apprised of the state of affairs at Annamaboe, and lost no time in sending assistance. Two ships were provided for the purpose, which sailed from the Cape on the morning of the 16th: but, from unavoidable circumstances, the re-inforcement the ships brought could not be landed before four o'clock in the afternoon. This re-inforcement consisted of twelve men and four officers; and their arrival in the fort afforded much satisfaction. This party was landed under cover of the smoke of some heavy guns, and was not fired at; but the canoe, on returning, was fired upon and one man wounded. It was the Governor's order that a flag of truce should be sent to the King, to endeavour to bring about an amicable understanding. A white flag was accordingly lowered over the wall, accompanied with the national colours; and when the emblem of peace was observed, it is impossible to express sufficiently the joy that diffused itself among the people: the multitude which crowded around the flags was inconceivably great, and it was with difficulty that the King's officers, who were known by golden swords and axes, could clear the way leading to his quarters: the air resounded with acclamations in praise of their King, and expressive of their satisfaction at the prospects of peace.

And here we cannot forbear remarking, that although the Ashantees are so remote from polished or civilized nations, they seem not to be unacquainted with the customs of a civilized people, as they are connected with the rules of war; for they paid every respect to the flag of truce: a few indeed of them were making towards the rock on which were a number of Fantees, but they well understood the signal of recall, when a musket or two were fired over their heads. The flag of truce returned about seven o'clock, with three messengers from the King; and they, in order to justify the King for his proceedings against the Fantees, entered into a long detail of the origin of the war, which we have been attempting to describe. The King was pleased that the flag of truce was sent, and expressed his satisfaction by giving the two soldiers who were the bearers of it a fat sheep. After a conference that continued beyond two hours, the messengers departed.

A communication was thus established with the King and his army; but it was considered prudent to keep the gates closed until a perfect understanding was effected. It appeared, however, that this could not be done, without a meeting between the chief Governor and the King. To accomplish this Mr. Meredith tried to persuade the King to go to Cape Coast, but in this he was disappointed; he however gained his Majesty's consent to send some of his confidential and chief men to wait upon the Governor, and to hear his sentiments.

It will, we doubt not, be gratifying to the reader, if we here subjoin the correspondence between Mr. Meredith and Mr. Torrane, the Governor in Chief, on this occasion.

Annamaboe Fort, June 17, 1807.

SIR,

MR. WHITE directs me to acknowledge the receipt of your letter to the Governor of Elmina. The state Mr. White is in, being much weakened with loss of blood and other causes, prevented him paying that attention to your letters which they demanded, and my duty was such, that I could not spare a moment to write you fully. I had a conference with three of the King's messengers last night, and at this instant there are two men with his Majesty; when they return, you shall be acquainted with the result. I have already mentioned to the King that Cheboo would be given up, and if it was agreeable for him to send his cane, and one or two of his gold-headed swords, I would engage their security by going to Cape Coast with them. The message received from the King was of a favourable tendency; and I trust he will perceive the expediency of putting an end to this sanguinary war. Be assured we are all so employed on various duties, it debars me more particularly of giving you a further detail of our proceedings. But I trust, by a messenger this evening, to relate fully every circumstance attending this very severe contest. The party were landed in safety, viz. twelve privates, one corporal, with Messrs. Bold, Galloway, and Woolbert. Both ships will remain here until to-morrow. I am well pleased with the attention and assistance afforded us by Captain Coley.

I am, &c.

HENRY MEREDITH.

Colonel Torrane, Governor in Chief, &c. &c. &c.
    Cape Coast Castle.

Annamaboe Fort, June 17, 1807.

SIR,

I WROTE you this morning, acknowledging the receipt of your letters, and, agreeably to my intentions then, I take the liberty of stating more particularly the occurrences in this garrison on the 15th and subsequent to it. I beg leave to remind you, that we were prepared for any attack that might be made upon us, by any body of men unaccustomed to the shock of artillery; and I believe Mr. White assured you of the confidence he placed in the officers and men under his command, and every soul was animated with a desire to do his duty.

[Here follows a description of the battle as before related.]

The re-inforcement you was pleased to send, got on shore without any opposition about four o'clock P. M.; and I assure you we were very glad to receive them, as, from the severe duty we had undergone the preceding day, we were much cut up by fatigue. About six P. M. the flag of truce, with a corporal and private from the detachment you sent, were conveyed to the King; and as they proceeded, they were warmly greeted by the Ashantees. The message the King returned was modest; he said, it was not his intention to commence hostilities with the fort, nor to distress any of the whites; his enemies were the Assins and Fantees, and he now conceived his anger against them pretty well assuaged. This morning (17th) according to agreement, his messengers came, and said, that the King wished to see the same person that conveyed the flag of truce, that they might hear from his own lips what he had to deliver. Accordingly I sent them with Dutton, a man of quick understanding, to hear more particularly the sentiments of his Majesty. After remaining some time hearing the opinion of his counsellors they returned, and after some preliminary discourse, they informed me that the King had deputed six of his principal men, with six deputed by the men of power in his train, to repair to Cape Coast to hear what you have to say, and to negotiate. In course of their communication the King deplored the number of lives that were lost in consequence of the fire from the fort.

As the messengers mean to repair to Cape Coast, I will forbear relating every particular. The King seemed to say that he must have those who sought protection in the fort: this he only hinted at, and probably the same may be hinted to you; but in giving them up, we ought to be assured of their being used kindly. I send a canoe with this, and have agreed with the messengers, that you will send canoes and a guard for their protection. Mr. White's travelling canoe is in good order, therefore be pleased to send eleven canoe-men for her. This canoe, with three more from the Cape, will, in my opinion, be fully sufficient to convey the whole twelve messengers with their guard. The number of persons here are reducing our provisions very fast, and if not removed soon, some of them will be most likely starved, or will be the cause of some serious malady: the sooner we are rid of them the better. But if you can gain their protection, it will be a humane act. Mr. White, who I am happy to say is in a fair way, desires his respects.

I am, &c.

(Signed) HENRY MEREDITH.

Colonel Torrane, Governor in Chief,
 &c. &c. &c.

SIR,

BOTH your letters of yesterday's date I have received; the latter has given me particular satisfaction, not only as it affords every prospect that this war will be terminated, but also as it removes great anxiety from my mind respecting the state of Mr. White's wounds. The assurances you now give me that he is in a fair way of recovery, are highly gratifying. I dispatch eleven canoe-men for Mr. White's canoe; and I also send three other canoes. I trust the King will appoint persons of sufficient consequence to negotiate with me: I have an earnest wish to see the King: make this desire known to him; tell him I think it may essentially lead to the arrangement of affairs of much importance; that I have greatly to deplore with him this war; that although these events cannot always be guarded against, they may even ultimately bring future good consequences; and herein I think much depends on our meeting. Assure the King, that notwithstanding the steps I have taken to give protection to the Fantees, I have ever held him in the highest respect, from the many reports I have heard of him, and that, had I seen any messenger from him antecedent to his attack on Annamaboe, I am of opinion we should have avoided the blow in that quarter. The King I understand to be a man of strong mind: it will naturally suggest itself to him, that a meeting between us may be of vast importance to the country. Assure him I have too high a consideration for my own character, as well as his consequence, to suffer the smallest indignity to be offered to him; that if he will come to the castle I shall be proud to shew him every honour, and that I will give every possible security for his personal safety. I have apartments ready for him, and officers shall be sent to attend him here. On receipt of this, send your accustomed messenger to the King, saying, that you have a letter from me, and that an officer will wait personally on him to explain the contents. This officer with this letter in his hand, you will send (say Mr. F. L. Swanzy) as early as you shall receive the King's reply. I know not whether you have a good flag for the occasion; I therefore send one. Mr. F. L. Swanzy will have two flag-bearers, one with a white flag, the other carrying the union; and he will be very particular in explaining every part of this letter, and do his utmost to persuade the King to visit the Cape. He may also add, that a ship can be procured, if he (the King) prefers coming that way, and that an officer of distinction shall be sent to accompany him. In a few words, Mr. F. L. Swanzy will do his utmost to persuade the King to visit the castle. An officer should come here, with the guard you send to protect the messengers. You must let me know of what consequence the messengers are, that I may treat them accordingly, and this it will be advisable to acquaint me of before their arrival.

I am, &c.

(Signed)   GEORGE TORRANE.

To Henry Meredith, Esq.

Although these men proceeded to the Cape, it was found that nothing important could be transacted without an interview with the King, and for this purpose Colonel Torrane was obliged to go to Annamaboe, and a day was fixed for a conference. To give as favourable and as respectable an opinion as possible of the British, a number of articles as presents were sent to the King, and as many officers and soldiers as the service could afford, were assembled to attend the Governor on the day appointed; but previous to those preparations, and a few days after the flag of truce was received by the King,

Cheboo (one of the men who was the cause of the war) was secured by the Governor at Cape Coast and sent to Annamaboe, to be delivered up to the King, in expectation that any further effusion of blood would be prevented, and that it would be the means of saving the Fantees from entire destruction.   These benevolent purposes were not realized: the King had proceeded so far in the war, that he could not recede without displeasing those auxiliaries he had with him, and who expected a vast deal of plunder; and besides, Apontay and Acoom were again in arms, and collecting all the Fantees they could to oppose the King's progress.   On the day appointed for the interview, the Governor and his party were put in motion, and although the procession was not very numerous, it was arranged with taste, and made no despicable appearance.   About twenty of the Company's artificers, habited in a neat manner, marched in front; a guard of forty men, and a band of music followed them; next walked the Governor, followed by ten officers, two and two, and some gentlemen traders (who were enticed from the Cape by curiosity), brought up the rear.   When the procession had got a short distance it was met by a principal man, who was sent by the King to conduct the Governor, and to keep off the multitude, which was assembling in great numbers, some of whom had never seen a white man. Notwithstanding the authority of this person, and the exertions of his attendants, the curiosity of the people was so great that every avenue was crowded; which, by preventing the circulation of air, augmented the natural heat of the day, and this inconvenience was farther increased by the putrid smell from the dead bodies, and the vast swarm of flies.   The Governor was obliged to visit each man of rank, before he could be received by the King; a ceremony that could not be prudently denied, and which occupied some time: for those men had their several courts, and collectively had formed an extensive circle.   Every one of them was seated under a huge umbrella, surrounded by attendants and guards, with young persons employed in fanning the air and dispersing the flies, which were numerous and troublesome.   One of those men and his attendants excited some curiosity and attention: his dress and appearance were so different from those of the others, that it evidently proved he must have come from countries situated a considerable distance inland.   He was a tall, athletic, and rather corpulent man, of a complexion resembling an Arab or an Egyptian.   His dress was heavy, and by no means adapted to the climate.   He wore a cap that came down below his ears, and being made of yellow cloth, it did not contribute to diminish his tawny complexion.   He was a follower of the Mohammedan religion, possessed much gravity; but was communicative, condescending, and agreeable.   He had about him a great number of sentences from the Alkoran, which were carefully incased in gold and silver, and upon which he set a high value.   He was a native of Kassina, a country that appears to be situated to the south of east from Tombuctou.   He said he had been at Tunis and at Mecca; had seen many white men and ships, and described the method of travelling over the great desert.   This person commanded a body of men who fought with arrows, as well as muskets: four of the arrows were found in the fort; they were short and pointed with barbed iron. He had many persons in his train who were of the same colour, but varied a little as to dress: they were all habited in the Turkish manner, but did not wear turbans. After the ceremony of visiting those persons was over, the Governor was conducted towards the King, who was surrounded by a number of attendants, whose appearance bore evident signs of riches and authority: chains, stools, axes, swords, flutes, message-canes, &c. were either of solid gold, or richly adorned with that metal: those dazzling appearances, added to damask, taffety, and other rich dresses, gave a splendour to the scene highly interesting. When the Governor approached the King, and when an interchange of compliments had passed, the air resounded with the noise of musical instruments, such as drums, horns, and flutes. After some conversation, during which much politeness was observed in the behaviour of the King, the Governor wished this ceremonial visit to be returned; which was agreed to, and a convenient place was found to receive the King and his train. The Governor, his officers, and attendants, were formed in a half-circle, and seated under the shade of some trees, and a passage of sufficient breadth was formed by the soldiers for the King and his attendants to pass through. It was full two hours before his Majesty was announced, so numerous was his train. Each man of rank, as he advanced, paid the necessary compliments agreeably to the custom of his country, and then filed off. It was previously directed, that the King should be received with arms presented and the grenadiers march when passing the soldiers. This mark of distinction and respect appeared to give him much satisfaction: he halted to observe the orderly behaviour and uniform appearance of the soldiers; and the martial air that was playing, seemed to produce the most agreeable sensations on his mind. The writer had an opportunity of seeing this man. He was of the middle size, well formed, and perfectly black, with regular features and an open and pleasing countenance. His manner indicated understanding and was adorned with gracefulness; and in all respects he exceeded the expectations of every person. His dress was plain: it consisted of a piece of silk wrapt loosely about him; a wreath of green silk ornamented his head: his sandals were neatly made, and curiously studded with gold. He was not distinguished by any gold ornaments, as his attendants were. One man who was dressed in a grotesque manner, and who appeared to act the buffoon, was, literally, loaded with gold.

As this was a visit of ceremony, no business of consequence was transacted. The King politely enquired after Mr. White, and expressed a hope that he would soon be well of his wounds. He said he would move from Annamaboe soon, as his army felt ill effects from the water, and from the dead bodies. After this visit, every confidence was placed in the King and his army, and as the gates were now opened, a free admittance was allowed: various conferences of a favourable nature were carried on between both parties;

but peace with the Fantees was considered impracticable. Apoutay had escaped the King's vigilance; and Acoom was at the head of a strong party, and marching towards Annamaboe to give the King battle. The King assured the Governor, that after he had subdued his enemies to leeward, he would return to Annamaboe for the purpose of making arrangements relative to the future welfare of the country, and the regulations of trade.

It was agreed, that those residing under British forts, provided they observed a neutrality, should not be molested, and that every respect should be paid to the British flag. The Governor likewise procured the release of those who sought refuge in the fort, although the King contested his right to them; for this reason, that as he destroyed the town, he had a claim to every person and to every thing belonging to it. On report of Acoom being in arms and making preparations to attack the Ashantees, the King ordered his army to collect and march to meet him. Two days subsequent to the King's departure (3d July,) Acoom's party and the advanced guard of the Ashantee's met; a battle was the consequence, which ended in the defeat of Acoom, who, with his party, would have been cut off, if a river, that was in their rear, had not favoured their flight; the fordable parts of which were known to them, but not to the Ashantees. After this defeat, the King's enemies dared not shew themselves in the field in any force; they however supported a kind of predatory warfare, and were sometimes successful in cutting off small foraging parties, As the Ashantees proceeded to leeward, desolation accompanied them; almost every town and village were laid in ruins; but disease, which got among them at Annamaboe, and which spread rapidly, carried off vast numbers. This unexpected calamity altered the King's intentions: he could not return to Annamaboe without risking the loss of his whole army; prudence therefore directed him to face towards his kingdom, leaving at Accra a sufficient force to dispose of prisoners, and to convey them in safety to Ashantee.

Cheboo and Apoutay, who appeared inseparable friends at the commencement of this war, and throughout it, fled to Cape Coast with about five hundred followers, as soon as they perceived the Ashantees approaching towards Annamaboe, on the 15th of June. The Cape Coast people were willing to afford them protection and assistance, but. when the Governor heard how things were at Annamaboe, he warned them of the danger; and advised them to be neutral. When an account arrived at Cape Coast of the desperate attack made on Annamaboe fort, the Governor came to the resolution of securing, if possible, both these men, and delivering them up to the King as the most probable means of not only putting an end to the war, but of securing the King's friendship. A party was accordingly selected for that purpose; but Apoutay, after a warm contest, wherein some were killed on both sides, effected his escape. Cheboo was not so fortunate; he was secured and sent to the King, as we have already mentioned; his followers too made a precipitate flight, leaving behind them some bulky articles, among which were the whole of Cheboo's regalia, which were carefully lodged for the King; and it had the effect on his disposition that was intended; it gave a favourable opinion of the British, and assured him of the Governor's friendship, and at the same time it abated the desire he encouraged, to be revenged for the loss his army had sustained on the 15th. For he concerted a design to attempt the fort by storm, and Wednesday the 17th was the day appointed for this enterprise. The plan was not badly arranged, and was to be conducted in the following manner. Six thousand men were to be selected; half of them destined not only to mount the walls, but to apply a quantity of gunpowder under them; the explosion from which was expected to shake the fort very much, and likewise to create such a confusion within as to cause the garrison to be off its guard; the other half were to keep up a continued firing. The plan was averted by the prudent policy of the Chief Governor, not only by his securing Cheboo, but by his alacrity in demanding a truce, whereby the King's resentment was cooled, and his inclinations diverted towards pacific measures.

APPENDIX. No. II.

Translations of a Manuscript descriptive of Mr. Park's Death.

Mr. Salame's Translation.

[The words in italics, so distinguished at that Gentleman's request, not being in the original.]

A literal translation of a Declaration, written in a corrupted Arabic, from the town of Yaúd in the interior of Africa.

In the name of God the Merciful and the Munificent.

This Declaration is issued from the town called (1) Yaúd in the Country of Kossa (2).—We (the writer,) do witness the *following* case; (statement.) We never saw, nor heard of the sea (River) called (4) Koodd; but we sat to hear (understood) the voice (report) of some persons *saying*, " We saw a ship, equal to her we never saw before; and the King of Yaúd had sent plenty of every kind

Mr. Jackson's Translation.

[Of this Gentleman's considerate politeness in anticipating my wishes by a spontaneous offer to translate this MS., I shall have occasion to repeat my acknowledgments in the Geographical Appendix.]

In the name of God the ..Merciful and Clement.

This Narrative proceeds from the territory in Housa (2) called (1) Eeauree. *We observed* an extraordinary event or circumstance (3,) *but we neither saw nor heard of the River which is called* (4) *Kude*, and as we were sitting, we heard the voice of children and *we saw a vessel* the like to which in size we never saw before ; and, *we saw* the King of Eeauree send cattle and sheep, and a variety of vegetables in great abundance: and there were two men and one

(1) Sir William Ouseley (who very obligingly communicated a hurried translation from Crickhowel, although the original had been but two hours in his possession) read this Yaur or Yaúur.

(2) Sir Wm. writes Husa or Haousa: the latter is occasionally the Moorish pronunciation, but Houssa is invariably the negro. I certainly never once heard that Houssa included Yawoorie, which has a distinct Sovereign, who is mentioned in the MS. : Perhaps it may be accounted for, from Yawoorie being one of the seven kingdoms tributary to Houssa or Mallowa.

(3) Mr. Jackson has preserved this apparent contradiction in his fidelity to the original, according to his reading. He considers, it may be reconciled by presuming that the writer only saw the vessel pass Yawoorie, and did not wit-

ness the ultimate catastrophe at Boussa, where he imagines the river may first receive the name of Kude, as African rivers frequently have a different name in every country through which they flow. This interpretation does not make the writer a mere reporter as in the other translation, but a witness of all that happened at Yawoorie, although not afterwards. I never understood the river to have any other name than Quorra or Quolla, from Shego to Foör, yet of this we ought not to feel positive.

(4) It is very extraordinary that the name of the Quolla should always be written Kude, Koad, or Koada, and that Mr. Hutchison, who was learning Arabic of the Moors, in Ashantee, should be taught to write and pronounce as Quolla, the same Arabic word which every European proficient reads as above. I cannot help

of food, with cows and sheep; *There* were two men, one woman, two male slaves and two maids in the ship; (5,) *The* two white men *were* derived from the race (*sect*) of Nassri; (Christ or Christianity.) The King of Yaúd asked them to come out to him; (to land (6); and they refused coming out, (landing,) and they went to the *King of the* Country of (7) Bassa, who is greater than the King of Yaúd; And *while* they *were* sitting in the ship and gaining a position (rounding) over the Cape of Koodd, and *were* in society with the people of the King of Bassa, the ship reached (struck) a-head of Mountain which took (destroyed) *her* away, (8) and the men and women of Bassa all together, with every kind of arms; (goods); And the ship could find no way to avoid the mountain; And the man who *was* in the ship, killed his wife, and threw all his property into the Sea, (River), and *then* they threw themselves *also* from fear (9): Afterwards

woman, and two slaves, and *they tied or fastened them in the vessel.* (5)

There were also in the vessel, two white men of the race called Christians (N'sarrah) and the Sultan of Eeauree called aloud to them to come out of the vessel (6,) but they would not.

They proceeded to the country of Busa, which is greater than that of the Sultan of Eeauree, and as they were setting in the vessel, they hung or were stopped, by the Cape or Head Land of Kude (7.)

And the people of the Sultan of Busa called to them, and poured their arms into the vessel, and the vessel reached the head-land or cliff, and became attached or fixed to the head of the mountain, and could not pass it. Then the men and women of Busa collected themselves hostilely together, with arms of all descriptions, when the vessel being unable to clear or pass the Cape, the man in the vessel

thinking that, from bad writing, ignorance, or perhaps some occidental difference, the *d* is put for the *l*, * and that it should be Kule or Koala, especially as there appears to be a town called Kula on its banks, (see routes in Appendix) which comes very close to Kulla, Mr. Brown's river. The identity of the Quolla and Kulla, seems confirmed by Mr. Dupuis reading the name of the kingdom, as written by the Moors, Koora, which seems as if they had written it for once, according to the negro pronunciation, (Quorra,) for as I have observed (p. 196) that the negroes always substitute r for the Moorish *l* (a defect also characterising a dialect of the Coptic, the Chayma, the Tamanack, &c. &c., and common, as Baron Humboldt observes, to every zone) Koora becomes Koola, for the same reason which the Quorra of the negroes was always

pronounced Quolla by the Moors; and Koola, it will be allowed, is very near to Mr. Brown's Kulla.

(5) Mr. Jackson writes وعقدان في السفينة Uakkadan fee sfeena, i. e. and tied or bound them in the vessel or ship, " adding, that he is at a loss to imagine how it can have been converted into "two maids in the ship."* Sir Wm., however, in his hurried notice, rendered it ' female slaves.'

(6) " Invited (or entertained them) until they left him," Sir Wm.

(7) Sir William, in his hurried perusal, read this, " and went on to the country of Besa, and (the Sultan of) this country is greater than the Sultan of Yaour: there they settled or halted, above Ras (Cape) Koumen. The people belonging to the Sultan of Besa saw the boat,

* I recollect one, but only one instance of the negroes substituting *d* for the Moorish *l*, which was in Toppodo for Toppollo, a town of Bornoo.

* *Ockdan fi ássafinat*, means either " *Two maids,* or *two female slaves,* in the ship," and no otherwise.—A. S.

they took one *out of the* water till the news reached the town of Kanji (10,) the country of the King of Wawí, and the King of Wawí heard of it, he buried him in his earth, (grave), and the other we have not seen (11); perhaps he is in the bottom of the water."—And God knows best. Authentic from the mouth of Sherif Abrahim.—Finis.

killed his wife (9) and threw the whole of her property into the river: they then threw themselves into the river, fear seizing them (the news of this occurrence was then conveyed to the Sultan Wawee) until it reached by water the territory of Kanjee (10,) in the country of the Sultan Wawee, and we buried it (a male body) in its earth, and one of them, we saw not at all in the water (11,) and God knows the truth of this report. From the mouth of the Shereef Ibrahim.—The end.

and they went into the boat, and it reached the Mountain Cape, (or Headland,) and was there stopped."

(9) " And *the man who was* * in the boat slew his woman (امرأة) and threw every article of his property into the river, and then cast *themselves* into the river through fear.

* I translate this in the singular, yet afterwards, there seems a confusion with the plural." Sir Wm. This act, which appears very improbable, and which I never heard of in the oral accounts which I received whilst in Coomassie, (Diary, p. 91) if it was committed, must have been by Lieut. Martyn, recollecting the difference of his and Mr. Park's dispositions, and Amadi Fatouma's anecdote of the former wishing to kill him for preventing him from firing any more at the people of the King Gotoijege. I should observe here, that Amadi Fatouma's *Poul* nation can be

no other than the Fillani, (p. 207) the Fullan of Ben Ali, for though it has been translated Poul, there is no *p* in the Arabic, and the Moors in Ashantee always wrote *f* for the negro *p*, as *fon* for *pon*. As Col. Maxwell merely observes in his letter, that " Isaaco's Arabic Journal was translated into English, by a person resident in Senegal, who probably had but an ordinary or colloquial knowledge of Arabic, it is to be regretted that the original was not transmitted with it, as a more careful perusal of it by Sir William Ouseley or some Arabic scholar in England, would probably reconcile the two accounts, at least in the names of places, if not in the circumstances, more than they can be from the translation remitted.

(10) See note; p. 202.

(11) " And the other did not,——from the violence of the water."—Sir Wm.

I have sent the original MS. to the African Association, the following is Mr. Jackson's transcript of it. I regret that Mr. Salamé did not also furnish a transcript of this MS.

بسم الله الرحمن الرحيم

هذه الوثيقه خرج من بلد حوسا يقال يّور و نحن راينا الامر لم نري ولا نسمع في البحر الذي يقال كوض انما نحن جلسنا نسمع عانح صبيان لرايت السفينه لم نري مثله قط فارسل سلطان يور لرايته مع البقر و الكبس مع انواع الطعام كثير دهما رجلان وامراة واحدة والعبدان و عقدان في السفينة رجلان بيضان خرجوا من نسب نصري و يدعودو سلطان يور الي ان خرجوا اليه و ابوا خروج و مشوا الي بلد بسا وهوا كبر من سلطان يور و هم يجلسون ويعلكون ملوك

علي راس كُوض و يصاخور اهل سلطان بسُا لرايته و هم ركوب في السفينة بلغ السفينة
راس جبل وياخد الجبل السفينة و رجال بُسا و النساه بسا يجمعون كلهم مع انواع السلاح
والسفينة لم يجد طريق المنع الجبل ورجل الدي في السفينة قتل امراته وري ماله كله في البحر
وروموا نفسهما في البحر لخوف ثم ياخدوا بلغ خير الي سلطان واوي حتي بلغ ماه به الي بلد
كنجي بلد سلطان وأوي ودفنه في ترابه وواحد منهما لم نره اقل في قهر الماه والله اعلم صح
في فم شريف ابراهيم * تمت *

APPENDIX. No. III.

ROUTES.

1.
To Dwabin.
Seepa
Marmpon
Pakooroo
Aquooquamong
Okimdaia
Weterkroom
Bunkooroo
Boomfeea
Kinnesoo

2.
To Quaoo.
1. Assiempong
2. Thro' Amoom R. to Oseemadoo
3. Obogoo,
Frontier Quaoo town.
4. Adumpong, the Government of the C. Coast Captain
5. Assebanasoo
6. Minidasoo,
Famous for Palm Oil.
7. Assoona
8. Wantomo

3.
To Accra.
1. Odossoo
3. Kroofoofroom,
Two hours from the lake.

4. Obirribee,
The 1st Akim town
5. Assinee
6. Over Boosempra to Gawasee
7. Meeasee
8. Monasa
9. Over the Aninnee, (rising in a hill called Quomshoo, 1 day to the W.) on a tree
10. Ashoosoo
11. Aquapong
12. Over Birrim to Measa
13. Asheeaqua
14. Kookrantoom
15. Aguiesso
16. Marmpon and Aboödee,
Visited by Issert, who calls it 24 miles from Christiansburg Castle.

4.
To Accra.
1. Ashiedumpong
2. Assaboo
3. Assuennie
5. Antarranaï
6. Ammoonoom
7. Akropong
9. Abirriwantoo
10. Aradntem

11. Kookrantoom
13. Aguiesso.

5.
To Elmina.
1. Thro' the towns Akasee, Kankawasee, Odasoo, Adiabin, Asakkraka, Adoonko, Agafrompon, to Adoomasa
2. Fiasee, Bonechumay, Asanasoo, to Becquoi
3. Inshuentem, (between waters) Abimpingua, to Atobiasee
4. Thro' Hoomassie, Assekosoo, Edoomassie, Akoorkerry, Akotokee, Yankeren, to Abateä, the frontier town of Dankara
5. Thro' Sewootcrasee, (put your head lower) Aboposoo, the frontier Tufel town, to Ensuaguesoo, (woman's town) the capital of Tufel
6. Morobim
7. Thro' Akoontarrem, (the 1st Warsawtown) Amodai, over Bopoquaw, (a high hill where there was formerly a large croom, now deserted) & Apachamba, to Kaïrakoo

8. Over Pra to Demamba
9. Dadiasoo
10. Asseecooma, Abannasoo, Abrädi, Elmina, or, as the natives call it, Addĭna.

6.
To Dankara.
1. Dakoon
2. Terrabooom, the frontier town of Dankara
3. Thro' Mosiasoo to Enquanta
4. Thro' Ofoo, Amasoo, to Dankara.

7.
To Buntookoo.
1. Barree * or to Passaroo
2. Beamasoo,
or to Dooniantiffee
3. Ensoota
4. Quanta
5. Across Tando,
to Odomassee
6. Suaterree
7. Birrakoomee
8. Yammee
9. Kirribeeö
10. Kickiwerree
11. Buntookoo

* When *or* appears between two names, it means that each town is equally close to the path, and indifferently visited.

8.
To Banda.
1. Tafoo
2. Ofeesoo
3. Abofoo
4. Kinkawasoo
5. Akomada
6. Tandosoo
7. Koontoosoo
8. Takima
9. Weäkee
10. Aousa
11. Soko
12. Namasa
13. Coransoo
14. Bimma
15. Banda

9.
To Boopee.
1. Esansoo, or Medina
2. Through Ofim, which rises close to the E. to

Bümsoo or Akimakasie
3. Soodroo
4. Takimenteä, or Quamang
5. Akommadeä, or Boomang
6. Boisoo
7. Coranza
8. Boibin
9. Koonquoontee
10. Dawdaw
11. Akrofroom
12. Oboosmosoo
13. Moboäsoo
14. On the path
15. Over Adirri
16. Boopee

10.
To Sallagha.
1. Marmpon
2. Aphwaguiasee

3 Gammasee a fetish temple
4. Akrofroom
5. Intonnasoo (Cloth Town)
6. Quanasee or Troabirree
7. Agwoona
8. Adoogan
9. Over rivers and mountains to Aguirra, or Poorra
10. Through Sennee to Amanting
11. Pattooda
12. Atoboboo
13. Weasee
14. Pannangha
15. Yadjee
16. Over Adirri to Sallagha

11.
To Source of Sennee.
1. Agamachasee

2. Aboiman
3. Yatirrim
4. Owceamasee
5. Anyanasue
6. Assekadoomasee

12.
To Odentee ferry.
1. Kokoofoo
2. Guia
3. Weeäsee
4. Bassa
5. Tarrisoo
6. Over Sennee, to ferry

13.
From Yahndi to Daboia
1. Through Patinga to Duetuem
2. Tampeūn
3. Through Nantong to Kompoongo
4. Through Boö to Dindinno
5. Daboia

Large Towns on the Route from Boornoo to Oongoora.

Deeagarra	Zogogdo	Goozirrinkoorra
Digza	Doobba	Dumgabalo
Gellaroo	Toppollo, or Toppodo	Potuskum, or Kuskum
Rakah		Dawaso
Zaghgah	Garaga	Woodbo
Ariggum	Gaskaia	Gummo
Madellarie	Matchella	Zega

Adagia, Mallagee, and Katanga, lay between Oongoora, and Kassina.

Towns adjoining, or laying close to the right and left of the above Route.

Serrakeelaia	Goobilwa	Danga
Dakum	Gobookalashee	Likhalalie
Lismaroo	Dazakou	Looha

The following transcripts of the most intelligible of the MSS. I brought, according to the different readings, with the Negro pronunciation as it was familiar to me in Ashantee, will show how careless or incapable the Moors are of writing the names of Negro kingdoms accurately.

according to the expression of the natives. The original MSS. will be sent to the African Association, to whom I had hoped to present the interesting itinerary of Shereef Brahima from Dagwumba to Mecca, but this valuable MS. which it had cost me so much pains to procure, after being kept three months by one gentleman before he discovered that he had not time to translate it, was lost or mislaid by another in the course of doing so, and I have the mortification of being unable to submit any other than the mere skeleton of it. See Geography, p. 205.

CHART No. I.

Course of the Niger or Quolla (by a Houssa Moor.)

Negro pronunciation.	Mr. Jackson's reading and transcript.		Mr. Dupuis' reading and transcript.	
Gebowa			Gebawa	جباو
Toro Jollabi	Futa Jelua	فوت جلوا	Foota Joolaba	فوت جلوب
Fota Tora	Futa Tura	فوت طور	Foota Tooroo	فوت طور
Hasoo	Kassua	خصوا	Khassoua	خصوا
Jaoona	Jāun	جعون	Jafoona	جفون
Gammoe	G⁻remua	غموا	Ghemoua	غموا .
Mallaia	Maly Faly	ملي فلي	Malia	ملي
Shego	Shag⁻ru	شاغ	Shagho	شاغ
Sansandin	Sansandia	سنسندي	Sansandia	سنسندي
Jennie	Janni	جان	Jinnie	جان
Mashina	Masheena	ماشن	Mashena	ماشين
Jimballa	G⁻rimbala	غمبل	*Ghimballa	غمبل

(G⁻r nearest sound to غ.)

Negro pronunciation.	Mr. Jackson's reading and transcript.		Mr. Dupuis' reading and transcript.	
Kabarra	Kabra	كبر	Kabara	كبر
Timbuctoo			Timbuctoo	تمبكت
Jolliba	Jilab Karihua	جلاب كريهوا	Jilleb Kareho	جلاب كريهوا

(or Garihua.†)

Negro pronunciation.	Mr. Jackson's reading and transcript.		Mr. Dupuis' reading and transcript.	
Uzzabin	Asabin	احبن	Azbene	ازبن
Gaw	G⁻raheh	غاي	Ghou	غاو

  * Mr. Dupuis renders the Arabic غ ḡh agreeable to Richardson. Mr. Jackson has insisted on preferring ḡr throughout. Mr. Dupuis, having sailed for Africa, has not had the advanage of correcting the press for himself, but every care has been taken.

  † Sir W. Ouseley remarks, that the letter *k* is frequently softened into *g*.

Negro pronunciation.	Mr. Jackson's reading and transcript.		Mr. Dupuis' reading and transcript.	
Kabi	Keb	كب	Kabi	كب
Yaoora	Eüra	يور	Yaoury	يور
			Hooman (Dhooman)	حمن
Raka	Baka	بَكا	Raka	رَكَا
Quarraraba	Kurauabee	كرَوبي	Koorawaba	كروب
Mafeegoodoo	Mafikadoo	مافقد	Mafhygodo	مافقعد
Cadie, Caudee, and Chadi	Shad	شد	Shada	شَد
Sharee R.	Shar	شر	Sharry	شِر
Foor	Fure	فور	Foor	فور
Weddai	Wadan	وادان	Wadana	وَادَان
	(i. e. two rivers.)			
Soonar	Sanar	سَنَار	Sanar	سَنَار
Shuar Benassa	Sheua benasser	شوا بنسر	Shewa ben Hassan	شوا بن حسن
	Shousuad	شوسواد	Shousooda	شوسواد
			Doulamba	دلنب
	Kalen or Falen	كالن or فالن	Kalana	كالن
Jefeesgo	Jafagr	جفغ	Jafegh	جفغ
Massar	Mass'r	مصر	Massir	مصر

MS. No. I.

Route from Boussa to Yarriba.

Wauwaw	Wou	واو
Kaiama	Kima	كيما
Godoobirrie	Khudubar	خدوبار
Gamba	Khamba	خمب
Kroomie Yarriba	Kurmi Yarabia	كرم يربي
Ageasee	Abashee	ابشي

A more familiar illustration of the difficulty or carelessness of the Moors in writing Negro names, is the following route to Sallagha, to which there are many paths, containing several Ashantee towns, which I have laid down in the map. I rather think, however, the corrupt Arabic of the interior is not quite understood.

MS. No. II.

Negro pronunciation.	Mr. Jackson's reading and transcript.	
	Jemakashee	جماكاشي
Gammasee	Khemashee or Ghemashee	خماشي
Akrofroom	Kukerume or Kuferume	كوكروم or كوفروم
	Ber kaleela (a narrow or close country)	برقليلا
Soota	U badha Shta	-
And afterwards Shta or an alluvial country		وبعده شتا
The people of Sudi in the territory of Shta		وحيل اسود كان في بلد شتا
Marmpon	U badha Mamefm	و بعده مـمفم
Aduarrie Kennie	D'keen Adjar	دكين ادجار
Aguira	Ajuee or Ajree	اجوب or اجري
Antonasoo	Anteenee	عنتيمي
	Akakuee	اككوي
Patooda (no P in Arabic)	Ketdee	كتدي
Atoboo	Atab	اتاب
Weasee	Hooashee or Weeashu	حوعشي or جوعشي
	Feneeueekee	فنيويقي
Perhaps meaning frontier of Booroom Bure		بور
Sallagha	Salag̃r	سلغ

I shall submit more translations or transcripts of routes and charts in Arabic, adding the Negro pronunciation, as the situations of most of the places were not so clearly confirmed as to enable me to insert them in my map, and consequently it is important to enable future travellers to refer to them; such outlines being a great assistance in directing and checking enquiry (which they frequently originate) and investigation. The original MSS. will be sent to the African Association, in case a further examination may be desirable hereafter.

MS. No. III.

Course of the Niger or Quolla (by a Bornoo Moor.)

Negro pronunciation.	Mr. Jackson's reading and transcript.		Mr. Dupuis' reading and transcript.	
Bambooch	Banbug̃r eladi eeakul بَنْبُغ الدي ياكل el Ham Abn Adam الحُم ابن أدم Banbug̃r, who eat the flesh of men.		Banboogho	بَنْبُغ
	Firmag̃ra	فرمَبغ	Fermagha	فرمَبغ
Hasoo	Hâsu	حاُس	Hasoo	حاُس
Jaoona	Jahunu	جَاحُن	Jahoonoo	جَاحِي

Negro pronunciation.	Mr. Jackson's reading and transcript.		Mr. Dupuis' reading and transcript.	
Gamoo	Jamu	جَم	Jamoo	جَم
Malay or Mallaia	Mali	مِلي	Malabi	ملبي
Shego	Shaegru	شيغ	Shagho	شيع
Sansandin	Sansandy	سنسند	Sansadia	سنسد
Jennie	Jany	جِن	Jinnie	جني
Mashina	Masina	مَاسِن	Massina	مَاسِن
Timbuctoo	Tunbûktu	تنبقت	Timbuctoo	تمبقت
Gauw	Ḡrau	غَاو	Ghaou	غَاو
Kolomanni	Kulman	كلمِن	Koolmani	كلمن
Zinberme	Dtanberma	ذنبرم	Danberma	ذنبرم
Cabi	Kabi	كَب	Kabi	كَب
Yawoorie or Yaoora	Eauri	يَاوِر	Yaouri	يَاوِر
Noofee	Nufy	نفي	Noufee	نفي
Boussa	Busâa	بوسَا	Boussa	بوسا
Rakka	Raka	رَاقَا	Rakka	رَاقَا
Bornoo	B'rn Bernu	برن	Bornou	برن
Chadee L.	(The lake drawn, but the name not written.)			
Bagarrimee	Baḡrarm	بَاغرو	Baghroom	بَاغرم
Kalamſarradoo	Kaferk or Kaferd كَافرك or كَافرد		Kaferda Kalferka	كَافرد
Weddaï	Wadana (two rivers)	وَدَان	Wadai	وَدَان
Soonar	Surnar	سرنبر	Soonar	سونبر
	Siua	سيوا	Sevva	سيوا
Schweess	Suis	سويس	Souisa	سويس
Zaloo	Jal	جَال	Jaloo	جَال
Kataëba	Katab	قتب	Kataibi	قتيب
Makidzue	Mek'duh	مقدوح	Mokad	مقدوح
Mertabass	M'rtabas	مرتبَاس	Mertabas	مرتبَاس
Hoodayba	Mamudeeb	مَمودِيب	Haoudeba	هودِيب
Taiboos	Teesuse	تيسوس	Tesoos	تيسوس
Jarooba	Jerub	جروب	Jarouba	جروب
Tabarrabass	Tidburse or Tidfurse	تدبرس or تدفرس	Tarbasa	تربَاس

Negro pronunciation.	Mr. Jackson's reading and transcript.		Mr. Dupuis' reading and transcript.	
Gedda	J'da	جدا	Jidda	جدا
Geddook	J'duk	جدوخ	Jidoukh	جدوخ
Limbarr'	Linbabahr	لنبحر	Linbahar	لنبحر
Tarrowm	Term	ترم	Taroom	ترم
Massar	M'nser	منصر	Minsor	منصر
Sakunderree or Askan-darie	Skender, a swamp or lake	سكندر مرج	Sakundria, Alexandria	سكندر

Route from Timbuctoo to Ferjan (from the same MS.)

	Tuan	توان	Toowano	توان
	M'brûk	مبروك	Mobaruka	مبروك
	Jeerban	حيربين	Joojebani	اجوجبين
	Abugiberk	ابوجبرخ	Kheerabi	خيربي
	Tehekeem	تحكيم	Tahkema	تحكيم

Bageeacha
Hootailee
Goosaicha } not written, but position marked, and thus pronounced.
Hayloon
Barrahese

	Ferjan	فرجان	Ferjan	فرجان

From Timbuctoo to Tunis (from the same Chart.)

Ziggie	Jak, Jik, or Juk	جتى	Jagha	جغ
Arowalla	Arun or Arul	عرون or عرول	Aaroon	عرون
Tarrabaleese	Trahesen	ترةيسن	Trabolas	ترەبليس
Mooquinassa	M'kenas	ممكناس	Mookanassa	مكناس
Hass	Has	حاس	Hhas	حاس
Landoloos	Lindalsu	لندلس	Lankalsoo	لنكلس
Toonis	Tunis	تونس	Tunis	تونس
	Near the sea	كباله بحر		

Other towns named on this route were

Hassaladee	Dizzaela	Maratooph
Hassazedeed	Dazeleel	Swamach
Hassat	Katerbaîlie	
Omattaras	Bahadzai	

MS. No. IV.

Course of the Niger or Quolla (by a Jennie Moor who had been to Egypt.)

Negro pronunciation.	Mr. Jackson's reading and transcript.		Mr. Dupuis' reading and transcript.	
Mallaia	Malh	ملح	Mahh	ماح
Shego	Shak	سك	Shako	سك
Sansandin	Sansandee	سنسندي	Sansandia	سنسندي
Jennie	Jin	جن	Jinnie	جن
Massina	Masheen	ماشين	Mashina	ماشين
Tinbuctoo	Tinbut	تنبت	Tinbuctoo	تنبت

(Here he draws the Jolliba flowing from or into the Quolla by Timbuctoo.)

Gauw	Gru	غو	Ghou	غو
Quoälla	Kula	كولا	Koualla	كولا
Askeä	Assaëe	اَساَي	Askea	اسكي
Zabirma	Zabuaä	زبوعا	Zaberma	زبرما
Cabi	Keb	كب	Kaby	كبا
Yaoora	Eeuë	يور	Yeory	يور
Boussa	B'sa	بسا	Bussu	بسا

(Here he branches off a southern route to Yarriba with precisely the same names as in MS. I. by the Houssa Moor.)

Noofee
Quolla-liffa
Atagara } not written, but position marked, and thus pronounced.
Sharee R.
Chadee L.

Foor	Foo	فو	Sour	صره
Weddai	Wadaee	وداي	Wadai	وداي
Joonar	Jusenaw	جوسناو	Joosnou	جوسناو
Shewa	Shuee	شوي	Shouy	سوي
Sooeess	Siuse	سوس	Sweis	سوس
Zale	Zal	زَال	Zal	زَال
Zaedooma	Zeehwam	زيدوم	Zeedouma	زيدوم
Lachtamoo	Lahellam	لاحلام	Lakhtamo	لاخطام
Makagoodoo	Mehed'twa	محذوع	Mohadzou	محذوع

Negro pronunciation.	Mr. Jackson's reading and transcript.		Mr. Dupuis' reading and transcript.	
Dalooba	Deeluba	ديلوبا	Djaoba	دجاوبا
Tarbass	Tubas	توباس	Terbasa	ترباس
Jaheesoo	Jekeesee	جكيس	Jakhesa	جخيس
Latooha	Lituh or Liauh	ليطوح or ليعوح	Letouh	ليطوح
Mabanoos	M'benuse	مبنوس	Mabanouso	مبنوس
Itkhame	Atekam	اتخام	Etakhamo	اطخمد
Massar	Missu	مصو	Massir	مصر
Sooryada	Sueed	سويد	Sourida	سويد
Nezoogoo	Teeawa	تياوع	Nezugh	نيزوخ
Kataramoo	Kateram	كترام	Kateramo	كترام
Dahloomoo	D'hclume	دحلوم	Dhalomo	دحلوم
Hateboo	Heteeb	حتيب	Hhateba	حتيب
Haheenie	Heneen	حنين	Hahhene	ححين
Hajamie	Khejam	خجام	Hajame	حجام
Tapasooloo	Tefawn	تفعون	Tafsoona	تفصون
Askandarie	.	.	Askundria	اسكندري
Bahar Mela	(Bahar Melhah the salt sea) Bahar al Malah			

MS. No. IV.

'This was written by an old Moor, a native of the Mallowa country, but unfortunately just as he had finished (for I made them all write at the moment in my own apartment, however hurried, rather than allow them to go home and compose for me) and was beginning to explain what he had written, a summons from the King obliged me to quit him, and he left Coomassie before I could procure another visit from him.   In the absence of all explanation, I can only conclude from some few names that are familiar to me, that it is a route from Berragoo over the Quolla, and then westward to Bergoo, known to Mr. Brown.   I am only induced thus to preserve a transcript of this ms. from its fortunate co-incidence in several names with the valuable lost itinerary of my friend Brahima, as far as can be collected from a mere sketch of a translation, which was made in anticipation of the perfect one.   I shall submit them collaterally, as they assist to elucidate each other, and agree very well in the relative positions of places, although the parties never saw each other, which is some satisfaction under the disappointment.

Outline of Brahima's Itinerary.   MS. No. IV.

Mr. Dupuis' reading and transcript.		Mr. Jackson's reading and transcript.		Other readings.
Bazao (Barao)	بَزَاوْ (اَبْراوْ)	Burgٰru	بَرْغ	Bouroughoo
		Babigry	بِيغِي	Babaghe
Kaikshi	كَيَقْشي	Keekesh	كِيقش	Keekash
Droo	درووْ	Serkune	سركون	Serkoon
Mashooko	مَشوكُوْ			
Banghoo	بَانغوا	Banaka	بازعقا	
Toonooma	تونوم	Tuee	توي	
Yajoury (doubtlels Yawoorie)	يَجووِر	Tenbykukmaetunby	تنب كوك مِيتنْب	
		Kenbua	كَنبوا	Kanboo
		Dendawy	دنداوِي	Danadoo
		Belgٰrua	بلغوا	Balaghou
Jabdgho	جبذْغ	Jebengٰrua	جبنغوا	Jabadghoo
Keemba or Keerba	كمبا (كصبا)	Kamba	كمبه	
Kadarkoo R.	الجركَدركْ	Kedugٰreh R.	كدوغه	Kadarko
Doodirba R.	نذربا	Dtedȷerba R.	نذربا	Dodarba
		Uwawfeh	وراوفه	
		Mhaka Kury (arrival at Kury)	محكا كوري	
		Saffer	سفر	
		Aäu Khashah	اعور كحاشه	
Shawanka	اشَوْنَكا	Shawangra	شاونغ	
Ghoufel	غوفل	Jafu	جافو	Japhoo
Simmer	سمر			
Yarkoo	يركو			
Daghm	دغم			
Bannanao	بننوا			
Doonkee	دنقِي	Dunka	دنقِي	Doonkot
Ghodau	غوضا	Gٰru'w	غوو	Ghouwa
Salamo	سلموا			
Janboodoo	جانبدوا	Jabendu	جبندوا	

Mr. Dupuis' reading and transcript.		Mr. Jackson's reading and transcript.		Other readings.
Soosoo	سسوا	Susu	سوسوا	
Kooreree	كررَ	Koos	كوص	
Barghoowa	برغوا	Berg¯rua		برغوا
Nak or Naka	نك			
Water of Wada	وض			
Douga (probably Donga)	ضوغا			
Mazim	مزم			
Kal	كل			
Makji	مقجي			
Tafkat	تفقت			
Shal L.	شل			
Koad or Koada	كوض			

Here the writer signified that he went back to *Kateen*, as appeared to the transcriber, but more probably *Kassina*, and thence proceeded to

Kano	كن
Bornou	برنو
Sher R.	شر
Shadda L	شاد
Foor	فر
Wada	وداء
Massir	سصر
Makata (Mecca)	مكة
Madina	مدينه
Shem (Damascus)	شام
Jerusalem, &c. &c.	بيت المقدس

APPENDIX. No. IV.

REPTILIA. (REPTILES.)

Gen. MONITOR, *Cuvier.*

Sp. 1. *Pulcher, Leach.*

M. Supra niger albo pulcherrime zonatus et maculatus: zonis dorsalibus e maculis effectis, ventre albido nigro transversim vage lineato, cauda compressa carinata.

This elegant species was found in Fantee. The whole upper parts of the body, the legs and tail, are black, most beautifully banded and spotted with white. The bands on the tail are alternately wide and narrow; the wider bands are each much and abruptly dilated above into a kind of spot, whilst the narrow ones become gradually wider in the inverse direction. The legs are spotted above with white; the under parts of them, as well as of the belly and throat, are also of the same colour with the spots.

Gen. CHAMÆLEON, *of authors.*

Sp. 1. *Dilepis, Leach.*

Ch. Capite supra sub plano utrinque bicarinato: carinis antice conniventibus, occipite utrinque squama magna instructo, dorso subspinoso-carinato.

This species may readily be distinguished from all that have been hitherto discovered, by the two large scales, affixed one on each side to the back part of the head. These scale-like processes, are covered by the same scaly integuments which cover the head and body.

Gen. ACONTIAS, *Cuvier.*

Sp. 1. *Punctatus, Leach.*

A. Supra brunneo-fuscus obsolete purpurascens, squamis postice macula ventreque fulvescentibus.

Fantee.

Gen. MACROSOMA, *Leach.*

1. *Elegans, Leach.*

Coluber elegans, *Shaw.*

Fantee.

Gen. COLUBER, *Cuvier.*

1. *Bicolor, Leach.*

C. Supra badio-niger subtus albidus, squamis dorsalibus elongatis gradatim angustioribus ; apice obtusiusculis.

Fantee.

2. *Irroratus, Leach.*

C. Badio-fuscus, gula pallida, squamis pulcherrime albido irroratis ; dorsalibus subelongatis apice rotundatis.

Fantee.

3. *Irregularis, Leach.*

C. Azureo-virescens, ventre albido, squamis simplicibus irregularibus : dorsalibus ovatis : lateralibus superioribus superne truncatis ; inferis subhexagonis.

Fantee.

The above three species of *Coluber* are decidedly new, as well as the *Acontias*; the latter is more particularly interesting, since it encreases the species of a very limited genus.

ARACHNOÏDA.

Gen. SCORPIO, *of authors.*

Sp. 1. *Afer, Fabr.*

Gen. MYGALE, *Latreille.*

The only specimen was too mutilated to enable me to make out its specific character.

MYRIAPODA.

Of this class you found two species in Fantee; a *Scolopendra*, and a gigantic *Julus*; neither of which are in a sufficiently good state to enable me to make out whether they be described or not.

INSECTA.

Gen. TEFFLUS, *Leach*, new genus.

Generic character.

CAPUT. *Mandibulæ* æquales edentulæ. *Palpi labiales* et *maxillares externi* articulo ultimo elongato-securiformi.

THORAX hexagonus antice et postice rectus. *Alæ* nullæ. *Elytra* coalita abdomen tegentia apicem versus utrinque sinuata. *Tibiæ* anticæ latere interiore apicem versus emarginatæ calcare elevato instructæ. *Tarsi antici* MARIS articulis duobus primis tenuiter dilatatis.

Habitus et Antennæ Carabi.

Sp. 1. *Meyerlei.*

Carabus Meyerlei, *Fabr. Syst. Eleut.* i. 169.—*Voet. col.* ii. *tab.* 39, *f.* 49.

Gen. ODONTOMERUS, *Dahl.*

Sp. 1. *Serratus.*

Buprestis serratus, *Fabr.*

Fantee.

Gen. Cetonia, *of authors.*

Sp. 1. *Marginata, Fabr.*

Fantee.

Gen. Phyllotoma, *Wm. MacLeay, MSS.*

Sp. 1. *Reflexa.*

Melolontha reflexa, *Fabr.*

Fantee.

Gen. Helops, *Fabr.*

Sp. 1. *Marginatus, Olivier.*

Fantee.

Gen. Upis? *Fabr.*

Sp. 1. Cuprea.

Tenebrio Cupreus, *Fabr.*

Fantee.

Gen. Lamia, *Fabr.*

Sp. 1. Tri-fasciata, *Fabr.*

Fantee. This species is also found at Sierra Leone, and in the Back Settlements of the Cape of Good Hope.

Gen. Petrognatha, *Leach.*

Character

Caput thorace paulo latius. *Antennæ* (*maris* corpore duplo longiores et ultra,) articulo secundo longiore flexuoso. *Labrum* lineare transversum nudum utrinque rotundatum. *Mandibulæ* petrosæ (maris interne apicem versus obtuse unidentatæ,) infra et externe irregulariter carinatæ. *Palpi maxillares* et *labiales* articulo ultimo basi subattenuato, apice externe oblique truncato-acuminato.

Thorax transversus utrinque 1-spinosus. *Elytra* humeris 1-spinosis, apiceque ad saturam spinoso-subproducto.

Sp. 1. *Gigas.*

Lamia Gigas, *Fabr.*

Fantee.

Gen. Callichroma, *Latreille.*

Sp. 1. *Festivum.*

Cerambyx festivus, *Oliv. Fabr.*

Fantee.

Gen. Mantis.

Sp. 1. *Superstitiosa, Fabr.*

Fantee

This species, as well as its congeners, is an object of superstitious veneration amongst the natives of north-western Africa, Syria, and India. It agrees in all points with the original specimen of *Superstitiosa*, so named by Fabricius in the Banksian Cabinet.

Gen. GRYLLUS, *Fabr.*

Sp. 1. *Squarrosus, Fabr.*

Fantee.

Gen. REDUVIUS, *Fabr.*

Sp. 1. *Barbicornis, Fabr.*

Fantee.

I have received this species from the Cape of Good Hope.

Gen. CANOPUS, *Rodhe.*

Sp. 1. *Punctatus, Leach.*

Supra olivaceo-ater impresso-punctulatus rubro punctatus, subtus ruber segmentis marginibus stigmatibus tibiis tarsisque nigris, capite rubro irrorato.

Gaboon.

APPENDIX, No. V.

Mr. TEDLIE'S *Account of the Thermometer.*

Date.	A.M.		M.		P.M.		Weather.
April 28	6	74					
29	7½	75					
	11	80					
30					2	88½	
					7	82½	
May 1	8	77					
2	8	76½			1	91	
3	6	76	12	89			

May 4. The Thermometer was broken last night at Asharaman.

At Coomassie, from the 7th June to the 14th, it varied from 80 to 85, between 12 and 2.

Date.	A.M.		M.		P.M.		Weather.
June 15					1	82	
16	10	79					
17			12	82			
18	9	79			2	84	
19	7½	73			2½	78	
					5	78	
20	10	78			1	81	
					2½	82	
21	8	74			2½	82	
22	8	76	12	82	1	74	Tornado.
23	8½	74			1	81	Tornado.
24	11½	76			2	73	Rain.
25	9	75			1	76	
26	9	76	12	76	2	78	
27	8½	79			3½	80	
28	8½	74	12	77			
29	9½	74			2	77	Fair.
30	9	77			1	80	Rain.
July 1	9	76			1	80	
2	8	73	12	78			
3	9	78			1	78	
					6	75	
4	8	72	12	74			
5	8	72			1	78	Fair.
6	6	71	12	76			

Date.	A.M.		M.		P.M.		Weather.
July 7	6	71			2	80	Rain.
					6	75	
8	6	72	12	78			Fair.
					3	80	Tornado.
9	6	72					Fair.
					1	79	Rain.
10	7	73			2½	81	
11	8	73			2	81	Fair.
					6	72	
12	6	72			2½	80	
					6	76	
13	8	77					
	11	73			3	77	Rain.
14	8	71			2	77	
15	8	70	12	74	6	72	Fair.
16	7	69			2	78	
					7	73	
17	7	69			2½	79	
18	8	71			3	79	
					6	76	
19	6	70					Fair.
					2½	76	Fair.
					7	74	
20	8	72			2½	78	
21	7½	71	12	75	2½	78	
					6½	75	
22	6	70			2	78	
					7	73	Rain.
23	6	70			2	78	
					8	72	
24	8	70			2	74	
					8	72	
25	8	69			1	74	
					6	72	
26	7	70			2	75	
					6	74	
27	7	68			3½	80½	
					8	71	

3 S

Date.	A.M.	M.	P.M.	Weather.
July 28	8 70			Fair.
			3 77	
			7½ 73	
29	7 70		2 78	
			8 73	
30	7 66½		2 78	
			7 73	
31	8 70	12 76	2 78	
			7 73	
Aug. 1	7 70		2 77	
			7 73	Rain.
2	7 71		2 73	
			8 70	
3	7 69½	12 72	3 73	Rain.
			8 70½	Fair.
4	7 70		2 78	
			8 74	
5	7 71		2 79	
			6 75	Rain.
6	7 70			Rain.
			2 78½	
			8 73	Fair.
7	7 71		2 78	
			6 76	
8	6 70	12 73	2½ 77	
			7 73	
9	6 70		2½ 78	
			7 75	
10	7 71		2 76	Rain.
			7 74	Rain.
11	7 71		2 78	
			8 73	Rain.
12	7 70½		3 76	Rain.
			6 73	
			8 71	
13	7 70		2 77	
			8 73	
14	7 70		2 74	Fair.
			6 73	
			8 71	
15	7 70		2 72	
			7 73	
16	7 70		2 75	
			7 73	
17	7 70		2 80	
			7 74	
18	7 71	12 77	2 80½	
			3 81	
			7 77	
19	7 71		2 75	Rain.
			8 73	
20	7 68½			Rain.

Date.	A M.	M.	P. M.	Weather.
Aug. 20			2 72½	
			6 71	
21	6 69			Fair.
			1 77	
			7 74	
22	6 68	12 73	2 77	
			7 71	
23	7 68		1 76	
			8 73	
24	7 69		3 74	
			7 71½	
25	6 68		6 74	
26	6 68		3 78½	
			7 74	
27	7 69			Hazy.
			1 72	
			3 72	
			7 70½	
28	6 69½			Rain.
			2 74	
			8 72	Rain.
29	7 70		3 78	Fair
			6 77	
30	7 70			Fair.
			2½ 76	
			7 73	Rain.
31	7 70½		3 77	
			7 73	
Sept. 1	7 71			Fair.
			3 80	
			7 77	
2	6 71			Hazy.
			2 75	
			7 74	Slight showers
3	6 71	12 74		Rain.
			1 80	
			6 74	
4	7 71	12 77	7 74	
5	5 71		3 79	
			7 76	Fair.
6	6 70		2 74	
			7 73	
7	8 71		3 76	
			8 73	Slight showers
8	7 71	12 76		
			2 80	
			8 73	
9	6 71		2 80	
			8 74	
10	7 71			Rain.
			3 80	
			7 76	

Date.	A. M.	M.	P. M.	Weather.
Sept. 11	6 72			Heavy rain.
			2 77	Rain.
			10 72	Rain.
12	7 72	12 78	3½ 80½	
			10 76	
13	7 22		2 78	
			3½ 80	Rain.
			9 76	
14	7 72			Hazy.
			2½ 79	
			6 76	
			8 75	
15	5 71		3 80	
			7 75	

Date.	A. M.	M.	P. M.	Weather.
Sept. 16	7 72		2½ 80	
			8 75	
17	7 72	12 78	2½ 81	
			9 75	
18	7 72		2 77	Rain.
			8 73	
19	7 71		3 81	
			9 75	
20	7 72		2 79	Rain.
			8 74	
21	7 72		2½ 81	Rain.
			8 72	
22	8 71			Hazy.
	12½ 71		2 82½	

Mr. Hutchison's *Account of the Thermometer, after the Departure of Mr. Tedlie.*

Date.	A. M.	M.	P. M.	Weather.
Sept. 23	8 73			Thunder, with [rain.
			2 80	
			8 75	
24	6 72			Rain.
		12 78		[dy.
			2 82	Fair, but clou-
			8 75	Rain.
25	6 71½			
	10 76			Fair.
		12 83		Rain.
			2 75	Violent tornado
			8 71½	Rain.
26	6 70			
		12 73		Hazy.
			2 80	Cloudy } thun-
			4 77	Wind } der.
			8 71	Heavy rain.
27	6 73			
	10 75			Fair.
		12 80½	6 75	
28	6 71		2 81½	
			6 74	
29	6 71½		2 82	
30	6 73			Cloudy.
			2 80	
			7 71½	
Oct. 1	6 72½		2 82	
	10 70		8 76	
2	6 70		2 79	Rain.
			8 78	Sultry.
3	6 71			Rain.
			2 82	Fair.

Date.	A. M.	M.	P. M.	Weather.
Oct. 3			6 80	
5	6 72		2 79	
			6 74	
6	6 72			Rain. [thunder.
			2 79	Much rain,
			8 75	
7	6 72		2 79	
			6 74	
8	6 71	12 79	2 73	
			6 71	[cloudy.
9	6 71		2 79	Sultry and
			6 78	
10	6 73			
		12 78		Fair.
			2 71½	[thunder.
			6 73½	Much rain,
11	6 73			Heavy fog.
			2 76½	Fair, cloudy.
12	6 71½			Sultry, foggy.
			2 80½	Fair.
			6 78	
13	6 73			Foggy.
		12 78		Sultry.
			2 79	
			6 77	Rain, thunder.
14	6 71½			Rain, foggy.
			2 78½	Fair.
			6 74	
15	6 72½			Rain, foggy.
			2 74	Hazy.
			6 73	
16	6 72½			Foggy.

Date.	A. M.	M.	P. M.	Weather.
Oct. 16			2 80½	Fair.
			6 75	
17	6 75½			Rain, foggy.
			2 78	
			6 74½	
18	6 73			Fair.
			2 80	[der.
			6 75	Rain and thun-
19	73½			
	71½			Much rain.
20	6 70½			Dense fogs.
			2 73	Foggy, with
			6 74	[showers.
21	6 72½			Fair.
			2 79	
			8 78½	
22	6 73	12 77		Foggy.
			2 82½	Fair.
			8 75	[showers.
23	6 72½			Foggy, with thr.
		12 80	2 83	
			8 77	
24	6 73			Foggy.
		12 80		Fair.
			3 78½	Rain.
			8 75	
25	6 74½	12 82		Foggy.
			2 82	Fair.
			6 74	
26	6 72½			Foggy.
			2 80	
			78	Rain, thunder.
27	6 72			Foggy.
			2 80	
	[illegible]			
			6 76	Thunder shrs.
29	6 7			Rain.
			2 82	Fair.
			6 75	
30	6 73			Foggy.
			2 83	Fair.
			8 78	
31	6 72½			Foggy.
			2 82	Fair.
			8 76	
Nov. 1	6 72½			Foggy.
			2 81	
			6 80	Sultry.
2	6 73			Fair.
			2 81½	
			8 75	Rain.
3	6 73			Rain.

Date.	A. M.	M.	P. M.	Weather.
Nov. 3			2 82½	Fair.
			6 78	
4	6 72		2 78	Rain, foggy.
			6 74½	Sultry.
5	6 72½		2 79½	
			6 78	
6	6 74		2 80½	Fair.
			8 79	Rain, sultry.
7	6 72½		2 82½	Fair, thunder.
			3 79	Rain.
			8 77	
8	6 72		2 78½	Thunder.
			8 75	Hazy.
10	6 71			Foggy.
			2 82	Fair.
			8 76	
11	6 72½			Foggy.
	2 81½			Fair.
			8 78	
12	6 74½		2 79	Cloudy.
			6 78	Sultry.
13	6 73		2 83½	Fair.
			8 75	
14	6 69		2 78½	
			8 75	
15	6 70½		2 82½	
			8 79	
16	6 69		2 82	
			8 80	
17	6 70½		2 82½	
			6 79	
18	6 72		2 82½	
			8 80	
19	6 72½		2 80½	
			8 78	
20	6 70½		2 81	
			8 76	
21	6 72½		2 83½	
			8 79	
22	6 72		2 83	
			8 78	
23	6 75		2 82	Rain.
			8 78	Foggy.
24			6 72	
			2 81	
			8 76	
26	6 71		2 83	
			8 75	

Date.	A. M.	M.	P. M.	Weather.
Nov. 27	6 73			Slight showers.
			2 80	Foggy.
			8 76	
28	6 70		2 80½	
			8 74	
29	6 78		2 82	
			8 75½	
30	6 78½		2 81	
			8 76	
Dec. 1			6 78	
			2 80½	
			8 74	
2	6 77½		2 80	
			8 74	
3	6 68½		2 79	Rain.
			8 74	Fair.
4	6 67		2 81	Foggy.
			8 77	
5	6 68		2 80½	
			8 77	
6	6 65		2 78	
			8 76	
7	6 63		2 80	
			8 77	
8	6 70		2 78½	
			8 76	
9	6 63		2 79	
			8 76	
10	6 71		2 79	
			8 75	
11	6 73		2 80½	
			6 74	
12	6 74		2 81	
			8 75	
13	6 74½		2 79½	
			8 77	
14	6 72		2 79	
			8 76	
15	6 73¼		2 79	
			8 76	
16	6 74		2 80½	
			8 74	
17	6 73½		2 80	
			8 75	
18			6 71½	
			2 79	Tornado.
			8 76	
19	6 68		2 79½	Foggy.

Date.	A. M.	M.	P. M.	Weather.
Dec. 19			8 74	
20	6 64½		2 79	Foggy.
			8 76	
21	6 75		2 80	Tornado.
			8 78	Rain.
22	6 76		2 81	Foggy.
			6 78	
23	6 76½		2 83½	
			8 80	
24	6 79		2 84	
			4 82	Thunder.
			7 80	Tornado.
				Foggy.
25	6 78		2 81	
			8 78	Tornado.
26	6 69		2 81	Foggy.
			6 80	Tornado.
27	6 70		2 82	Foggy.
			8 76	
28	6 74		2 82	
			8 78	
29	6 73		2 80½	
			8 76¼	
30	6 74		2 79	
			8 76	
31	6 72		2 81	
			8 78	
Jan. 1 1818.	6 70½		2 81	
			8 78	
2		6 72		
3		6 72	2 85	Thunder.
			8 76	Rain.

From sickness, the Thermometer was not attended to till the 10th, during the interval the weather was excessive cold, and the fogs very dense.

Date.	A. M.	M.	P. M.	Weather.
10			2 74	Foggy.
			8 68	
11	6 62½		2 76	
			8 70½	
12	6 60		2 77	
			8 70	
13	6 61½		2 74½	
			8 68	
14	6 58		2 74	
			8 66	
15	6 60		2 75½	
			8 70	
16	6 61½		2 76	

Date.	A. M.	M.	P. M.	Weather.	Date.	A. M.	M.	P. M.	Weather.
Jan. 16			8 72½		Jan, 25	6 64		2 84	
17	6 62		2 76¾					8 80	
			8 71		26	6 68		2 83½	
18	6 60		2 74					8 67½	
			8 73		27	6 68½		2 84	
19	6 62½		2 79					8 80½	
			8 75		28	6 72		2 84¼	
20	6 64		2 78½					8 78	
			8 76		29	6 72		2 85	
21	6 64½		2 79					8 80	
			8 74		30	6 74		2 85	
22	6 66		2 80					8 80	
			8 78		31	6 76		2 85	
23	6 64		2 82					8 80	
			8 76		Feb. 1	6 74		2 84½	
24	6 62		2 82½					8 79	
			8 74		2	6 73½		2 86½	

APPENDIX. No. VI.

I WILL now submit the numerals of 31 nations, which, with the exception of three, the Fantee, the Accra, and the Bornoo, (and those but imperfectly,) have never been reported before. I will arrange them according to their geographical approximation, remarking any apparent affinity which occurs to me, in notes. I shall place the Inta first, because it is the most remote, inland, which can be assimilated to the Fantee, Ahanta, Aöwin, and Amanaheä; and may, probably, from that circumstance, be the root of these languages; as it has been shewn, in the history, that the nations of the water side have been gradually pressed down, or have emigrated from the interior, and it is consequently to be expected that the etymology of the names of these countries are not to be found in the languages of the people who *now* inhabit them, but more probably in the languages of their southern neighbours. Thus,

Inta is likely to be derived from the *Booroom* word *inta, water,* as it has been noticed as an alluvial country.

Yngwa, a northern province of Dagwumba, from the Ashantee *anggwa, fat, rich,* or the Booroom, *yngia, a wood.*

Soko from *Soko, one,* in the Badaggry (below Dahomy) as *Yahndi* the capital of Dagwumba was so called from *yahndo* the numeral *one,* to indicate its pre-eminence.

Assin from the Ashantee *Assoon,* an elephant. But this expectation is not further supported in the two or three other probable etymologies which occur to me, as *Takima* from the Ashantee *takramma,* tongue. *Akim* (formerly the greatest trading country,) from the Booroom *Akimmie,* cloth.; *Booroom* from *boora,* full, in that language.

It is curious how nearly the *word* for God in the Malemba, *M'Poungoo,* approaches the native name, *Empoongwa,* of the country Europeans call *Gaboon. Wonga* is fear in the Malemba, and *Woonga-woonga* is the name of an uninhabited savannah of three days extent, between Empoöngwa and Adjoomba.

	1. *Inta.*	2. *Booroom.*	3. *Ashantee.*	4. *Aöwin.*	5. *Amanaheä.*
One(*a*)	Koko	Ekoo	Akoon	Aconĕ	Aconĕ
Two(*b*)	ʼAnyoe	Enoo	Anoo	Enyow	Enyow

(*a*) The words for the numeral one assimilate in the specimens 1, 2, 3, 4, 5, 6, 7, 8, 9: again, but distinctly, in 14, 12, 15, 16: also in 26, 25, 13: in 21, 18, 20, 19 : in 27, 28, 29, (making apparently five roots), but they remain solitary in 11, 17, 22, 23, 24 30 and 31. The numeral one in 14 is not unlike the two in 8, 9, 2, 3, and the one in 12, would, with

Three(c)	Assa	Essa	Mensa	Inza	Insa
Four(d)	Anna	Enna	Ennung	Inna	Enna
Five(e)	Annoo	Annoo	Ennoom	Noo	Enoo
Six(f)	Assee	Esseä	Inseëä	Inzeah	Inseah
Seven(g)	Assoonno	Assoono	Inshong	Inzoo	Insoon
Eight(h)	Adoobrooa	Aquiay	Woquee	Motteä	Mottuay
Nine	Digrakoono	Akonno	Oonkonnong	Ongoona	Ongona
Ten(i)	Koodoo	Edoo	Edoo	Boloo	Booloo

	6. *Ahanta*	7. *Fantee*	8. *Affootoo*	9. *Inkran†*	10. *Adampë*
One	Akoon	Akoor	Achoomee	Ekkoo	Kakee

the prefix of y, be precisely the same as the two of 25. Excepting *Kakee, one,* the Inkran numerals seem to have been adopted as those of Adampë, for the convenience of trade and intercourse, but I will add a few words, to show that the languages are radically different :

	Adampë.		*Inkran.*
House -	- Aoosoo	- -	Wheay.
Fire -	*Odja	-	Lla.
Man -	Ossa	- -	N̄oon.
Woman -	Ossë	- -	Yeo.
Victuals -	Odë	- -	Neeaynee.
Father -	Attay	- -	Tchay.
Mother -	Awoo	- -	Nneay.

(b) The numeral *two* is the most general word, and may be assimilated in 2, 3, 8, 9, 4, 5, 1, 6, 12, 13, 14, 15, 16, 17. There is little difference between the numerals *two* and *five* in most of these, and *five* in 15 and 16, precisely answers to *two* in 1 and 2.

(c) *Three* may be assimilated in 1, 2, 4, 5, 6, 7, 8, 12, 13, 14, 15, 16, 17. In 12, 13, 14, 16, it approaches to the Congo and Mozambique *tatoo* and *atatoo.*

(d) I have observed that in most African languages there is less distinction in the words for four and five, than between any other of the numerals ; and that frequently the word for *five* in one language, is identical with that for *four* in another, geographically remote. *Four* may be assimilated in 1, 2, 3, 4, 5, 7, 8, 11, 6, 14, for the two latter deviate only in the substitution of one liquid for another, which is as common in the languages of Africa as in those of America. The words for four in the above suite do not seem of a different root from those in 12, 13, 14, 15, 16, and 21, from which it only varies in 20 by the prefix of *nabo.* With the difference of a single letter, the same word for *four* is found in the Yngwa (13) and the Empoöngwa (31) which are 1000 miles distant. Four in Congo is *m'na*, in Empoöngwa, *nqhee.* *Sanu*, the Kaffer *four*, is approached in 18.

(e) *Five* may be assimilated from 1 to 17, (11 excepted) one liquid being substituted for another in 14, an *leer* being prefixed in 13. It is remarkable too that we again identify this numeral in the Malemba, Embomma, and Empoöngwa languages, by removing the prefixes *t, to,* and *neh,* from the words *tanoo, toanoo,* and *nehanee.* Below five, the numerals in the Inkran lose all identity with those of the languages with which it has been hitherto assimilated.

(f) *Six* assimilates from 1 to 9, in 12 to 17 (14 excepted) in 20, 23, 24, in 17 and 22 ; but remains distinct in all the others. The Sanbal of Oöngobai (30) approaches the Sambanoo of the Embomma.

(g) *Seven* assimilates in 1 to 9 ; in 12, 13, 16, but in no others.

(h) *Eight* assimilates in 2, 3, 6, 7 ; in 11 to 17, (14 excepted) all of which, with 31, approximate to E'nana, the word for eight in the Malemba.

(i) *Ten* assimilates in 1, 2, 3, 7, 8, 12, in 4, 5, 6, in 17, 19, 25, 26, 29, in 13, 15, and in 14, 20, 22, 23, 24.

---

* This word approximates to *ogha, ogiah,* and *egah,* the words for *fire* in the Booroom, Ashantee, and Fantee : but all the other Adampë words I have ever heard, cannot be assimilated to those which denote the same objects in any other African language.

† *Inkran*, an *ant,* is the native name of the country Europeans call *Accra*, which name was probably given by the Portuguese to their settlement there (the earliest they made according

Two	Ayue	Abeeën	Ennuë	Ennuë
Three	Assan	Abiasseh	Assah	Ettayh
Four	Arra	Anan	Annah	Edjuë
Five	Aoonoo	Ennoom	Ennoo	Ennoomó
Six	Ayshing	Asseeä	Isshin	Eghpah
Seven	Assooa	Ashong	Isshennooh	Paghwooh
Eight	Awotchay	Awotwee	Ettchee	Paghnue
Nine	Awonna	Akoon	Assan	Nahoon
Ten	Boonoo	Edoo	Eddoo	Nongmah

	11. *Kerrapay*	12. *Dagwumba*	13. *Yngwa*	14. *Hio*	15. *Mosee*
One	Eddee	Yahndo	Lakoo	Innee	Yimbo
Two	Effee	Ayee	Ayee	Eygee	Ayeeboo
Three	Eltong	Attah	Attah	Etta	Ataboo
Four	Ennay	Nasee	Anähee	Ernee	Annasee
Five	Altong	Ennoon	Leerennoo	Aroon	Annoo
Six	Adday	Yohbee	Ayoboo	Effa	Ayobee
Seven	Adrinnee	Poice	Ayapaï	Eggay	Owhi
Eight	Ennee	Nehenoo	Annee	Eggo	Ennee
Nine	Indee	Wyhee	Awai	Essun	Aïhopoi
Ten	Owoo	Edoo	Peä	Eywaw	Peega

	16. *Kumsallahoo*	17. *Gaman*	18. *Kong*	19. *Fobee*	20. *Callana*
One	Yumbo	Tah	Kiddee	Koroom	Kodoom
Two	Yeebo	Noo	Filla	Nalay	Naboolla
Three	Tabo	Sah	Sowa	Poompevarra	Nawedazoo
Four	Nasee	Nah	Nanoo	Leetaynalee	Nabonaza
Five	Annoo	Taw	Looroa	Kakwassee	Nabonoa
Six	Yobo	Torata	Wora	Mannassa	Lodoo
Seven	Poihee	Toorifeenoo	Ooranfilla	Noottoosoo	Logwa
Eight	Nehee	Toorifeessa	Leeaygee	Borafay	Littaïzoo
Nine	Wahee	Toorifeena	Konunto	Pirrifay	Nako
Ten	Pega	Noonoo	Tah	Nanooa	Yewoo

	21. *Bambarra*	22. *Garangi*	23. *Mallowa.*	24. *Kallaghee*	25. *Bornoo*
One	Killi	Kerriminna	Daia	Gadee	Leskar
Two	Foolla	Ferriminna	Beeyoo	Silill	Ahndee
Three	Sabba	Sowaninna	Okoo	Quan	Yaskar
Four	Nani	Firrima	Odoo	Foolloo	Deegah
Five	Looroo	Fahtima	Beä	Vydee	Ooögoo
Six	Wora	Tata	Seddah	Zoodoo	Araskoo
Seven	Worroola	Mannima	Becquay	Etkassa	Tooloor
Eight	Sagi	Pirima	Tacquass	Shiddowka	Woskoo
Nine	Konunto	Missirima	Tarra	Woollaä	Likkar
Ten	Ta	Gwahee	Gwoma	Woma	Meeägoo

	26. *Maïha*	*Quolla-liffa* by Mr. Hutchison.	*Badaggry* by Mr. Hutchison.	27. *Sheekan*	28. *Kaylee*
One	Lagen	Da	Soko	Ilwawtoe	Woto
Two	Indë	Bue	Auwee	Ibba	Ibba
Three	Eäska	Okoo	Atong	Bittach	Battach
Four	Daäger	Hodoo	Inna	Binnay	Binnay

to the traditions of the natives) to commemorate the voyage of Hanno; Accra being one of the five cities raised by him between the Soloe Promontory, or Cape Bojador, and the River Lixus or Ouro.

3 T

	Maïha.	*Quolla-liffa.*	*Badaggry.*	*Sheekan.*	*Kaylee.*
Five	Ohoo	Bakwee	Ato	Bitta	Bittan
Six	Araska	Shida	Trukoo		
Seven	Tooloor	Bockwa	Chauto		
Eight	Weska	Sidda	Quouie		
Nine	Lekar	Tarra	Kennee		
Ten	Inagoon	Goman	Owoo	Duĕoom	Duĕoom
Twenty				Emboomebba	
Hundred				Kama	

	29. *Oongoòmo*	30. *Oongobaï*	31. *Empoöngwa.* See p. 439 for character.
One	Wootta	Rappeek	Hemoödee
Two	Beeba	Ramboise	Mban
Three	Bittach	Mittasee	Ntcharoo
Four	Binnay	Binnay	Nahee
Five	Bitten	Bittan	Nehanee
Six		Sambal	Oroöba
Seven		Bittooba	Ragginnoömoo
Eight		Bissamen	Ennanahee
Nine		Bwoi	Eno go öm
Ten		Deĕoom	Hegoöm

The following is the skeleton of a *Vocabulary*, of which the enlarged or perfect copy was blown out of the cabin-window, in a sudden squall, (with some specimens of music), during my voyage home.

English.	*Ashantee.*	*Fantee*.*	*Booroom.*	*Various.*
Above	wattefee			
Advice	matoorh			
Afraid	osooroh		efweedammee	
Afternoon	inumirree	ingubirh	ennie	
Again	impray		meära	
Alike	oninnisie		ninnamata	
Alive	nannuwomie	uannekan	issaboobwaw	n'chema Malemba Inchema a fruit in Empoöngwa.
All	nenarra		inkaken	
Alone	waunkoo		ohwoorie	
Angry	mŏbwaf	moboäf	moohiaf	
Another	ebissoo		ekoo	
Arm	wabow		serrekoonkoo	
Ashamed	wennatoo		woifarrie	
Asleep	werda	wadda	awdirrie	
Awake	waihen		otinnie	
Back	wakee		atterra	
Bad	omoo		ohmara	
Bead	aoonee		aboroo†	

* Where there is no word in the Fantee column, it is the same as the Ashantee.

† I have before stated (Superstitions, p. 270.) that *aggry* is a generic name, probably exotic, of the derivation of which the Negroes are wholly ignorant. It is remarkable that the Boo-

English.	Ashantee.	Fantee.	Booroom.	Various.
Beard	aboidwee		annoque	the same as *chin*, a frequent surname.
Beat	whaoonoo	wabomĕ	babeëm	
Bed	empa		kerray	
Before	wawquoorasoo	waw*quan*	oïyo	ovetide *quande* Malemba.
Beg	ekkaydie	empoikeöw	dibbim	*mpanou.* Malemba.
Behind	owakee		odioterra	the noun *back* with *o* & *odiu* prefixed
Below	asnadie			
Big	kookrookoo		otchwaw	
Bird	anima		abooree	for names of animals, see p. 328.
Bite	whakum		inkadooa	
Black	tintoom		oboobie	
Blind	frafoo		atenna	
Blood	mugga		moogga	*menga.* Mal. Emb.
Boil	woaroo	wowoorh	ohfoo	
Bone	ebiou		ebou	
Boy	afra		ayebee	
Burn	whahim		ohwho	
Buy	mekoto		meashoor	
Call	aferen	afren	ateëm	
Carry	atooron		dumta	
Catch	makin		mekeeram	
Change	wahseesun			
Cheeks	wafoon		afeehe	
Child	ebbah		obee	
Clean	wafie		aulay	
Cloth	ettum	en*tama*	*akim*mie	
Cold	oiwoo		afoo	differs little from *boil*
Come	rraba			
Cry	oroosoor		orissoo	
Cut	witwa		wawtung	
Dance	saw		attcha	
Dark	oiheesoom		mayoo	
Daughter	mebăbā		mebee	*coomba.* Em. which is a common female name in Fantee

rooms call these beads *sikka koonkoorie,* and never use the common word for *bead* (aboroo,) when they speak of them: this name imports their value (*sikka* being *gold*) and one would fancy something connected with their locality, *Koonkoorie* being a range of hills seven days northward of Kong, (see p. 182.) but I never could obtain the least explanation on this subject from the natives.

English.	Ashantee.	Fantee.	Booroom.	Various.
Day*				
Dead	wow		ohoo	
Deaf	nasheeasie	teetïfoo	sinteelaboo	
Deep	eboonie			
Devil	ayen†			Amoonie a proper name
Dig	amoonna			
Door	aboo		ebunabooná	
Drink	noom		noo	noa. Mal. noi. Em.
Drop	wawto	awtarradi	otore	
Drown	eboon			
Drunk	wassoo	wawboo	hassoo	
Ear	assoor			
Eat	edce			dea. Mal.
Egg	kessua	kirrifooa	akaddie	
Empty	eppun			
Enough	ojëay		obahrìe	
Eye	wunnie	ennua	ennyass	
Eyebrow	wunnĕwee	entun		
Face	wynim		anyasirra	
Far	akirh'		aterh'	
Fat	anggwa		oomfoä	
Father	aggáh		missee	
Fear	sooroo		efweedam	
Feather	takirrie		eetta	
Feel	suomwhay		kirrada	seembede. Mal. Kirradee, a river of Booroom.
Fetch	ekkoon		becquaw	a town in Booroom
Fifty	edoonoom			10. 5.
Fight	orrokoo		obuquooa	
Fill	eënnama		boorra	
Find	maoo	maoon	maioom	
Finger	insa		eserrïbee	
Fire	ogiäh	egah	ogha	boogoom. Mosee
Fish	enum		eyay	
Flower	nadjua		ewooda	
Fly	watoo		oqueshoo	
Fool	woigimmie	abooa	woigimmie	booba. Mal.
Foot	wannunsa		aïah	
Forget	moorafie		sessĕro	

* They distinguish different times of the day, thus

Morning, or before 12.	napa.		
Mid-day, or 12.	aweeabillee	aweeabil	emfass.
Afternoon, 4.	ingubee		noobwawss.
Evening, 6.	adiasa	adjasa	eybeen.
Night	noofa		aniaberra

† This reminds me that I ought to have noticed, in the Superstitions of Ashantee, that they believe the devil to be a wandering evil spirit, occasionally entering into a human being, imme-diately to be destroyed for the safety of mankind.

English.	Ashantee.	Fantee.	Booroom.	Various.
Forgive	edimämoo		iukawffinsow	
Fowl	akoo		karrabee	
Friend	ankoo		oonkoosïba	
Fruit	quadiäteä	impooa	quadiateä	
Girl	biseä		otchay	
Give	fummum		täsämi	
Glad	yam	yamma	amirra	
Go	kaw		narry	
God	yankoompon		oodoobwarrie	
Gold	sikkä			
Good	oëyay		obwärie	
Green	boioöma			
Grow	owynee	ocen	ohodan	
Hair	hewhee		hemoonie	{ Amoonie, a proper name.
Half	effch		baggah	
Hand	mensa		assaddie	{ Mensa, a proper name.
Handsome	oia		obweefay	
Hang	osesan			
Hard	oiätin		oöqua	
Head	tirrie'		egnoon	
Hear	matr'		maynoon	
Heart	akoomo		akirräbie	
Heavy	oiadoor		obodoor	
Here	hah		oomboh	
Hide	mōhoo		manghoo	
High	essoor		oskasoor	
Hill	cooqua		iffoo	
Hit	aboor		odum	
Hold	soom		karrara	
Hole	watchoo		osarrie	
Horn	aben		abay	
Horse	panquaw			
Hot	oiayuc		owuegua	
House	efee	odan	eban	{ paseebah, Kumsallahoo. deeo, Dagwumba. gidda, Mallowa. koopella, Mosee. Kokoopella, capital of ditto.
Hundred	ehha			
Hungry	oquandummie	comagin	aquandum	
Husband	mookoon		mookooddie	
Idle	nehuff			
Iron	dadee			
Jump	oroo		fay	
Keep	intamaseea	ysee	afeeërra	
Kick	chayche		orraychum	
Kill	coom		bamoem	
King	ohennie			
Knot	eppo		ippo	
Know	innim		nayoom	
Lame	opakkie		ebbeä	

English.	Ashantee.	Fantee.	Booroom.	Various.
Land	fum	dadi	sebooroo	{ tenga. Mosee kaisa Mallo.
Last	naddou		afoorinay	
Laugh	sicroo	sroo	orroomuss	
Law	widdooffoo			
Lead	soomwie			
Learn	akirren		ekērow	
Leg	asirrie		inwoonnie	
Lie (down)	daoo		oyadee	
Lie (falsity)	etwapō		afoorenie	
Little	kakra	kakrabi	bahttee	
Long	ohwar'		ohbissay	
Look	fway		kaye	
Love	poopa			
Mad	same as ' fool'			{ pagga, Kums. boodasa, Dag.
Man	binin		oninnie	{ noon, Accra. nedda, Mosee. moottanee, M. moontau, Male. muntu,Mozam.
Many	peenarra		otuä	
Market	egwass	egoom	ebiass	
Mat	keraw	empa	kerray	
Mend	pam		bärä	
Moon	serrānee	boossoom	ofoorie	{ wattacha, Ku. marraga, Dag. oüota Mallowa. choogoo, Mos.
More	mambissoo		samoko	
Mother	mna	minna	minnee	nneay, Accra.
Mouth	wannoom	ennoom	annoo	
Much	dooroo		otchoo	
Nails	oomboiray		ungwarrie	' unguis'
Name		dgin	ekkoona	
Neck	ekkone		ekkoona	
Nest	anïmaboo			{ anïma, a bird. Annămāboo, a Fantee town.
Net	ebbwau			
Never	dabbiada		as no!	
New	fofoor		ofroofoo	
No	dabbi			{ an inarticulate noise with the lips closed
Noise	deddie		boolāo	
Nose	ewhin		ewhoonie	
Oil	engoo		oomfwaie	
Old	quodda		aquŏdä	
Open	boi		booë	
Owe	mintēka	dinnekow	indāqua	
Pay	tchamkou		kamëquow	
Play	agoor'		feearee	
Poison	otoowādoo		otoowādoo	
Poor	haynil		ohēä	

English.	Ashantee.	Fantee.	Booroom.	Various.
Pot	quonsun		adinna	
Pregnant	orrŏhoo			
Present (gift)	wahoo		okŏë	
Pull	twin		sheeay	
Quarrel	irriquaw	orriyow	batŏë	
Quick	tetimrĭka		serrie	
Quiet	gyaë	yafoo	yaië	
Rain	osoorăba	yankoom	bwārie	
Rat	quissie			
Red	memmia	betcheä	okooquaw	
Ring	inkaä		apateä	
River	bāk		oboom	
Rob	odomādi		odoiyā	
Round	kandinginnŭma		koorookooddie	
Run	gwan		serrie	{ as ' quick,' B. { sirr, run, Arabic.
Salt	inkkim		imfoorie	
Sand	aghwëä		issay.	
Say	assie	ass	aberrie	
Sea	eppoo			
See	aweeh		akayh	
Sell	tum		fah	
Send	wahsmum		ocheow	
Shake	wosoo		ediddie	
Shell	oorabba		owoora	
Short	takoteä	tchaba	akoteä	
Shut	toom		toroo	
Sick	yirrie	yarrie	mimmiclal	
Silver	gwettay		odume	
Sing	enyoom		ennum	
Sister	akirrawa	akirrāba	moofwa	
Sit	tinnahoe	kooaugh	tchinna	
Sleep	waughda		oädie	
Smell	gwooa			
Smoke	wishshue		djessie	
Soft	mirrou		omooqua	
Son	ebba		ebee	
Sorry	oimiyow		boomega	
Speak	akas		osasin	
Stand	ginnaoh	ginnah	yerrie	
Steal	wawwoo	weyweädie	oëwee	{ windega, Kum. { wintanga, Dag. { lana, Mallowa.
Strong	waginna	ohwidein	oshoneyöo	{ As an exclama- { tion of wonder.
Sun	ayowea		oöe	
Swear	shua.			
Sweet	oiaday	oiadow	obooding	
Swim	abhoorh		abboor	
Soil	afoonna		affung	
Tail	dooah		odoo	
Take	afwa		maytah	
Tell	abim		aiyow	
Thief	krumfoe	niwee	ohwie	
Throat	komen		ekoonnie	
Throw	too		ohtoo	
Tie	tittieh	kikhieh	keay	

English.	Ashantee.	Fantee.	Booroom.	Various.
To-morrow	otchinna	akinna	otchay	
Tongue	takramma		dannoo	
Tooth	essie		engyie	
Touch	kah		tah	
Town	croom		eban	
Tree	dooa		assah	dawgo, Kums. dawro, Dagw. rahoo, Mosee. ittachee, Mall. chee, Embom.
True	umpa		kerram	
Turn	dahen		darie	
Twenty	eddooän		edooh	
Wake	wyen		otinnie	
*Walk	nanchoo		narree	
Warm	oyahue		obiguh	
Wash	gwarr		orrohooroo	
Water	inshoo	insoo	inta	kome, Kumsal. looa, Mallowa. quom, Mosec.
Weep	oroosoo	oroosoo	oreesh	
White	foofoo		intoofoofoorie	Intiffa, a proper name.
Wife	ayerh		mekkah	
Wild	wadoohem	wadoohem	dooafay	
Wind	ooframma		affoo	
Wing	ataban		ittay	
Woman	bisea		tchee	
Work	adjooma		orilaloo	adawwah, Ku. matah, Mallow.
Year	affrieyay		otee	
Yes	yeö		matee	
Yesterday	endodra	ennida	indeay	

  * It is curious that in both these radically distinct languages, the verb *walk* should assimilate so closely to the noun *cow*.

London : Printed by W. Bulmer and Co.
Cleveland-row, St. James's.

Lightning Source UK Ltd.
Milton Keynes UK
UKOW03f1504190615

253731UK00001B/33/P